WHY AMERICA FIGHTS

WHY AMERICA FIGHTS

PATRIOTISM AND WAR PROPAGANDA FROM THE PHILIPPINES TO IRAQ

SUSAN A. BREWER

OXFORD
UNIVERSITY PRESS

OXFORD
UNIVERSITY PRESS

Oxford University Press, Inc., publishes works that further
Oxford University's objective of excellence
in research, scholarship, and education.

Oxford New York
Auckland Cape Town Dar es Salaam Hong Kong Karachi
Kuala Lumpur Madrid Melbourne Mexico City Nairobi
New Delhi Shanghai Taipei Toronto

With offices in
Argentina Austria Brazil Chile Czech Republic France Greece
Guatemala Hungary Italy Japan Poland Portugal Singapore
South Korea Switzerland Thailand Turkey Ukraine Vietnam

Published by Oxford University Press, Inc.
198 Madison Avenue, New York, NY 10016

www.oup.com

First issued as an Oxford University Press paperback, 2011

Oxford is a registered trademark of Oxford University Press.

Library of Congress Cataloging-in-Publication Data
Brewer, Susan A. (Susan Ann), 1958–
Why America fights: patriotism and war propaganda
from the Philippines to Iraq / Susan A. Brewer.
p. cm.
Includes bibliographical references and index.
ISBN 978-0-19-538135-1; 978-0-19-975396-3 (pbk.)
1. United States—Foreign relations—20th century.
2. Politics and war—United States—History—20th century.
3. Patriotism—United States—History—20th century.
4. Propaganda, American—History—20th century. I. Title.
E744. B6977 2009 303.6'60973—dc22 2008050360

To Bob

CONTENTS

ACKNOWLEDGMENTS

I first grasped the value of propaganda when it was time to pick up toys. As the eldest of four children who were allowed to make elaborate messes, I led the clean-up. With delight, I discovered that the effort went easier with music, Sousa marches or show tunes. Later, I became interested in the stories that Americans tell about their country and its role in the world. In particular, I was intrigued by the way the people in charge used patriotic versions of history to win support for their foreign policy, especially during wartime when so much was at stake. As any big sister knows, the power to manipulate can be used for good or nefarious purposes. I write this book for my brothers, sister, students, and anyone else who wants to understand how a nation can be inspired with truths and deceptions when it goes to war.

The research and writing of this book were made possible by generous fellowships and grants. My thanks to the Institute for Research in the Humanities at the University of Wisconsin–Madison, the National Endowment for the Humanities, and the University of Wisconsin–Stevens Point University Personnel Development Committee. I am grateful to the splendid staffs at the National Archives for assistance with documents, still pictures, and motion picture, sound, and video records, the Library of Congress Manuscript Division and the Prints and Photographs Division, the John F. Kennedy Library, the Franklin D. Roosevelt Library, the Harry S. Truman Library, and the Wisconsin Historical Society. For resources from work in progress to silent films and Operation Enduring Freedom Trading Cards, I am grateful to Stephen Badsey, Laura Belmonte, Nick Cull, Leslie Midkiff DeBauche, Mitchell Hall, David Langbart, Neil Lewis, Chester Pach, John Regnier,

Mitchell Robinson, Eric Rohmann, Mark Tolstedt, and Helena Vanhala. At the University of Wisconsin–Stevens Point, I am beholden to my dedicated colleagues and engaged students, with a special thanks to research assistants Scott Butterfield, Clinton Huffmann, Amanda Lorge, and Chris Solberg. For their assistance, I thank Sandy Bauman, Rachel Mahoney, Doug Moore, Tom Reich, Jan Swinford, and Justin Thomas.

Why America Fights covers a lot of time and territory. I am deeply indebted to the outstanding work of scholars from many disciplines. In particular, I have benefited enormously from the wise counsel of Paul Boyer, Walter LaFeber, and William Skelton, who generously shared their expertise in cultural, diplomatic, and military history as they vigorously critiqued the entire manuscript. At conferences, I benefitted from the comments of Jim Baughman, Paul Boyer, Patricia Clavin, Lloyd Gardner, Chester Pach, Emily Rosenberg, and Robert Schulzinger. I am most fortunate to have insightful readers who reviewed all or parts of the manuscript, including Jim Baughman, Chris Bort, Scott Butterfield, Patricia Clavin, Leslie Midkiff DeBauche, Corinne Dempsey, Bob Erickson, Nick Garigliano, Anne Greer, Bruce Hall, Gene Kadish, Theresa Kaminski, Mary Statzer, and Greg Summers. I am grateful for the excellent support and careful reading of editor Susan Ferber at Oxford University Press. I thank Joellyn Ausanka for her skill and assistance during the production stage. Thanks to Thomas Schneider and Hans Wagener for the publication of a version of Chapter 2 in *"Huns" vs. "Corned Beef": Representations of the Other in American and German Literature on World War I* (Göttingen, Germany: V&R unipress, 2007).

I am grateful for the many kindnesses of my friends and family without whom I would not have completed this book. Candy Fleming and Eric Rohmann encouraged and advised me. For their hospitality and conversation, I thank Patricia Clavin, Linda Nemec, Chris Bort, Anne Greer, Steve DeJulio, and Marjorie Thompson. I thank my family, who with love has seen me through another elaborate mess. Finally, this book is dedicated to Bob Erickson, who never imagined he would watch so many war movies.

WHY AMERICA FIGHTS

INTRODUCTION

The first casualty when war comes is truth.

Senator Hiram Johnson, 1917

ON THE FIRST ANNIVERSARY of the terrorist attacks of September 11, 2001, President George W. Bush launched a campaign to promote war against Iraq. "We will not allow any terrorist or tyrant to threaten civilization with weapons of mass murder," he declared. The president's prime-time speech was broadcast from Ellis Island where White House staffers had expertly staged the scene by illuminating the Statue of Liberty in the background. The previous day the attorney general raised the terror alert level to orange and the White House announced that Vice President Richard Cheney had spent the night at a "secure, undisclosed location." Following the speech, the president's top advisors appeared on television news shows to describe the immensity of the Iraqi threat. Secretary of Defense Donald Rumsfeld warned, "Imagine a September 11 with weapons of mass destruction." Americans must go to war, announced officials, to secure their own safety, liberate the Iraqi people, and spread democracy in the Middle East.[1]

In promoting Operation Iraqi Freedom, the Bush administration drew on a long history of government efforts to rally popular support for war. When Americans are called upon to fight, they want to know why Americans must kill and be killed. They expect their leaders to prove that war is right, necessary, and worth the sacrifice. This book explores the official presentation of war aims in six wars: the Philippine War, World War I, World War II, the Korean War, the Vietnam War, and the Iraq War. From William McKinley

3

to George W. Bush, the chief message has been that Americans must defeat the enemy in order to create a safer, more prosperous world in which freedom and democracy will thrive.

To explain to Americans why they fight, government leaders translate war aims into propaganda—the deliberate manipulation of facts, ideas, and lies. To do so they condense complex foreign policies into easily communicated messages: "to make the world safe for democracy" or "to lead the Free World." They seek to "bring the whole story together in one official narrative," as Secretary of State Dean Acheson put it in 1950 when the United States embarked on a worldwide Cold War.[2] The official narratives have presented conflict as a mighty clash between civilization and barbarism in the Philippines and World War I, democracy and dictatorship in World War II, freedom and communism in Korea and Vietnam, and, most recently, civilization and terrorism in Iraq.

These official narratives show that Americans fight for both their ideals and their interests. The wars considered here were fought overseas and caused few American civilian casualties. Compared to its enemies and allies, the United States suffered far less devastation and, in the case of the world wars, emerged a stronger and richer country. For many U.S. policymakers, observed historian Tony Judt, "the message of the twentieth century is that war works."[3] To sell that message to the public, leaders equated the expansion of a U.S.-dominated international order with the aims of spreading democracy and freedom. The official narratives served to camouflage any contradiction that might exist between America's pursuit of power and its principles. Indeed, propaganda projected the appealing notion that America's global ambitions and democratic traditions are one and the same.

The message that what is good for America is good for the world drew on the belief in American exceptionalism. This treasured myth claimed that the United States, as the world's morally superior nation, had special responsibilities and privileges. Leaders declared that Americans had a duty not only to protect their valued system of democracy and capitalism, but to extend it to others. The assumption of American superiority also explained why the rest of the world was incapable of achieving the "American way of life" on its own. The United States therefore had to provide direction. To assert what Presidents Woodrow Wilson and George H. W. Bush called the "new world order," the United States expanded its influence into Latin America, Asia, Africa, Europe, and the Middle East. It acquired military bases around the globe and protected access to trade routes and natural resources for itself and its allies. And it engaged in numerous conflicts against aggressors and insurgents. As long as the United States seeks to remake the world in its own image, observed historian Joan Hoff, it has a mission without end.[4]

In wartime, the idea of the American mission takes on vibrant patriotic trappings. The rituals of stirring speeches, parades, and martial music fill the imagination. They recall ancient traditions of war cries and drum beats, when warriors painted their faces and donned bearskins to embolden themselves and terrify the enemy. War destroys, noted historian Drew Gilpin Faust, but it also "exhilarates and intoxicates." It summons up stories of national honor, tests of manhood, and moral redemption. We Americans "wish to advance from where we stand," commented writer Randolph Bourne in the months before the United States entered World War I. More than "flag reverence" or "patriotic swagger," he thought, Americans craved "unity of sentiment, for service," to lift themselves out of the "uneasy pettiness" of day-to-day life. Bourne knew that for some, military action satisfied that longing. It offered adventure with purpose. "War is a force that gives us meaning," concluded war correspondent Chris Hedges in 2002.[5]

Wartime propagandists defined that meaning by ennobling geostrategic objectives with patriotic purpose. They solemnly outlined the evidence of aggression against civilization or the Free World and the steps necessary to defeat it. They organized spectacles to honor heroic warriors in their fight against dehumanized enemies. They described the rewards of victory. By invoking past glories and promising a happy ending, the official narratives provided a persuasive framework for understanding the current conflict. They also served to distract from reality. For example, in World War II, propagandists appealed to American confidence in their national mission while they shielded civilians from a full knowledge of the immense struggle they faced to defeat Nazi Germany and Imperial Japan. And in the lead-up to the Iraq War, officials recalled the triumphs of World War II as they exaggerated the threat presented by Iraqi dictator Saddam Hussein in order to justify invasion. Propaganda can inspire and unite a nation in time of crisis; it can also deceive.

It is important for citizens to understand wartime propaganda, for controversial as it is, it is also essential. Even though war notoriously is fought in a fog, leaders must endow it with clarity and purpose in order to maintain morale and justify sacrifice. The president typically needs bipartisan consensus because the U.S. Constitution divides war powers between the executive and legislative branches. As commander-in-chief, he may require the flexibility to act forcefully and quickly. The president does not want to have his hands tied

Sailors march up Fifth Avenue in the Fourth Liberty Loan Parade, New York City, September 1918. (National Archives, 165-WW-2350-2)

by Congress or public opinion. Therefore the administration will urge unity and present the crisis in a way designed to achieve it. For all these reasons, wartime propaganda, to some extent, has to be simplified and uplifting. Its role, wrote veteran World War I propagandist Edward Bernays, is to "help bring order out of chaos."[6]

Official narratives therefore serve a vital purpose. In their dramatic completeness, they purport to address all the rational and emotional reasons why Americans must fight. These persuasive stories reveal a great deal about how Americans see themselves in the world. But as fascinating as they are in the way they weave together current events with myth, history, and popular culture, the official narratives deserve closer scrutiny. As packaging, they must be unwrapped in order to investigate the war aims that are being sold. The question to consider about official propaganda is how closely what people are told aligns with the government's objectives. Does it illuminate or obscure the actual war aims? The fundamental issue after all is the worthiness of the policy. As we will see, propaganda can promote a legitimate war such as World War II or a flawed conflict such as Vietnam. Whether "propaganda is good or bad," noted Bernays, "depends upon the merit of the cause urged."[7]

This book examines overt propaganda, typically called information, directed by U.S. officials at the home front. Americans long have associated the term propaganda with lies and dictators. "We call our stuff information and the enemy's propaganda," said an American colonel in 2005, summing up the conventional distinction. Even so, as scholar Richard Alan Nelson points out, propaganda is "as American as apple pie."[8] The First Amendment to the Constitution protects the right to communicate persuasive messages through speech and the media. Moreover, in the United States, industries of persuasion—marketing, advertising, and public relations—flourish. As opposed to covert propaganda, which comes from hidden sources and tends to be false, overt propaganda comes from a known source and is understood to be based on facts. It can be a "self-interested selection of the facts," as a former presidential press secretary once defined "spin control."[9] To rally Americans around the flag, officials have manipulated facts, exaggeration, and misinformation. The primary purpose, after all, is not to inform, but to persuade. In the end the propaganda campaign seeks to disguise a paradoxical message: war is not a time for citizens to have an informed debate and make up their own minds even as they fight in the name of freedom to do just that.

Wartime administrations have created a variety of organizations to construct and disseminate one-sided stories of "us versus them." The president, noted political journalist Richard Reeves, serves as the "first explainer."[10] In this effort, the chief executive has been assisted by officials with backgrounds in politics, diplomacy, the military, the media, business, advertising, public relations, education, and the arts. In the two world wars, temporary propaganda agencies called the Committee on Public Information and the Office of War Information were set up to mobilize the nation for total war. In the Korean War, Vietnam War, and Iraq War, officials from the White House, State Department, Defense Department, and the military services crafted persuasive messages. In these wars, the goal was not to mobilize the population, but to elicit its passive support for a faraway conflict.

In their messages, officials have used appeals to emotion and self-interest calculated to resonate with public opinion as they perceived that opinion. In doing so, they drew on contemporary beliefs about race and ethnicity, class, gender, and religion. For example, President William McKinley described the Philippine War as an effort to bring Christian civilization to "little brown brothers." His successors would apply a modified version of the "white man's burden" to the Koreans, Vietnamese, and Iraqis, all people portrayed as somewhat backward, but assumed to be desirous of the benefits of western civilization once liberated from tyranny. Such portrayals of the conflict focused attention on romanticized images of Americans rather than strategic or economic interests. But leaders have not neglected practical concerns. During the Korean War, President Harry Truman's aide John Steelman warned television viewers that if the communists were not stopped, they would rob Americans of their cars and TVs.[11]

Wartime administrations have delivered their propaganda through speeches, cartoons, advertisements, posters, radio shows, films, and the news media. They especially relied on news management to convey their interpretation of events, called "perception management" by Secretary Rumsfeld. Leaders have voiced respect for the freedom of the press and its role, according to democratic theory, of providing citizens with the information they need to make informed decisions. That said they have sought to manipulate the content of that information. Officials usually embraced the tradition of fact-based propaganda teamed with censorship. They wanted to maintain credibility with the press and the public because then their version of events was more likely to be transmitted by the one and accepted by the other. And, as essential sources of war news, civilian and military leaders could deliver it in the interpretative framework of the official narratives. The patriotic narrative appealed to producers, publishers, and reporters as citizens and as professionals, who knew a good story when they saw it. War, no one could deny, was a boon for the news business, especially if the coverage was not too upsetting. Thus, it was expected, that in time of crisis, the mass media would be on the same team with the government and the armed services. "Yes, we wrote only a part of the war," recalled novelist turned World War II correspondent

John Steinbeck. "But at the time we believed, fervently believed, that it was the best thing to do."[12]

Despite their considerable efforts to inspire popular support, wartime leaders have always contended with skepticism or opposition from Americans who question the need to fight or disagree with the conduct of the war. Organized protests such as the Anti-Imperialist League in the Philippine War and Another Mother for Peace during the Vietnam War have denounced U.S. foreign policy. Satirists from author Mark Twain to comedian Jon Stewart have skewered the self-righteousness and hypocrisy of official pronouncements. From the front lines, war correspondents have reported that all was not going according to plan. The troops have recounted their experiences to reveal that fear, incompetence, and greed were as much a part of war as bravery, skill, and generosity. "Are you correspondents telling the people back home the truth?" demanded a furious and exhausted lieutenant in Korea of *New York Herald Tribune* reporter Marguerite Higgins. "Are you telling them we have nothing to fight with, and this is an utterly useless war?"[13] When confronted with such challenges to their uplifting version of events, officials have sought to marginalize dissent and revise their own messages.

The official narratives, intended to unify, could provoke contention precisely because they drew on the idea of Americans as a chosen people with a global mission. In earlier wars when Americans fought enemies they viewed as tyrants or savages who threatened their way of life, they considered what the United States stood for. During the Mexican War in the 1840s, for example, advocates of the idea of "manifest destiny" declared that expansion across the continent was the way to secure what Thomas Jefferson called the "empire of liberty." Others, like army lieutenant Ulysses S. Grant, thought the Mexican War was an unjust fight waged by the strong against the weak in which the American republic behaved like the European monarchies. Americans both for and against the Mexican War believed the United States should live up to its ideals; they disagreed over how to go about it. American national identity and purpose would continue to be debated in every conflict.[14]

Through wartime propaganda, leaders sought to prevail in that debate. The book begins with the pivotal Philippine War of 1898–1902, which marked the emergence of the United States as a global power and allowed President McKinley to set a number of precedents for "perception management." When the United States took over the Philippines during the Spanish-American War, McKinley and other expansionists thought the acquisition of the Pacific islands would enhance U.S. economic opportunity in Asia. The president called Filipino resistance an "insurrection" and described the war as a humanitarian mission. He pioneered the management of news coverage in his effort to persuade Americans that a war to control an overseas colony did not violate their democratic principles.

The second chapter analyzes the powerful deployment of propaganda and censorship by the Woodrow Wilson administration during World War I. To mobilize the nation in 1917, the Committee on Public Information embarked on a "vast enterprise in salesmanship." Propagandists extolled American greatness and condemned German barbarism by using sensational stories of atrocity, which were later discredited. Coercive laws reinforced prowar patriotism. In Montana, for instance, a man was sentenced to twenty years hard labor for refusing to kiss the flag.[15] The administration incited support for defeating Germany but did not build a consensus for Wilson's grand vision of an American-led peace. Its efforts left many Americans distrustful of both war and propaganda.

The Japanese attack on Pearl Harbor and the Philippines in December 1941 united Americans who had disagreed over intervention in another European war even as Nazi Germany conquered country after country. The administration of Franklin Roosevelt sought to succeed in World War II where Wilson had failed in World War I by winning both the war and the peace. The third chapter shows how officials portrayed the war as an all or nothing contest against the "slave world" of the Axis powers. To regain public trust in official instruction, the Office of War Information deployed the "strategy of truth" as it blanketed the nation with messages "like new snow." Propagandists wanted to convince civilians and soldiers that the long, difficult fight in distant places would be worth it. "The hope of something better after the war is necessary," they concluded.[16] To keep the peace, officials asserted, Americans this time must commit to international leadership.

Five years after the Allies defeated the Axis, the outbreak of war in Korea tested the new U.S. role as "leader of the Free World." The fourth chapter analyzes President Truman's promotion of a limited war dedicated to the containment of communism. Officials portrayed Korea as a battleground on a far frontier where Americans fought with "good Asians" to defend civilization from "bad Asians"—or else they would have to fight communists at home. The Truman administration adopted a strategy of credibility as it expanded public affairs departments throughout the executive branch and coordinated the official line from the White House. As the stalemate in Korea became unpopular, officials sought to construct a public consensus in support of a global Cold War.

The fifth chapter examines the serious gap between the war aims of the Kennedy, Johnson, and Nixon administrations and the propaganda they adopted during the Vietnam War. Secretary of Defense Robert McNamara concluded in 1965 that Vietnam was a war the United States could not win but feared that losing the war would damage its international prestige. Policymakers conducted a low-key propaganda campaign, relying on Cold War rhetoric and news management. Media coverage conveyed the official messages of spreading democracy and containing communism until events in Vietnam challenged those objectives. Although by 1968 most Americans thought that the war was a mistake, U.S. forces fought in Southeast Asia for five more years. The legacies of a failed war and a divided nation haunted future wartime policies and propaganda.

As it promoted a preventive war against Iraq, the George W. Bush administration used "iron-message discipline" and a strategy of credulity. The sixth chapter describes how the administration appealed to fear following the September 11, 2001, terrorist attack and faith by calling upon Americans to believe in a mission of liberation in the strategically vital Persian Gulf. It relied on "infoganda," the blurring of news, propaganda, and entertainment, to sell war aims based on flawed intelligence and false allegations. The campaign drew on mythic memories of World War II and distorted lessons of Vietnam. As familiar as it appeared, the administration's official narrative was, to an unprecedented degree, disconnected from the actual war on the ground in Iraq.

In the end, war aims must be achieved in the real world, not in the dramatic version presented by propaganda. When wars have to be fought, propaganda is necessary to explain how and why. It simplifies and encourages. The clarity of the official narratives may be blinding, however, not only to the public but to the officials who deliver them. The messages reflect the assumption that the world welcomes American-sponsored democracy and freedom, when many people at home and abroad point out that Americans themselves have not always lived up to such ideals. Propaganda assures Americans that the expansion of their wealth and power benefits them and everyone else when it may not. In none of the wars covered here were the war aims achieved as promised, but some were closer than others. It depended on how much officials relied on fact or fiction to make the persuasive case that Americans fought for both their ideals and their interests. The results have had significant consequences. Like generals, propagandists often fight the last war.

Office of War Information poster, 1943. Bernard Perlin, artist. (National Archives, NWDNS-44-PA-356)

Over time, official strategies of persuasion have favored a public of misinformed spectators over informed citizens. By employing news management and censorship, leaders delivered a mighty array of selected facts and colorful narratives. At the same time, propaganda did not simply flow down a one-way street from the top. Citizens had their own ideas about what it meant to be a patriot. For some it meant unquestioning loyalty. To others, like Francis Bellamy, who wrote the Pledge of Allegiance in 1891, it meant a commitment to the principles "with liberty and justice for all."[17] In wartime, leaders typically blurred these views of patriotism by praising individual freedoms and democratic ideals while demanding conformity and obedience. As they made the case that the United States must lead the world, government leaders exerted greater dominance over the American people.

Wartime propaganda's portrayal of the United States as a generous liberator, spreading democracy as it defends civilization, was designed to appeal to what Americans wanted to believe about themselves. It showed Americans answering the patriotic call for unity and embarking on a blessed mission. Such compelling messages are worth investigation.

I

The "Divine Mission"

War in the Philippines

And of all our race He has marked the American people as his chosen nation to finally lead in the regeneration of the world. This is the divine mission of America, and it holds for us all the profit, all the glory, all the happiness possible to man.

Senator Albert J. Beveridge, 1900

I thought it would be a great thing to give a whole lot of freedom to the Filipinos, but I guess now it's better to let them give it to themselves.

Mark Twain, 1900

AT THE TURN OF THE TWENTIETH CENTURY, Americans and Filipinos fought bitterly for control of the Philippine Islands. The United States viewed the Pacific islands as a stepping-stone to the markets and natural resources of Asia. The Philippines, which had belonged to Spain for three hundred years, wanted independence, not another imperial ruler. For the Americans, the acquisition of a colony thousands of miles from its shores required a break with their anti-imperial traditions. To justify such a break, the administration of William McKinley proclaimed that its policies benefited both Americans and Filipinos by advancing freedom, Christian benevolence, and prosperity. Most of the Congress, the press, and the public rallied to the flag, embracing the war as a patriotic adventure and civilizing mission. Dissent, however, flourished among a minority called anti-imperialists. Setting precedents for all wartime presidents who would follow, McKinley enhanced the power of the chief executive to build a public consensus in support of an expansionist foreign policy.

By promoting national unity and progress, McKinley successfully navigated the transition of the United States to great power status. A skilled politician with years of experience as a congressman and governor of Ohio, McKinley knew the power of symbolism. In the presidential race of 1896, he conducted a "front porch" campaign from his hometown of Canton, projecting a comforting image of small town values even as his party platform supported the fast-paced industrialization that was transforming the nation. As president, McKinley turned to familiar themes from the past to win support for far-reaching changes in foreign policy. The last Civil War veteran to serve as president, he celebrated the coming together of the North and South to fight a common enemy.[1] He portrayed American expansion in the Pacific as a continuation of Manifest Destiny, comparing the Filipinos to Native Americans, calling them savage warriors or "little brown brothers." Appealing to popular attitudes of the times, he encouraged Americans to fulfill their manly duty to spread Christian civilization.

To influence the media of the day, the McKinley administration mastered the latest communication technology. Since the Civil War, Congress had been the power center in Washington, attracting almost all of the press coverage. During the Cleveland administration, one lone reporter from the *Washington Evening Star* started to cover the president by hanging around outside the Executive Mansion, later called the White House, to question visitors as they left. McKinley was the first to have his inauguration filmed and to have a secretary who met daily with the press, "for a kind of family talk," as journalist Ida Tarbell put it. Reporters were provided with a table and chairs in the outer-reception room where they could chat with important visitors and even the president if he approached them first. Outside on "newspaper row," more reporters gathered to interview officials as they left, tossing their scoops to waiting messenger boys. McKinley paid special attention to the representatives of the wire services, the news agencies that sent syndicated stories by telegraph to subscribing newspapers across the country. The president's staff, which grew from six to eighty, monitored public opinion by studying hundreds of newspapers from around the country daily. To make sure that reporters accurately conveyed the president's views, his staff issued press releases, timing the distribution so that reporters on deadline filed only the administration's version of the story.[2]

In contrast to the more rambunctious expansionists of the day, the genial McKinley exuded calm and dignity. As noted by his contemporary, the British historian and diplomat James Bryce, American leaders put considerable effort into leading opinion while appearing to follow it. The president spoke publicly of America's expanded influence in the Caribbean and the Pacific as though it had happened by chance or been willed by God. His actions, however, made the acquisition of an empire no accident. In addition, his public position of passivity made it difficult for critics to challenge his policies until they were well under way. McKinley, observed the astute Henry Adams, a grandson and great-grandson of presidents, was "a marvelous manager of men." While politicians, members of the press, and military men freely expressed their criticisms of U.S. policy, the president and his fellow expansionists took the country to war with Spain, built a consensus for keeping the Philippines, and maintained support for waging war against Filipinos who fought for their independence.[3]

"Remember the *Maine*! To Hell with Spain!"

THE WAR BETWEEN THE AMERICANS AND THE FILIPINOS was just one of many colonial wars taking place in the late 1800s and early 1900s as the world's industrialized powers scrambled for dominance in Africa and Asia. Britain doubled its imperial territory, France acquired three and a half million square miles including Indochina, and Russia expanded east. The aging Austro-Hungarian, Ottoman, and Spanish empires struggled to hang on to what they had. Up-and-coming nations—Germany, Japan, and the United States—sought to extend their influence. Imperial powers clashed over faraway frontiers and subdued native peoples who resisted foreign rule. New technologies often made these fights one-sided. At the battle of Omdurman in 1898, British soldiers lost forty-eight of their own in the few hours it took them to kill 11,000 Sudanese with Lee-Enfield rifles and Maxim guns, the first light, reliable machine gun, which shot eleven bullets a second. To fuel economic expansion, businessmen and traders competed over investments, raw materials, and markets, backing railroad construction in China, digging copper mines in Africa, and selling sewing machines to Pacific Islanders. Missionaries of many faiths crusaded for the souls of the "heathen," by preaching ancient beliefs as well as western attitudes about culture and consumer goods. Explorers raced to plant their flags. Claims of national glory accompanied many of these exploits, along with justifications of spreading progress and stability. Such fierce competition for territory, economic gain, and souls often produced upheaval instead.[4]

His goal, McKinley told Governor Robert LaFollette of Wisconsin, was to "attain U.S. supremacy in world markets." The United States had settled its western frontier, wrapping up thirty years of conflict with the Native Americans. With their own continental empire to manage, American expansionists seemed more interested in indirect imperialism—informal dominance through economic power—than direct imperialism, which entailed hands-on governance. For instance, U.S. companies already had made fortunes out of bananas and minerals from Latin America. To further economic expansion, Captain Alfred Thayer Mahan of the U.S. Navy advocated the construction of a canal through Central America, the buildup of a strong navy to protect trade routes, and the acquisition of refueling bases in the Caribbean and the Pacific. Mahan's ideas had powerful support from McKinley, Senator Henry Cabot Lodge (R-MA), Assistant Secretary of the Navy Theodore Roosevelt, and other expansionists, called "jingoes." In particular, the United States wanted access to China with its millions of potential customers. So did Japan, Britain, Germany, Russia, and France. The imperial powers threatened to divide up China as they had Africa. In January 1898, the U.S. Minister to China warned Washington, "partition would tend to destroy our markets." Within months, McKinley sought to prevent such a partition by turning the United States into a Pacific power with the ability to conduct direct imperialism in the Philippines and advance indirect imperialism in China.[5]

American expansionists of the white, Anglo-Saxon, and Protestant middle and upper classes were confident that they should lead at home and overseas. Citing Social Darwinism and scientific studies that demonstrated the superiority of the white race, they considered white American men to be dominant by virtue of their evolved good character, civilized self-control, and successful creation of a functioning North American empire. The men of decadent Spain, they thought, had gone soft. They considered nonwhite people to be no more than children, primitive and wild, in need of the guidance of a big brother or great white father. Women, viewed as weak and passive, also required protection. Such attitudes reassured these leaders of their natural supremacy at a time when millions of Catholic and Jewish immigrants arrived from Southern and Eastern Europe, the women's suffrage movement agitated for the vote, African Americans challenged the "color line" drawn by segregationists in the South, and workers and farmers demanded radical reforms. These prominent men typically preferred the status quo at home. War overseas provided an escape from "the menace and perils of socialism and agrarianism," thought Henry Watterson, the editor of the *Louisville Courier-Journal*, just "as England has escaped them, by a policy of colonialism and conquest." He concluded, "We exchange domestic dangers for foreign dangers." In a nation at war, expansionists believed, everyone would know and accept their place in society whether at the top or the bottom. Freedom was only for "people capable of self-restraint," said Theodore Roosevelt, who ironically was seen as a bit of a wild man himself.[6]

American expansionists drew on these beliefs and interests to justify war with Spain in the summer of 1898 and the fighting in the Philippines that followed. For most Americans, the conflict with Spain was about the liberation of Cuba. By 1896, Cuban rebels, who carried out ruthless economic warfare by destroying cane fields, sugar mills, and railroads, had taken charge of more than half the island. To prevent civilians from supporting the rebels, Spanish Governor-General Valeriano Weyler forced Cubans out of their villages into guarded "reconcentration camps," where 100,000 died of disease and starvation. Then Weyler, who, as an admiring young military observer, had accompanied Union General William T. Sherman on his march through Georgia, ordered his troops to lay waste to the countryside. As Cubans and Spaniards fought on, American investors in Cuban railroads and sugar plantations lost millions of dollars. At his inauguration in March 1897, President McKinley declared that the United States wanted "no wars of conquest." What the United States did want in Cuba was stability and economic access. McKinley informed Spain that it should put an end to the revolt, institute reforms, stop the reconcentration policy, and respect the human rights of the Cubans. Madrid recalled Weyler and proposed some reforms that satisfied no one. As the upheaval continued, McKinley stepped up the pressure by ordering the new battleship U.S.S. *Maine* to Havana to protect American lives and property.

Americans followed the story of the Cuban Revolution in their many newspapers. New Yorkers alone could choose among eight morning and seven evening papers. They could read the Republican or Democratic papers for news that shared their politics. Or they could turn to the independent and, at three cents a paper, high-priced *New York Times*. For the less highbrow readers, there were the sensational "yellow journals." To increase circulation, publishers Joseph Pulitzer of the *New York World* and *St. Louis Post Dispatch* and William Randolph Hearst of the *New York Journal* and *San Francisco Examiner* competed for readers (and advertisers) with exposés, stunts, comics, sports coverage, women's features, and exciting accounts of foreign conflicts. They believed that war, especially the way they reported it, sold papers. Some histories have blamed yellow journalism for stirring up such a frenzy for bloodshed that McKinley was compelled to give in and fight a war with Spain. Although McKinley's actions do not support this view, the stories

featured in the yellow press d'
contrast to the anti-war pap
problems and atrocities cor
press filled their pages wi'
rape, and murder.[7]

When the *Maine* bl
cans were stunned by
of their ship. The a'
of inquiry to inve
of sympathy. Sp
Washington woula
Charles W. Fairbanks (R-IN,
into war until it is ready for it."[8] The ,
anticipation for war. Luck was with them wi..
consulting the navy's ordnance expert or chief engin..
external explosion caused by a mine had destroyed the *Main..*,
was widely interpreted to mean that Spain was culpable even thou
report did not say so. In a later investigation, the U.S. Navy determined that
an internal explosion involving the fueling system most likely had destroyed
the ship. At the time, however, McKinley fed the widespread impression of
Spain's guilt by saying that anything that happened in Havana was ultimately
Spain's responsibility.

McKinley prepared for war by calling for a military buildup. Congress
appropriated fifty million dollars, three-fifths of which went to the Navy. The
rest went to the Army, which assumed that only small forces would be needed
to take beaches and aid the Cubans and so used most of its appropriation
on coastal fortifications. In late February, without permission, the gung-ho
Assistant Secretary Roosevelt put naval units on alert. Although all attention
was on the Caribbean, he did not ignore Spain's colony in the Philippines.
He ordered George Dewey, the commander of the Asiatic Squadron, who
had been busy searching the coast of China for the best site for an American
port, to proceed to Hong Kong and stand at the ready. Secretary of the Navy
John Long and the president countermanded most of Roosevelt's orders, but
not the one to Dewey. As for Spain, it had 150,000 troops in Cuba exhausted
by fighting and disease, 20,000 in the Philippines, and an antiquated navy.
Well aware that a single U.S. battleship could take out one of their entire
squadrons, Spanish officers steeled themselves for what they hoped would be
an honorable defeat.[9]

WHY AMERICA FIGHTS

searched for a compromise solution, the Euro-
nether they should take sides. From the Vatican,
y to avoid a war by accepting Spain's promise of an
els. Germany, which had its eye on Spanish posses-
, and France proposed mediation. McKinley politely
s. The British decided to support the Americans by doing
esident received reports that American business leaders had
war might enhance opportunities for trade, investments, and
gressional support consolidated after Senator Redfield Proctor
eturned from Cuba with a vivid description of the suffering under
reconcentration policy. His colleague from Wyoming, Senator Francis
arren, expressed growing indignation "that we, a civilized people, an
ightened nation, a great republic, born in a revolt against tyranny, should
ermit such a state of things within less than a hundred miles of our shore as
that which exists in Cuba."[10]

Once ready to wage war, McKinley explained his reasons to Congress on
April 11, 1898. By custom, he did not deliver his message in person but sent it
to be read out loud to the legislators by clerks. The turmoil in Cuba, stated
his message, had "caused enormous losses to American trade and commerce."
The "cruel, barbarous, and uncivilized practices of warfare" had shocked and
offended. The issue of Cuba had caused such unrest at home that it was
distracting Congress from "that close devotion to domestic advancement that
becomes a self-contained commonwealth whose primal maxim has been the
avoidance of all foreign entanglements." The president defined U.S. aims as
ending the war between Spain and Cuba, establishing a stable government
in Cuba, and ensuring peace and security for both the citizens of Cuba and
the United States. After calling for the use of force to achieve these purposes,
the president mentioned in passing that Spain had proclaimed a suspension of hostilities in Cuba. In other words, Spain had made one more major
concession. He closed by asking Congress to consider this development as it
pondered action true to "our aspirations as a Christian, peace-loving people."
The Philippine Islands were never mentioned.

As Congress prepared to declare war on Spain, the big debate was not over
whether to go to war, but whether the United States should recognize the
revolutionary government in Cuba. The debate illustrated the gap between
the public's and the administration's perceptions of what the war was about.
McKinley's aim was American access to a stable Cuba, not Cuban independence. As historian Louis Pérez has pointed out, the Cuban rebels were on

the verge of achieving independence on their own. If they did, they might decide to pursue freedom from foreign domination by kicking out not only Spain, but also the United States. McKinley persuaded the lawmakers not to recognize Cuban independence. The United States and Spain declared war on each other at the end of April.[11]

As much as he could, McKinley centralized war news in the Executive Mansion. In the war room, he installed twenty telegraph wires and fifteen phone wires with direct connections to the executive departments and Congress. From the Executive Mansion, it took a speedy twenty minutes for a message to reach army headquarters in Cuba. To protect the secrecy of troop movements, McKinley ordered military censorship in Florida and in New York City, home of the wire services. The press complained, but complied. On May 17, the Associated Press (AP) resolved "to loyally sustain the general government in the conduct of the war" by avoiding publication of "any information likely to give aid to the enemy or embarrass the government."[12]

To expand the regular army, McKinley called up 200,000 volunteers from National Guard units; each state was given a quota based on population. The commander-in-chief personally chose officers, considering party obligations, competence, and his theme of national unity. Most famously he gave commands to former Confederates, General "Fightin' Joe" Wheeler and Fitzhugh Lee, nephew of General Robert E. Lee who had surrendered to Union General Ulysses S. Grant in 1865. The lack of preparation of the troops was remarked upon by Kansas newspaper editor William Allen White. "The principal martial duty the National Guards had to perform before they were mustered out," noted White, "was to precede the fire company and follow the Grand Army squad in the processions on Memorial Day and the Fourth of July." White was confident that American citizen soldiers, as clumsy as they were, soon would be transformed into a disciplined regiment, a "human engine of death."[13]

As ordered by President McKinley, George Dewey sailed his fleet from Hong Kong to the Philippines and into Manila Bay on the first of May in 1898. Dewey gave the order "You may fire when ready, Gridley," and oversaw the efficient destruction of Spain's Pacific naval force without losing a single American sailor. Ships from the British, French, and German navies witnessed his triumph. As Dewey's fleet attacked, a British naval band showed their support by playing "The Star-Spangled Banner," a song whose lyrics had been composed by an American as the British bombarded Baltimore during the War of 1812. The Germans, with their five warships in Manila Bay, proved more troublesome as time went on, making clear their interest in any available islands. The British for their part much preferred the United States as a partner in the Pacific to Germany. To control information from his end, Dewey cut the transoceanic cable, which meant that news of his victory was transmitted through Hong Kong and reached the United States on May 7. The dramatic reports of Joseph L. Stickney of the *New York Herald*, who blurred the line between reporter and participant by serving as Dewey's aide during the battle, Edward W. Harden of the *New York World* and the *Chicago Tribune*, and John McCutcheon, cartoonist of the *Chicago Record* made Dewey a national hero. Quick to capitalize on the victory, entrepreneurs slapped Dewey's picture or name on songs, dishes, shaving mugs, baby rattles, neckties, and chewing gum.[14]

McKinley adopted a public face of reluctance and uncertainty about the Philippines while he moved to take control. He remarked that "old Dewey" would have saved him a lot of trouble if he had sailed away once he defeated the Spanish fleet. Although certainly true, McKinley followed up Dewey's victory by sending 20,000 troops under General Wesley Merritt to the islands. The president decided, "While we are conducting war and until its conclusion, we must keep all we get. When the war is over we must keep what we want." He told committed expansionist Henry Cabot Lodge that he had doubts about keeping all of the islands, but "we are to keep Manila." The president continued, "If, however as we go on it is made to appear desirable that we should retain all, then we will certainly do it." Over the next several months, Senator Lodge and his fellow jingoes dedicated themselves to make it "appear desirable." As for the American troops, they were shipped overseas on an open-ended mission with inadequate intelligence. Caught by surprise, the War Department could provide Merritt's staff with only an encyclopedia article on the Philippines. Even so, Lt. Col. Edward C. Little of the 20th Kansas Volunteer Infantry Regiment had a good idea of their objective. He told his men, "We go to the far away islands of the Pacific to plant the Stars and Stripes on the ramparts where long enough has waved the cruel and merciless banner of Spain."[15]

On their way to the Philippines, U.S. forces stopped to take the island of Guam from Spanish officers who didn't know they were at war. At the same time, McKinley stepped up plans to acquire the Hawaiian Islands. The president told his secretary, "We need Hawaii just as much and a good deal more than we did California. It is manifest destiny."[16] Five years earlier, U.S. marines and warships had provided support for the overthrow of Queen

Lili'uokalani led by pro-American plantation owners. Urging annexation during the war with Spain, Senator Lodge made the case that if the United States didn't take the islands now someone else would, an argument that he would use again regarding the Philippines. Congress made Hawaii a U.S. territory by joint resolution despite petitions of protest from Hawaiians. With the islands of Hawaii, Guam, and the Philippines, the United States possessed the refueling bases for naval and merchant ships across the Pacific so desired by expansionists.

Meanwhile, the news that the Navy was as effective against the Spanish fleet around Cuba as it had been in the Philippines cheered Washington, which had received troubling reports from the Army. One problem for an army unaccustomed to fighting overseas was the lack of transport. The Navy reluctantly loaned two cruisers, which it never got back, while the Army scrounged around Florida for boats. In mid-June, the Tenth Army Corps led by General William Shafter landed in Cuba. His 17,000 troops traveled with Cuban generals, several European military observers, and eighty-nine journalists all serenaded by brass bands. Famed war correspondent Richard Harding Davis described "a most happy-go-lucky expedition, run with real American optimism and readiness to take big chances, and with the spirit of a people who recklessly trust that it will come out all right in the end." Ambitious for combat and fame, Theodore Roosevelt volunteered and organized his own unit, the Rough Riders, a team of Ivy League graduates and cowboys. The African American 9th and 10th Cavalry deserved much of the credit for the successful attack on the San Juan hills, but Roosevelt and the Rough Riders took it for themselves. Spanish forces surrendered in mid-July. Newspapers extolled the victories but also reported on the terrible sicknesses that devastated American forces in the Caribbean, ultimately causing the deaths of 5,083 soldiers as opposed to the 379 who died in battle. Davis, who publicly dismissed stories of awful camp conditions, wrote his brother, "I have written nothing for the paper because if I started to tell the truth at all, it would do no good, and it would open up a hell of an outcry from all the families of the boys who have volunteered."[17]

In the Philippines, the big problem for the U.S. military was not Spain, but the army of Filipinos headed by the twenty-seven-year-old Emilio Aguinaldo. Spanish colonial administrators had faced a growing nationalist movement led in 1897 by Aguinaldo who declared the Philippines independent, named himself president, and called for rebellion. When Spain began to use the same repressive tactics it employed in Cuba, Aguinaldo accepted a truce, which

SOMETHING LACKING.
Uncle Sam—Well Sonny, What Is It?
Phil Ippines—Where Do I Come In on This?—July 30.

Uncle Sam, wearing the badge "World's Humane Agent," considers what to do with the Philippines as Porto Rico and Cuba look on, July 1898. Charles L. Bartholomew, *Minneapolis Journal.* (*Cartoons of the Spanish-American War by Bart*, Minneapolis: Journal Printing Company, 1899)

included his exile to Hong Kong. He remained there until Dewey had him returned to the Philippines to help the Americans in their fight against Spain. In short order, Aguinaldo resurrected an army; took control of all of the islands with the exception of Manila, a few ports, and the areas inhabited by Muslims; issued a declaration of independence; and set up an elite-dominated government with a national assembly of lawyers, doctors, educators, and writers. Then U.S. army troops arrived, carrying instructions that they were not to share authority in the islands with the Filipinos. General Thomas M. Anderson sent Aguinaldo a message: "General Anderson wishes you to inform your people that we are here for their good and that they must supply us with labor and material at the current market prices."[18]

Recognizing the Filipino people as the real threat, the American command worked out a deal with the Spaniards to stage a mock battle of Manila on August 13, 1898. They would shoot at each other and then Spain would surrender before the Philippine Army of Liberation could take part. As the Americans raised their flag over Manila, the outraged Filipinos cut off the city's water supply. General Merritt was forced to negotiate and allow Filipinos access to their capital city. Merritt sailed for the Spanish-American peace conference held in Paris. He left General Elwell S. Otis, a graduate of Harvard Law School and a veteran of Gettysburg and the Indian wars, in command. Relations between the Filipinos and the Americans were both tense and friendly. Manila was an "odd place," wrote volunteer Wheeler Martin to his family in Idaho. "They cant talk english nor we can't understand them," but there lived "some of the prettyest women I ever saw in my life." A number of U.S. soldiers, who referred to the Filipinos as "niggers" and "gugus," expected deference from the "natives." Filipinos, who knew something about the tragic history of Native Americans and African Americans, expressed their belief that it might be better to die fighting than live under U.S. control.[19]

Its victory over Spain meant that the United States had become a world power. "Our army's greatest invasion of a foreign land was completely successful," eyewitness Davis concluded, "because the Lord looks after his own." Other commentators were from "the Lord helps those who help themselves" school of analysis. *McClure's Magazine* ran an article replete with statistics and charts showing that the United States had become so strong it could prevail in war if attacked by any combination of European nations. Blue and gray had fought together, celebrated McKinley. Theodore Roosevelt trumpeted the uniting in battle of the economic and social classes so divided by industrial strife between business and labor. The fashion magazine *Vogue* wasn't so sure that class unity was a positive development. It expressed regret that "our democracy" required gentlemen to mingle with the other classes in military units. "Constant contact with the rougher element," *Vogue* feared, would "effect changes in a man's character." Spain, which had been so vilified in the weeks leading up to war, was now seen as gallant in defeat. The peoples of Cuba and the Philippines who the Americans had pledged to liberate began to be portrayed by the administration and the press as violent, incompetent, and untrustworthy.[20]

Campaign to Keep the Philippines

AS THE PEACE TALKS WITH SPAIN began in the fall of 1898, McKinley announced that he would make a speaking tour to "sound out" opinion on what to do with the Philippines. His real purpose was to build support for keeping them. In fifty-seven appearances, McKinley linked patriotism with holding the islands. At train stops, he frequently commented with pleasure on seeing children waving "the glorious old banner of the free." He also sought approval to keep troops in the Pacific, even though, as Democratic leaders pointed out, the men had enlisted to free Cuba. McKinley's aides made sure that his appearances in midwestern towns reached a wide audience. They took along a train carload of reporters from the wire services, national magazines, and big city newspapers. The president's staff distributed advance copies of formal speeches along with numerous bulletins complete with human-interest anecdotes, which frequently appeared word for word as news stories. Newspaper editors got the message and reported that it looked like the United States would be keeping the Pacific islands.[21]

McKinley struck two major themes, unity and progress, as he spoke to cheering crowds in Iowa. To the people of Clinton, he said, "North and South have been united as never before. People who think alike in a country like ours must act together." He suggested that where war and foreign policy were concerned politics should stop at the water's edge. At Denison, he said, "Partisanship has been hushed, and the voice of patriotism alone is heard throughout the land." In Chariton, he spoke of the peaceful acquisition of Hawaii in addition to the Spanish territories. "And, my fellow-citizens, wherever our flag floats, wherever we raise that standard of liberty, it is always for the sake of humanity and the advancement of civilization," proclaimed McKinley. "Territory sometimes comes to us when we go to war for a holy cause, and whenever it does the banner of liberty will float over it and bring, I trust, blessings and benefits to all the people." At Hastings, the president was direct about the rewards of war: "We have pretty much everything in this country to make it happy. We have good money, we have ample revenues, we have unquestioned national credit; but we want new markets, and as trade follows the flag, it looks very much as if we were going to have new markets." To the people of Arcola, Illinois, the president spelled out what it meant to

President McKinley greets the citizens of Alliance, Ohio, from the rear platform of his train, 1900. (Library of Congress, LC-USZ62-102871)

have foreign markets: "When you cannot sell your broom-corn in our own country, you are glad to send the surplus to some other country, and get their good money for your good broom-corn." When McKinley returned to Washington, he remarked that "the people" seemed to expect that the United States would keep the Philippines.[22]

The administration always had wanted Manila as a base and decided early on to hold the island of Luzon to protect the capital city. When the Navy argued that it would be better to have all of the islands, McKinley agreed. He accepted General F. V. Greene's favorable report on the commercial opportunities of the islands. Numerous articles and books about "our new possessions" outlined their potential for supplying Americans with coffee, sugar, and mineral wealth. Washington instructed U.S. authorities in the Philippines not to promise anything to "the natives" or to treat them as partners but to avoid an outright conflict. For their part, Aguinaldo and his supporters, committed to the goal of independence, were divided on how best to proceed, unsure of whether to ask for American protection of their independence or formal recognition.[23]

McKinley organized the Peace Commission so that expansionists would dominate the delegation to Paris, carefully including prominent Senators since the Senate would have to ratify any treaty. During their deliberations, the commissioners were briefed by General Charles A. Whittier, who said that based on his meetings with Aguinaldo, the Filipino leader would not be difficult to manage. Furthermore, he reassured them as to "the ease with which good soldiers could be made out of the natives, provided they were led by white officers."[24] With Spain, the commissioners negotiated a treaty that gave the United States control of Cuba, Puerto Rico, Guam, and for twenty million dollars, the Philippine Islands.

Shortly after the president signed the treaty, but before it was submitted to the Senate for ratification in late December 1898, he sent orders to General Otis in the Philippines announcing that "the mission of the United States is one of benevolent assimilation." McKinley continued, "In the fulfillment of this high mission, supporting the temperate administration of affairs for the greatest good of the governed, there must be sedulously maintained the strong arm of authority, to repress disturbance and to overcome all obstacles to the bestowal of the blessings of good and stable government upon the people of the Philippine Islands under the free flag of the United States." This elaborate message expressed the desired combination: a free United States and a stable Philippines. The War Department instructed Otis to "prosecute the occupation" with tact and kindness, avoiding confrontation with the insurgents by being "conciliatory but firm." Aguinaldo, convinced that the Senate would reject the treaty because it so grievously violated American principles, maintained a siege of Manila. His envoy Felipe Agoncillo traveled to Paris where both sides at the peace talks ignored him. He returned to Washington to make the case that the "greatest Republic of America" should recognize the first Republic of Asia or there would be conflict, but no official would see him.[25]

As McKinley's plan to take the Philippines became clear, a number of Americans spoke out in opposition for a variety of reasons, some principled and some practical. Anti-imperialists included former presidents, the Democrat Grover Cleveland and the Republican Benjamin Harrison, industrialist Andrew Carnegie, labor leaders Samuel Gompers and Eugene V. Debs, philosopher William James, and writer William Dean Howells. Satirists Mark Twain and Peter Finley Dunne mocked the high-sounding rhetoric of humanitarianism and morality, which they saw as a cover for racism and greed. Dunne's famous character, the barkeeper Mr. Dooley, said it was a case

Emilio Aguinaldo (second seated man from right) and other insurgent leaders.
(National Archives, 391-PI-34)

of hands across the sea and into someone's pocket. African American leaders
Booker T. Washington and W. E. B. DuBois believed that the Filipinos could
govern themselves and certainly would do a better job than the United States
judging by the American record with nonwhite people at home. Other anti-
imperialists were white supremacists who believed that any effort to prepare
Filipinos for self-government would fail. Women's rights groups, still fighting
for the vote, sympathized with the Filipinos facing the prospect of being
governed without their consent. Those with strategic concerns pointed out
that the United States always had depended on the Pacific Ocean as a barrier,
protecting it from attack. Acquisition of hard-to-defend bases at Manila and
Pearl Harbor would make the United States more vulnerable.[26]

Despite the organization of the Anti-Imperialists League with its 30,000
members, the Senate ratification of the peace treaty appeared likely in early
1899. The economy was booming and the Republicans did well in the 1898
congressional elections. The president's critics accused him of either being
a genial hack, the tool of bosses and capitalists, or a mastermind, craftily

forging an empire by trampling over the Constitution and Congress, a sure indication that they were demoralized and did not know how to challenge him. The president made another tour to promote his Philippines policy, this time through the South, where in Savannah he asked, "Can we leave these people, who, by the fortunes of war and our own acts, are helpless and without government, to chaos and anarchy, after we have destroyed the only government they have had?" He answered, "Having destroyed their government, it is the duty of the American people to provide for a better one." The president dismissed as unpatriotic any suggestion that the American people were incapable of creating a new government for others. On February 6, 1899, the Senate ratified the treaty with one vote to spare. The Senate vote divided largely along party lines, which meant that partisan politics may have had more to do with the outcome than the outbreak of fighting in the Philippines the day before.[27]

War in the Philippines

NO ONE KNOWS FOR SURE who fired the first shot. The opening battle followed weeks during which both sides had engaged in provocations. Most accounts identify American sentries from the 1st Nebraska Regiment as the ones who opened fire when three or four Filipinos failed to halt as ordered. But the story that first reached the Executive Mansion courtesy of the *New York Sun* reported that the insurgents had initiated the attack. McKinley never wavered from this version, later elaborating on it by claiming that the attacking insurgents had violated a flag of truce and shot down U.S. soldiers while they treated wounded Filipinos. How the Filipinos came to be wounded went unexplained. The president was confident that the United States would easily and quickly pacify the islands. Reports of the first battle in which forty-four Americans and seven hundred Filipinos were killed helped to inspire such confidence. Washington called the conflict an insurrection; the Philippine Republic considered it a fight for independence.[28]

Between February 1899 and November 1899, Americans and Filipinos fought a conventional war with regular armies and set battles. The American forces maintained an average troop strength of 40,000 men and the Filipinos between 80,000 to 100,000 regulars. Military historian Brian McAllister Linn described the Filipino Army as intrepid and courageous with an impressive infantry but suffering from inadequate training and lack of weapons and ammunition. The Americans had greater skills, effective and powerful

"Insurgent dead just as they fell," February 5, 1899. (National Archives, III-AGA-3-22)

weapons, and a navy that shut down coastal and island traffic. Late in the year, Filipino forces turned to guerrilla tactics designed to hit the Americans at their weak points. U.S. troops occasionally sighted and pursued the enemy, only to come upon farmers working hard in a field. Private Frederick Presher of New Jersey suspected they were "quick change artists," but had no proof. Aguinaldo exercised less control over his forces in the guerrilla phase, and the fighting continued after he was captured in 1901. The Filipino strategy aimed to wear out the Americans and make their occupation too costly to continue.[29]

To carry out benevolent assimilation, the U.S. Army pursued a "carrot and stick" policy developed during the Civil War and Indian wars. It rewarded cooperation with reforms and punished opposition with coercion, destruction of property, and death. General Otis applied his significant administrative skills to civic action programs. McKinley established a Philippine Commission to visit the islands and determine what should be done to maintain "order, peace and the public welfare." The commissioners reported that the Filipinos were not ready for independence. McKinley set up a second commission, led by William Howard Taft, a fellow Republican from Ohio, to serve as the U.S. governing authority. The U.S. civilian and military authorities attempted to woo Filipino elites with promises of opportunity and privilege. General Arthur MacArthur ordered his soldiers to establish "friendly relations with the natives."[30] Otis, like McKinley, was confident of success because he mistakenly thought only a small percentage of Filipinos opposed American rule.

At home, millions of viewers saw the administration's optimism about the war reflected in films. The new motion picture companies discovered that audiences were eager to watch dramatic scenes of their military forces in victorious action. The films, each less than a minute long, served as a "visual newspaper and as propaganda," according to film historian Charles Musser. Some films featured actual footage of troops marching and ships sailing. Others were faked and called "reenactments." For example, the box office hit *Battle of Manila Bay* was made on top of a roof in New York City with cardboard ships floating in a table turned upside down and filled with water. Thomas Edison's company produced six reenactment films set in the Philippines and shot in New Jersey. In *Advance of Kansas Volunteers at Caloocan*, made in June 1899, white American soldiers wave the flag as they triumphantly defeat the Filipinos played by African Americans. Such films and others in which actors in blackface played Filipinos reinforced the perception that the war was about superior, white Americans subduing a dark and inferior enemy. Theater owners further enhanced the spectacle with the sound of gunfire or by spreading smoke through the audience, which would hiss at the enemy and cheer the raising of the American flag. Musser concludes that during the war, the movie showmen "evoked powerful patriotic sentiments in their audiences, revealing the new medium's ideological and propagandistic force."[31]

Press reports from the Philippines indicated that victory might not be as imminent as the film reenactments or Otis's official reports suggested. The military placed few restrictions on war correspondents, who traveled, ate, camped, and sometimes joined in combat operations with the troops. Reporters wrote that Otis "never visited the lines" and refused to heed the analysis of those at the front. In the popular magazine *Collier's Weekly*, Frederick Palmer noted, "General Otis does not impart his plans to anybody either before or after they have failed." One general told Palmer that he disagreed with Otis on strategy: "I want to lick the insurrectos first and reason with them afterward. He wants to reason with them and lick them at the same time." In June 1899, correspondent John Bass, who reported for *Harper's Magazine*, observed that the "whole population of the islands sympathizes with the insurgents" and that "the American outlook is blacker now than it has been since the beginning of the war."[32] Reporters, who for the most part endorsed expansionist policies, criticized what they saw as Otis's ineffectiveness because they wanted the U.S. military to succeed.

Reporters also objected to what they saw as excessive censorship. The Army controlled the one telegraph line out of Manila and reviewed all press reports. Otis assured Washington that his censors allowed reporters to cable "established facts" but not the "numerous baseless rumors circulated here tending to excite the outside world." In the summer of 1899, the censor blocked a story reporting that General Henry Lawton thought it would take at least 75,000 troops to pacify the islands, a story that reinforced the impression that all was not going as well as Otis claimed. When correspondents objected, Otis threatened to expel or court-martial anyone who sent a formal letter of complaint from Manila. The frustrated reporters transmitted their complaint to the United States via Hong Kong and charged that censors clamped down on news not because it would harm operations but because it would upset people back home. They accused Otis of attempting to make things look better than they were by fixing casualty reports, overrating military accomplishments, and underestimating the Filipinos' commitment to independence. The administration was implicated in these charges because it released Otis's official reports, making it hard to tell, as the *Cleveland Plain Dealer* pointed out, just who was misleading the public, Otis or the administration. Even the expansionist press joined in the criticism, except the McKinley loyalists who argued that only the president could be in the position to know what news of the war was safe to report. The president announced that he would continue to support Otis's censorship policies.[33]

Although soldiers and reporters tended to believe that Filipinos were inferior to Americans, some learned to respect their opponents' tenacity. For example, Colonel Frederick Funston told a correspondent that the enemy was "an illiterate, semi-savage people, who are waging war, not against tyranny, but against Anglo-Saxon order and decency." Palmer's reporting, however, gave the Filipinos credit for effective fighting. "But the island of Luzon is large," he wrote, "and the Lawton expedition, such is the excellence of Aguinaldo's intelligence bureau, was not more than fairly started before the Filipino army appeared on the flank of MacArthur's division opposite to where it was wanted and began taking pot shots at the worn and cynical

Montana regiment."[34] William Oliver Trafton, a twenty-two-year-old Texas cowhand who enlisted for adventure, referred to the enemy as savages, wild varmints, and Indians. When he endured more hardship than adventure, he developed some admiration for the Filipinos. Before a battle Trafton talked with his friend:

> He says, "Hell, they sure won't kill only 40 of us."
> I says, "You told me that we could whip the whole thing in two weeks."
> He says, "Haven't we licked them every time that we have had a fight?"
> I says, "Yes, but the damn fools won't stay whipped."[35]

Like many Americans, Trafton had underestimated the Filipinos' determination to resist.

The Debate over Empire

THE RESISTANCE OF THE FILIPINOS to U.S. rule required some adjustment in the administration's presentation of its policy. McKinley still portrayed the American cause as humanitarian. He expressed his sorrow that certain "foolish" Filipinos had failed to recognize the benefits of American generosity. A year after the sinking of the *Maine*, McKinley stood in the Mechanics' Hall in Boston, the capital of the anti-imperialist movement, before portraits of Washington, Lincoln, and himself labeled "Liberators," to explain to an audience of almost six thousand that the United States sought to emancipate the Philippines. "No imperial designs lurk in the American mind," he asserted. Dismissing controversy, McKinley said it was not "a good time for the liberator to submit important questions concerning liberty and government to the liberated while they are engaged in shooting down their rescuers." Ironically, the news that the Filipinos were fighting for their independence was used to justify the argument that they weren't ready for it. With exasperation, the anti-imperialist *Nation* commented, "McKinley is one of the rare public speakers who are able to talk a good deal of humbug in such a way as to make their average hearers think it excellent sense and exactly their idea."[36]

As opposition to the war grew at home, McKinley linked support for the troops with support for his policies. The president spoke at the August homecoming of the Tenth Pennsylvania Regiment in Pittsburgh. He expressed his confidence in General Otis, his praise for the troops who served their country "in its extremity," and his disdain for critics who said the soldiers should be brought home. He argued that without U.S. soldiers, the Philippines would be in chaos and suffering under the rule of "one man, and not with the consent of the governed." Here he somehow implied that the Filipinos themselves prevented the establishment of "the consent of the governed," but in the same speech he stated that the goal was the creation of a government there under the "undisputed sovereignty" of the United States. The most dramatic moment of the ceremony came when McKinley slowly read a list of the regiments engaged in the Philippines: "First California, First Colorado, First Idaho, Fifty-first Iowa, Twentieth Kansas, Thirteenth Minnesota, First Montana, First Nebraska, First North Dakota, Second Oregon, Tenth Pennsylvania, First South Dakota, First Tennessee, Utah Artillery...." As he did, the soldiers of Pennsylvania roared their appreciation for each regiment. By celebrating unity with a roll call of the states, the president, with the help of cheering soldiers, could drown out dissent.[37]

President McKinley reviews the state militia in Los Angeles, 1901. (Library of Congress, LC-USZ62-122820)

McKinley and his fellow expansionists linked national glory to power and economic interests. Just before he left on another autumn tour to promote his policies, the president spoke to close associates at the Executive Mansion. "One of the best things we ever did was to insist upon taking the Philippines and not a coaling station or an island, for if we had done the latter we would have been the laughing stock of the world," said McKinley. "And so it has come to pass that in a few short months we have become a world power." The president, who tended to be less specific about American power in public, left the more assertive statements to his supporters. In *Collier's Weekly*, Lodge made the persuasive case that if left alone, the Philippines would be vulnerable to takeover by some European power not bothered by issues of self-government. He described the islands as rich in natural resources and a large potential market "as the wants of the [Filipinos] expand in the sunshine of prosperity, freedom and civilization." Moreover, the possession of the islands secured access to even greater markets. "No longer will it be possible for other powers to shut the gates of China upon us," declared the Massachusetts senator. "Will the American people reject this opportunity?" Lodge asked. "Will they throw away all this trade, and all this wealth?" He didn't think so.[38]

The expansionists mustered racial arguments to justify U.S. policies. Senator Albert J. Beveridge (R-IN) told the Senate that race was more powerful than the Constitution. "God has not been preparing the English-speaking and Teutonic peoples for a thousand years for nothing but vain and idle self-contemplation and self-admiration. No!" he declared. "He has made us the master organizers of the world to establish system where chaos reigns."[39] Without U.S. control, Lodge predicted "bloody anarchy" among the eight million people of many different races and tribes speaking fifty or sixty languages and dialects on the 1,725 islands of the Philippines. He denounced Aguinaldo as "an irresponsible Chinese Mestizo" (Aguinaldo's maternal grandfather was Chinese) and a "self-seeking dictator of the ordinary half-breed type" leading one portion of a tribe in rebellion. Theodore Roosevelt compared the Filipino insurgency to the Indian wars when he accepted the Republican vice-presidential nomination in 1900; the parallels, he declared, were so "exact" that self-government to the Philippines "would be like granting self-government to an Apache reservation under some local chief." War correspondent John Bass shared some of the racial views of the expansionists but was less confident that the use of force in the Philippines would succeed. Writing in *Harper's Magazine* about the Moros or Muslims of the islands of Sula and Mindanao, he predicted that these people, like the Native Americans, would succumb eventually to the superior race. In the meantime, although their "land of promise" could flourish with tobacco and coffee plantations, it was best to leave the Moros with their wives and their Koran alone, concluded Bass. If they were forced to change, he correctly predicted, they would fight.[40]

Much was made of manly duty. In Madison, Wisconsin, McKinley announced that since the army and navy had "brought us" new territories, Americans must meet their responsibilities "with manly courage" and "respond in a manly fashion to manly duty." Theodore Roosevelt, advocate of the strenuous life, insisted that military service toughened American manhood, which too much civilization tended to undermine. American men, in particular, had an obligation to set an example. "The eyes of the world are upon us," stated Philippine Commissioner Dean C. Worcester in a speech before prominent Chicagoans. Worcester echoed John Winthrop, who in 1630 had defined the Puritan mission with the declaration "we shall be as a city upon a hill." To this founding inspiration, Worcester added a quotation from the new poem by British poet Rudyard Kipling. In "The White Man's Burden," Kipling urged Americans to take up their imperial responsibilities over their "new-caught, sullen peoples, half-devil and half-child."[41]

As later recalled by a minister, McKinley's most quoted explanation for his Philippines policy was oddly personal. Speaking to a delegation of Methodists in 1899, he insisted that he had not wanted the Philippines and "when they came to us, as a gift from the gods, I did not know what to do with them." He described praying on his knees for guidance when it came to him that it would be "cowardly and dishonorable" to give the islands back to Spain, "bad business" to give them to commercial rivals Germany and France, and impossible to leave them to "anarchy and misrule" under unfit Filipinos. "There was nothing left for us to do," he concluded, "but to take them all, and to educate the Filipinos, and uplift and civilize and Christianize them." In this account of divine guidance, McKinley neglected to mention that most of the Filipinos were Roman Catholic or that the Philippines had a university older than Harvard. This explanation, nevertheless, summed up the key principled, pragmatic, and prejudiced justifications of the president's imperial policy.[42]

Anti-imperialists also cited principles and national self-interest to argue against U.S. policy in the Philippines. To state the opposing position, *Collier's Weekly* invited Republican George F. Hoar, the respected senior Senator of Massachusetts and Lodge's counterpart. The debate, Hoar argued, was between republic and empire, between liberty and slavery, between the Declaration of Independence and imperialism. Standing by its traditional principles, the United States had become "the strongest, freest, richest nation on the face of the earth." Americans would deny their own heritage, he asserted, if instead of dealing with the people of the Philippines as Christians who desired independence, they treated the Filipinos as primitives to be subdued so that Americans could "use their land as a stepping-stone to the trade of China." Other anti-imperialists used satire to contrast U.S. policy with Christian values. William Lloyd Garrison, Jr., the son of the noted abolitionist, rewrote a popular hymn.

> Then onward, Christian soldier! Through field of crimson gore,
> Behold the trade advantages beyond the open door!
> The profits on our ledgers outweigh the heathen loss;
> Set thou the glorious stars and stripes above the ancient cross!

The *New York Evening Post* justified such opposition, saying, "Anti-Imperialism is only another name for old-fashioned Americanism."[43]

For imperialists and anti-imperialists interested in expanding American trade in the Pacific, the debate centered on the question of whether the Filipinos on their own were capable of providing the Americans with the economic opportunities they wanted. In his Annual Message, now called the State of the Union address, President McKinley told the nation that the Filipinos "should be helped...to a more scientific knowledge of the production of coffee, india rubber, and tropical products, for which there is demand in the United States." The anti-imperialist Senator George Turner of Washington acknowledged the need to protect the "vast interests" of the United States in Asia but pointed out that if Manila became a great trading port, it would be at the expense of American ports on the Pacific coast. "It will profit principally a motley population of foreigners, for whom we care nothing," Turner concluded. He suggested that by letting the Filipinos govern themselves, the United States could then make commercial treaties with the islands without the burdens of governing. Even Senator Hoar desired access to Asian markets; he simply objected to the means by which the United States was obtaining it. So did the editors of *Harper's Weekly*, who felt that the United States had made a mistake in the Philippines. Echoing the president, however, they concluded that once the country was at war, everyone must pull together to support the troops.[44]

Also fueling anti-imperialist anger was the perception that the administration had abused its power and deceived the public. Senator Hoar believed that the American people had been misled when they were told that the Filipinos were "barbarous and savage" and had made "an unprovoked attack...upon our flag." Referring to "McKinley's War," anti-imperialists charged the president with waging war by military authority, not a congressional declaration. Mark Twain thought that the American people and the Filipinos were being "sold a bill of goods," which featured two different brands of civilization. "For home consumption," he thought, the "blessings of civilization"—justice, gentleness, Christianity, law and order, temperance, liberty, equality, education—were prettily and attractively displayed. For export to "the heathen market," in contrast, "civilization" meant blood, tears, destruction, and loss of freedom. The war, he felt, betrayed the Filipinos and the "clean young men" sent to fight them. Twain tried to imagine what the Filipinos thought: "There must be two Americas: one that sets the captive free, and one that takes a once-captive's new freedom away from him, and picks a quarrel with him with nothing to found it on; then kills him to get his land." He said he wished he could see how the United States was going to get out of what had become "a mess, a quagmire."[45]

The debate over the war became more politicized in the 1900 presidential election. The Democratic candidate, William Jennings Bryan, called for Congress to consider granting independence to the Philippines. Anti-imperialist and philosopher William James hoped that if the Filipinos held out long enough, Americans would come to their senses and reject "imperialism and the idol of a national destiny, based on martial excitement and mere 'bigness.'" The administration and the military condemned the anti-imperialists for, as they saw it, encouraging the Filipinos to resist by denouncing U.S. policies. William Howard Taft thought with justification that the insurgents would fight on in hope of a Democratic victory in November.[46] Bryan centered much of his campaign on the Philippine issue. He declared McKinley's policy to be a violation of the sacred mission of America. The victorious McKinley spoke of jobs and economic growth. Roosevelt, with his escort of armed cowboys, campaigned for virile, nationalistic Republicanism. At his second inauguration in March 1901, McKinley began his speech talking about currency and ended with the Philippines. "We are not waging war against the inhabitants of the Philippine Islands. A portion of them are making war against the United States," he declared. "By far the greater part of the inhabitants recognize American sovereignty and welcome it as a guaranty of order and of security for life, property, liberty, freedom of conscience, and the pursuit of happiness."[47]

After McKinley's reelection, U.S. forces escalated the repression. In May 1900, Otis had been succeeded by MacArthur who rejected "benevolent assimilation" and with it the belief that most Filipinos really wanted American rule. In December, MacArthur ordered U.S. forces to wage war against the civilian population in hostile areas. The Americans employed torture, executed prisoners, raped women, looted villages, and destroyed the rural economy. The most effective way to punish a guerrilla fighter, explained General Robert P. Hughes, was to attack his women and children. Funston, now promoted to brigadier general, tricked Aguinaldo into surrender by pretending to be a prisoner of disguised Filipino scouts, entering the leader's camp, and then taking him captive. Aguinaldo called for the end of resistance; several of his generals surrendered and many guerrillas went home. Where the fighting continued, both sides carried out atrocities. In Batangas province in 1901 and 1902, the Americans used reconcentration camps that had caused such outrage when Spain used them in Cuba. An estimated 200,000 Filipinos died from disease and starvation. The punitive policies succeeded in breaking the resistance. Colonel Arthur Murray, who had opposed brutal actions that would make enemies out of civilians assumed to be friendly, concluded that if he had it to do over, he would have had done "a little more killing and considerably more burning."[48]

The conciliation side of U.S. policy was the responsibility of Taft, who was confident of the ability of the United States to bring justice and order to the islands. He believed that once laws governing land, mining, banking, and transportation were in place and schools, roads, and hospitals were built, enterprise and prosperity would follow. Yet, he was dogged by problems everywhere. The Filipinos were ignorant and superstitious, he reported. "We shall have to do the best we can with them." Taft's deeper frustrations were reserved for his fellow Americans. He condemned the U.S. military officers who treated the Filipinos with cruelty and prejudice, because such behavior inspired more recruits for the insurgents. To Secretary of War Elihu Root, Taft complained about the behavior of U.S. civilians. "You know we have the rag tag and bob tail of Americans, who are not only vicious but stupid," wrote Taft. "They are most anxious to have Congress give an opportunity to open this country and develop it, but instead of facilitating a condition of peace and good feeling between the Americans and the Filipinos, they are constantly stirring up trouble." Taft, who was trying to win over the Filipino upper class, despaired when a visiting congressman announced at a press interview in Manila that the Filipinos were "nothing but savages, living a savage life and utterly incapable of self government and without the slightest knowledge of what independence is." The same attitudes about Filipino inferiority that expansionists had expressed to justify the takeover now interfered with the administration's efforts to carry it out.[49]

Taft also had to respond to Washington's concerns about news reports that described Manila as a den of sin, drunkenness, and prostitution. In contrast to the administration's claims that their purpose was to bring Christian uplift to the Philippines, it looked instead as though the occupation of the islands had corrupted the morals of U.S. troops. Taft blamed the negative press for upsetting the people at home but had to admit the characterization was valid. He defensively noted that Manila at least was more sober than American cities of its size. The army, alarmed by the spread of venereal disease, established a system for examining prostitutes and confining the diseased to hospitals. As historian Kristin Hoganson has noted, such news prompted anti-imperialists to challenge the administration's portrayal of its policy as a civilizing mission. Critics declared that instead of enhancing masculine nobility, imperialism led to degeneracy or "going native."[50]

At home, McKinley concentrated on spreading the word of progress. In his last speech given in September at the 1901 Pan-American Exposition in Buffalo, New York, the president praised the fair for recording "the world's advancement." Extolling industrial growth, commercial advantage, and new communications technology, he declared, "Isolation is no longer possible or desirable." For the instruction and entertainment of millions of fair-goers, the fair directors constructed a Filipino Village—their idealized version of the Philippines—alongside Mexican, Hawaiian, Cuban, Eskimo, and Japanese villages. To enter the eleven-acre Filipino Village, fair-goers passed U.S. soldiers on parade at the gates. Once inside they saw one hundred Filipinos at work and play, thatched huts, water buffalo pulling carts, a Catholic church, and a theater where a Filipino band played "The Star-Spangled Banner." The organizers included representatives of the more "primitive tribes" and had decided against putting Aguinaldo on display. The exposition's artificial global order was shattered when Leon Czolgosz, an anarchist and the son of Polish immigrants, shot the president. After McKinley died eight days later, anarchists and socialists were arrested around the country, demands escalated for restrictions on immigration, and the price of souvenirs at the exposition skyrocketed.[51]

Peaceful Filipinos display economic productivity in the Philippine Village at the Pan-American Exposition in Buffalo, New York, September 1901. Frances Benjamin Johnston, photographer. (Library of Congress, Lot 2967 (G) Box 1)

Theodore Roosevelt's administration defended the ongoing conflict and the extreme methods used to fight it. Under pressure from Senator Hoar, the Senate investigated the conduct of the war in April and May 1902. News stories of the reconcentration program and torture practices had appeared in the press. Anti-imperialists bypassed military censorship in the Philippines by publishing eyewitness accounts of atrocities reported by returning soldiers. Chaired by Senator Lodge, the hearings led to light fines for a few officers and a court martial for General Jacob H. Smith, who had ordered his troops to kill every person over ten years old on the island of Samar. Smith's court martial actually ended in only a reprimand. Lodge said that he regretted the atrocities but blamed American behavior on Filipino culture. "I think they have grown out of the conditions of warfare, of the war waged by the Filipinos themselves, a semicivilized people, with all the tendencies and characteristics of Asiatics, with the Asiatic indifference to life, with the Asiatic treachery and the Asiatic cruelty, all tinctured and increased by three hundred years of subjection to Spain," he explained. Roosevelt dismissed reports of

U.S. atrocities. He thought that American troops had behaved worse at the massacre of the Sioux at Wounded Knee in 1890. Moreover, he denounced the army's critics "who walk delicately and live in the soft places of the earth" for dishonoring the "strong men who with blood and sweat" suffered and died "to bring the light of civilization into the world's dark places."[52]

Power in the Pacific

ON JULY 4, 1902, President Roosevelt declared the war in the Philippines over. The editors of the *Washington Post* noted that between the two of them, Presidents McKinley and Roosevelt had tried to pronounce the war over six times already. The Philippine Commission defined any continuing Filipino insurgence as "banditry."[53] Forty-two hundred Americans and hundreds of thousands of Filipinos had died. The fighting between Filipinos and Americans continued until 1910 and against the Moros on Mindanao until 1935. Six years later, in December 1941, the Japanese attacked the Philippines and defeated U.S. forces led by General Arthur MacArthur's son, General Douglas MacArthur, who vowed to return and liberate the islands. Aguinaldo, his father's old adversary, sided with the Japanese. After World War II, the United States granted the Philippines independence on July 4, 1946, but kept major naval and air bases on the islands until the early 1990s. Aguinaldo, ever the survivor, marched in the first Philippine Independence Day parade waving the revolutionary flag he first had raised in 1898.

President McKinley announced a new global role for the United States when he acquired the Philippines. For years, the U.S. government ran the Philippines in the interests of powerful Americans, specifically those with influence in Washington. "Any connection between these interests and those of the Filipino people at large—or, for that matter, of the American people at large—was basically coincidental," concluded historian H. W. Brands. The United States had become a Pacific power, but the costs of running its colony exceeded the profits. The experience of the Americans in the Philippines reinforced their preference for economic expansion in Asia without direct imperialism. McKinley did not hesitate to assert U.S. interests. For instance, in 1900, the president dispatched 5000 troops from the Philippines to China to join the other imperial powers as they put down the Chinese government-backed rebellion against foreign influence known as the Boxer Rebellion. By ordering U.S. forces to fight overseas against a recognized government without congressional approval, McKinley had created a new presidential power. And

UNCLE SAM—DID ANYONE SAY HE WISHED TO TREAD ON THE TAILS OF MY COAT?
December 3.

Uncle Sam spreads his coat tails to cover the Philippines, Hawaii, Cuba, and Puerto Rico, December 1898. Charles L. Bartholomew, *Minneapolis Journal.* (*Cartoons of the Spanish-American War by Bart*, Minneapolis: Journal Printing Company, 1899)

he had proven Senator Lodge to be right. The acquisition of the Philippines meant no other power could "shut the gates of China" on the United States and that included China.[54]

McKinley, who, according to Root, "always had his way," claimed to follow the will of the people as he shaped opinion.[55] He established the White House as the producer of news and, through the emerging mass media, delivered his messages that balanced principles and interests with something for almost everyone: gung-ho expansionists, do-gooders and missionaries, businessmen, and flag-waving audiences at train stations across the country. He presented the United States and himself as servants of a higher power, fulfilling an extended version of Manifest Destiny. He declared that "trade follows the flag" and the flag must be honored wherever it waved. Although he spoke of the benefits of new markets, access to natural resources, and enhanced prestige, McKinley assured Americans that this policy was not mainly one of self-interest. It was a "divine mission" in which Americans took on the responsibility of guiding Filipinos. Popular films, cartoons, and fair exhibits reinforced the official messages that this mission meant profit and glory. At the same time, such assertions of America's moral and material superiority were challenged by a drawn-out war, heavy loss of life, and reports of atrocities. Critics expressed concern that war for empire could damage the republic. And the argument made by anti-imperialists—that Americans should not just preach their democratic traditions overseas but actually practice them—would survive.

With gusto, President Theodore Roosevelt associated American expansion with the progress of civilization. It was the task of the "masterful race," announced Roosevelt in 1901, to make the Filipinos "fit for self-government" or leave them "to fall into a welter of murderous anarchy." In his Annual Message of 1902, he asserted that as civilization had expanded in the last century, warfare had diminished between civilized powers. "Wars with uncivilized powers," Roosevelt explained, "are largely mere matters of international police duty, essential for the welfare of the world."[56] It would be the job of his successors to define who was civilized and who was not.

2

Crusade for Democracy
Over There in the Great War

We go forth in the same spirit in which the knights of old went forth to do battle with the Saracens. Notwithstanding the sacrifices, we shall gain from it a nobler manhood and a deeper sense of America's mission in the world.... The young men of America are going out to rescue Civilization. They are going to fight for one definite thing, to save Democracy from death. They are marching on to give America's freedom to the oppressed multitudes of the earth.

Pershing's Crusaders, 1918

We have come back hating war, disgusted with the prattle about ideals, disillusioned entirely about the struggles between nations. That is why we are quiet, why we talk little, and why our friends do not understand. But the populace refuses to be disillusioned; they force us to feed their own delusions. Soon we will take on the pose of brave crusaders who swept the battlefields with a shout and a noble charge.

Captain Will Judy, 1919

AS A RESULT OF WORLD WAR I, President Woodrow Wilson sought nothing less than the creation of a new world order based on American principles and interests and led by the United States. After three years of staying out of the European conflict, the president decided that the United States must take a hand in ending it. Confident of American moral and economic superiority, he believed the United States would save civilization from barbarism. To the war, he brought a plan for peace. It challenged old world imperialism by advocating the principle of self-determination, which allowed people to choose their own governments. He called for open door capitalism and advocated an international collective security system. Wilson's brand of liberal internationalism projected a world order in which the United States would

46

thrive. Americans would go to war, he declared, to make the world safe for democracy.

The son of a Presbyterian minister, the devout Wilson believed that God had ordained his presidency. A former professor of history and politics, president of Princeton University, and Democratic governor of New Jersey, he bested incumbent Republican William Howard Taft and third party candidate, former president Theodore Roosevelt, in 1912. Wilson oversaw the adoption of progressive reforms intended to restore morality, order, and economic opportunity in a time of corporate consolidation and social unrest. He brought this same reform agenda to international affairs, offering it as an alternative to war and revolution. Although famous for his brilliant speeches espousing democratic idealism and internationalism, he frequently used American power to assert national self-interest. Between 1913 and 1917, he ordered U.S. military interventions in Cuba, Haiti, the Dominican Republic, Honduras, Nicaragua, and Mexico to restore order and protect American economic interests. For Wilson, the contradictions between the promotion of democratic ideals and the assertion of U.S. power through military intervention were resolved by his conviction that what was best for the United States was best for the world.

When he led the United States into World War I, Wilson set up a propaganda agency, the Committee on Public Information (CPI), to rally public support. It combined the most modern methods of persuasion with messages of American greatness. The prominent image of the crusader, seen in film, posters, and advertisements, showed Americans as the redeemers of civilization, rescuing innocent allies and defeating a vicious enemy. Following in McKinley's footsteps, Wilson celebrated the unity of north and south in time of crisis. Born in Virginia, he was the first Southerner to be president since the Civil War. Wilson extolled "the old spirit of chivalric gallantry" before a convention of Confederate veterans on Registration Day in June 1917 when ten million men registered for the draft.[1] The unity theme did not include everyone equally. Racial and religious minorities received little attention in propaganda images that echoed popular histories of the crusades as a fight between white Christians and dark-skinned heathens. To fit the role of the enemy, the Germans, although white and Christian, became dehumanized barbarians called Huns, after the fifth century Mongolian invaders led by Attila. Even as the crusader image upheld conservative values of elite, masculine leadership, it also satisfied progressive reformers who promoted moral virtue and social justice. Significantly, propagandists turned an image from medieval Europe into one that celebrated American unity, progress, and idealism.

The Wilson administration combined propaganda with news management. The president's speeches and "the story of our boys in the trenches are the finest propaganda the world has ever seen," crowed James Kerney of the CPI.[2] The administration thought that news stories should back up the government's interpretation of events. When Wilson decided in 1916 to send troops under General John Pershing into Mexico to punish rebel leader Pancho Villa for raids across the border, the White House asked reporters to "be good enough to assist the administration in presenting [its] view of the expedition to the American people."[3] Its view was that the expedition did not constitute an intervention. In Mexico, the advance of 10,000 U.S. troops certainly looked like an intervention, especially when they clashed with Mexican government forces. As for reporters, they found themselves on the receiving end of, in the words of Associated Press (AP) reporter Arthur Sweetser, "some fine stories and of course much propaganda."[4]

In addition to using news management to define policies, the Wilson administration also enacted extensive censorship to protect military operations overseas and to crush dissent at home. It identified disagreements with the official line as enemy propaganda. When Wilson declared that "the only possible antidote for the German poison that is being spread...over the land is the TRUTH," by truth he meant his version of events.[5] This attempt to control war messages and news from the top down reflected the belief of Wilson and his aides that they knew what was best for the public to know. Not everyone agreed. A *Boston Daily Globe* editorial stated that Americans would not endure the conscription of their men and their property "if the truth were also conscripted" and declared, "In fighting for the truth, democracy must know the truth." Such sentiments turned out to be wishful thinking during World War I.[6]

The Wilson administration's heavy-handed deployment of propaganda and censorship directly affected the success of its war aims. First, it had to build enough domestic opposition to Germany to move from its initial position of neutrality to war. Second, during the war it promoted a dramatic and oversimplified portrayal of a clash between civilization and barbarism, playing down differences among the allies and presenting Americans as disinterested rescuers. Finally, once the war ended, Wilson failed to achieve most of his war aims at the peace talks and then also failed to obtain enough support for the Senate ratification of the peace treaty. The administration had stirred up

fervent nationalism in war but did not build a consensus for liberal internationalism in peace.

American Neutrality

WHEN EUROPE WENT TO WAR IN 1914, the belligerents all claimed their cause
was noble, while pursuing self-aggrandizement. Of the Central Powers,
Germany was the most ambitious. It planned to extend its eastern frontiers,
acquire more territory from France, occupy the channel coast, and control
Belgian foreign relations. The weaker Austro-Hungarian and Ottoman
Empires struggled to retain their territories. The Entente or Allied Powers,
led by the British and the French, sought to prevent German domination
of Europe, liberate Belgium, and return the Alsace region to France. They
also wanted to gain territory, particularly in the Middle East where British
forces allied with the Arabs against their Ottoman rulers. Their eastern ally,
Russia, had an eye on access to the Mediterranean through the Turkish
straits.

Both sides recalled ancient glories, using the symbol of the warrior knight
to portray battle as an exercise in manly honor and aristocratic leadership,
while using modern technology to fight a war of attrition. At the Battle of the
Somme, begun in July 1916, British forces bombarded enemy lines for eight
days and then advanced from the trenches shoulder to shoulder. German
machine gunners killed 20,000 of them the first day. After four months the
German forces had fallen back a few miles at the cost of 600,000 Allied dead
and 750,000 German dead. In contrast to the colonial conflicts familiar to
all the imperial powers involved, the death toll on both sides was appallingly
high.

President Wilson proclaimed American neutrality. He considered the
president the "only national voice" in public affairs, especially in a society
divided between business and labor, conservatives and reformers, and natives
and immigrants. Wilson was worried about the possibility that Americans,
millions of whom had family ties overseas, might turn against each other if
the United States took sides. He asked the press to assist him in keeping the
country calm. The president held regularly scheduled news conferences once
or twice a week, presenting White House reporters with a prepared statement
on an issue of his choosing. A year into the war, however, he distanced himself
from regular contact with the press, leaving it up to his popular press secretary, Joseph Tumulty, to meet with reporters every morning. The president

also wished to be able to reach the public directly without having to rely on the press to deliver his messages correctly. He proposed that his call for neutrality be printed and displayed in Post Offices across the country, which the State Department agreed to fund. Wilson and Secretary of State William Jennings Bryan also arranged for movie theaters to project this appeal: "President Wilson has asked Americans to preserve absolute neutrality during the war abroad. Please refrain from partisan applause in viewing this picture."[7]

As much as Wilson proclaimed neutrality in public, he repeatedly took the side of the Allies. An admirer of British political traditions, he also knew that the Royal Navy's dominance of the seas had protected decades of American economic expansion. And now the war boosted the U.S. economy. American bankers loaned two and a half billion dollars to the Allies and $27 million to the Central Powers. American companies sold billions of dollars of food, fuel, and steel to both sides, but increasingly to the Allies. The British and German navies tried to prevent American supplies from reaching their enemies with brutal results. The British blockade intended to starve civilians on the German home front; German submarines torpedoed ships traveling in the Atlantic war zone.

These naval strategies presented Americans with a dilemma. Should the U.S. government concern itself with protecting American citizens who traveled and traded around the world? Concerned that the deaths of Americans would prompt calls for war, Bryan wanted to ban all civilians from travel on belligerent ships. Representative Jeff McLemore (D-TX) and Senator Thomas Gore (D-OK) offered popular resolutions calling on the president to warn civilians against such travel. Wilson disagreed. He persuaded members of Congress to back off by arguing that they shouldn't interfere with the president's authority to conduct foreign affairs and that congressional debate on such matters showed weakness to the world. On this issue, legislators such as Senator Henry Cabot Lodge (R-MA), who normally asserted Congress's foreign policy powers, remained quiet because they supported Wilson's position. The president declared that Germany would be held responsible for the destruction of any American life or property. Americans had to have access to the world, he believed. In 1916, Wilson told a meeting of salesmen in Detroit that they should compete aggressively for markets abroad carrying with them "liberty and justice and the principles of humanity" wherever they went. "Go out and sell goods," the president urged, that "will make the world more comfortable and more happy, and convert them to the principles of America."[8]

Meanwhile the German and British governments launched their own propaganda campaigns in the United States. Germany wanted to keep the United States neutral, but its propaganda betrayed a lack of understanding of who held the power in American society. It appealed to German Americans, thereby escalating the already significant suspicion of immigrant groups and the foreign born. The Germans also reached out to African Americans with promises of support for equality at a time when the Ku Klux Klan was undergoing a rebirth. In addition, German agents committed acts of sabotage, smuggling bombs on board ships carrying arms to the Allies. The British, who wanted to get the United States into the war, were more effective. They cut the telegraph cable between the United States and Germany, making the Americans dependent on British sources for news of the war. They targeted the mainstream press, business leaders, and university professors as influential transmitters of their cause. Finally, they made a vivid case for their portrayal of the war as a contest between civilization and barbarism.[9]

The British presented exaggerated versions of actual events, creating a portrayal of the Germans that American propagandists later adopted. When a German submarine torpedoed the British luxury liner *Lusitania* off the coast of Ireland in May 1915, it sank a thousand passengers, including 128 Americans, and ammunition destined for Allied forces. The British and American press denounced the Germans as killers of innocent women and children. The Germans pointed out that their embassy had placed ads in the New York papers warning Americans against travel on British ships, while at home they honored the U-boat captain as a national hero. Rightly suspecting that the *Lusitania* carried ammunition, Bryan thought the United States should set an example of Christian democracy by protesting both Britain's use of passengers to shield bullets and Germany's submarine warfare against civilians. He resigned when Wilson refused to challenge Britain's policy and demanded that Germany stop attacking nonmilitary ships without warning. In May 1916, Germany agreed to Wilson's demands, in part because it needed time to produce more U-boats.[10]

A few days after the sinking of the *Lusitania*, the British released the Bryce report on German atrocities in Belgium committed following the German invasion in 1914. Compiled by Lord Bryce, the respected former ambassador to the United States, the report was based on an unverified combination of eyewitness and hearsay evidence collected from civilians. Although most of the unconfirmed accounts named adult males as the victims of German brutality, the few that detailed the rape of women, the slaughter of children, and the mutilation of children provoked outrage among Americans. The alleged "severing of hands," noted in the report, was widely accepted as fact. The British and later the Americans charged the German military of conducting a deliberate and systematic policy of terror against civilians. The Germans tried to counter the Bryce report's blending of fact, myth, and rumor with their own report that emphasized the atrocities committed by French and Belgian civilians turned guerrilla forces. For example, German Chancellor Theobald von Bethmann Hollweg told American war correspondents, "Belgian girls have gouged out the eyes of German wounded soldiers on the battlefield." The German military provided supervised access for American correspondents to the front lines. Five signed a statement denying the atrocity charges, while three refused; all agreed that the invasion caused extensive death and destruction. The British version condemning the evils of German militarism nevertheless dominated the American media, reinforced as it was by the news that German forces destroyed historical and artistic treasures as they conducted industrial warfare on the western front. Germany's violation of Belgium's neutrality guaranteed by international law was popularized as the "rape of Belgium."[11]

Americans accepted or rejected these propaganda campaigns depending on their position regarding the war. The stories of German barbarism justified the call of nationalists Theodore Roosevelt and his former secretary of war, Senator Elihu Root (R-NY), for military preparedness. Avoiding an outright demand for war, the preparedness movement instead called for military buildup, universal military training, and "patriotic education" in the schools. According to Henry Stimson, Root's protégé who had served as President Taft's secretary of war, the movement sought to teach Americans to be more dutiful and disciplined. Roosevelt condemned those who disagreed as cowards. Tens of thousands marched at the Preparedness Parade up Fifth Avenue in New York in May 1916. One big electric sign read, "Absolute and Unqualified Loyalty to Our Country." Radical literary critic Randolph Bourne caustically observed that the same people who managed to ignore the peacetime horrors of exploitive labor and oppressed minorities at home were roused to outrage by the wartime horrors of atrocities in Belgium. Although others joined Bourne in questioning the march to war, pressure mounted to equate loyalty with support. When Bryan resigned, the AP adopted a resolution that nothing "unpatriotic" said by the recent secretary of state should be reported. Accused of being un-American, Bryan wondered, "When did it become unpatriotic for a citizen to differ from a president?"[12]

Opposed to the preparedness movement, pacifists argued that no good could come of going to war. Senator Robert LaFollette (R-WI) believed that hard-fought progressive reforms would be lost if the country mobilized. Settlement house founder Jane Addams organized the Women's International League for Peace and Freedom, which called on the president to pursue disarmament, an end to colonial empires, and the creation of an international peacekeeping organization. Other Americans rejected the civilization versus barbarism dichotomy for one of their own. Radical unions and socialists opposed the war in Europe as a capitalist war, denouncing the treatment of British and German workers as cannon fodder. They pointed out that if leading American businessmen who supported war had their way it would be working-class men who would be sent to fight. African American spokesman W. E. B. DuBois saw the war as a continuation of imperial competition, writing that the "civilized nations are fighting like mad dogs over the right to own and exploit...darker peoples."[13]

The Wilson administration talked of peace but shifted toward intervention as it defined an enhanced global role for the United States. Tumulty advised the president that the people did not wish to follow Bryan's pacifism, nor did they embrace Roosevelt's militarism. They needed, Tumulty thought, "entertainment and guidance."[14] Wilson reached out to the public, as had President McKinley, by undertaking a national speaking tour by train in 1916, a presidential election year. He embraced preparedness, calling for a buildup of the navy and doubling the size of the army. "We are participants, whether we like it or not, in the life of the world," declared Wilson. "The interests of all nations are our own also."[15] Appealing to both sides, Wilson ran a careful and ultimately close reelection campaign on strong defense and the slogan "He Kept Us Out of War." Wilson again tried and failed to mediate an end to the war by calling for peace without victory. Privately, Wilson's new secretary of state, Robert Lansing, viewed with satisfaction the shift of economic power from Europe to the United States. "They must come to us for money. That's certain," said Lansing in November 1916. "And with that power we can dominate them."[16]

On April 2, 1917, Wilson, escorted to Capitol Hill by U.S. cavalry troops, broke with tradition by personally asking a joint session of Congress to declare war. American grievances against Germany had stacked up. Faced with serious food shortages, Berlin gambled on resuming submarine warfare against U.S. ships in January 1917. The German command believed it could force the Allies to surrender before the U.S. military would be ready for battle.

In addition, German Foreign Minister Arthur Zimmermann sent a telegram inviting Mexico to join with Germany and fight the Americans in order to regain Texas, New Mexico, and Arizona. Intercepted in February before it reached Mexico City and leaked to the American press, the Zimmermann telegram raised the fear of invasion. In March, German submarines sank three American merchant ships. Even then the administration wondered about the strength of public support for war. In the days before the invention of public opinion polling, Lansing asked reporter Arthur Sweetser if the AP could canvass its Midwest correspondents about public opinion in the region thought to be least inclined toward war. Sweetser replied that such action would be against AP rules and suggested that the Internal Revenue people could do it. Lansing said they could, as could the postmasters, but the government did not wish to appear to be behind the canvass.[17]

In his war message, Wilson declared that the United States would fight to liberate the peoples of the world, including the people of Germany. Recalling the Declaration of Independence, Wilson pledged, "We dedicate our lives and our fortunes" to make the world free. His stirring speech, greeted with loud applause by members of Congress, called for the inalienable rights of

President Woodrow Wilson's famous slogan does duty on an enlistment poster. (National Archives, 46-WP-277)

Americans to become universal rights. LaFollette spoke against the president's case. He said that Britain as well as Germany had violated international law but that the president had cooperated with one and called for war on the other. If the United States really was going to fight for democracy, the senator asked, why not fight for the dissolution of the British Empire and home rule for Ireland, Egypt, and India, as well as for the end of German autocracy? Finally, he believed the American people had been misled, fooled, and silenced. As he spoke, most of his fellow senators left the floor. Congress voted to declare war by a margin of 82 to 6 in the Senate and 373 to 50 in the House. "I join no crusade," said Senator William Borah of Idaho as he voted in favor. "I make war alone for my countrymen and their rights."[18]

"The Greatest Adventure in Advertising"

WILSON DECIDED TO RAISE AN ARMY of three million men, train and equip them, and ship them past German submarines to Europe. He knew this meant total mobilization: "It is not an army we must shape and train for war, it is a nation."[19] The Selective Service Act of May 18, 1917, required men between the ages of 21 and 30 (later extended to 18 and 45) to register for the draft and provided two-thirds of the army. In contrast to the Civil War, the Spanish American War, and the Philippine War, when most soldiers volunteered and served in the uniforms of their states, the World War I era saw a draft as a fair and efficient way to raise a national army. Ninety percent of those drafted were single. Seventy percent were laborers or farmhands. About 100,000 could not speak English.[20] To mobilize industry and labor, the administration set up the War Industries Board and the War Labor Board. To mobilize public opinion Wilson created the CPI by executive order, charging it to present the "absolute justice of America's cause" and the "absolute selflessness of America's aims."[21]

Launched in the progressive reform spirit, the CPI believed that the war might bring out the best in the American people if they had the proper direction. At its head was former muckraking journalist George Creel. Dedicated, energetic, and deeply loyal to Woodrow Wilson, Creel brought together government officials, professors, journalists, artists, and advertising professionals. The CPI's Domestic Section was staffed by reformers who thought that mobilization could further their goals of uniting the classes, assimilating immigrants, and spreading democracy. Experienced at using investigative reports to arouse public indignation against child labor, boss rule, and corporate corruption, they wanted to extend their achievements in domestic reform to the world to make it a better place to live. The CPI's Foreign Section conducted propaganda overseas with offices in thirty countries. Embracing progressive notions of expertise and efficiency, the CPI used the mass media to call upon Americans to enlist, to conserve, and to buy bonds, all the while explaining why the United States must fight. In this era before radio and television, the CPI ideally wanted all Americans to hear and see the same propaganda messages at the same time, delivered by posters in public spaces, speakers at club meetings, newsreels at the local theater, ads in magazines, and reporting in the newspapers. Creel called the CPI "a vast enterprise in salesmanship, the world's greatest adventure in advertising."[22]

Secretary of War Newton Baker pronounced CPI's philosophy as "faith in democracy . . . faith in the fact."[23] From the beginning, however, CPI officials would find it difficult to stick to the facts and appeal to reason rather than resort to sensationalism. As early as May 1917, Press Secretary Tumulty, concerned that the "righteous wrath" of the people had not yet been aroused, suggested to the president that the story of German outrages against the Belgians would show Americans what "our own people might suffer if German autocracy should triumph."[24] Indeed, German atrocities and the German threat to the United States emerged as key themes of wartime propaganda. Instead of educating Americans about what might be involved in creating a new international order, these messages suggested that once the enemy was defeated, the world would be safe.

Creel thought the press was the greatest power on earth because "we know only what it tells us."[25] Through its Division of News, the CPI told the press what to tell the public. At the time, reporting in the nation's capital had a reputation for being casual and haphazard. "As far as I can see," described Sweetser, "the newspapermen hang around pretty close to the big people, meet them regularly at certain hours for conferences, wander the rest of the time, play poker in the press room occasionally, and do a whole lot of gossiping and imagining."[26] For Creel, this practice of wandering and hanging around left too much to chance. Who knew what reporters might ask officials and what those officials might answer? What the situation required, he believed, was the preparation, coordination, and release of all official war news by the CPI on behalf of the White House, the Army, the Navy, the Department of Justice, the Department of Labor, and wartime agencies including the National War Labor Board, the War Industries Board, and the War Trade Board. President Wilson frequently decided what information would be released and when. Tumulty deferred to the CPI by canceling his daily press conferences. The State Department, where the colorless Lansing detested the flamboyant Creel, ran its own publicity bureau without collaborating with the CPI. The department asked the press not to print articles about government policy without the department's approval, which it then refused to give, or so complained the liberal magazine *New Republic*. Washington reporters, who, by and large, wanted to support the war effort, grumbled about official distrust but accepted their new role, described by Sweetser, as "messenger boys for handouts."[27]

The CPI's Division of News ran twenty-four hours a day to produce stacks of information, which the press used voluntarily and frequently. It printed the *Official Bulletin*, a daily report on the activities of government departments, wartime regulations, and presidential proclamations, an exercise that proved that "faith in the fact" at times could be dull. One exception was the closely read casualty lists, which increased the bulletin's length from eight to forty pages in 1918. For the more entertaining sections of the newspaper, the CPI's Division of Syndicated Features recruited novelists and short-story writers to write patriotic stories for the Sunday editions. Every week the Bureau of Cartoons sent the nation's cartoonists suggestions for topics collected from thirty-one government departments. These included instructions to call for more nurses or discourage Sunday motoring. Others discredited homegrown criticisms of the war. For example, to counter the charge of radical unions that the United States had gone to war to protect the billions of dollars that financiers and bankers had loaned to the Allies, cartoonists were told to show that the characterization of the war as a "rich man's war" was a lie spread by German propaganda.[28]

The Division of Civic and Educational Cooperation best exemplified the CPI's inner struggle between educating and inflaming the public. Run by Guy Stanton Ford, professor of history at the University of Minnesota, the division produced more than ninety pamphlets explaining the war. In *German War Practices*, issued in November 1917, CPI writers emphasized authenticity by citing German generals, political leaders, and ordinary soldiers, thereby letting the enemy condemn himself. The most famous quotation was from Kaiser Wilhelm's speech in 1900 to German troops about to embark to fight the Boxers in China. The Emperor commanded them to show no mercy like the Huns under King Attila and to "Open the way for Kultur once for all." The pamphlet explained that numerous German political leaders denounced this speech in the Reichstag, thus showing Germany as a nation with a parliament, political parties, and diverse opinion, a Germany that seldom appeared

The mission of the CPI's Bureau of Cartoons was to direct "the scattered cartoon power of the country for constructive war work." For the October 26, 1918, cover of the "Bulletin for Cartoonists," James Montgomery Flagg drew this portrait of himself and Kaiser Wilhelm. (National Archives, CPI, RG 63, Entry 19, Box 2)

in most CPI materials. Yet, most of the quotations selected for this pamphlet featured Germans recommending the use of excessive force in wartime, thereby reinforcing the image of Germans as terrorizing brutes.[29]

The Division also targeted material to reach 22 million students in 100,000 school districts and, through the children, their parents. For the teachers and pupils of Wisconsin, Albert H. Sanford of the State Normal School at LaCrosse compiled from CPI documents a course of study called "Why the United States is at War." The number one reason was "Because we were attacked by Germany and Austria." Sanford failed to provide evidence of an actual attack on the United States but listed such aggressive acts as German submarines sinking ships carrying American citizens, German and Austrian plots to stir up American workers and commit industrial sabotage, German efforts to arouse disloyalty among Americans of German heritage, and German collusion with Mexico against the United States. Another reason was Germany's merciless treatment of small nations, especially the horrible atrocities committed in Belgium. The final reason was Germany's ambition to dominate the globe with an empire extending from the North Sea to the Persian Gulf. Germans claim, Sanford explained, that "they are a race chosen by God to rule the world." He acknowledged that the Germans had a right to believe in their superiority, "but not to *impose* their systems upon other people." If Germany won in Europe, Sanford concluded, it would invade the United States.[30]

Artists turned these explanations into vivid posters showing German monsters out to conquer the world. The CPI's Division of Pictorial Publicity led by famed illustrator Charles Dana Gibson and the Division of Advertising wanted to arouse emotions. So did the Treasury Department, which persuaded people to buy bonds. Bonds paid for two-thirds of the war's price tag of $33.5 billion. Increased taxes, which placed a greater burden on corporations and the wealthy, to the dismay of such senior Republicans as Senator Lodge, paid the other third. These Divisions were more enthusiastic about using atrocity propaganda than the rest of the CPI. Government agencies, such as the Department of Agriculture, the Fuel Administration, and the Treasury Department, and nongovernment groups including the YMCA, the YWCA, and the Red Cross defined the messages and CPI artists provided the pictures.[31]

To encourage enlistment, the CPI printed five million copies of the most famous World War I poster, James Montgomery Flagg's Uncle Sam, who says, "I Want You." Its artists created 2500 eye-catching and instructive designs

Movie star Douglas Fairbanks, the most popular action hero of the silent screen era, calls on Americans to buy liberty bonds during the Third Liberty Loan Drive, New York, April 1918. (National Archives, 111-SC-16569)

from which twenty million posters were printed, more than all the other nations at war combined. Previously used for advertising, posters became political instruments employing symbols, slogans, and familiar stories to persuade. Enlistment and liberty bond posters called on American men to defeat the hulking, ape-like attackers of women and children, using the slogan "Remember Belgium." In contrast, American soldiers were pictured as "our boys," full of youthful courage and cheer. Recruiting posters showed a mother handing her son over to Uncle Sam and the army building boys into men with the character of a crusading knight. Posters for the YMCA, Red Cross, and Salvation Army showed reassuring pictures of the "boys" in France having coffee and doughnuts and singing songs. The Salvation Army "doughnut girl" represented the virtuous American woman the "boys" were fighting to protect. Their reward for a job well done would be to return home and marry someone just as nice.[32]

The CPI's Division of Advertising, located on Madison Avenue in New York, supplied advertisers with text and illustrations ranging from the gory

World War I propaganda poster. Henry Patrick Raleigh, artist. (National Archives, NWDNS-4-P-226)

to the light-hearted. One ad, showing German soldiers cutting off the hands of a boy and strangling a woman, proclaimed that the civilization of German Kultur must be "mended or ended."

> To carry on this crusade of modern righteousness means not merely that our young men shall cross the seas to fight the Hun.... It means that we shall give up many things that are dear to us: sacrifice, that our Crusaders may save us and our children from the horrors that have come to the little ones of Belgium and France.[33]

This ad copy, calling on Americans to subscribe to the Fourth Liberty Loan, was meant to appeal to all, regardless of their politics or views on postwar policies. Another ad used humor to illustrate German ambitions with a rewritten map of the United States as New Prussia, turning Boston into The Kulturplatz, Chicago into Schlauterhaus, and San Francisco into San Sweitzerkase. Bismarck was left unchanged.[34]

Ads, like cartoons, equated rumors and dissenting views among Americans with German propaganda. One showed two women having tea with the headline "Gossip that Costs Human Lives!" Readers learned that by spreading rumors such as "this is a business man's war," they would increase discontent and prolong the war. These lies, started by German spies, the ad explained, "will kill our boys in France!" Other ads encouraged Americans to hide any worries and be upbeat. Only write cheerful news to soldiers at the front, said one. Another instructed readers that if "our boys can go smiling and singing" into battle, civilians should cheer up, buy bonds, and keep business going normally by shopping.[35] Readers would usually have seen these ads in magazines one at a time. When viewed together, they present a dizzying range of messages from beware invasion by Germans who mutilate children to be cheerful and go shopping.

The CPI promoted unity by targeting people typically removed from leadership and responsibility. Posters urged children to do their part. Three hundred thousand Boy Scouts sold bonds, distributed CPI pamphlets, gardened, and patrolled the coastline. To mobilize women, the Division of Women's War Work collaborated with women's organizations and sent instructive stories to newspapers and magazines. Posters encouraged women to take up nursing, knitting socks, and jobs left behind by soldiers. The CPI secretly funded and ran the American Alliance for Labor and Democracy, allegedly labor's own organization run by American Federation of Labor leader Samuel

Gompers. This group, with 150 branches in forty states, distributed millions of pamphlets, held mass meetings, and advocated the eight-hour day and worker participation in management. By appealing to their patriotism, the CPI hoped to keep workers quiet and productive. Gompers and employers denounced as disloyal those workers who demanded more radical reforms. Even as the CPI's message of inclusion gave new legitimacy to women and workers, it advocated loyalty and deference.[36]

Loyalty was the message directed at immigrants as well. The administration promoted the War Americanization Plan to teach English and citizenship. CPI's Division of Work with the Foreign-Born set up "Loyalty Leagues," organized twenty-three foreign-born groups, and translated CPI materials into foreign languages. July 4, 1918 was proclaimed Loyalty Day, celebrated with parades and pageants across the country. In New York City, forty nationality groups with floats paraded up Fifth Avenue for ten hours. Spectators saw a woman dressed as Joan of Arc, Albanians saluting the president as the "protector of small nationalities," Bolivian llamas, Chinese baseball players, Lithuanian knights, Spanish toreadors, and Swiss Guards, as a dirigible released from above copies of the "Star Spangled Banner." Such a display of unity was the result of extended negotiation. For example, the Italians, Slovaks, and Bohemians threatened to boycott the parade unless the Hungarians agreed not to wear their national costume. The *New York Times* pronounced the pageant to be proof of "incomplete" assimilation. Such sentiments echoed Wilson's speech to new citizens: "You cannot become thorough Americans if you think of yourselves in groups. America does not consist of groups."[37]

Seventy-five thousand volunteers called the Four Minute Men summed up the major propaganda themes. These volunteers, who had to be approved by three prominent men in their community, gave approximately one million speeches reaching four hundred million people. They spoke at schools, picnics, churches, fairs, and civic clubs. Their primary venue was the movie theater where they spoke during the four minutes it took to change the film reel. The Four Minute Men had assistance from College Four Minute Men, a Women's Branch for matinees, and, in New York, Four Minute speakers in Yiddish and Italian. Washington sent bulletins instructing Four Minute Men to mention local boys fighting in France as they encouraged audiences to subscribe to the liberty loans, conserve food, and register for the draft. The CPI told the speakers to contrast the backwardness of the autocratic German system to the progress and principles of the American spirit of 1776.[38] By 1918, the

CPI directed the Four Minute Men to use atrocity stories. Speakers described Prussian *Schrecklichkeit*, defined as "the deliberate policy of terrorism," which forced German soldiers "to carry out unspeakable orders against defenseless old men, women, and children, so that "respect" might grow for German "efficiency."[39] As an alternative to speeches, some theaters held a Four Minute singing of patriotic songs. Since theater owners participated in the Four Minute program voluntarily, the CPI warned its speakers not to exceed the time limit and upset the management or annoy the audience.

The CPI was not just interested in reaching the audience between films, but also through the movies themselves. President Wilson wrote to the head of the National Association of the Motion Picture Industry, "The film has come to rank as a very high medium for the dissemination of public intelligence, and since it speaks a universal language it lends itself importantly to the presentation of America's plans and purposes."[40] Movies reached millions. At the approximately 1750 movie theaters in the United States, audiences saw silent films typically accompanied by live music. As Sweetser put it, "Personally, I have given up reading war books. But if ever any pictures come to town, I'm in the front row."[41] The CPI used film in a number of ways. The Division of Films made Army Signal Corps footage into documentaries and newsreels. Early in the war, military censorship in Europe prevented newsreel companies from obtaining actual war footage, so they had shown Swiss army maneuvers or the New Jersey National Guard or staged battle scenes for the camera. By 1915 European governments and military authorities allowed censored "official films" to appear. Eventually the "Official War Review," a compilation of Signal Corps footage and footage from Allied nations, appeared in approximately half the movie theaters in the country.[42]

The CPI made and promoted feature-length films as patriotic community events. Its first, *Pershing's Crusaders*, featured an opening sequence of German soldiers crawling through woods, destroyed Belgian villages, refugees fleeing, the *Lusitania* sailing, a German submarine, and burning East Coast factories. The editing of these clips of what appears to be for the most part actual footage tells a story in which the Germans first attacked Belgium, then civilians crossing the Atlantic, and, finally, the United States. Following these scenes of destruction, the film documented the orderly mobilization of an industrialized nation: workers at defense plants mass producing uniforms, artillery shells, and ships "for our great soldier family." Then it showed thousands of young men drilling and marching at training camps as they were transformed into soldiers, and, once in France, passing in review before General Pershing and his French counterparts. In April and May 1918, the CPI staged week long "official screenings" of *Pershing's Crusaders* in flag-draped theaters in twenty-four cities. It engineered a contest among theater owners for the most bookings. The CPI asked movie critics, schools, department stores, churches, and business organizations to promote attendance. It recruited local politicians and society leaders to endorse the film and attend gala openings. In Washington, the president, the Cabinet, and Congressmen attended the official screening of *Pershing's Crusaders.*[43]

Quite different in tone was the CPI film *The Training of Colored Troops* (1918). Justifiably skeptical of calls to make the world safe for democracy, African Americans served in a segregated military in World War I. The film sought to reassure black audiences by presenting a view of boot camp that neglected to show the unheated tents that served as winter housing and inadequate medical care. Instead viewers saw a family proudly listening to the mother reading a letter from her son in the Engineer Corps. To reassure white audiences, the film accompanied scenes of disciplined and armed black troops with stereotypical shots of black soldiers eating watermelon and happily tap dancing. The CPI film portrayed African Americans as playing an important role in the war, while satisfying white notions of superiority.[44]

The CPI knew it had to prove to movie producers that "government propaganda could be made so interesting that audiences would cheerfully accept it as part of the entertainment they had paid to receive." The Division of Film supplied scenarios for short films, while the producer made and distributed the picture to thousands of theaters. In 1918 this collaboration produced *Keep 'Em Singing and Nothing Can Lick 'Em* with Paramount-Bray Pictograph about musical morale in the services and *Feeding the Fighter Over Here and Over There* with the Pathé Exchange Company showing why civilians had to cut back on beef and flour in order to feed the troops. *The American Indian Gets into the War Game*, made with Universal, showed American Indian men voluntarily enlisting and women doing Red Cross work with the result, according to CPI official Rufus Steele, that "the white man is shamed into a higher patriotism."[45]

The U.S. government had little direct involvement in the making of feature films; however, the motion picture industry willingly adopted CPI themes of Allied honor and German frightfulness. Only one out of five films (about 500 were released each month) made during the war was about the war, but movies with war-related themes tended to be some of the biggest box office hits. At the movies, Americans saw their soldiers portrayed as rescuers

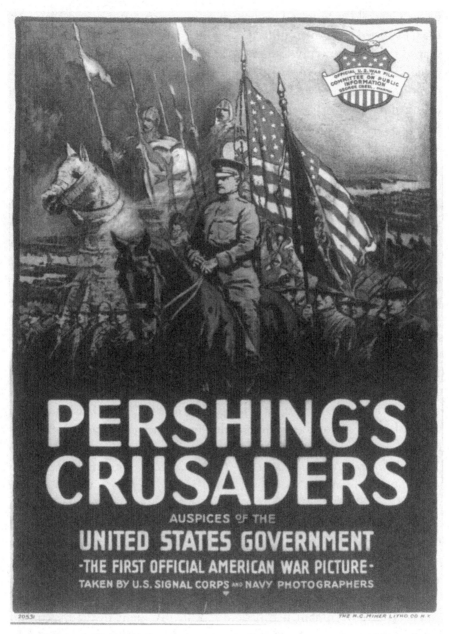

The American Expeditionary Force carries on the tradition of medieval Christian crusaders in the CPI official war film *Pershing's Crusaders*, 1918. (Library of Congress, LC-USZ62-712-72)

of threatened women. Although the CPI objected to the extreme nature of hate films *To Hell with the Kaiser* and *The Kaiser, Beast of Berlin*, the agency itself repeatedly promoted the theme of German brutality. Feature films ridiculed "slackers," the term used during the war for those who refused to fight, and condemned pacifist mothers who prevented their sons from joining up. A popular theme, also promoted by the CPI, was that men find redemption in war. In *The Unbeliever* (1918), made with the cooperation of the U.S. Marine Corps, the rich and scornful Phil learns that "class pride is junk" as he watches his chauffeur die in battle, finds faith after seeing an image of Christ walking across the battlefield, and falls in love with a beautiful Belgian girl who barely escapes rape by a German officer. Even Charlie Chaplin in his wartime comedy *Shoulder Arms* (1918) saves a French girl from rape just before he captures the Kaiser and then awakens from his boot-camp dream.[46]

Director D. W. Griffith had already triumphed with a formula that combined war with melodrama in his controversial masterpiece *The Birth of a Nation* (1915). In this widely seen historical drama of the Civil War and Reconstruction,

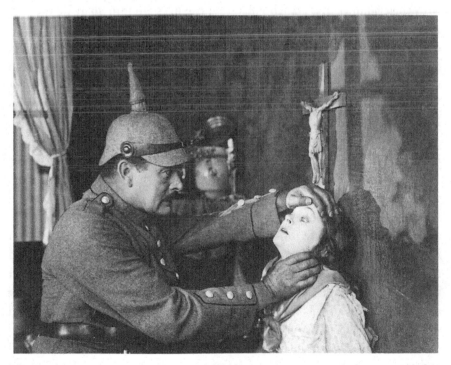

Mae Marsh, as a Belgian girl, and A. C. Gibbons, as a German soldier, in Goldwyn's all-star Liberty Loan picture, 1918. (National Archives, NWDNS-53-LL-8-1)

the members of the Ku Klux Klan, wearing crosses on their robes like crusading knights, are heralded as the defenders of white supremacy and the protectors of women's virtue from depraved black men, themes that would implicitly and explicitly be repeated in wartime America. For example, in Raoul Walsh's *The Prussian Cur* (1918), Klansmen on horseback save the day by preventing German sympathizers from breaking a German spy out of jail. Hoping to repeat his success with a modern war epic, Griffith went to France in 1917 to film battle footage of the western front and found to his dismay that there was nothing romantic about it. "The life of a soldier in modern war," he told an interviewer, "is the life of an underpaid, overworked ditch digger compelled to live in discomfort and danger."[47]

Griffith cobbled a film together from his footage of a more exciting mock battle with charging men and horses that he directed in England, documentary footage of Austrian troops in action, and trench scenes restaged in Hollywood. The result, *Hearts of the World*, opened on March 12, 1918, the same day as the Third Liberty Loan drive. The movie told the story of "Girl" (Lillian Gish) and "Boy" (Robert Harron), affianced Americans living with their families in a French village, whose lives are torn apart by the war. Boy enlists and Girl endures the destruction of her home, a whipping by one German soldier, and an attempted rape by another. Reunited and facing death, Boy and Girl are saved by French and American troops. At the end, viewers see parading Yanks, American and Allied flags, a portrait of President Wilson, and the happy Boy and Girl. The title reads, "America—returning home after freeing the world from Autocracy and the horrors of war forever and ever." Even as the film displayed Griffith's misgivings about modern war, it showed that virtue would triumph over evil.[48]

To sell the movie, advertisements proclaimed that viewing the horrors of *Hearts of the World* was an act of patriotism: "If You Are a Red Blooded American—If you doubt the savagery of German kultur—don't fail to be at the Olympic Theatre tomorrow night." When the film censor board in Pennsylvania wanted to cut out a few atrocity scenes, the film's promoters placed newspaper ads that accused the censors of being pro-German and pointed out that their names were Oberholtzer and Audenreid. The ads appealed directly to movie-goers' fears: "The same things that are shown in Hearts of the World in Mr. Griffith's great drama, can happen to *Your Wife, Your Sister, Your Sweetheart, or Your Mother* if the methods of the Philadelphia censors are to prevail and are to crush the Truth and keep it from the great American public." *Hearts of the World* became the most popular film of World War I.[49]

The CPI's goal of deluging Americans with patriotic messages was realized at the movies. Draped in flags, theaters displayed propaganda posters and portraits of President Wilson. The military services set up recruitment booths in the lobby. On special nights, theater managers announced that ticket sales would be donated to the Red Cross, and that soldiers and sailors would be admitted for free, as would anyone with a letter from a soldier overseas. Shows opened with the singing of the "Star-Spangled Banner." Newsreels featured local men in uniform and black and white war scenes of the "blood-red battle-fields of France." Audiences listened to a Four Minute Man speech or sang along in a Four Minute Sing. Audiences saw shorts produced in collaboration between the government and the motion picture industry, often featuring movie stars who sold bonds on and off the screen. One called *100% American* starred "Uncle Sam's favorite niece," beloved actress Mary Pickford, who threw a softball named "Fourth liberty loan" at the Kaiser knocking him into the soup. For some showings of *The Unbeliever*, bugles sounded and marines brandishing bayonets marched across the stage. There in the audience were the CPI's ideal American citizens, receiving stirring instruction from the government, the military, and Mary Pickford.[50]

The desire of the CPI and its willing volunteers to arouse "white hot" patriotism had unintended consequences. The slogan, "100% American," meant to be inclusive, was turned into a weapon against Americans suspected of being traitors because of their ethnic heritage. In 1900 the greatest concentration of Germans in the world outside of Berlin was in the city of New York. One of the largest immigrant groups in the United States, German Americans had been prosperous, respected, and outspoken, but the pervasive dehumanization of Germans took its toll. To avoid harassment and to prove their loyalty, many German Americans tried to assimilate by changing their family names and no longer speaking German at home. At times the harassment turned violent. In April 1918, a mob in St. Louis attacked a German American named Robert Prager who had tried to enlist in the Navy, wrapped him in the flag, and lynched him. Considered a case of "patriotic murder," the jury found the mob leaders not guilty.[51]

Convinced that anything German could harm American society, people moved to eradicate all traces of it. East Germantown, Indiana, changed its name to Pershing. Sauerkraut became "liberty cabbage." German shepherds were called police dogs. Nebraskans held book-burning rallies to rid their communities of German books. Patriotic organizations agitated for the banning of German music. Schools prohibited the teaching of the German

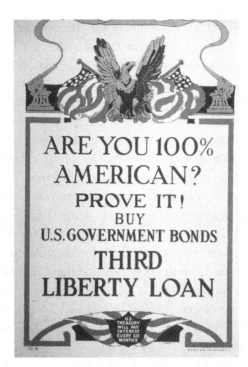

World War I propaganda exhorted citizens to prove they were "100% American" by supporting the war. (National Archives, NWDNS-45-WP-120)

language. "Ninety percent of all the men and women who teach the German language are traitors," said an Iowa politician. President Wilson privately wrote to Creel that opposition to teaching German in the schools was "childish." Yet, the CPI had portrayed Germans as monsters and stressed that they were behind any challenges to the official position on the war.[52]

The authorities suppressed dissent. "We must have no criticism now," announced Senator Root.[53] The Censorship Board, consisting of CPI Director Creel and representatives of the military services, the postmaster general, and the War Trade Board, coordinated government censorship. For the news media, the CPI set up a system of voluntary censorship asking editors to submit for official approval any stories that might harm the war effort. With the support of the Justice Department, the American Protective League, a group of 250,000 private citizens, spied on neighbors and workers, opened mail, burglarized homes, bugged telephones, intercepted telegrams, slandered people, and advocated assault on dissenters. Congress restricted civil liberties with the Threats against the President Act, Espionage

Act, Trading-with-the-Enemy Act, Sedition Act, and Sabotage Act. Although fears of sabotage and spies abounded, there was not a single proven case of sabotage after the country entered the war, nor were any German spies caught under the Espionage Act.[54]

Under these federal security acts, Americans could be arrested, tried, fined, and jailed for spoken threats against the president, discouraging men from registering for the draft or enlisting, and making any criticism of the conduct of the war and war aims, American or Allied. Postmaster General Albert Burleson suppressed one journal that said the war should be financed by higher taxes and less borrowing, and another for quoting Thomas Jefferson's opinion that Ireland, which in 1918 was still under British rule, should be an independent republic. A Wisconsin farmer was sentenced to one year in Leavenworth prison for saying, "This is a rich man's war and we would not have this war if it had not been for the rich girls in the United States marrying English lords." An Ohio judge sent a farmer named John White to jail for saying that the German troops had done the same thing in Belgium that American soldiers had done in the Philippines. Socialist leader Eugene Debs received a ten-year sentence for making an antiwar speech in Ohio. The producer of *The Spirit of '76*, a film about the American Revolution that showed British redcoats bayoneting women and children in the Wyoming Valley of Pennsylvania, was sentenced to ten years for making a film that sowed dissension and interfered with the war effort.[55]

Over the Top

The combination of propaganda and censorship gave Americans on the home front a misleading picture of their troops in France. "If the people really knew, the war would be stopped tomorrow," British Prime Minister David Lloyd George observed. "But of course they don't and can't know. The correspondents don't write and the censorship would not pass the truth."[56] Before the United States entered the war, Major Douglas MacArthur, appointed censor at the War Department in 1916, had expressed his preference for the British system that released only what the government wanted. During times of war, he believed, everyone should aid the military. Foreign correspondent and muckraker Arthur Bullard, who had observed the British model, disagreed. He argued in the *Atlantic Monthly* and in letters to President Wilson's closest advisor, Colonel Edward M. House, that strict censorship protected incompetence, became politicized, and over the long run undermined public confidence. The best way, true to democratic tradition, Bullard felt, was to trust the public with the truth.[57] General Pershing agreed with MacArthur.

Pershing, the stern, ambitious commander of the American Expeditionary Force (AEF), had a law degree, spoke fluent French, and after a career of fighting American Indians, Spaniards, Filipinos, and Mexicans, now led an unprepared army on the western front. Contrary to CPI propaganda on American and Allied harmony, Wilson and Pershing viewed the United States as a distinctive force fighting in its own way for its own reasons. The president announced that the United States was an "associate" power, not an allied power. He and Pershing insisted on maintaining a separate American army. Wilson told foreign correspondents off the record that he thought "the American people would feel a very much more ardent interest in the war if their men were fighting under their own flag."[58] More to the point, Wilson, looking ahead to American postwar leadership, did not want U.S. troops to vanish into the French and British armies. Pershing, moreover, espoused the classic American strategy of the direct, overwhelming offensive in contrast to the Allies who were fighting a defensive war of attrition. But Pershing found mobility to be a big problem, along with the lack of trained troops and over-stretched supply lines.

To organize the press, Pershing took along his close friend, long-time war correspondent Frederick Palmer. To be accredited to the AEF, correspondents had to swear that they would "convey the truth to the people of the United States" and not disclose information that would aid the enemy. Each reporter or his newspaper had to post a $10,000 bond as a guarantee that he would conduct himself as "a gentleman of the Press." Reporters had to rely on official bulletins, photographs, and press releases praising U.S. operations handed out by Palmer. Correspondents wanted to report on the supply problem that left the Americans dependent upon the British and French for equipment. Although the War Department refused to let out the story, Heywood Broun of the *New York World* returned home and did a series on supply mishaps: of trucks delivered without motors, mules without harnesses, and tractors instead of motorcycles. In response, the War Department revoked Broun's accreditation and the *New York World* lost ten thousand dollars. In the late winter of 1918, the War Department, responding in part to domestic complaints, ordered that the censors allow more realistic and speedier reporting from the front.[59]

The censorship of information or photographs that would have a negative effect on the home front, soldiers, or allies served to reinforce CPI messages.

Censors banned a story that the French had presented wine to the Americans because it might offend the temperance movement back home. Also banned were photos of U.S. soldiers improperly equipped or out of uniform, the wreckage of a fallen plane, an operating room at a military hospital, and any American dead. "Such pictures caused needless anxiety to those whose friends and relatives were at the front, and tended to foster the anti-war spirit that was always so persistently cultivated by the enemy," said Major Kendall Banning of the War Department. Dead Americans, identified by name, hometown, and as the son or brother of someone, were pictured in formal portraits, some in civilian dress and some in military uniform, in the *New York Times' Mid-Week Pictorial* "Roll of Honor." In contrast, released photos of enemy dead showed their crumpled and twisted bodies on the battlefield. According to the photographic record, as photojournalist Susan D. Moeller observed, the horrors of war happened to the enemy; Americans remained serenely untouched even in death.[60]

As for why they fought, soldiers cited both their own reasons and those promoted by the CPI. Broun reported on a YMCA frontline survey asking soldiers why they had enlisted. One of the most common answers he called "swanking and swaggering," as in "To fight for my country, the good old United States, the land of the free and the starry flag that I love so well." The other most common answer, "Because I was crazy," he pronounced cynical. One practical soldier wrote that he joined up "to improve my mind by visiting the famous churches and art galleries of the old world." The reasons that Broun considered the most sincere included: "Because they said I wasn't game and I am too" and "Because she'll be sorry when she sees my name in the list of the fellows that got killed." Adventure called many such as ambulance driver John Dos Passos who said, "I wanted to see the show." Others simply said they were there to kill Germans.[61]

Soldiers, seeing the castles and cathedrals of Europe they had known only from history books and novels, read in the army newspaper, *Stars and Stripes*, that they were the "spiritual successors" to the "Knights of King Arthur's Round Table." Many wrote in their letters home about knights, grails, feats of valor, and the crusade, accepting as their own the epic cause outlined for them by the government.[62] William Judy, who had volunteered even though he thought the United States was unwise to go to war, heard a chaplain explain, "We fight that we may never need to fight again." Other than that, the army field clerk from Chicago rarely heard anyone talk about the principles they were fighting for, even though they could be read everywhere. Nor did the

The Eighteenth Infantry, Machine Gun Battalion, in advance on the St. Mihiel Front, France, September 1918. (National Archives, NWDNS-111-SC-20936)

soldier discuss strategy or often even know where he was. One demonstrated his imperviousness to CPI propaganda when he asked which side Belgium was on. Soldiers, Judy noted, talked about women, where to buy wine and cigarettes, their next bath, what the censor did to the last letter, and popular songs back home. "What's the idea of fighting for France when they charge us high prices," they asked and, most important of all, "When do we eat?"[63]

In contrast to the soldiers in *Pershing's Crusaders*, the troops in the trenches dealt with mud, shelling, rats, lice, spoiled food, and rotting bodies. In 1918 poison gas caused between 20 and 30 percent of American casualties. Most gas attacks were not fatal but resulted in blindness and blistering skin. Heavy artillery bombardments could cause shell shock, which manifested in numbness, panic, nightmares, loss of speech, or loss of memory. The 200,000 African American troops faced added difficulties of rigid discrimination. The all black 92nd Division, referred to as the "Rapist Division" by its white commanding general, was inadequately trained and did not perform well. White officers said it was because the troops were black, ignoring the fact that poorly trained white soldiers had panicked as well. Four black infantry regiments fought with distinction under French command; the men of the 369th Infantry Regiment received the prestigious Croix de Guerre for bravery. But no African American troops marched in the victory parade in Paris. One news story that reinforced the heroic image of American forces in battle was the celebrated account of Alvin York, a white man from Tennessee and a former conscientious objector. York, armed with an Enfield rifle and a Colt .45 sidearm, single-handedly defeated an entire enemy machine gun battalion, killed 25, and captured 132 Germans. Less attention was paid to the more common sight of the men of American rifle companies lying dead in a line, casualties of machine gun fire.[64]

When the war ended in an armistice in November 1918, Americans felt that they had won the war. More accurately, it could be said that the presence of American troops and the potential for many more had made a difference. Back home, CPI ads promised the families of American soldiers, "He Will Come Back a Better Man!" Showing the returning soldier greeted by a proud father, loving mother, and hero-worshipping little brother, the ads said, "When that boy of yours comes marching home a Victorious Crusader he will be a very different person from the lad you bravely sent away with a kiss, a tear and a smile. He will be strong in body, quick and sure in action, alert and keen in mind, firm and resolute in character, calm and even-tempered."[65] Some soldiers did return in fine condition. After the war, however, three out of five beds at government hospitals were filled with veterans suffering from shell shock or what would now be diagnosed as post-traumatic stress disorder. Others, describing themselves as jumpy or unstable, fought the war in their dreams for years.[66]

Will Judy felt like "some god" at his homecoming when a hundred girls threw flowers as his outfit paraded on State Street in Chicago. He soon learned that people at home expected him to confirm the official version of the war. "We must say that the enemy were fiends, that they butchered prisoners, that they quaked in fear as we came upon them in their trenches, that they were not nearly as brave as ourselves, that Americans are the best and bravest fighters of all nations," he noted. He blamed propaganda in the press for creating this image of the American soldier in France, "rushing mid shot and shell across No Man's Land, and plunging the knife into the cowering enemy."[67] Judy believed that most veterans would feel compelled to stick to the script expected of them or be silent. Filmmaker D. W. Griffith thought the opposite. Griffith, who observed that modern war "is nothing but filth

Propaganda often portrayed American action on the Western Front as romantic and patriotic as in this Liberty Loan poster, 1918. Sidney H. Riesenberg, artist. (Library of Congress, LC-USZC4-9850)

and dirt and the most soul sickening smells," believed that when the men came home they would expose the romance of war as a lie and peace would reign forever.[68] What both eyewitnesses of the western front agreed on was that the portrayal of the Great War on the home front had little in common with the real thing.

To rally the country, the CPI had informed, educated, exaggerated, and misled. Most of its propaganda ignored Wilson's claim that the United States was going to war to liberate the peoples of the world, including the Germans. For his part, the president announced in January 1918 that the "new international order" would be based on the Fourteen Points, which spelled out American principles and interests such as open diplomacy, freedom of the seas, disarmament, self-determination, and equal access to trade. Wilson advocated the creation of an international organization called the League of Nations to guarantee the rights and territorial integrity of all nations.[69] The United States must no longer isolate itself, Wilson repeatedly told his audiences; it must take on its full responsibility. On the day the war ended, the president called on Americans to be patient as the victors constructed a peace out of "disinterested justice" and "humane temper." After his administration demonstrated that it could successfully incite fierce emotions, the president set out to bring a moderate peace to Europe as the basis for a democratic world order.

To Rescue the Old World

PRESIDENT WILSON TOOK THE UNPRECEDENTED STEP of heading his own peace commission and sailed on the *George Washington* to Paris in November 1918. To the Europeans, the CPI's Foreign Division had delivered the messages that America could never be beaten, that America was a land of freedom and democracy and could therefore be trusted, and that because of President Wilson's vision of a new world order and his power of achieving it, the Allied victory would usher in an era of peace and hope.[70] The leaders of the victorious Allies would meet to thrash out the details. Wilson hoped to use his prestige to moderate the imperial excesses of the British and French. Still maintaining a separation from the Europeans, he had announced the Fourteen Points without consulting them. Confident of the righteousness of his plan, Wilson assumed that if nations had the right of self-determination they would choose democracy. In his war message, for example, he said that the Russians, who had just overthrown Czar Nicholas II in their first revolution of 1917, always had been "in fact democratic at heart." He was also aware that a policy of open door trade would benefit the United States as the world's new number one economy the most. Wilson had, he believed, not only principle on his side but also power. The United States had a million troops in Europe and a navy as big as Britain's. Besides, the Allies owed the Americans ten billion dollars.

As Wilson realized, his vision of world order seemed far removed from the smoldering confusion of postwar Europe. Four empires—the German, Russian, Austro-Hungarian, and Ottoman—had crumbled. The upheaval caused by the war created fertile ground for revolution. In November 1917, Vladimir Lenin and the Bolsheviks took power in Russia and promised peace, bread, land, and the end of the capitalist exploitation of workers. To show his contempt for the ambitions of Russia's former allies, Lenin published secret deals exposing British and French plans to divide up the spoils in the Middle East. Italy wanted Austro-Hungarian territories in the Alps and on the Adriatic. Japan demanded German holdings in China. The war left survivors

The American flag dominates the display of allied flags in this World War I poster for the U.S. Food Administration. Adolph Treidler, artist. (National Archives, NWDNS-4-P-247)

shattered by the losses of sixteen million soldiers and civilians killed, twenty million wounded, and twenty million dead from the global flu epidemic of 1918. Viewing the devastation with pity and revolution with horror, President Wilson was more certain than ever that the world needed progressive American leadership to steer between the extremes of imperialism and communism. Sailing across the Atlantic, Wilson said, "The conservatives do not realize what forces are loose in the world at the present time. Liberalism is the only thing that can save civilization from chaos—from a flood of ultra-radicalism that will swamp the world."[71]

It was the new world coming to rescue the old from itself. This mission was the culmination of what the CPI had explained to the American public during the war. The Old Idea of autocracy, militarism, and aggression would give way to the New Idea of democracy, liberty, and equality embodied in the spirit of 1776. The Bolsheviks in Russia, however, had their own New Idea. Bowing to Allied pressure, Wilson had ordered 14,000 U.S. troops to Archangel and Siberia from 1918 to 1920 officially to protect supplies and Czech prisoners of war; unofficially the Americans wanted to intervene in the civil war against the Bolsheviks. The CPI sent a baffled Arthur Bullard to Siberia to explain the American presence. "We are rather in the position of advertising something and not knowing what it is," he observed.[72] Wilson, torn between his opposition to the Bolshevik regime and his disinclination to commit enough U.S. forces to overthrow it, later admitted he had no policy. At home, the left condemned the president's hypocritical claim that the United States was not taking sides in internal Russian affairs, while conservatives berated him for not going all out to remove the Bolsheviks, who had pledged to wipe out capitalism. The Allied intervention failed. Confronted with foreign troops, many Russians preferred to support Lenin. Distrust and antagonism continued between Soviet leaders and western governments.

The CPI celebrated the origins of the New Idea in allied nations France and England, always seeking to downplay the inconvenient history that Americans had twice fought the British. The Four Minute Men were instructed to point out that in the British Empire, the New Idea inspired "moderation and justice in dealing with colonists."[73] From Paris, the CPI's Kerney informed Tumulty that America's allies had not embraced the New Idea. The president "has an enormous task ahead of him, because, frankly Joe, there isn't much idealism in these countries," warned Kerney. "The French have a mad love of their land," he reported, "but it is the actual land itself, not any real ideals for the good of the world, that most of them love and die for."[74] Yet, the cheering of the French and British people, who poured into the streets to welcome the American president, confirmed Wilson's belief that the peace belonged to him.

It turned out that the New Idea embodied in the Fourteen Points held much more appeal for colonial peoples than for the Allied leaders who wanted revenge and reward. To render Germany incapable of future aggression, the French insisted that Germany accept terms widely perceived as humiliating, including responsibility for the war, demilitarization, and reparation payments of 33 billion dollars. Britain rejected freedom of the seas and open door trade, fearing infringement on its naval and imperial power. The Allies agreed to self-determination for a number of new countries in Eastern Europe, but the controversial boundary lines mixed Germans with Poles and Czechs, Slovaks with Hungarians, and Serbs with Croats and Bosnians. As Walter Lippmann, Wilson's disillusioned young aide, observed, these weak new nations, intended to serve as a buffer between the west and the threat of communist expansion from Russia, were hardly capable of doing so.[75] With many of his Fourteen Points compromised, Wilson pinned his hopes on the League of Nations to prevent future conflicts by creating "collective security." To many astute observers, however, the world did not seem safer.

Indeed, the victors did not extend self-determination to the colonial peoples whose expectations had been raised. Syngman Rhee, the Korean nationalist and Princeton graduate who had been introduced around campus by Woodrow Wilson as "the future redeemer of Korean independence," wanted to go to Paris to advocate his country's freedom from Japan. The State Department denied Rhee's request for a passport because the United States already had recognized Japan's annexation of Korea. Ho Chi Minh, the young Vietnamese nationalist who worked in the kitchen of a Parisian hotel, tried but failed to see Wilson to tell him he wanted self-determination for French Indochina. Arab hopes for independence went largely unanswered as the British and French divided up the Middle East into "mandates." Lloyd George mused, "Mesopotamia...yes...oil...irrigation...we must have Mesopotamia." The British constructed Iraq out of three Ottoman provinces, Basra, Baghdad, and Mosul, put down a rebellion, and installed a king, all the while planning to exercise control through indirect rule. Back in Washington, Secretary of War Baker wondered what all the fuss was about over American support of "mandates" when, after all, the United States had one in the Philippines. In Europe, Asia, and the Middle East, the seeds of future conflicts had been sown.[76]

The Wilson administration's successful wartime management of the news fell apart in Paris. Wilson took muckraking journalist and friend Ray Stannard Baker to be press liaison, but since the talks were held in secret Baker had nothing to say. CPI Director Creel, along to do Peace Commission publicity, had lost the trust of reporters. Out of the 500 correspondents covering the conference, 150 were American; most of them were local Washington reporters who did not speak French and found it difficult to establish news sources in Paris. British and American reporters organized a protest against the secrecy. Of the leaders of the Big Four—Britain, France, Italy, and the United States— Wilson alone called for more openness. He followed through by releasing daily communiqués and opening the plenary session to the press. As it turned out, nothing important happened in the plenary session and so the reporters enjoyed an empty victory.[77] Two of Wilson's fellow Peace Commissioners, Secretary Lansing and Colonel House, made statements that did not match the president's views. In addition, the president had failed to heed McKinley's example of naming senators to the commission who might then help persuade their colleagues to support the resulting treaty. News accounts of differences among the Commissioners encouraged the president's growing opposition at home. In return, reports of Wilson's lack of domestic support fueled Allied doubts that the United States would uphold its share of the peacekeeping burden, thereby weakening the president's bargaining position in Paris.[78]

An anxious Tumulty, left behind in Washington to monitor the press, wrote that it looked bad that the president was living in a palace guarded by soldiers. He urged that this image be corrected with a human-interest story of a presidential visit to an American military hospital. Take reporters and "sit beside beds of common soldiers," Tumulty advised.[79] The hospital visit accomplished, the president kept up a demanding schedule of secret negotiations in Paris with little time to exercise his skill at public persuasion. Nor did he seem to think it was necessary. Wilson maintained his conviction that he had the support of the American people. The president tried to keep the peace treaty, signed June 28, 1919, from the press until ratification. When it leaked, the debate over its content and the secrecy surrounding it was angry. If this way of doing international diplomacy was part of the new world order, a number of Americans didn't like it. About the president, Sweetser, now a press aide to Ray Stannard Baker, privately noted, "Never knew a man who had such a faculty for doing the right thing in the hardest way."[80]

Wartime unity at home, in part genuine and in part an artificial construction of propaganda and censorship, was disintegrating. Progressives, who had supported the Fourteen Points, denounced the treaty for violating those principles. LaFollette thought it too harsh on Germany. Middle-class reformers were troubled by the repression of civil liberties at home. "The time has come," wrote progressive historian Charles Beard, to "release political prisoners whose offense was to retain Mr. Wilson's pacifist views after he abandoned them." Socialists and radical workers were more convinced than ever that their cynicism regarding Wilson's noble expression of ideals was justified. Conservatives were wary of Wilson's global commitments, fearing that entanglement in the League would prevent Americans from taking independent action in pursuit of their own interests. Industrialists Henry Clay Frick and Andrew Mellon helped to finance an anti-League campaign. Lodge, the formidable chair of the Senate Foreign Relations committee, raised the specter of Bolshevism, claiming that Wilson asked the country "to move away from George Washington to...the sinister figure of Trotsky the champion of internationalism." Critics in Congress voiced their concern that the League's Article 10, requiring member nations to provide troops if the League requested, overrode their constitutional power to declare war. From France Kerney warned Tumulty that most of the American soldiers he ran across opposed the League because they believed it meant involvement in other European wars. "They don't want any more of Europe," he wrote. "Surely they don't want any more war."[81]

The president was on the defensive. Although he had spoken about his vision for postwar peace before the United States had entered the war, he had not laid out in any concrete way just how he would realize this vision. Now the treaty faced criticism from conservatives, liberals, and citizens who did not want to be involved in another European conflict ever again. Once he returned from France, Wilson tried to bypass his critics in Congress and the press by reaching out directly to the public. He planned a 10,000-mile train tour across the country. Accompanied by twenty reporters and movie cameramen, the president gave thirty-two major speeches over twenty-three days in September 1919. In an early version of "equal time," Senators Borah and Hiram Johnson of California trailed Wilson, countering the president's eloquence with some of their own. Both expressed their fears that the United States would end up defending the imperial ambitions of Britain and France. In a bid to resurrect McKinley's success, Tumulty presented his boss with highlights from the Ohioan's last speech at the Buffalo Pan-American Exposition. McKinley had portrayed a prosperous world tied closer together by transportation and communication in which the vast business of the

United States flourished and isolation was "no longer possible or desirable." Wilson, however articulate in opposition to isolationism, seldom approached McKinley's sunny view of the future.[82]

Wilson warned that if the United States did not commit to keeping the peace, an even more devastating war would break out. Even though he said he preferred not to consider international relations in terms of business, he did, saying, "[Y]ou can make more money out of friendly traders than out of hostile traders." Wilson declared that a commitment by the United States to the League of Nations would not demean national sovereignty. Before a San Francisco audience, the president explained that the Monroe Doctrine gave the United States the authority to act independently in the western hemisphere. Wilson addressed fears that Article 10 of the League covenant would drag American troops into combat around the world. In Indianapolis, he explained that nations would use the "terrible remedy" of an economic boycott to punish offenders. Furthermore, he elaborated, any action by the League

On his national tour, President Wilson declared, "The peace of the world cannot be established without America." Here he is speaking in Tacoma, Washington, on September 18, 1919. (Library of Congress, LC-USZ62-106648)

Council, charged with enforcing Article 10, would be unanimous. Americans therefore would not fight in any action they did not support. Besides, the president assured the citizens of St. Louis, the financial, industrial, and commercial strength of the United States made it the "senior partner." Finally, the president warned what would happen to the United States if it stood alone. It would require a great army, universal conscription, high taxes, and a powerful commander in chief. Militarized government, Wilson warned, was "absolutely antidemocratic in its influence."[83]

The impressive rhetorical skills of the exhausted president faltered as he sometimes rambled and relied on generalizations. Press coverage fell off. When he became seriously ill in Colorado, his debilitating stroke was covered up. The public was told there was nothing to worry about, and the president returned to Washington where he was not seen for weeks. In the meantime, Lodge announced his reservations to the treaty. The senator insisted that Congress's power to declare war be preserved. He wanted a guarantee of the Monroe Doctrine and a rejection of the provision that turned German control of China's Shandong province over to Japan. Although Wilson had agreed to many of these reservations in his speeches, he refused to compromise on the treaty with the senators, even though most of them supported a league in some form. In March 1920, the Senate failed by seven votes to ratify the treaty. A year later, the United States formally ended the war with Germany, Austria, and Hungary. The League of Nations was set up without the United States as a member.

Hun or Home

The CPI's short-term success of arousing "white hot patriotism" to fight the war did not translate into long-term support for an internationalist foreign policy. To convince Americans to support the switch from neutrality to war, propagandists had demonized the German enemy. While they dramatized what the United States fought against, they were less clear about what the country fought for. Moreover, the silencing of dissent on the home front did not encourage the kind of open debate on liberal internationalism out of which some sort of popular consensus might have developed. When he returned home from Paris to promote the treaty, President Wilson tried to construct such a consensus. He used the emotional argument that mothers believed their sons had died to save the "liberty of the world," which, he explained, meant an ongoing American commitment to peacekeeping.

Notably, much more of his appeal focused on U.S. economic and security interests than it had during the war. But it was late in the process to start convincing people that his policy fulfilled both their ideals and their interests. At the end of World War I, Americans celebrated their national greatness but differed over how to exercise their power. The public had seen the United States portrayed as the home of democracy, decency, justice, freedom, and progress. Its enemy was barbarism, autocracy, and militarism. The simple choice—Hun or Home—was, in the style of effective propaganda, no choice at all. Even more misleading was the CPI's projection that once the Hun was defeated, the rest of the world would embrace an American-led new world order.

World politics turned out to be much more complicated. Wilson, despite his intention to offer a moderate path between imperialism and communism, ultimately sided mostly with the empires of Britain and France. At the same time, oppressed colonial peoples seized upon his stirring call for self-determination. They turned to resistance and revolution. At home, returning black veterans embraced a short-lived crusade for racial justice against white supremacists. Civil rights leaders called for the defeat of the "Huns of Georgia" in order "To Make America Safe for Americans."[84] Wilson claimed that Americans must save the world by taking the lead. Others argued that Wilson's version of internationalism meant entanglement in old world problems. The United States, stronger than ever, would do best without being tied down, they felt. Through the 1920s, Americans pursued their global economic interests and stayed out of the League of Nations. When depression and another world war followed, however, many concluded they had made a mistake and turned again to Wilson's ideas.

The U.S. government's effective mobilization of public opinion also left a mixed legacy. The Wilson administration made official propaganda central to the war effort by applying progressive notions of bureaucratic efficiency, scientific management, and innovative dissemination. Creel, pointing to pressure from citizen groups for more extreme hate propaganda, claimed that the CPI had been a moderating force. Yet, the CPI had shifted from its emphasis on education and information to the promotion of unquestioning patriotism. Its atrocity propaganda tended to be remembered more vividly than advice to be cheerful and go shopping. In the 1920s, investigations exposed much of the wartime atrocity propaganda as fabrication, leaving many convinced that propaganda meant lies. CPI veteran Edward L. Bernays concluded that the term propaganda had earned such a negative reputation that he would replace it with public relations, a classic PR makeover that launched a dynamic new industry.[85] Disbanded in the summer of 1919, the CPI provided a model of public mobilization for its World War II–era successor, the Office of War Information, to emulate without appearing to do so.

Their experiences with a crusade for democracy left Americans divided. Randolph Bourne observed that in the modern era, all the wartime home front really needed was the efficient cooperation of the "big men," the industrialists and financiers. Most citizens had only to acquiesce. They supported the war by going on with their daily lives, working and paying taxes. As a result, he thought, "we do not feel the war to be very real." Walter Lippmann worried that the gap between what was really happening in the world and people's perceptions of what was happening could be exploited by propagandists who appealed to "the pictures in our heads" or, as he dubbed them, "stereotypes." Urging people to embrace reason and objectivity, he reluctantly acknowledged, "Prejudices are so much easier and more interesting."[86] While Bourne and Lippmann voiced concerns about the detrimental effects of war on democratic government, war correspondent turned military press officer Frederick Palmer explained away such doubts. Americans must have confidence in their productivity, their manhood, and their cause, he wrote, because "to have lacked faith would have been un-American." The new veterans group, the American Legion, formally created in Paris in 1919 by American Expeditionary Force officers, called for honoring war service and opposing left-wing radicalism. Espousing a virile Christian nationalism, they considered calling themselves the "Crusaders" before settling on Legionnaires. As Will Judy expected, these veterans fulfilled the official version of their experience. He concluded, "The truth will never be known about this war or about any other war past or future."[87]

3

The Good War

Fighting for a Better Life in World War II

We are fighting today for security, for progress and for peace, not only for ourselves, but for all men, not only for one generation but for all generations. We are fighting to cleanse the world of ancient evils, ancient ills.

President Franklin D. Roosevelt, 1942

People see a new world is needed.... But they are skeptical as hell.

Citizen Response to Office of War Information Survey, 1943

PRESIDENT FRANKLIN D. ROOSEVELT declared that the United States was determined not only to win World War II but also to secure the peace that would follow. To win the war would be tough. By early 1942, Nazi Germany had conquered most of Europe. Following a surprise attack on the U.S. Pacific Fleet at Pearl Harbor in December 1941, the Japanese crushed the Americans in the Philippines and the British at Singapore. The United States began to mobilize, but it would be months before its forces were ready to take on the enemy. In the meantime, it counted on its chief allies, Great Britain and the Soviet Union, to carry on the fight. As for securing the peace, the Roosevelt administration planned to succeed where Woodrow Wilson had failed, by making sure that this time the United States would commit to the role of international peacekeeper. FDR was confident that the economic and military power of the United States would ensure its postwar dominance over the alternative agendas of its wartime allies. American internationalism presumed American leadership.

The Roosevelt administration was well aware that it would have to persuade the American people to commit to an internationalist foreign policy. Still disillusioned from their experiences in World War I, Americans had wanted to stay out of a second one. Once attacked, they fought for survival, not ideals.[1] In total war, officials knew, waving the flag would not be enough. Millions must fight, produce, ration, conserve, and buy bonds. In April 1942, a memo prepared for Archibald MacLeish, poet, Librarian of Congress, and wartime propagandist, raised the question, "What will unify this nation affirmatively and effectively for the desperate war which lies ahead?"

    1. Should this war be presented as a crusade?
    2. If so, a crusade for what? What do men want?
       a. Order and security? World order, etc.?
       b. Better life?
    3. How do you get these things?[2]

Right from the start, propagandists retooled the civilization versus barbarism theme to portray the war as an all out fight between democracy and dictatorship. In an important change, however, they emphasized the pragmatic rewards of victory—a better life and a safer world. And the way to "get these things" was through internationalism.

The propagandists of World War II followed in the footsteps of the Committee on Public Information (CPI), while attempting to avoid their predecessors' mistakes. The Office of War Information (OWI), set up in 1942, adopted the "strategy of truth," which honored the idea that informed citizens could be trusted to make up their own minds. Their goal was to regain public confidence in official propaganda. Following the CPI's example, the OWI had domestic and overseas bureaus dedicated to the dissemination of messages through the mass media, which became, according to journalism historian James Baughman, "voluntary propagandists."[3] The OWI pledged to avoid the rousing "over the top" exhortations of the CPI and instead instruct the public in a straightforward and practical way. Its messages, however, made it absolutely clear what was the right thing to do. As historian Lary May pointed out, the conversion narrative popular in wartime movies described an American maverick who learns to become part of the platoon or bomber crew. He decides to commit to the war effort for the good of the country and its future.[4] In contrast, Americans saw that the peoples of enemy nations were not allowed the freedom to make their own choices. Enemy dictatorships controlled the media, staged massive pageants glorifying the leader, the nation, and the military, and silenced anyone who spoke out in opposition.

The "strategy of truth" complemented the portrayal of the war as a clash between democracy and dictatorship.

Wartime propaganda blended facts with inspiring and reassuring cultural beliefs, blurring what was true with what people wanted to believe was true. As a result, it delivered mixed messages. As the U.S. government mobilized the nation, it held up citizen soldiers as symbols of national unity and called for the participation of women and minorities in war production and military service. For much of mainstream America, these changes were tolerated as temporary "win the war" measures. For them, a better life meant the restoration of the old social order once the crisis had passed. So as the government called upon industrial, urbanized America to ship millions of troops overseas to fight, its propaganda projected images of small-town serenity and traditional family life. Even as officials sought to educate Americans about the importance of making a long-term commitment to international peacekeeping, they sold the war with the promise that once it was over everyone could come home to enjoy a prosperous peace.

The promise of a better world guaranteed by American internationalism required the greatest stretch of the "strategy of truth." After all, no one knew what the future would bring. The one hope everyone had was "This time we will all make certain...we won't have to do it again," as sung by marching troops in the big finale from Warner Brothers' *This Is the Army* (1943).[5] Hanging over propagandists was the conviction that Americans had rejected the League of Nations because they believed their leaders and their allies had lied about war aims. Doubts about allies persisted. Polls showed that Americans suspected the British fought to preserve their empire and would again fail to pay their war debts as they had after World War I. The Soviet Union, with its one-party communist rule, state-run centralized economy, and intolerance of religious faith, they felt, was incompatible.[6] To reassure the public, propaganda portrayed the allies as "just like us," sharing not only a common enemy, but also common war aims. Such a portrayal sought to inspire the popular endorsement of internationalism desired by President Roosevelt. He wanted to create bipartisan support at home for whatever commitments he might make overseas.[7]

What Americans wanted this time was not to make the world safe for democracy, observed one pollster, they wanted to make the world safe—period.[8] Wartime propaganda, in a broad appeal to both principles and interests, told them they could have both. To understand the administration's persistent promotion of internationalism, it is important to examine the period from 1939 to 1941 when Americans debated the virtues of isolationism while the Roosevelt administration fostered public support for U.S. aid to nations resisting Nazi aggression. In the months following Pearl Harbor, official propaganda deployed an arsenal of patriotic imagery, defining the Americans, the Allies, and the enemy as combatants in a fight for freedom against slavery. They called upon Americans to convert to internationalism with the explicit message that the United States must cooperate with allies to set up a democratic and capitalist world order and the implicit message that in doing so, the United States would be in charge. Once the war turned in the Allies' favor in 1943, propagandists took care to warn of the hard fight ahead. They projected the creation of a stable peace in which the United States would prosper.

"Fiddle-Dee-Dee...War, War, War!"

WITH THESE WORDS, Scarlett O'Hara, the heroine of the Civil War epic film *Gone With the Wind* (1939), expressed her exasperation with talk of war when she preferred to discuss parties. As Germany's invasion of Poland triggered war in Europe that same year, many Americans were as disdainful of distant war as the self-absorbed Scarlett. After World War I, the failed peace, and the economic hard times of the 1930s, they distrusted war and its consequences. The out-of-work World War I veterans who marched on Washington in 1932 seeking their bonuses were seen as casualties of the Depression. Retired Marine Corps General Smedley Butler denounced the huge fortunes made during war in his 1935 polemic, "War Is a Racket." In particular, he decried the suffering of families and soldiers who, "having patriotism stuffed down their throats," died or returned wounded, mentally broken, or unable to readjust. "They have paid their part of the war profits," he declared.[9] In the 1930s, protesting college students joined "Veterans of Future Wars." At the University of Minnesota, a student leader shouted, "And next time, when they come and tell us we must invade the land of some other, some equally innocent and misguided people, to 'defend our wives and sweethearts,' we know what we will do—we shall defend them by preserving our lives, by staying at home with them. We will not listen to the scream for slaughter."[10] The U.S. Senate investigated the war profits made by bankers and munitions makers, dramatically called "merchants of death." Congress passed a series of Neutrality Acts designed to keep the United States out of another European war.

At the same time Americans watched warily as fascist Italy invaded Ethiopia in 1935, Nazi leader Adolf Hitler ordered German troops to reoccupy the Rhineland in violation of the Versailles treaty in 1936, and Japan attacked China in 1937. In a major speech in Chicago in 1937 President Roosevelt called for a "quarantine" of aggressor nations, but little action followed. During the Munich Conference of September 1938, Roosevelt sent messages to the leaders of Germany, Italy, Britain, and France saying he hoped they would settle peacefully Germany's demand for Czechoslovakia's Sudetenland. The British and French, unprepared for a major war, practiced appeasement by giving in to Hitler, who assured them he wanted no more territory. They soon learned that war had only been postponed, not prevented. The Soviet Union, looking out for itself, signed a nonaggression pact with Germany. When Germany attacked Poland in September 1939, Britain and France declared war. Following a quick defeat of Poland, Germany invaded and conquered Denmark, Norway, the Netherlands, Belgium, and France in the spring of 1940. From London, Winston Churchill, the new Prime Minister, eloquently declared that his nation would fight on, but many wondered how long the British would last. The Japanese, proclaiming Asia for Asians, threatened the vulnerable European colonies of French Indochina, British Malaya, and the Dutch East Indies. Sharing common enemies, Germany, Italy, and Japan, known as the Axis powers, formed a military and political alliance called the Tripartite Pact in September 1940.

The debate among Americans over the Axis move to control Europe and Asia centered on the following question: Could the United States, looking out for itself, live with this new international order? Isolationists, who included conservatives, liberals, socialists, communists, and pacifists, answered yes. They viewed the American entry into World War I as a mistake not to be repeated. Some feared war would mean bigger government or the dismantling of New Deal reforms or another crackdown on civil liberties. Members of the America First Committee believed the western hemisphere could be defended as a "Fortress America." A few, like America First spokesman, the famed aviator Charles Lindbergh, admired the German Luftwaffe and aspects of Nazi ideology. Others believed that the United States could best maintain what they saw as its moral superiority by avoiding contamination with foreign troubles. Most isolationists did not envision a self-sufficient United States cut off from the rest of the world, however. Rather, they advocated global neutrality allowing Americans to trade with whomever and wherever they pleased.[11]

Internationalists, also a diverse group of conservatives, liberals, and social-ists, countered that the United States could not survive in a world dominated by the Axis. Some pointed to the malevolent Nazi belief in a thousand-year Third Reich that seized territory for an Aryan master race and persecuted Jews, the disabled, and anyone else the Nazis deemed unfit. Internationalists called for the United States to assist nations under German attack. When isolationists in Congress defeated initial attempts by internationalists to revise the Neutrality Act, Roosevelt asked the esteemed Kansas editor and Repub-lican William Allen White to organize a Non-Partisan Committee for Peace through Revision of the Neutrality Act to press for revision. In November 1939, lawmakers repealed the arms embargo and thus allowed Britain and France to purchase weapons. As the British struggled on after the fall of France, a number of internationalists began to advocate direct U.S. intervention. Henry Luce, the influential publisher of *Time, Life*, and *Fortune* magazines, argued that in 1919 the United States had bungled its opportunity to assume world leadership but that in 1941, it must act to create the "American Century." To Luce this meant that the United States must spread its free enterprise system, its technological skills, its humanitarianism, and its ideals across the planet.[12]

A number of Hollywood producers showed their interventionist leanings with such films as *Confessions of a Nazi Spy* (1939), *Foreign Correspondent* (1940), and *Sergeant York* (1941). Warner Brothers' *Sergeant York* told the real story of the devout Tennessee farmer, played by Gary Cooper, who wrestled with his conscience about the commandment "thou shalt not kill," decided World War I was a good cause, and became a national hero in 1918 at the battle of Meuse-Argonne. Upon his return from Europe, the war hero had turned down thousands of dollars in movie deals and commercial endorsements, saying, "Uncle Sam's uniform, it ain't for sale." Producers Jesse Lasky and Hal Wallis made sure that Alvin York approved of their film version of his life. Their efforts paid off when York himself attended the film's premiere in New York along with first lady Eleanor Roosevelt and General John Pershing. Speaking before the Veterans of Foreign Wars, York stated that if Americans stopped fighting for freedom, "then we owe the memory of George Washington an apology" because if so, "he wasted his time at Valley Forge." Taking advantage of the movie's success, the U.S. Army produced a recruiting pamphlet based on York. Isolationist senators charged Hollywood with carrying out pro-war propaganda, some pointing a finger at the number of foreign-born and Jews in the movie industry. In Hollywood's defense, Wendell Willkie, the Repub-lican who had lost to FDR in the 1940 presidential election, asserted the right of freedom from government censorship. No matter where anyone stood in the debate between isolationism and internationalism, all felt Hollywood was an influential force.[13]

So was the news media. Radio brought the war into the living rooms of America. Reporters, like most Americans, sympathized with the invaded, not the invaders. Radio networks used their own reporters and newspaper correspondents in international roundups from London, Paris, Vienna, and Berlin. From Berlin, William L. Shirer of CBS tried various stratagems to cope with Nazi censorship. Forbidden to call Germany's attack of Holland and Belgium an "invasion," Shirer instead quoted directly from German government sources, counting on his listeners to figure out what was happening. In London, Edward R. Murrow of CBS had the support of the British Ministry of Information as he covered the bombing ordered by Field Marshal Hermann Goering to "soften up" Britain for invasion. Murrow described the courage of Londoners during the Blitz as they put out fires, pulled the living and the dead from the rubble, cleared the streets, and started each new day expecting more of the same.[14] The measured reports of these war correspondents sounded restrained, however, compared to New York-based Walter Winchell, the most popular radio broadcaster in the United States. A fan of FDR and proud of his insider reputation, Winchell volunteered to use his show on NBC to promote the administration's foreign policy. Dramatically delivering his reports as "flashes" or "exclusives," Winchell pushed U.S. intervention in the European conflict as he did celebrity gossip, denouncing isolationists as "ratzis" in a sensational blend of news and entertainment.[15] Public support for aid to Britain grew, but most Americans continued to agree with both isolationists and internationalists. They did not want to go to war and they did not want Hitler to win.

Although he preferred to be the main source of official news, Roosevelt created a number of propaganda agencies. In September 1939, he established the Office of Government Reports (OGR) to track public opinion and to provide the media with information about the growing defense program. The Division of Information at the Office of Emergency Management churned out between ten and twenty press releases a day about the buildup of America's "arsenal of democracy." The Office of Civilian Defense, created in May 1941 and headed by the pugnacious mayor of New York, Fiorello La Guardia, was given the job of promoting civilian safety and national morale. To deal with propaganda abroad, the Coordinator of Inter-American Affairs, headed by Nelson Rockefeller, the multimillionaire grandson of the founder of Standard

Oil, promoted hemispheric solidarity. The Coordinator of Information (COI), led by Colonel William Donovan, conducted covert operations and directed "black propaganda" or disinformation at the enemy. It would later evolve into the Office of Strategic Services (OSS), the forerunner of the Central Intelligence Agency. At COI, Pulitzer-prize winning playwright and presidential speechwriter Robert Sherwood ran the Foreign Intelligence Service, which oversaw radio's "Voice of America." In addition, the State Department, the War Department, the Navy Department, and the Treasury each had its own public information office. Finally, to coordinate it all, FDR set up in October 1941 the Office of Facts and Figures (OFF) headed by MacLeish. "Here's Where We Get OFF," announced the fed-up editors of the *New York Herald Tribune*, dismissing the need for another agency to "explain what those who explain what the explainers of the explanations mean."[16]

President Roosevelt made sure that his propaganda agencies did not interfere with his sometimes less than candid pronouncements on U.S. foreign policy. Running for a controversial third term in 1940, he pledged, "Your boys are not going to be sent to any foreign wars," while he moved the United States ever closer to the fight. Behind the scenes the White House supported the Committee to Defend America by Aiding the Allies with its 300 local chapters, the interventionist group Fight for Freedom, which used its connections to push its position on national broadcasts, and the Council for Democracy, founded by Luce and other prominent journalists and businessmen to promote the American system. The White House and its supporters, who believed that most isolationists were misguided, selfish, or at best naive, nevertheless proceeded to discredit them by calling them disloyal, un-American, Nazi sympathizers, and "fifth columnists" or subversives who deliberately paved the way for German takeover of the United States.[17]

FDR avoided dealing with isolationists in Congress by using an executive order to send U.S. destroyers to Britain in exchange for the lease of British bases from Canada to South America. Congress passed (by only one vote in the House) the Selective Service Act of 1940, the first peacetime military draft in U.S. history, and, after impassioned debate, it approved Lend-Lease in March 1941. Through Lend-Lease the United States delivered supplies to Britain and later to the Soviet Union. At a press conference, the president compared Lend-Lease to the neighborly act of loaning a hose to the man next door when his house is on fire. Although critics scoffed at such a misleading analogy, the president's story appealed to the spirit of humanitarianism as well as the desire for self-preservation. In the fall of 1941, FDR, again evading

Congress by using his commander-in-chief powers, ordered U.S. naval convoys to escort supply ships across the Atlantic.

Most important for propaganda purposes, Roosevelt announced war aims. When he returned from a secret meeting with Prime Minister Churchill off the coast of Newfoundland in August 1941, he was greeted by a furious White House press corps who had been told along with the rest of the country that the president had gone fishing. FDR described the moving Sunday service held aboard the British battleship *The Prince of Wales*, during which he and Churchill, their highest-ranking military officers, and sailors from both navies sang "Onward Christian Soldiers." During this secret meeting, Roosevelt and Churchill had drawn up the Atlantic Charter, pledging that the postwar order would respect the self-determination of nations, equal access to trade and raw materials, freedom of the seas, economic security, and disarmament. They said they wanted to acquire no new territory and made a vague reference to some future international security system.[18] The Atlantic Charter principles served as a propaganda weapon against the Axis. For home front audiences, the Atlantic Charter was often represented by the Four Freedoms—freedom of speech, freedom of worship, freedom from want, and freedom from fear—spelled out by FDR in January 1941.

Roosevelt had maneuvered the United States into a state of undeclared war in the Atlantic and had announced U.S. aims in a war that it wasn't officially fighting. He believed that he had done as much as he could; only a shocking crisis would change isolationist attitudes. Always convinced that Hitler was the most serious threat, FDR committed the United States to a Germany-First strategy and tried to negotiate with Japan. When the Japanese expanded south into French Indochina, the United States responded with a trade embargo, which included shipments of scrap iron and petroleum. Japan, dependent on oil imports, had to decide whether to abandon its goal of dominance over Asia or obtain oil elsewhere, most likely from the Dutch East Indies. In diplomatic talks, Japan asked for U.S. acceptance of its conquests on the Asian mainland and the United States demanded that Japan withdraw from China. Neither side would compromise. When General Hideki Tojo took power in October 1941, Japan prepared to attack U.S. forces in the Pacific. At Pearl Harbor in December it delivered the worst naval defeat in American history.

Japan's attack on Pearl Harbor and the Philippines united the Allies and the American home front. On December 8, Congress declared war on Japan with only one dissenting vote. Hitler, long disdainful of America's mixed race population and democratic government, declared war on the United States three days later.[19] On January 1, 1942, twenty-six countries signed the Declaration of the United Nations, dedicating themselves to achieving the war aims laid down in the Atlantic Charter. Critics later accused Roosevelt of knowing in advance that Japan planned to attack Pearl Harbor. Although historians acknowledge that FDR schemed against the Axis, they have found him not guilty of deliberately allowing an attack on the U.S. Pacific fleet. Taken by surprise despite intelligence warnings of Japanese troop movements, the Americans had underestimated Japan, believing it to be without the initiative or know-how to launch such an attack. Japan, in turn, underestimated the United States, believing that before the easy-going Americans managed to mount a challenge, it could consolidate its Pacific holdings and negotiate a compromise peace.

More suspicion at the time centered on the lack of information about U.S. losses at Pearl Harbor. Official statements minimized the destruction by saying that only the battleship *Arizona* had been lost, other ships had been damaged, and the Japanese had suffered heavy casualties. Rumors spread that the entire Pacific fleet had been wiped out and 11,000 men killed. In a radio broadcast on February 23, 1942, Roosevelt addressed the exaggerated reports. He announced that three of the ships hit at Pearl Harbor were beyond repair and that 2,340 U.S. servicemen had been killed. FDR said the Japanese did not know how many planes they destroyed and he was not going to tell them. Enemy pilots, Americans would learn later, had wrecked most of the U.S. military aircraft and, in doing so, had themselves lost twenty-nine planes out of three hundred. Speaking several weeks after the December 7th attack, the president said, "Your government has unmistakable confidence in your ability to hear the worst." He was not talking about Pearl Harbor, but the fact that the United States would lose more ground to the enemy before it would regain it. He admitted that it would be "hopeless" to aid the Philippines.[20]

Americans knew little about what was happening in their Pacific colony where, under Japanese bombardment, Private John Lemke of Wisconsin crawled into a foxhole with a letter from home. "Dear Son," it read, "I'm so glad you are in the Philippines, because I am afraid that war with Germany is inevitable."[21] General Jonathan Wainwright led the 80,000 ill-equipped Filipino–American forces as they retreated to the Bataan Peninsula, while Commanding General Douglas MacArthur issued misleading press communiqués from the island fortress of Corregidor. When the president ordered MacArthur to safety in Australia, the general's formidable public relations skills helped to cover the disaster with glory. He pledged, "I shall return" and

FDR urged his radio audience to have world maps at the ready as it listened to his addresses. Speaking from the White House on February 23, 1942, the president explained supply and communication lines across oceans that had become battle-fields. In a new kind of global war, he insisted, allies were indispensable. (© Bettman/CORBIS)

was lauded as a hero back home. The desperate men he left behind were not so complimentary, but Washington would not know what happened to them for more than a year. After running out of food, medicine, and ammunition, they surrendered to the Japanese in April 1942. About 600 Americans and 7000 Filipinos died on an eighty-mile forced march known as the Bataan Death March to prisoner of war camps where thousands more perished.[22]

The events of 1939 to 1941 would inspire propaganda messages throughout the war and in the years to follow. The failure of appeasement at Munich had shown that the aggressors must be stopped by force. The attack on Pearl Harbor demonstrated that the world's oceans could not protect the United States. Isolationists called for a Pacific-First strategy and remained highly critical of Britain and the Soviet Union, but few doubted America's pressing need for allies if the Axis powers were to be defeated. To pave the way for postwar cooperation, FDR wanted the Allies to be called the United Nations.

Almost everyone preferred to say Allies, although British and American officials frequently used the president's term. They called the proposed successor
to the League of Nations the United Nations Organization or UNO, a deliberate conflation of the wartime alliance with postwar peacekeeping. As he had
shown when he returned from his "fishing trip" with Churchill, FDR enjoyed
keeping secrets as well as being the chief news source. His administration,
from White House aides to the new information agencies, had constructed a
partnership with prominent voices in the news media, Hollywood, and internationalist groups. The result, concluded historian Richard W. Steele, was "a
propaganda din so pervasive and so diverse in its sources" that by the time of
the Pearl Harbor attack the public was resigned about going to war even if it
didn't want to.[23]

The Strategy of Truth

The job of the OWI, directed the president in June 1942, was to "formulate
and carry out, through the use of press, radio, motion picture, and other
facilities, information programs designed to facilitate the development of an
informed and intelligent understanding, at home and abroad, of the status
and progress of the war effort and of the war policies, activities, and aims of
the Government." The widely respected Elmer Davis, the CBS news commentator with a "Hoosier twang as reassuring as Thanksgiving," reluctantly took
the job as director. He oversaw hundreds of information campaigns dedicated
to morale, recruiting, conservation, rationing, manpower, and food, as in "on
account of Hitler our meat is littler."[24] The OWI's objective, acknowledged
privately, was "the coordination, synchronization, embellishment, emphasis,
manipulation and distribution of facts as information rather than...gross
overstatements and exaggerated misrepresentations."[25] To mobilize the population, the OWI drew on familiar advertising techniques such as repetition,
catchy slogans, and celebrity endorsement. Yet, too much salesmanship might
project the wrong message. If commercial advertisers pitched their products
with slogans such as "win the war by looking lovely," worried propagandists,
they would identify patriotism with consumption rather than hard work and
sacrifice. Davis announced, "To tell the truth at home is to mobilize behind
the war the support, initiative, imagination, and genius of the American
people."[26]

It wouldn't be easy to tell the truth about war aims because of the many
versions floating around wartime Washington, including several in the OWI.

In an effort at more efficient coordination of government information, the new agency absorbed OFF, the Office of Government Reports, the Information Service of the Office of Emergency Management, and the Foreign Intelligence Service. But because not all the existing information agencies were included, the OWI never had the same centralized authority as the CPI had in World War I. Many of the deeply antifascist men and women already engaged in propaganda work were frustrated that so many Americans had been ambivalent about the threat posed by Nazi Germany. As much as they might have believed in the ideal of the informed citizen knowing the right thing to do, they thought the common man was in need of enlightenment and education. A large number were liberal New Dealers, committed to carrying on social and economic reforms. In addition, the OWI employed thousands of colorful, independent-minded writers, professors, artists, radio and film professionals, advertising executives, and news reporters who were not at home in a federal bureaucracy under the scrutiny of politicians. Conservatives on Capitol Hill felt that the OWI was too pro–New Deal, pro-Roosevelt, and pro–civil rights. In the summer of 1943, the House voted to eliminate the OWI's domestic branch; the Senate saved it, but reduced its budget. Rather than produce its own information, the OWI would coordinate the distribution through the media of information from other government agencies.[27]

To coordinate the government's propaganda policy, OWI Director Davis met regularly with representatives from the Joint Chiefs of Staff, the War Department, the Navy Department, the State Department, the Office of the Coordinator of Inter-American Affairs, the Board of Economic Warfare, the War Production Board, and the Office of Censorship. Each had its own agenda, Davis discovered. Reacting to this set-up, former CPI director George Creel sent Davis his regrets that his World War II counterpart had no real control over the Army, Navy, and State Departments. Creel recounted that when anyone had disputed CPI's authority, he won out because "Woodrow Wilson hammered them down." Creel refrained from pointing out what was obvious—Davis did not have that kind of backing from FDR. Creel offered little hope other than wishes of good luck and the warning that for Davis, "amiability can be a vice." Although observers praised the OWI director for his skill in dealing with high-powered colleagues, Davis later noted that Creel was "about right on all points."[28]

From the beginning, the OWI's "strategy of truth" confronted many obstacles. First, there was the issue of censorship. On December 16, 1941, President Roosevelt set up the Office of Censorship, headed by Associated

Press (AP) executive news editor Byron Price. The Office of Censorship had authority over all civilian communication. It withheld information that would aid the enemy, including defense matters, shipping, weather reports, and the president's travels. Price, who believed that press censorship violated the "democratic creed," nevertheless accepted its necessity in wartime. He set up a voluntary system, providing news outlets with guidelines of what was and was not all right to print or broadcast. By asking the media to police itself, Price maintained good relations with the press throughout the war. Before news organizations released a story, Price wanted them to ask themselves, "Is this information I would like to have if I were the enemy?"[29] In a 1942 press conference, he and Davis explained the relationship of the Office of Censorship and the OWI with the news media. Price announced, "We tell what they cannot print." Davis said, "We give them stuff we hope they will print."[30] Teamed with censorship, the "strategy of truth" meant selections of the truth, not the whole truth.

Most significantly, the military's heavy censorship made the job of the OWI a difficult one. Reeling from Japan's successful attack, the Army and

The OWI News Bureau in Washington, D.C., ran twenty-four hours a day. Note the posters on the walls. (Library of Congress, LC-USZ62-90303)

Navy enhanced public distrust by releasing conflicting information. On his first day on the job, Davis visited Secretary of War Henry Stimson and Secretary of the Navy Frank Knox, both prominent Republicans who had joined the Roosevelt administration to bring bipartisanship to the national government. Stimson, seated beneath a portrait of his mentor Elihu Root, lectured the OWI director on military secrecy and gave him a "polite brush-off." Knox, a fellow newspaperman, expressed a wish to cooperate, but Davis was not optimistic because he knew that Admiral Ernest J. King, the Chief of Naval Operations, preferred an information policy that would tell the American people about the war only when it was won. By withholding bad news, which meant almost all of the news in early 1942, the armed services allowed rumors and suspicion to flourish. This policy infuriated Davis who believed the truth should be told as long as it did not harm operations. The OWI and the services conferred daily, but the situation improved only when the navy could report victories at Coral Sea, Midway, and Guadalcanal later in 1942.[31]

Telling the public the truth about war aims was challenging because policymakers did not agree on nor did they wish to spell out what those aims were. The propagandists wanted to do a better job than their World War I counterparts of preparing the public for peacetime commitments.[32] OWI Deputy Director Arthur Sweetser, who had covered the State Department as a reporter in World War I and had spent the interwar years with the League of Nations, tried to find out what U.S. war aims were and how they would be achieved. Sweetser visited President Roosevelt who told him that he did not favor a revised League of Nations, which he dismissed as "a lot of talky-talk." Instead, FDR preferred a plan for the postwar order in which what he called the Four Policemen—the United States, Britain, the Soviet Union, and China—would enforce peace. "If you don't like the Russians, you've got to have them anyway," explained FDR. "They're too big and powerful to disarm and you'd better proceed on the good old political theory, if you can't beat 'em, join 'em. Then you'd have a colossal power."[33] The Four Policemen, Roosevelt insisted, would keep the peace by responding to any violation with what he called his old quarantine idea. The policemen would cut off the violator from trade with every part of the world; if economic sanctions did not work then military force would be applied. The president thought his Four Policemen plan could keep the peace for twenty-five years at least, but he did not explain to Sweetser how a plan based on great power dominance would fulfill the Atlantic Charter principles.

While the White House concentrated on security, the State Department, Sweetser learned, was focused on the postwar economy. Secretary of State Cordell Hull, the dignified former Democratic senator from Tennessee and long-time advocate of free trade, was more interested in expanding access to global markets then he was in creating the United Nations. He told Sweetser he believed that Americans should not interfere with British rule in India where Mahatma Gandhi was leading a mass movement for independence, because if in turn the British "butted in" on Argentina, the Americans would brandish the Monroe Doctrine and tell them to mind their own business. Undersecretary of State Sumner Welles told Sweetser that propagandists should correct the impression that to ensure "freedom from want" the United States would be playing Santa Claus to the world, extending the New Deal overseas, and bringing "bounty to the suffering humanity everywhere." Although Welles thought that the United States should spread the bounty, he didn't think American taxpayers would like the idea so it would be better not to tell them about it. Sweetser had found out that the White House and the State Department planned to expand American military and economic power as the key to postwar peace. However, they did not want the public to know much about their admittedly sketchy plans. That left the OWI with the noble concepts of the Atlantic Charter and Four Freedoms to promote.[34]

To convey these aims, propagandists counted on cooperation from the mass media, which was dedicated to patriotic service and also to making profits. Although the OWI had set up the Victory Speakers program on the model of the Four Minute Men of World War I, it quickly recognized that radio, movies, and newsreels made the Four Minute Men idea old-fashioned. Surveys showed that the public thought that radio—especially speeches by the president—was the best way for the government to get out its message. Indeed, President Roosevelt already had mastered the use of radio to reach people in their homes with "fireside chats." Ninety percent of Americans listened to four hours of radio daily. They listened mostly for entertainment, but the amount of radio broadcasts dedicated to news was up from 5 to 20 percent in the war years. Convinced that "radio propaganda must be painless," the OWI and radio companies integrated war messages into variety shows, comedies, soap operas, sports coverage, and news programs.[35]

To Hollywood, the OWI sent the *Government Information Manual for the Motion Picture Industry*, asking it to consider, "Will this picture help win the war?" The OWI suggested messages, reviewed scripts, and asked the studios to cut out objectionable scenes and dialogue. The film industry, according to historian Thomas Doherty, voluntarily became "the preeminent transmitter of wartime policy," even as it preferred to blend propaganda with tried and true entertainment formulas. Officials sometimes winced at the ludicrous plots of war films and the "pepped-up" heartiness of newsreels in which the terrain was always impossible and the action always vital. In return, *Life* magazine spoofed OWI directives with a "mystery-adventure-love" story about Dorothy, a fictitious café-society blonde guilty of "decorative leisure," who is rescued from a "cruel and crafty" Japanese spy by a defense worker who drives only thirty-five miles an hour to save his tires. Indeed, film, radio, and print media sometimes did poke fun at propaganda instructions even as they delivered them. Either way, they helped the OWI to achieve its goal: "when the worker leaves the factory that he does not leave the war."[36]

As propagandists surveyed their audience, they considered whether to tell Americans what they should know or what they wanted to hear or some combination of the two. The OWI Bureau of Intelligence took advantage of new methods of monitoring opinion by using polls and correspondence panels made up of clergyman, editors, labor leaders, social workers, businessmen, educators, and others. The members of these panels, representing what the OWI conside___ ___ ind articulate faction," were individuals who were in ___ ___ ct and shape opinion in their communities. Their co_ ___ e statistics gathered by pollsters. Initiating what w_ ___ ite House practice, Roosevelt worked with poll- ste ___ ents. For instance, when polls showed that the pu ___ president admitted mistakes, FDR, speaking be ___ hat errors were bound to happen in a world- w_ ___ ...ought the postwar period was "going to be terrible," observed the OWI. Surveys showed that about 70 percent of the public said that they expected to be worse off when the war was over. But they also showed that Americans were thinking internationally. According to polls, more than 80 percent of Americans supported the formation of a world police force to keep the peace after the war, the improvement of living conditions for people all over the world, and the guarantee that "all nations get a fair share of raw materials." Propagandists resolved to appeal to the public's hopes and assuage its fears. Aware that when it came to global affairs, Americans feared being taken for "soft, sentimental and starry-eyed suckers," the administration constantly described its foreign policies as "realistic," "hard-headed," and "practical."[38]

In its promotion of war aims, therefore, the OWI showed Americans that their ideals and self-interest were one and the same, even though such a portrayal would turn out to be at odds with the "strategy of truth." The truth, after all, did not always make the most persuasive propaganda, which was why the White House, the State Department, and the military preferred at times not to tell it. Nor did the mass media with its tendency to dramatize, reassure, and entertain always embrace it. Well aware of the many voices of wartime Washington, as well as Allied capitals, the OWI attempted to promote generalized war aims while trying not to look too much like propagandists. OWI Associate Director Milton Eisenhower, the respected youngest brother of General Dwight D. Eisenhower and a Republican New Dealer with years of experience in government information work, pronounced "OWI's role in stimulating American thinking about the kind of peace we want is just about the toughest of all." The best they could hope for, he predicted, was that the people's "decision this time will be *very much better* than it was the last time."[39]

Free World versus Slave World

IN AN IMAGE THAT WAS INSPIRING and misleading in its simplicity, propaganda portrayed two worlds at war. "This is a fight between a slave world and a free world," declared Vice President Henry Wallace. The message found historical roots in Abraham Lincoln's civil war era pronouncement that the nation cannot live half slave and half free. Academy Award–winning director Frank Capra quoted Lincoln in the orientation film *Prelude to War* (1942), the first of seven in a series called *Why We Fight*, which he was commissioned to make for American troops by General George Marshall, the Army Chief of Staff. To show GIs what was at stake, the film described two worlds, one light and one dark. In the dark world of the Axis powers, the people had in hard times turned to gangster-like leaders who promised national immortality, squashed any political opposition, burned books, closed places of worship, invaded defenseless countries, and turned the conquered people into slaves. The people of the light world, shown as Americans, had turned to peaceful solutions to the Great Depression, kept their freedoms, and shunned war. The film contrasted the carefree children at play in the world of light with the disciplined children training for combat in the dark world. Pleased with Capra's film, the president ordered that it be released to the public in 1943. Viewers watched animated maps showing the inky black spread of the Axis into Europe, Africa, and Asia aiming at the Middle East, South Asia, and the Americas.[40]

World War II propaganda posters and films showed children in danger. Lawrence Beale Smith, artist. (National Archives, NWDNS-44-PA-124)

Propagandists recoiled from stirring up hatred against the enemy to the level expressed in World War I because they wanted to pave the way for postwar reconciliation. Analysts concluded that the antagonism Americans felt for the Germans and especially for the Japanese needed to be directed against the evil of their political systems rather than the people. The OWI issued the "Policy Directive on the Nature of the Enemy," declaring the Axis leaders to be the real enemy. It explained that the German, Italian, and Japanese people were enemies as long as they followed their leaders but had the potential to be converted to the Allied position. Until then, the directive stated, "All who are not with us are against us."[41] The OWI's most successful radio propaganda series, *You Can't Do Business with Hitler*, sought to foster an "enlightened hatred" of the Nazi regime by focusing on the destruction of family life, the abuse of women compelled to have children to fill Hitler's armies, and the indoctrination of those children. The radio audience found the OWI shows "grim and realistic." Up to the spring of 1944, 65 percent of

Cast rehearsal for OWI radio series *You Can't Do Business with Hitler*, 1942–1943. The fifty-six episodes included "The Anti-Christ," "Swastikas Over the Equator," "Trial by Terror," and "No God for Poland." Abrasha Robofsky on the left played Hitler. (Library of Congress, LC-USE6-D-010243)

Americans continued to believe that the German people wanted to be free of their leaders; only 13 percent thought the Japanese wanted to be free of theirs. American attitudes about the Germans as victims of Nazi rule changed when German soldiers killed tens of thousands of GIs following the D-Day invasion of France in June 1944.[42]

Concerned about the pervasive stereotyping in popular culture, government officials warned against underestimating enemy forces. The comics, they noted, represented the Japanese as "toothy, short, evilly slant-eyed . . . and violently yellow." The movies, they observed, tended to show the enemy as brutes and fools. In RKO's *Tarzan Triumphs* (1943), for example, Tarzan (Johnny Weissmuller) rejects isolationism when he joins forces with the natives and jungle animals to defeat vicious Nazis, who invade Africa in search of oil and tin. At the end a German general jumps to salute as he mistakes Cheetah's radio chatter for a speech by Hitler.[43] Propaganda guidance warned, "we fool only ourselves" by treating the Japanese "as funny little men." In reality, the guidelines noted, "the Japanese are tough fighting men, ruthless and fanatical in their military aspirations."[44] Posters often presented the enemy as omnipresent in everyday life. They showed Axis leaders or spies listening for any piece of military information or expression of discontent. Posters cautioned, "Loose lips sink ships" and reminded civilians that slacking off aided the enemy. For all their ethical intentions, propagandists did draw on the prejudices of the American public to enhance the emotional power of their messages. Official propaganda, however, relied less often on crude stereotypes than popular culture.[45]

Instead of acknowledging real differences among the Allies or even among Americans themselves over war aims, the OWI focused on how enemy propaganda played up those differences with the purpose of dividing and conquering. Those who brought up the incompatibility of the Atlantic Charter principles with British imperialism or Soviet communism could then be accused of doing the work of Joseph Goebbels, the Nazi Minister of Propaganda. In 1942 U.S. officials especially wanted to show that all the allies were on an equal footing because they worried that with armies other than American doing most of the fighting, the United States could be frozen out of the peace.[46] To avoid these complications, the OWI presented the Four Freedoms as an established part of everyday American life with the suggestion that they eventually would be spread to the rest of the world. If not, all might suffer. "The world is all one today," declared the OWI pamphlet *Four Freedoms*. "A hungry man in Cambodia is a threat to the well-fed of Duluth."[47]

The OWI portrayed America as a land of equality and tolerance where everyone pitched in to do his or her part. Backed by policies that allowed a 40 percent growth in union membership, a poster announcing "Together We Win" showed labor and management united in the war effort with the blessing of Uncle Sam. In the cartoon *Spirit of '43*, made by Walt Disney in cooperation with the U.S. government, Donald Duck must choose to spend his wages or save them to pay his taxes. His bad conscience, dressed in the zoot suit fashionable among urban African Americans and Mexican Americans, tempts Donald to enjoy himself and spend his money in a saloon with a swinging door that resembles a swastika. His good conscience, sporting a Scottish accent and a kilt, explains why Donald must save and pay his taxes, which the government will turn into ships and planes. After wrestling with his consciences, Donald decides to pay his taxes. The cartoon ends with a display of American weapons destroying the Axis.[48]

As illustrated by Disney's outfitting of Donald's bad conscience in a zoot suit, the OWI found it a challenge to apply the unity message to all races and religions. It worried that the history of discrimination against minorities in the United States undermined the claim that Americans would spread the Four Freedoms around the world. Nelson Rockefeller told Davis that the treatment of Mexicans in Texas and New Mexico raised the "danger of bad publicity."[49] In addition, although few Americans tuned in to enemy broadcasts, Radio Tokyo repeatedly pointed out U.S. hypocrisy. It cited past race riots, saying that President Roosevelt "did nothing about giving the people of the colored race freedom from fear." Nazi shortwave broadcasts, observed officials, blamed everyone's problems on the Jews.[50] The OWI made sure to associate prejudice with the enemy's doctrines, not America's. It thought Hal Fisher's comic "Joe Palooka," about a good-natured boxing champion, with its forty million readers, was "doing an amazing job." In one strip, Joe's manager Knobby explains why he just hauled off and socked someone. "This guy makes a crack about a certain people, never mind who, pulling Goebbels stuff, underhand and sly, trying to divide us and meanwhile Americans of every race, creed, color and religion are fighting over there for what? So that lugs back here can still go on preaching hatred of other Americans?" asks Knobby, declaring that no one should be complacent about what he calls treason.[51]

Still, the OWI compromised its promotion of the Four Freedoms when it came to African Americans. The U.S. government needed African American men and women to serve in the military. More than one million did, typically in segregated units. And to address inequality in the workplace, President Roosevelt created the Fair Employment Practices Commission, which was somewhat successful at closing the pay gap between whites and blacks. But U.S. propaganda typically portrayed African Americans making a contribution to the war effort in the name of duty and faith rather than freedom. Although it did not advocate equal treatment, the OWI instructed radio and films to treat African Americans with more respect: "avoid the Stepin Fechit type, the minstrel man, the stooge, the dumb domestic, the guy always being chased by ghosts." It saw some sadly limited improvements. In Paramount's *Star Spangled Rhythm* (1942), for example, African Americans have an "included but separate" status. In the finale, famous entertainer Bing Crosby sings "Old Glory" in front of a giant American flag and a reproduction of Mount Rushmore. He celebrates the unity of north and south, urban and rural, by asking white men from New Hampshire, Georgia, and Brooklyn to tell what home means to them. After the Georgian talks about red clay hills and football, the camera cuts to a black chorus singing a spiritual under the head of Abraham Lincoln, and then back to the white Americans clustered around Crosby who sings about the Washingtons, "George, Martha, and Booker T." The efforts of the OWI satisfied few people. African American leaders complained that there was too little emphasis on equality, and Southern segregationists felt there was too much.[52]

Careful as it was to treat American citizens of German and Italian heritage with respect, the U.S. government failed to do so with Japanese Americans. Military authorities, politicians, and pressure groups accused Japanese Americans on the west coast of disloyalty and treason, although they had no evidence to back up these charges. In February 1942, Roosevelt ordered the internment of 120,000 Japanese Americans in "concentration camps." Eighty thousand, born in the United States, were U.S. citizens. MacLeish raised the question of honoring civil liberties but to no avail. Dropping the term "concentration camp," officials adopted language chosen to deflect comparisons to Nazi policies that called for rounding up people because of their race or religion. They described the Japanese Americans as "evacuated," as if a natural disaster had occurred, who were then transported to "assembly centers" for "relocation" to "internment camps." The official government film, *Japanese Relocation*, emphasized the cheerful cooperation of Japanese Americans as they were moved hundreds of miles away from their homes into "pioneer communities." When violations of civil liberties had to be referred to at all, propagandists stuck to their theme of unity. The term "Jap" applied to a hated enemy, the

OWI pointed out to radio broadcasters. "Remember, incidentally, that loyal Japanese-Americans—now in western U.S. relocation camps—strongly resent being called 'Japs.'"[53] As in their portrayals of segregated African Americans, the OWI emphasized loyalty, not freedom and equality.

Hollywood also rarely included racial minorities in its wartime portrayals of the united national family. War movies told the story of soldiers from all classes, ethnic backgrounds, and corners of the country coming together. As historian George Roeder has noted, Brooklyn did wartime service as an unofficial state, the melting pot home of the street-smart patriot, who roots for the Dodgers and goes to war with a wisecrack. In movies servicemen recreated the family unit by calling the oldest member "pops" and the youngest, "the kid." When they were not fighting, they talked about baseball, their hometowns, and their wives or girlfriends. In one of many scenes involving letters from home, a soldier or a sailor might find out that he has become a father. At some point, someone would explain what they all fought for—to make the world a decent place to live in or a safe place for children. An unusual racially mixed platoon appeared in MGM's *Bataan* (1943). Led by Sgt. Bill Dane (Robert Taylor), the makeshift unit included Jake Feingold (Thomas Mitchell), Felix Ramirez (Desi Arnaz), African American Wesley Epps (Kenneth Spencer), F. X. Matowski (Barry Nelson), and Filipino scouts, who are ordered to protect the chaotic retreat from the advancing Japanese. "It don't matter where a man dies as long as he dies for freedom," says one of the doomed men.[54]

Women, according to the OWI, were "on the same team" with men while the nation was at war. Collaborating with industry and the media, the OWI launched a major "womenpower" drive with the slogan, "The more women at work, the sooner we'll win."[55] Although the most famous illustration of "Rosie the Riveter" shows a proud woman flexing her muscles saying "We Can Do It," a more representative poster of the effort to recruit married middle-class women showed a businessman husband bestowing approval on his war worker wife. More popular than Rosie among servicemen was Betty Grable, the perky blonde movie star whose pin-up was prized by five million GIs. As historian Robert Westbrook observed, pin-ups of movie stars, wives, and girlfriends symbolized what men fought to protect and possess. "We are not only fighting for the Four Freedoms," said soldiers in New Guinea, "we are fighting also for the priceless privilege of making love to American women."[56] Although propaganda praised women in the military or factory, it also used the image of women, symbolizing domesticity and sexual contentment, as a reward for men's service. Advertisers reinforced this image with depictions of the happy postwar home, lavishly furnished with the latest appliances. An ad for Eureka vacuum cleaners told women that in "fighting for freedom and all that means to women everywhere, you're fighting for a little house of your own, and a husband to meet every night at the door."[57]

While propaganda succeeded in projecting the image of a national family, restricted as it was, it struggled with the portrayal of a global family of United Nations. Surveys showed that while Americans admired the British for their accomplishments in North Africa and felt indebted to the Russians for their magnificent stand on the eastern front, they did not necessarily apply these good feelings to peacetime cooperation. As though launching a new brand, the OWI planned a massive "saturation" promotion of the United Nations Organization to coincide with Flag Day on June 14, 1943. It handed out almost a million United Nations posters, distributed "Facts about the United Nations" to radio stations, newspapers, newsreel editors, schools, and libraries, and requested that department stores install United Nations window displays. It sent speeches to 9,000 American Legion posts, editorials to 750 local newspapers, and scripts to 500 local radio stations. The OWI had created a news event and reported with satisfaction that the resulting press coverage was "very heavy." Fifty percent of news stories and forty-three radio network programs mentioned or featured a United Nations angle.[58]

In addition, propagandists reversed the tactics they used to present the enemy. Instead of focusing on powerful leaders, they presented members of Allied nations as ordinary individuals. The "Produce for Victory" posters directed at defense workers showed grateful British and Chinese soldiers dependent on American weapons and manpower. Hollywood promoted U.S.–Soviet relations in films that featured attractive Russian peasants as wholesome freedom fighters and downplayed the brutalities of dictator Joseph Stalin's rule. Warner Brothers' *Mission to Moscow* (1943) was such a whitewash that critics from the left and right condemned its falsifications. Hollywood's Britain and China also were filled with dedicated freedom fighters who embraced democracy and modernity.[59]

Warner Brothers' *Casablanca*, the 1943 winner of the Academy Award for best picture, illustrates both the successes and the shortcomings of the promotion of internationalism. Released in New York shortly after the Allied invasion of North Africa in November 1942, the film appeared as Americans were beginning to consider more closely their postwar role. While the administration advocated internationalism, Republican Senator Robert Taft of Ohio called for maintaining tradition. "We can't crusade throughout the

The poster series "This Man Is Your Friend...He Fights for Freedom" featured British, Dutch, Australian, Ethiopian, Canadian, and Russian soldiers. (National Archives, NWDNS-44-PA-2097C)

world for the Four Freedoms," he declared in 1943, "without making ourselves thoroughly hated."[60] The son of President William Howard Taft urged that the United States maintain its freedom of action overseas by avoiding foreign entanglements—a position similar to that of *Casablanca*'s hero Rick (Humphrey Bogart), an American café owner in Morocco who just wants to run his business and stay out of politics. *Casablanca* opens with a narrator explaining the importance of the French Moroccan capital to refugees fleeing the dark world of the Axis. Everybody—the Germans and Italians of the Axis, the collaborationist Vichy French who govern Morocco, refugees who dream of reaching the United States, members of the resistance, and thieves—comes to Rick's Café Americain.

The cynical Rick asserts, "I stick my neck out for nobody," which the corrupt French police captain Louis Renault (Claude Rains) pronounces "a wise foreign policy." His pose of isolation is challenged by his lost love, Ilsa Lund (Ingrid Bergman), and her husband, the Czech freedom fighter Victor

Laszlo (Paul Henreid). Rick commits and takes charge when he decides to rescue Laszlo and Ilsa by tricking Captain Renault and shooting the German Major Strasser (Conrad Veidt). Rick sends Ilsa away with Laszlo, telling her that he has a job to do, a phrase Americans in military service and war production heard many times. In farewell, Laszlo welcomes Rick to the fight, saying, "This time I know our side will win."[61]

The OWI Motion Picture Bureau praised the film for conveying the theme of sacrifice as well as presenting the fight between the free world and the fascist world. It approved of the portrayal of Major Strasser as a "typical Nazi" out to "enslave the world." In addition, the movie included "good Germans" such as Carl (S. K. Sakall), the kind-hearted waiter who attends underground meetings. It thought the characters of Laszlo and Berger (John Qualen), the Norwegian resistance member, demonstrated the "courage, determination, and self-sacrifice" of the underground movement. It approved of the decision of Captain Renault to side ultimately with Rick against the Germans as showing that "the French were not all collaborationist." Finally, the OWI viewed with satisfaction what it considered to be a dignified portrayal of Sam (Dooley Wilson), the African American piano player.[62]

Even as the film delivered explicit OWI messages, it also conveyed the implicit message that Americans should take the lead. According to Gallup poll editor William Lydgate, a national survey conducted in 1942 showed that Americans had "a marked superiority complex." Those surveyed were asked to rank seventeen nationalities. The five, in rank order, considered "as good as we are in all important respects" were 1. Canadians (76%), 2. English, 3. Dutch, 4. Scandinavians, and 5. Irish (56%). At numbers six and seven, the French and Germans were designated as "not quite as good as we are in all major respects." Further down the scale and deemed "definitely inferior" were 8. Greeks, 9. South Americans, 10. Jewish refugees, 11. Poles, 12. Russians, 13. Chinese, 14. Spaniards, 15. Italians, 16. Mexicans, and 17. Japanese. At the Café Americain, the white American is the boss and the Norwegians Ilsa and Berger and the Czech Laszlo rank highly. There are good Germans and bad. The French, in the words of Captain Renault, "blow with the wind." Ugarte (Peter Lorre), the thief, and Signor Ferrari (Sidney Greenstreet), the head of the black market, are Italian, and there are nameless Chinese, Arab, and refugee patrons. All compose a hierarchy that Americans would have understood.[63]

As propagandists were well aware, they often called for a portrayal of the United States as they wished it to be rather than the way it actually was. For example, they welcomed *Casablanca's* presentation of the United States as "the haven of the oppressed and homeless" where refugees were "assured of freedom, democratic privileges and immunity from fear." The OWI knew, however, that most Americans supported strict immigration policies. Surveys showed that people were worried refugees would compete with American workers, especially when the soldiers returned, and feared that "we will get the dregs of foreign populations." In particular, the OWI detected an increase in anti-Semitism expressed in frequent references to concerns that many immigrants would be Jews. The State Department rigorously enforced immigration restrictions, which frequently prevented refugees, including those who actually made it to Casablanca, from reaching the United States.[64]

In contrast to the fictional Rick's café where the American handily sorted out friend from foe, the real situation in Morocco was messy and controversial. When the Allies landed in North Africa they faced the possibility of conflict with French troops under orders from the Vichy regime to fight. General Eisenhower made a deal with Admiral Jean François Darlan, the Vichy military commander, a fascist who had collaborated with the Germans for two years. In exchange for his cooperation, Darlan became the head of the civil government in French North Africa. Back in Washington, Elmer Davis struggled to figure out what to say about teaming up with fascists.[65] The OWI drafted a press release for the president explaining that the Darlan deal was a temporary military expedient, "justified only by the stress of battle," and sent Milton Eisenhower to North Africa to discuss public relations fundamentals with his brother. Darlan's assassination by a Frenchman in late December 1942 did not end the misgivings surrounding U.S. policy. An OWI survey found Americans to be confused, asking, "Who are our allies, with whom and against whom are we fighting?" Moreover, they seemed to assume, noted one analyst, that U.S. conduct overseas would be governed by "righteous and inflexible moral principles," at the same time it practiced expediency, sacrificing not "a single American soldier for some abstract ideal."[66] It seemed that Americans who heeded propaganda messages promising that U.S. policy would honor both their ideals and interests had been, as Rick would say, misinformed.

Contrary to Americans' assumption of superiority, reinforced by films like *Casablanca*, their major allies held greater authority when it came to the actual fighting. In January 1943, Roosevelt and Churchill met for a summit conference in the French Moroccan capital, code-named Rick's Place. The primary purpose was the coordination of Allied military strategy, especially the already delayed invasion of France. For months Stalin had demanded a second front to divert some of the three and a half million enemy troops facing the Russian Army on its thousand-mile-long front line. The fully mobilized British, still dominating Anglo–American military strategy, objected to launching the massive continental offensive advocated by the U.S. command. The Americans, struggling to build up for a continental invasion while supporting forces in the Pacific and North Africa, deferred to the British. The western allies agreed to advance from North Africa into Italy, again postponing an invasion of France until 1944. The Kremlin suspected that the delay might be deliberate if the British and Americans wanted Russians to bleed. At the cost of hundreds of thousands, the Red Army had begun to turn back the enemy at Stalingrad. Meanwhile, Stalin wondered if the Americans and the British, quick to make a deal with a French fascist, might negotiate a separate peace for themselves. As reassurance, FDR dramatically announced that the Allies would accept only an "unconditional surrender" from Axis forces.[67]

For propagandists the image of the free world versus the slave world was useful in a number of ways. It hid the uncertainty and confusion in Washington over postwar policies. By showing all Allies as members of the free world, it helped to gloss over differences such as Stalin's insistence that Soviet security required the communist absorption of Latvia, Lithuania, Estonia, and at least the eastern half of Poland. Its sympathetic portrayal of the Nationalist Chinese ignored reports that Mao Zedong's communist guerrilla forces did a better job of fighting the Japanese invaders than Chiang Kai-shek's Nationalists. The image of the free world versus the slave world also helped to put in perspective the nation's own shortcomings. Joe Louis, the African American world heavyweight boxing champion who lent his considerable presence to propaganda posters and bond drives, was asked why he enlisted in a white man's war for a white man's country. Louis replied, "Lots of things wrong in America, but Hitler ain't gonna fix it."[68] Few could argue. Indeed, for oppressed people whether under imperial rule or Axis domination, the fight for the free world promised liberation, independence, and justice. U.S. propaganda declared that the liberators would stand by these pledges even as they pursued their own interests.

As much as the OWI bombarded Americans with messages about the war, it realized that civilians and servicemen longed to see idealized images of home untouched by conflict. Irving Berlin's song "White Christmas," the number one hit of 1942, summed up the mood of dreamy nostalgia.[69] Soldiers overseas made clear their preference for broadcasts featuring dance music and

The "This Is America . . . For This We Fight" poster series celebrated pastoral America, not the industrial giant breaking production records. (National Archives, NWDNS-44-PA-2072)

comedians, because, as one wrote, "we see enough war without having to hear about it every time we turn on the radio."[70] A lieutenant colonel with the 12th Fighter Command in North Africa wrote to tell General Marshall how much he approved of the movie *Star Spangled Rhythm*, especially dancer Vera Zorina. He wrote, "Keep the comedies and 'girl shows' coming." They will speed up the war, he explained, because "we'll get it over with so we can get home to the girls, the music, and the life we've left behind us."[71]

The Better Life

SECOND ONLY TO WINNING THE WAR, Americans by 1943 worried about postwar problems from "what's going to happen to us in Podunk" to "what are we fighting for," observed Dorothy Johnstone of the OWI.[72] Surveys showed that even as the war boom brought an end to the Depression, the public was anxious about jobs, housing, and losing the peace a second time. In the latter years of the war, propaganda, with the enthusiastic support of the business community, presented the rewards to come. At the same time, the announcement of unconditional surrender meant that the country was in for a long fight. To prevent civilians from becoming too complacent, the OWI pushed for more realistic coverage from the front lines. It promoted internationalism as the key to securing American strategic and economic interests. To this effort, the Treasury and State Departments contributed a nationalistic overtone. "The best way to sell bonds," concluded the Treasury Department, "was to restore to the American people faith and confidence in their destiny as a nation."[73]

Official propaganda promoted the American way of life, associating it with jobs, opportunity, and free enterprise. Business organizations launched their own PR effort identifying American business with American progress. Their goal was not only to improve their image, but also to make the point that any future New Deal-style government intervention was unnecessary. As one OWI analyst observed, business groups were turning "freedom of enterprise" or "competitive capitalism" into the Fifth Freedom.[74] The celebration of capitalism or free enterprise, the preferred term, raised consternation at the OWI when it reduced the role of the citizen to consumer. Some members of the staff were dismayed by what they saw as a shift from honest education to slick advertising, indicated in part by the takeover of the Graphics Division by a Coca-Cola executive. As an expression of their disgust, they produced a fake poster of the Statue of Liberty holding four bottles of Coke with the caption, "The War That Refreshes: The Four Delicious Freedoms." Then they resigned.[75] The War Advertising Council, the industry executives who worked with the OWI to incorporate propaganda into thousands of ads, welcomed the change. It disapproved of the "old poetic pamphleteering" and "ivory tower days" of early OWI educational efforts, saying that the American people hated dullness. The Council's chairman, Chester J. LaRoche, announced, "The new OWI is a practical realist." He urged that large problems be scaled down so that the individual could see how his life was affected.[76]

Patriotic ads told the story of Americans who cheerfully went without while working overtime in order to win the war and enjoy abundance in peace. Advertisers defined "Freedom from Want" as the freedom to buy consumer goods once factories made toasters again instead of tanks. A General Electric ad, for example, featured a soldier and his girlfriend drawing in the sand their dream house with "better living built in." As historian Mark Neff pointed out, the "mystique of unconditional sacrifice" disguised the real reluctance

This is America..

. . . where every boy can dream of being President. Where free schools, free opportunity, free enterprise, have built the most decent nation on earth. A nation built upon the rights of all men ★ *This is your America*

. . . Keep it Free!

The "This is America . . . Keep It Free" poster series included free enterprise as one of the freedoms Americans fought for. (National Archives, NWDNS-44-PA-2067).

of Americans to give up daily comforts. Although his pollsters cautioned him against "scolding," FDR could not resist speaking out against "the whining demands of selfish pressure groups who seek to feather their nests while young Americans are dying." In a letter to the armed forces newspaper *Yank*, a sarcastic soldier pointed to ads that detailed the suffering endured by the civilian who was going without a rib roast, a new car, or "nylons for his honey," so that the troops could have everything they needed. As if that weren't hard enough to stomach, he continued, advertisers had figured out what soldiers were fighting for and wanted when they got home. "It will be homey, and new, and shiny and soft, and robust and restful, and cheap and expensive, and thick and thin, and sharp and dull," he wrote. "It will be everything and nothing." Certainly, the implication in advertisements that the end of the war meant the end of sacrifice did not help prepare Americans for any ongoing international commitment. Nor did they reflect OWI's earlier goal of encouraging the individual, informed about global events, to see himself or herself as part of something bigger.[77]

Norman Rockwell's famous depiction of the Four Freedoms in small town New England seemed to satisfy almost everyone's idea of the American way of life. The OWI initially rejected Rockwell's "Four Freedoms" because it did not consider Rockwell, who illustrated ads for Jello and Crest toothpaste along with magazine covers, a "real artist." This "old OWI" view, the despair of the War Advertising Council, reflected its preference for raising public tastes rather than embracing them. The OWI changed its mind when nationwide acclaim greeted the publication of the "Four Freedoms" in the popular *Saturday Evening Post*. At the time the conservative *Post* was working on improving its own image. When in 1942 it published an article called "The Case Against the Jew," angry readers threatened to boycott the magazine. The new editor, Ben Hibbs, celebrated self-reliance, family, and community. Rockwell's illustrations fit the bill.[78]

The "Four Freedoms" resonated with both liberals and conservatives. The *Post* described them as portrayals of the "Common Man," who "raised no clenched fist and carried no banner demanding anything, and he didn't incite anyone to riot." Foreshadowing Richard Nixon's Vietnam era salute to the "silent majority," the *Post* article explained that the Common Man "asked only his rights as an American and silently pledged his faith in the promise of his country and in the system under which he lived and raised his family." In Rockwell's "Freedom of Speech," the working-class man does not incite a riot, but he is not silent. He is shown instead speaking up and being listened to by

OURS...to fight for

Freedom of Speech

Freedom of Worship

Freedom from Want

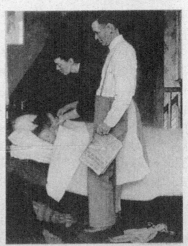

Freedom from Fear

Poster of Norman Rockwell's "Four Freedoms." (National Archives, NWDNS-44-PA-189; printed by permission of the Norman Rockwell Family Agency. Copyright © 1943 Norman Rockwell Family Entities)

white-collar businessmen at a town meeting. President Roosevelt congratu-
lated Rockwell on "bringing home to the plain, everyday citizen the plain,
everyday truths behind the Four Freedoms" and contributing "to the common
cause of a freer, happier world." FDR wanted the paintings to be presented to
Allied leaders. For him, the "Four Freedoms" represented goals of rights and
securities to be achieved at home and abroad.[79]

To raise funds and "sell the war," the OWI and the Treasury Department
teamed up with the *Saturday Evening Post*, the news media, the entertainment
industry, and retail stores to produce the Four Freedoms War Bond show,
which traveled to fifteen cities from April 1943 to May 1944. The OWI printed
two-and-a-half million copies of the "Four Freedoms," wrote radio programs,
and with Paramount News made a newsreel with Rockwell in Vermont staging
his neighbors at the Thanksgiving table, even though the artist had worked
from photographs, not live models. The show had its own logo, the torch
of the Statue of Liberty, and slogan, "Keep the Light of Freedom Burning."
City leaders organized parades, speeches by dignitaries, school essay contests,
choirs singing patriotic songs, traditional dances by local ethnic groups, and
ceremonies at shipyards or factories. Advertisers donated ad space to promote
the event and radio stations provided free airtime to cover the show. Major
retail stores such as Kaufman's in Pittsburgh, Tisch-Goettinger Company in
Dallas, and Bullock's in Los Angeles hosted the exhibit. Visitors who bought
bonds received reproductions of the "Four Freedoms" and were invited to
sign the "Freedom Scroll"—to be presented to President Roosevelt—pledging
their commitment to the principles of the Four Freedoms.[80]

Cities competed to see who could put on the best show and sell the most
bonds, with Chicago going so far as to take its eye off the real enemy and
adopt the motto "Beat New York" in its promotion. New York's show at
Rockefeller Center featured radio star Kate Smith, famous for her hymn-
like rendition of "God Bless America," and the cast from the hit musical
Oklahoma!, while selling $13.6 million in bonds. Chicago did beat New York
by blanketing the city with ads in milk bottles, bank statements, and taxis.
Chicagoans bought $17 million in bonds during the eleven-day show star-
ring Rita Hayworth and Orson Welles at the Carson Pirie Scott department
store. All in all, the show, starring 450 celebrities, including Bing Crosby, Bob
Hope, and Ronald Reagan, was seen nationwide by 1.2 million people who
bought $133 million in bonds.[81]

As they toured the nation, Rockwell's illustrations of the freedoms of the
common man had been accompanied by the latest techniques of promotion,

blurring the selling of the war with the sale of retail goods, celebrities, and civic pride. Radio, too, blended propaganda with entertainment and advertising. In order to stay healthy and win the war, "Gargle with Pepsodent Antiseptic regularly," heard the audience of Bob Hope's popular radio show. Although *Harper's* columnist Bernard DeVoto complained to his friend Elmer Davis that the OWI and Treasury radio ads were "so phony and hoked up that they stink violently," Americans responded to the combination of a good cause with star-studded entertainment and consumer goods.[82] One of the results was a significant gap between the war as sold and the war as fought.

"The Guts to Look at It"

CENSORSHIP AND WAR REPORTING contributed to that gap. "It seems to me that the folks at home are fighting one war and we're fighting another one. They've got theirs nearly won and we've just got started on ours," said a gunner on a Flying Fortress named *Mary Ruth, Memories of Mobile*. Based at a bomber station in England in June 1943, he told correspondent John Steinbeck, "I wish they'd get in the same war we're in."[83] For the first twenty-one months after the United States entered the war, the government allowed no pictures of American dead to be published. This restriction did not apply to enemy dead. Newsreel footage from Guadalcanal, for instance, showed dead Japanese, but only live U.S. marines, filthy and exhausted as they were. The July 5, 1943, cover of *Life* featured six servicemen carrying a flag-draped coffin; inside it listed the names by state and hometown of the 12,987 troops so far killed in action.[84]

Polls showed the public resented and distrusted "sugar coated" war coverage. In August 1943, a fed-up Davis threatened to resign unless the military allowed the OWI to show civilians what was going on. Roosevelt backed Davis. General Marshall ordered military photographers to send back to Washington pictures that would "vividly portray the dangers, horrors, and grimness of War."[85] Even then newspapers and magazines were reluctant to publish them. Rejecting a photo of a GI whose foot had been blown off, the photo editor of the *New York Daily News* said, "I personally try to select pictures that will go down well when I have my coffee in the morning." The press didn't want "sugar coating" or "stomach-turning" pictures, summed up the managing editor of the *Seattle Post-Intelligencer*.[86]

Despite such concerns, the media did run more graphic images of Americans in battle in the last two years of the war. The military continued to

In September 1943, *Life* published one of the first photographs of American dead released by the censors under the new policy. The *Life* editorial, "Here lie three Americans," defended the publication by referring to an earlier story about a soldier named Bill from Wisconsin who was killed by the Japanese in New Guinea. "If Bill had the guts to take it," wrote the editors, "then we ought to have the guts to look at it." George Strock, photographer. (Time & Life Pictures/Getty Images)

censor the most gruesome photographs and any in which the American dead could be personally identified. Propaganda posters and ads used pictures of wounded or dead GIs to sell bonds, call on workers to stay on the job, or demand silence about troop movements. A *Time* reviewer observed that in the big budget tear-jerker *Since You Went Away* (1944), the wounded men really looked wounded for almost the first time in a Hollywood war film. One short government film made in 1944 announced that every two-and-a-half minutes an American soldier fell in combat. War production, promised the film, would bring "the boys back sooner."[87] Americans saw vivid combat documentaries made by Hollywood directors in uniform, such as John Ford's *The Battle of Midway*, John Huston's *San Pietro*, and William Wyler's *The Memphis Belle*. Using navy and marine footage from Iwo Jima, Fox and Paramount produced ten-minute newsreels of that terrible battle. Film critic James Agee praised the results but wondered whether the act of watching even the best war film degraded the viewer and betrayed the fighting man. "We tell ourselves sincerely that we sit in comfort and watch carnage in order to nurture our patriotism, our conscience, our understanding, and our sympathies," he thought, but maybe "we have no business seeing this sort of experience" unless we are there ourselves.[88]

By 1943, propagandists recommended a "judicious, but more extended use of confirmed atrocities." After World War I so many Americans were leery of atrocity propaganda that it hadn't seemed effective to use it. For example, the news story of the Bataan Death March was greeted with suspicion in part because the government released it at the same time a war bond drive was launched. In addition, the OWI feared that atrocity propaganda might stir up more hatred of ethnic groups at home or provoke retaliations against American prisoners of war. In early 1944 experts concluded, however, that if the ban on reporting Japanese atrocities were lifted, it would not affect the treatment of American POWs. Moreover, officials felt, public knowledge that Japanese forces had mutilated prisoners and used them for bayonet practice would serve to deflect criticism of the United States as it began firebombing Japanese cities.[89] This change in policy undermined the distinction earlier propaganda had drawn between enemy leaders and enemy people. For many GIs, the distinction had long been moot. In the Pacific theater, especially, Americans and Japanese adopted a ferocious kill or be killed attitude.

The same concern regarding the effectiveness of atrocity stories influenced the OWI's decision to say little about reports that the Nazis were carrying out the systematic mass murder of European Jews. In 1941 and 1942 news stories reported the deportation of Jews from Germany and occupied territories, some saying they were going to a "reservation" in Poland, others to slave labor camps, and others to be murdered. Although the U.S. government confirmed in late 1942 that it had proof that the Nazis were exterminating Jews, the OWI held off, saying it lacked documented facts. It worried that "horror stories" might depress rather than boost morale. Bowing to the presence of anti-Semitic prejudice in American society, officials did not want to reinforce Nazi allegations that the Allies fought on behalf of the Jews. When it did refer to German atrocities, it frequently avoided naming the victims as Jews. Even after the Allies began to liberate the death camps and send home eyewitness reports and film footage, people still questioned what they saw and heard. An exasperated Henry J. Taylor of the *New York World Telegram* noted, "in the last war only a few of the German atrocity stories were true, yet most of them were believed. In this war the atrocity stories are true yet few seem to be believed."[90] Seasoned radio broadcaster Edward Murrow admitted that "for most of it I have no words" as he tried to report what he saw in April 1945 at Buchenwald—20,000 of the living dead crawling around a camp located in a pleasant countryside surrounded by well-fed Germans. He told CBS listeners, "If I've offended you by this rather mild account of Buchenwald, I'm not in the least sorry."[91]

War reporting, most of the time, was not supposed to offend anyone; it was expected to contribute to the war effort. "Correspondents have a job in war as essential as the military personnel," said General Eisenhower. "Fundamentally, public opinion wins wars."[92] Commanders were forthcoming, but correspondents could not report on everything they knew. Censors not only protected operations, but sought to boost morale or reputations. They did not want the public to see photographs of U.S. soldiers maimed in combat, crying or losing control, killed in accidents or by "friendly fire," or suffering from self-inflicted wounds or psychological trauma. Also banned were scenes of black GIs in integrated social scenes and fights between American and allied soldiers. When they blocked United Press (UP) reporter Walter Cronkite's story about the Eighth Air Force carrying out a blind bombing of Germany through heavy cloud cover, Cronkite successfully appealed by arguing that the Germans already knew about such attacks. His story, however, did contradict official claims that all U.S. bombing was exactly on target and hit only military installations. In addition, correspondents sometimes censored themselves. For example, they helped Eisenhower temporarily cover up an incident when the volatile General George S. Patton Jr. slapped two soldiers hospitalized for psychological stress, called combat fatigue in the 1940s.[93]

Overall, war reporting tended to validate the official version of events. The military required civilian correspondents, photographers, and newsreel units to be accredited, be given officer status, wear military uniforms, and obey military law. The military's public relations officer (PRO) and staff assigned correspondents to individual combat units. The services also used a "pool" system in which one print correspondent, one radio correspondent, and one photographer would be selected to represent all of the rest. Pool reporters or correspondents assigned to a particular unit depended on theater headquarters for the big picture, relied on symbolic stories to convey it, and focused on the U.S. role. In the dramatic fulfillment of his pledge to return to the Philippines, MacArthur waded ashore more than once so the cameras could get the best shots. For the long-awaited D-Day invasion of Normandy, the PROs arranged for 100 military photographers and 400 civilian correspondents, including 237 Americans, to cover the landing. Half of them reported from Eisenhower's headquarters in London and the others went in with the army, navy, or airmen. A delighted Davis pronounced the resulting press coverage "the best coverage of any military operation in all history." Less enthusiastic, the British Ambassador in Washington expressed dismay over those U.S. headlines that suggested the Americans had invaded France by themselves.[94]

The most famous news photograph of the war, the flag raising on Iwo Jima in February 1945, represented a hard-won victory at the cost of 30,000 U.S. casualties (6000 deaths) and a propaganda success. The command decided it needed a morale-boosting symbol for the troops on the island that also would demonstrate progress to the public at home uneasy about the high casualty rate. It ordered the taking of Mt. Suribachi and the raising of the Stars and Stripes. Marines of the Third Platoon, accompanied by photographer Lou Lowery from the Marines magazine *Leatherneck*, raised the flag to cheers from the GIs below and gunfire from Japanese soldiers ordered to defend their positions until they died. The command directed that one of the marines show up at the admiral's flagship for press interviews. Don Pyror of CBS introduced the weary Sgt. Ernest Thomas to his radio audience as a "modest but tough 20-year-old fighting man from Tallahassee" and the "first American in history who has ever raised Old Glory over a part of the Japanese home empire." To the dismay of Sgt. Keyes Beech, the marine's publicity officer, Thomas corrected the reporter saying, "No Mr. Pryor, I don't want to give that impression. The honor belongs to every man in my platoon."

Beech spiced up Thomas's self-effacing account in the official version given to the wire services. Before his story hit the front page, a Japanese sniper killed Thomas. In the meantime, the battalion commander decided a bigger flag would be easier to see and some men on Mt. Suribachi quickly switched flags. The raising of the new flag happened so fast that Joe Rosenthal, an AP pool photographer, didn't know what or who was in the picture he had taken when he shipped off his film to be developed. His stunning shot became a national sensation. *Leatherneck* withheld Lowery's photographs so they would not compete with Rosenthal's iconic image, and the names of the marines who actually took the mountain were forgotten.[95]

President Roosevelt demanded that the men in the picture immediately return home for a hero's welcome and to appear in the seventh war bond drive show, which had already chosen the Rosenthal photo as its official symbol. It took weeks to locate them. Three out of the six were dead. The survivors, Marine private Rene Gagnon of New Hampshire, Marine private Ira Hayes of Arizona, and Navy corpsman John Bradley of Wisconsin, escorted by Sgt. Beech, embarked on a national tour, leading parades, touring factories, kissing movie stars, and reenacting the flag raising. They had become "Hollywood marines." The handsome Gagnon was good at it, the quiet Bradley found it disturbing that civilians had to be entertained before they would pay for the war, and Hayes, who received a lot of curious attention because he was a Pima Indian, felt deeply guilty about the recognition, which he believed belonged to the men buried on Iwo Jima and those still fighting. The politicians, the military, the press, and the public embraced the heroic myth symbolized in the photograph; the blurring of fact and fiction seemed to bother only a few.[96]

Soldiers themselves preferred news coverage that captured their experience. War correspondent Ernie Pyle became a favorite because his human interest stories conveyed the hardships and waste of the war even as he gave it a sense of purpose. With a circulation of fourteen million, Pyle's columns celebrated the citizen soldier on the front line, always citing a man's hometown. Pyle's own fatigue and disillusion crept into his last stories from the Pacific where he was killed by a Japanese machine-gunner in April 1945.[97] Another favorite chronicler of war was twenty-three-year-old Sergeant Bill Mauldin, whose cartoons for the Army's *Stars and Stripes* were carried by U.S. newspapers. Mauldin drew incidents in the lives of the bedraggled dogfaces Willie and Joe. "They wish to hell they were someplace else, and they wish to hell they would get relief. They wish to hell the mud was dry and they wish to hell

The Iwo Jima flag-raising photograph turned poster, 1945. (National Archives, NWDNS-44-PA-1422)

their coffee was hot. They want to go home," summed up Mauldin. "But they stay in their wet holes and fight, and then they climb out and crawl through minefields and fight some more."[98] His cartoons mocked spit and polish officers and the upbeat tone of wartime news coverage. With their focus on the individual soldier, Pyle and Mauldin put a human face on a war the Allies were winning with brute force, a war that made a man feel, as one bombardier put it, like "a cog in one hell of a big machine."[99]

Selling Internationalism

THE MORE COSTLY THE FIGHT, the more determined Americans became to prevent another war. No one, the OWI found, wanted to be called an isolationist. Polls showed that anywhere from 70 to 90 percent of the public agreed that the United States should join a union of nations. Gratefully recognizing these views to be a reversal of the rejection of the League of Nations, officials noted that the spirit of cooperation was decidedly weaker when it came to economic issues. Sixty-eight percent said the United States should keep out foreign goods and 43 percent thought the Axis should be made "to pay for the war even if it breaks them." Still, Americans supported the U.S.-sponsored reconstruction of war-torn countries, even though they feared that their own standard of living might decline. "You can sell the postwar plan better when and if it is brought forward in the light that it will help American business and economics, as well as the rest of the world," advised one correspondent. "Americans are thinking more this time about 'How is this going to help us?' than they were when we were saving the world for democracy." Surveys revealed that some Americans worried that if the United States took on the role of world policeman "walking the beat and keeping order," it might turn imperialist "at the slightest provocation." Others showed no such fear, embracing the attitude, "this country must and will boss the world."[100]

To counter isolationist and imperialist attitudes, the OWI instructed radio broadcasters to emphasize security. The guidelines recalled the failure of appeasement at Munich and the attack on Pearl Harbor, "The world has shrunk. Our safety—we know now—can be threatened through an act of aggression thousands of miles away. There is no security for any, unless there is security for all." Moreover, the guidelines warned, "Modern wars tend to spread and become world wars." Even before Americans saw photos of the awesome mushroom cloud, they knew that another world war might be their last. In the spring of 1945, an OWI radio spot warned, "Scientists and military experts tell us that a third World War would be even more devastating than this one... that whole cities might be destroyed in one great blow... that it would mean the end of the civilization we have fought so long and hard to build and preserve." Therefore, "world peace requires world cooperation."[101] And that meant working with allies. Avoid "the superior viewpoint that the Yanks are coming and now the world's worries are over," the OWI instructed broadcasters. "Over-zealous patriotic programs have not yet reached the point of closing with 'Heil America'—but sometimes the effect is almost the same." Each American's responsibility, explained the OWI, was to study peace proposals and write to his or her newspaper and elected representative.[102] It projected the image of an engaged citizen who advocated internationalism.

The State Department, like FDR, was more interested in avoiding any domestic constraints on the administration's foreign policy than in creating fully informed citizens. Secretary Hull chaired what he referred to as the committee on political problems, attended by top department officials, professors, prominent journalists, Republican and Democratic legislators, and MacLeish, now at State to promote the United Nations Organization. While the administration prepared detailed diplomatic policies, it wanted a "less precise" program for educating the public, carried out by the sort of people sitting on the committee. Senators, it advised, should present resolutions affirming general principles, "couched in terms of American traditions and interests." When the administration negotiated postwar policies at allied conferences in Teheran, Quebec, Yalta, and San Francisco, it did so behind closed doors, which left critics little to object to, except the secrecy itself. Columnist Drew Pearson complained that there was no news in State Department handouts. "What purports to be news becomes propaganda," he wrote in his syndicated column. While Davis at the OWI and prominent columnists Pearson, Walter Lippmann, and James Reston pressed for more openness, the State Department preferred to have senators, foreign affairs specialists, and journalists encourage popular acceptance of vaguely defined policies. The goal was to avoid "disruptive public controversy."[103]

To that end, the Roosevelt administration projected an activist foreign policy that used internationalist means to achieve nationalist ends. Raising again the specter of the United States as Santa Claus, the members of Hull's committee were concerned that some Americans feared that the United States would be expected to "feed, clothe, reconstruct, and police the world." It decided to convince the public that U.S. foreign policy had "two very practical objectives." One was to safeguard America by preventing another war. The second was to protect the American economy "by providing free access to raw materials and fostering international commerce." The phrase "free access" was a significant rewording of the Atlantic Charter provision for "equal access."[104] "Free access" meant that as the world's strongest, the U.S. economy would dominate; "equal access," which guaranteed access to all, might result in limits on the United States if it had to share with other nations. FDR and State Department officials cited the expansionist foreign policies of McKinley and Theodore Roosevelt, now deemed "great American traditions," as their model. They emphasized the historical continuity of a foreign policy, "which for fifty years has been projecting the United States further and further into world affairs."[105] Their theme song might have been the 1944 Cole Porter hit "Don't Fence Me In." "Just turn me loose," sang Bing Crosby, the Andrews Sisters, and Roy Rogers.

U.S. military planners wanted a global system of strategic bases in the Atlantic, Mediterranean, Persian Gulf, Indian Ocean, and the Pacific. Charges that such acquisitions violated Atlantic Charter principles were brushed aside.

FDR agreed, reported interviewer Forrest Davis. The president explained that the United Nations flag would fly over "commercially valueless" atolls in the Pacific, but the Stars and Stripes would be run up over islands with "strategically valuable" bases for planes or ships.[106] Newspapers such as the *Pittsburgh Post Gazette* declared it was nonsense to think that the Atlantic Charter would prevent the United States from holding as a security measure the Pacific bases won in the war. A reporter in Chicago asked the three flag raisers from Iwo Jima whether the United States should turn over captured islands in the Pacific to some international body after the war. "Hell no," answered Rene Gagnon. "The Marines fought and died to take those islands."[107] Along with bases, Americans wanted access to airfields around the world. At the 1944 International Civil Aviation Conference, the United States successfully negotiated what Senator Joseph Ball (R-MN) called "the five freedoms for international air transport." Participating nations granted each other the privilege to fly across territory, land, and put down and take on passengers, mail, and cargo. Ball noted, "Some of our allies seem fearful, perhaps with cause, that America will dominate international air transport in the future."[108]

As for obtaining access to oil, U.S. policy was such a deviation from the announced war aims that the OWI could not touch it. In 1940 the United States produced 63 percent of the world's oil. By 1943, however, the Secretary of the Interior, Harold Ickes, warned, "if there should be a World War III it would have to be fought with someone else's petroleum, because the United States wouldn't have it."[109] The largest known supplies of someone else's petroleum were in the Persian Gulf nations. U.S. companies controlled 42 percent of known oil reserves in the Middle East, mostly in Saudi Arabia, and sought access to British-controlled oil fields in Iran and Iraq. The OWI realized that the U.S. policy of exerting great power dominion over Arab oil reserves was so out of line with the Atlantic Charter principle of "equal access" to raw materials that, in this case, the "strategy of truth" was silenced.[110]

Avoiding specific issues of oil or bases, the OWI simply equated American interests with the interests of everyone else. It wanted radio listeners to be reminded that once the slave world was defeated, the Allies, using the Atlantic Charter provisions, "must build for *all* men a better world in which horrors like the Axis can never again occur."[111] Treasury Secretary Henry Morgenthau voiced the administration's prevailing theme, "Today the only enlightened form of national self-interest lies in international accord," as he introduced the results of the 1944 United Nations Monetary and Financial Conference, better known as the Bretton Woods agreement.[112] Describing it as complicated and even mysterious, the newly created International Monetary Fund (IMF) and the World Bank, explained administration spokesmen, had the simple purpose of ending "economic warfare" and making possible a free, fair, and stable system for the exchange of goods. As the largest financial contributor, the United States would control these international organizations. The Soviets, suspicious of capitalist expansion, refused to participate. The forty-four Allied nations that did hoped that global economic cooperation would prevent future depressions and wars of conquest.

Roosevelt, always difficult to pin down, continued to be imprecise on how his Four Policeman plan in which the United States, Britain, the Soviet Union, and China maintained world order meshed with Atlantic Charter principles. Confident that the United States would grow only stronger, FDR preferred to delay agreements on postwar policies. His British and Soviet counterparts did not want to wait. Churchill, anxious to preserve British dominance in the Mediterranean, met with Stalin in October 1944 to divide up control over the Balkans. The British would have 90 percent predominance in Greece, the Russians 90 percent in Romania, and so on. This agreement, known to Roosevelt, was not made public, but some of the results were hard to keep secret. Americans criticized Britain's move to install a reactionary king in liberated Greece where fighting broke out between monarchists and the left-wing faction, which had led the resistance to Nazi occupation. Nor did the Americans approve of the Russians sitting outside Warsaw for weeks while the Germans crushed the Polish underground Home Army, deported the population, and destroyed the city. After the Red Army resumed its advance, Soviet-sponsored Polish communists set up a provisional government without much opposition.

In December 1944, a reporter asked the president what he thought about the growing feeling "that we are losing the purposes, or that they are slipping away from us." FDR answered evasively, saying he thought the Atlantic Charter, like the Ten Commandments or "Christian living," was "a pretty good thing to shoot for." Then he said he did not mean to compare the Atlantic Charter to the Ten Commandments or Christian living; he meant that the Atlantic Charter, like the Fourteen Points, was "a step toward the better living of the population of the world."[113] The president tried to redefine the Atlantic Charter aims as goals for the distant future rather than aims to be achieved with victory. Americans, who found it fairly easy to rationalize their own adjustments to Atlantic Charter principles, were discomforted by their Allies' brutal pursuit of self-interest. Asked how they felt about the way the Big Three were cooperating with each other in January 1945, 46 percent said they were satisfied and 43 percent said they were dissatisfied.[114]

At his last summit conference held at Yalta on the Black Sea in February 1945, Roosevelt demonstrated his preference for great power pragmatism. FDR wanted the Russians to help defeat Japan in a fight he expected to last for two more years. Stalin promised to assist in the Pacific and to support Chiang's nationalists in China, not Mao's communists. In exchange, FDR and Churchill agreed that the Soviet Union would regain islands lost to Japan in 1905 and access to Chinese ports and railroads. The Big Three agreed on occupation plans that divided up Germany, pledged support for the United Nations Organization, and compromised on Poland. The Soviets would get Polish territory in return for allowing the Poles to vote for a new government. Stalin asserted that because the great powers had shed blood to liberate the small powers, the small powers had no right to criticize them. When a U.S. diplomat suggested that Americans would disagree with that point of view, the Russian deputy foreign secretary replied, "The American people should learn to obey their leaders."[115] About the compromise, the president admitted privately that it was the best he could do. The Russians already controlled most of the territory they asked for. Churchill, worried as he was about Soviet expansion in Europe, recognized that the Russians remained essential allies while the Germans still had almost 300 divisions on the front lines. Speaking before a joint session of Congress, FDR was vague but positive about the Yalta agreements. He died a few weeks later, concerned about Soviet policies in Poland, but convinced that the Allies must find a way to work together. The administration did not arouse great interest in the summit conference. Seventy percent of the public did not know about the agreements reached at Yalta; 20 percent had never heard of Yalta.[116]

Much more fanfare was directed at the San Francisco conference in May 1945 where international delegates set up the United Nations Organization. In 1944 the State Department had charged MacLeish as assistant secretary of state for public affairs with "informing the public" and "maintaining popular support for the country's foreign policy." Francis Russell of the Public Liaison branch wrote that most Americans viewed foreign policy the same way they viewed Einstein's theory of relativity: they knew it was important but not worth trying to comprehend. He thought the department needed to translate what he called "the present burning desire to avoid another war" into sustained support for U.S. international involvement. MacLeish met with representatives of the major news organizations to encourage feature stories, not on conference policymaking, but on the role of the United States as host. Officials arranged for more than 200 interested organizations, such as the U.S. Chamber of Commerce, to send distinguished "observers" to San Francisco where they attended off-the-record forums with the American delegation and had the opportunity to express themselves. The State Department was making an effort to establish diplomatic relations with the American people, noted *New York Times* columnist Anne O'Hare McCormick.[117]

Viewed as a tribute to the fallen president, the conference was promoted as a symbol of the Allied commitment to the Atlantic Charter war aims and American acceptance of internationalism. McCormick, one of the columnists who had served on Hull's committee on political problems, described the significance. Roosevelt had told her that he wanted the conference held in the United States to dramatize it for the American people, to strengthen their feelings of responsibility, and to demonstrate "America's world-wide interests by directing attention to the Pacific battlefield."[118] After witnessing a week of ceremonial speeches, *New Yorker* writer E. B. White compared the emerging United Nations Organization to an Airedale puppy. "One minute you look at it and you are sure it will grow rabid and destroy the family," wrote White. "The next minute you look again and feel certain it will someday pull a drowning child from a stream and win the gratitude of the whole community."[119] Defending the secrecy surrounding the actual negotiations, Lester Markel of the *New York Times* observed that intricate details might better be discussed without the distracting media spotlight.[120] Everyone was distracted by the news that Italian partisans had shot Mussolini and Hitler had committed suicide in his Berlin bunker. All rejoiced on May 8 at the news of Germany's surrender.

The new United Nations Organization had a General Assembly, which included representatives from all the member nations. At Yalta FDR had agreed to Stalin's insistence on two extra Soviet votes in the Assembly. FDR thought the concession more embarrassing than important. The British, after all, could count on Canada, Australia, and New Zealand, the United States had Latin America, and, in FDR's mind, the General Assembly was just for "talky-talk." This concession, however, raised suspicions about what else FDR might have given to Stalin at Yalta; these suspicions would grow in the years to come. The real power in the U.N. went to the Security Council, where each of the five permanent members—the Four Policemen plus France— held veto power over the use of military and economic sanctions. In addition, Article 51 allowed regional alliances including one between the United States

The American flag appears top and center of the United Nations flags. (National Archives, NWDNS-44-PA-2195)

and Latin America. The rules permitted the United States to intervene to keep the peace in Europe and Asia, while giving it freedom of action in the Western Hemisphere. War Department official John J. McCloy declared that Americans would "have our cake and eat it too." The negotiations left the British and French empires intact and gave the United States control over the Pacific islands it had wrested from Japan. The *New York Post* captured the resulting contradiction between ideals and interests with its headline: "U.S. Stand Perils Colonial Freedom." Of the 95 percent of Americans who had heard or read about the San Francisco conference, 45 percent believed that the conference would be able to work out a plan to prevent another world war for at least fifty years, 30 percent said they did not, and 20 percent said they did not know.[121] The Senate approved the U.N. treaty in July 1945 by a vote of 89 to 2.

For Americans, the war came to a close as it had started, with a shock. It took only one atomic bomb, harnessing "the basic power of the universe," announced the White House, to destroy a city. President Harry Truman announced that the first bomb had been dropped on Hiroshima, which he called a "military base" because Americans wished to spare civilians. This statement favored image over reality. Hiroshima was one of only five Japanese cities that had escaped General Curtis LeMay's "blanket of fire" strategic bombing campaign of 1944–1945 that killed somewhere between 240,000 and 300,000 Japanese, mostly civilians. The atomic bombs dropped on Hiroshima on August 6 and on Nagasaki on August 9 killed 180,000 people immediately. Reports that tens of thousands more died from radiation poisoning were denounced as Japanese propaganda by U.S. military authorities, as they tried to shift reporters' attention to the story of liberated American POWs. Japan agreed to surrender only after negotiating terms that would allow the Emperor Hirohito to remain in power.[122]

The news of the atomic bomb was greeted with elation by GIs who thought that if they didn't have to invade the Japanese home islands they might survive the war. Yet, the celebration of the war's end was tempered by anxiety over the implications of the new weapon. U.S. leaders appealed to faith and national destiny. "It is an awful responsibility which has come to us," declared President Truman in a nationwide radio address on August 10, 1945. Referring to the bomb, he said, "We thank God that it has come to us instead of to our enemies; and we pray that He may guide us to use it in His ways and for His purposes." At the formal surrender ceremony held on the *Missouri* on September 2, General MacArthur said the hope of mankind was "that a better world will emerge out of the blood and carnage of the past."[123]

Victory

AS WARTIME PROPAGANDA HAD PROMISED, by uniting together, the free world of the Allies had defeated the slave world of the Axis. Given the emphasis on Axis leaders as the real enemy and the restraint regarding atrocity stories, the slave world in actuality turned out to be worse than presented. Few were prepared for the terrible revelation of the Nazi extermination camps. As for the Japanese, racist attitudes contributed to the dehumanization of an enemy already deemed dastardly for the sneak attack on Pearl Harbor. Confronted with such enemies, Americans from Donald Duck to Humphrey Bogart's Rick had a choice to make. There was never any doubt, according to propagandists, about the right choice. The sacred roll call of states, whether celebrated by Hollywood or quietly conducted by Ernie Pyle, illustrated the effectiveness of parts uniting to make a whole. So it made sense to suggest a link between the United States and the United Nations. "We need to establish a union of nations," said the OWI, "just as we once established our own great and peaceful Union of States... to keep the peace." The Union could not live half free and half slave, nor could the world, claimed propagandists, holding up the United States as a model for the rest of the world to follow. The conversion narrative first called upon Americans to commit to the war and then it called on them to commit to keeping the peace. Again the stakes were high, declared the OWI, "Work today for peace that your children may live tomorrow."[124]

Of course, the propagandists of World War II were not the first or the last to see the postwar world fail to live up to their portrayal of it. An estimated fifty to seventy million people had died in the carnage. Millions more were without shelter, food, or clean water as they began the ordeal of reconstruction. It was hard to tell whether the two new superpowers, the United States and the Soviet Union, now poised to assert themselves, would continue to get along. Colonial peoples, encouraged by the Atlantic Charter's call for self-determination and Japan's smashing, if temporary, defeat of the western imperial powers, agitated for independence. Civil wars broke out or threatened in China, Greece, and Korea. Jewish survivors stubbornly made their way to British-controlled Palestine despite British and Arab opposition. The world war was over, but peace seemed elusive.

The only nation to emerge from the war years richer and stronger was the United States. The Americans held two-thirds of the world's gold, made one-half of the world's manufactured products, dominated the oil, shipping, and electronic industries, and had the biggest navy, the biggest air force, and a monopoly on atomic weapons. They had the power not only to join an organized international community, but to dominate it. The United States had reinforced its influence in the Americas, expanded its power in the Pacific, especially when it took on the occupation of Japan by itself, ran its zone in Germany, and increased its presence in Africa and the Middle East. It proved to be generous in many ways, giving $48 billion in Lend-Lease aid; donating almost 70 percent of the funding to the United Nations Relief and Recovery Administration, which provided food, shelter, and medicine to victims of the war; establishing itself as the world's banker through the IMF and the World Bank; and hosting the new United Nations organization. Convinced that the world was better off with U.S. leadership, it expected others to follow.

By accepting global commitments, Americans, as one OWI correspondent put it, had adopted "enlightened selfishness." Still, FDR, in the last months of the war, was unsure just how much international peacekeeping Americans would support. For instance, at Yalta and elsewhere, he expressed the view that the U.S. occupation of postwar Germany would have to be short because the public would insist on the return of the troops. Treasury bond drives and wartime advertising had reinforced the idea that after their sacrifices, Americans could enjoy their well-deserved material rewards. What we Americans want, concluded pollster Lydgate, is "a permanent world peace that will allow us to go about our business."[125] Their model was not only the noble, self-sacrificing hero of the wartime conversion narrative. It was also Scarlett O'Hara, Hollywood's unscrupulous Southern belle, who sees her home devastated by war and vows, "I'm going to live through this and when it's all over I'll never be hungry again."[126]

Wartime propaganda was criticized for being at once too much and too little. By collaborating with the mass media, the government had been able to reach people in their homes, workplaces, and neighborhoods. Henry Luce concluded that "big government" dominated the news with its endless supply of press releases, communiqués, and pictures.[127] Yet, even though people had been connected to the war by film, radio, posters, magazines, United Nations store displays, and Four Freedoms pageants, they had also been distanced from the real thing by censorship and simplistic messages. "I still say that you are not permitted by the Army and Navy or by the administration to treat the

American people as adults or as functioning members of a democratic society," deplored Bernard DeVoto to Davis. "I still say we know far less, dangerously less, than the tolerable minimum of what is going on in the war and what the government is doing about our relations with other countries."[128]

A discouraged Edward R. Murrow wrote to Davis saying, "I decline to be at a rebirth of the illusion that international relations are simple, easy or mysterious." He blamed the broadcasting business for too often reporting only what they thought the people would like to hear. "The refusal to face unpleasant facts was the primary reason for this war happening as it did," stated Murrow, "and it will also be the reason why a vast number of the boys who are fighting this war will feel within three years of its end that they have been betrayed."[129] Captain Horace R. Hansen of the War Crimes Branch confirmed Murrow's prediction when he wrote from Dachau, Germany, to his folks in Minnesota saying that the GIs felt bitter.

> It is highly discouraging to have gone thru a war with such high hopes for a good future, only to see the occupation job going to pot, everybody dipping in our purse and our prestige being frittered away. Then on top of all this we read with utter disgust how England, France, Holland and others are right back at the old game— maneuvering, pushing, even fighting to grab all they can get all over the world. We often wonder what we fought the war for and what has happened to the Four Freedoms, the Atlantic Charter and other solemn pledges.[130]

As postwar policies exposed the contradictions between ideals and interests, Americans had reason to remain skeptical.

In the end, the uplifting and misleading propaganda version of World War II survived and the "strategy of truth" did not. As he closed down the agency in September 1945, Elmer Davis concluded that the OWI had enjoyed a limited success. He noted that it was difficult to coordinate information without the full cooperation of the services and the State Department, or, as he diplomatically put it, when officials and news reporters preferred the prestige of a White House announcement. FDR always had remained the chief news source, at times using his formidable communication skills to be forthright with the public and at other times not. Next time, Davis advised, war propaganda should be conducted from the White House. The head of an office of war information should ideally be the president's press secretary, the person with the confidence of and access to the president. In addition, Davis suggested wryly, he should have the talents of a lobbyist, a traffic policeman, and the impresario of an opera company.[131] Future wartime White Houses would follow Davis's recommendation, running their propaganda campaigns from within.

As stretched and selective as it had been, the OWI's "strategy of truth" had been dedicated to the idea that if informed, the American citizen would make the right decision, especially if it was made obvious what that decision should be. It had sought to regain the confidence in official propaganda that had been lost after World War I, emphasizing the practical over the sensational. It had attempted to replace the isolationism that constrained U.S. foreign policy before Pearl Harbor with broad support for internationalism. The OWI urged that civilians should be trusted with the harsh realities of war, yet it was unable to convince the administration to divulge much about postwar policies. In future wars, which would not be total wars requiring mass mobilization, most citizens would not be asked to sacrifice or make decisions. During the wars in Korea, Vietnam, and Iraq, government propagandists, building on the precedent set by the Roosevelt administration, would instead point out that given the complexity of global policies it was best to leave the details to those in charge. The "strategy of truth" would not be considered necessary or effective.

"Good war" propaganda was considered effective. Americans, as historian David Kennedy has observed, did not wish to recall how they ignored the Nazi danger through much of the 1930s, how they had shut out refugees seeking shelter, how they had mishandled Japan, how they had fought with production for three years while the Russians bled on the battlefield, how they violated the constitutional rights of thousands of Japanese American citizens, how they again asked African Americans to fight in a world war for freedoms they didn't have, and how they carried out morally questionable terror and fire bombing against civilians. Americans preferred to remember the propaganda version of a noble war fought for democracy and freedom by innocent people forced to defend themselves against a vicious enemy, a war fought overseas by decent men while on the home front everyone contributed, a war in which Americans played the starring role and the Allies had bit parts, and a war that delivered a better life.[132] This version ignored the skepticism expressed by people during the war years so it could present the conversion to internationalism as complete and whole-hearted. Americans, it proclaimed, had embraced their role as leader of the Free World and keeper of the peace. The propaganda version of the good war would be conscripted to serve in the wars to come.

4

War in Korea

"The Front Line in the Struggle between Freedom and Tyranny"

The future of civilization depends on what we do.

President Harry Truman, 1950

Someone gave old Harry the wrong dope on this war. He can find someone else to pin his medals on.

GI in Korea, 1950

THE KOREAN WAR WAS A LIMITED WAR with far-reaching consequences. The U.S. government viewed North Korea's invasion of South Korea in 1950 as part of a communist plot to achieve global domination. Acting on the belief that the Soviet Union ordered the attack, President Harry Truman sent U.S. forces to Korea to contain the spread of communism. Korea, he declared, had become "the front line in the struggle between freedom and tyranny." Despite Truman's clear public pronouncement of Korea's significance, the president and his advisors feared that Korea wasn't the real front line. They worried that the war there might be a distraction intended to draw the United States away from the real target in Europe or the Middle East. Therefore, wary of possible Soviet aggression elsewhere, it designated Korea a limited war. Meanwhile the U.S. government tripled the military budget; committed to supporting anticommunist forces in the Philippines, Vietnam, and Taiwan; and rearmed its recent enemies, West Germany and Japan. The United States geared up to fight a global Cold War.

To win the support of the American people for this ambitious policy, the Truman administration set out to, in the words of Secretary of State Dean Acheson, "bring the whole story together in one official narrative."[1] Following the model of World War II propaganda, the official narrative depicted two worlds in conflict. The so-called Free World of law and order, prosperity, and security opposed the "communist world" of corruption, subversion, and terror. Referring to communism as "red fascism," the administration pointed to lessons learned from World War II. Appeasement did not work; only force could stop aggressors from destroying the American way of life. In 1950, after years of depression and war, two-thirds of Americans had achieved middle-class status and they wanted to enjoy it. Instead, they were told that everything they had could be taken away. Truman warned that if Americans didn't fight communists in Korea, they would end up fighting communists in Wichita.

The administration and its supporters identified Korea as a battleground on the frontier where Americans fought to defend civilization from savages. It drew on malleable racial stereotypes to identify Asians as members of the Free World or the communist world. The "Good Asian" image, which had been applied to Chinese allies during World War II, shifted to the Koreans, meaning South Koreans. The people of Asia wanted what Americans wanted, explained the president, "better health, more food, better clothes and homes, and the chance to live their own lives in peace."[2] Implied in the "Good Asian" image was the assumption that Koreans not only wanted what Americans wanted, but as obedient allies would do what the Americans wanted. The "Bad Asian" image—sly and inscrutable—which had been applied to the Japanese during World War II, now shifted to the North Koreans and the Communist Chinese. This enemy moved in hordes or swarms, as in United Press (UP) reporter Robert Miller's description of the North Koreans: "The Communists came by the thousands in fanatical, screaming waves."[3] Moreover, "Bad Asians" were viewed as dangerous because they must be someone else's puppets. Indeed, in U.S. rhetoric, the North Koreans lost their nationality as Koreans and became reds or commies. And, unlike "Good Asians," they would not be considered as potential members of western civilization. North Koreans, stated the Army Handbook, "have the Oriental disregard for human life."[4] To emphasize the divide between east and west, policy-makers frequently pointed out that the Russians themselves were an Oriental or Asiatic people. These stereotypes divided Asians into people who did or did not want to be like Americans, suggesting that there was no need to learn anything more about them.[5]

As the nation assumed an ongoing state of war, government propaganda became permanent and professional. Following the recommendation Elmer Davis had made in his final report on the Office of War Information (OWI), the White House took over its coordination. Instead of calling on poets, historians, and artists to serve in a temporary wartime agency, the government expanded the role of policymakers, public relations specialists, and journalists in public information departments throughout the executive branch. For example, the career of Edward Barrett, the assistant secretary of state for public affairs from 1950 to 1952, included a stint at the OWI, being executive editor of *Newsweek*, doing public relations at the high-powered firm of Hill and Knowlton, and serving as dean of the Columbia School of Journalism. His career illustrated why it was easy to consider government information officers, private sector public relations specialists, and members of the news media as being on the same team.

Moreover, the president's press office expanded to include the secretary and two assistants who not only briefed the 300 or more reporters who covered the White House, but also prepped the president for press conferences with notebooks of background material and answers to expected questions. In addition, the three wire services, the two radio–television networks, and the major Eastern daily newspapers assigned reporters to cover the president at all times, forming a permanent press corps of ten to twenty correspondents who accompanied Truman even on his early morning walks. Truman heartily detested the press, telling the powerful publisher Henry Luce that he must have trouble sleeping at night because he misinformed rather than informed people. Yet Truman personally answered questions at 347 press conferences during his years in office, including several held during the Korean War. As *U.S. News and World Report* outlined in a chart, "How the Government Conditions the Public to Ideas It Wants to Put Over," the executive branch developed the official line and disseminated it through the press to the public. In the process the president "gets big headlines."[6]

The goal was to construct a bipartisan consensus in support of Cold War foreign policy. Opinion surveys showed that most Americans paid much less attention to international events than they did to domestic issues such as jobs, prices, and housing. Therefore, the public opinion that the Truman administration cared most about was the 25 percent of Americans—businessmen, journalists, academics, labor leaders, and members of interest groups—who it believed followed international events and foreign policy. Officials courted their support with special briefings and appointments to presidential advisory boards and committees. In turn, these committees, such as the Committee on the Present Danger, set up in the fall of 1950, advocated administration foreign policy. Officials figured that if these notables endorsed their product the rest of the public would buy it. In this effort they were aided by the Ad Council, set up during World War II as the War Advertising Council, which promoted free enterprise and American international leadership. With advice and funding from the White House, the Ad Council launched campaigns such as United Nations Week, Pan-American Week, World Trade Week, Patriotic Rededication Week, and United America Week. "Communism thrives on dissension!" announced the ad for Brotherhood Week in 1948. Gabriel Almond, political scientist and former OWI analyst, wrote in 1950 that the American people "will follow the lead of the policy elites if they demonstrate unity and resolution."[7]

The World War II era "strategy of truth" was replaced with a strategy of credibility. President Truman cultivated a reputation as a straight talker, which, however much it suited his small town Missouri background, he used at times to mislead the public. His administration interpreted unfolding events and international flare-ups, no matter how complicated, in the simplistic terms of the "Free World vs. communist world" framework. As in World War II, the government told the news media that their support during the Cold War crisis was essential. According to historian Nancy Bernhard, "broadcasters used the freedom of the press to volunteer as propagandists."[8] With such assistance, the administration delivered its messages through speeches, press conferences, films, radio shows, and television programs. Even though freedom of the press was celebrated in Cold War rhetoric, secrecy and censorship, both formal and informal, played a role in limiting news coverage, especially in the repressive climate of the Red Scare on the home front.

All of these efforts could not make Korea a popular war. In the first phase, from June to September 1950, the war aim was the liberation of South Korea from communist invasion. Although the first American troops arrived in time to join the South Koreans in retreat, they turned the fight around and pushed back the enemy to the North. In the second phase from September to November, the war aim shifted to rollback, the more ambitious goal of running the communists out of Korea altogether. After the Chinese entered the war in November 1950 and delivered American forces one of the worst defeats in U.S. military history, the war aim reverted back to keeping communism out of South Korea. Fighting interrupted by temporary cease-fires distinguished the third and longest phase of the war, as peace talks dragged on for months. When in April 1951 Truman fired commanding general Douglas MacArthur, who openly disagreed with the last shift in war aims, Americans at home engaged in a debate over "why we fight." The administration defended its turnaround in Korea by reducing the war's significance, saying that the United States must concentrate on the global threat and not over-commit to one of many fronts in the fight against communism. Not surprisingly, Americans felt confused, with many concluding that the war in Korea was a mistake. Throughout, the Truman administration confronted a problem its successors would face in future wars: how to persuade Americans that they were fighting for the highest stakes in a limited war in a small faraway country about which they knew nothing.

Americanism versus Communism

IN 1945 THE TWO BIGGEST WINNERS of World War II viewed each other's agenda for the peace with suspicion. Truman, like Wilson and FDR, believed that the whole world would benefit if it belonged to a stable international order based on American values and interests. Policymakers thought that U.S. industries needed to be able to sell their products overseas or else the country would slump back into depression. National security no longer meant just defending borders. It required the promotion and protection of an international market economy. With a monopoly on the atomic bomb and one-half of the world's wealth, Truman estimated that the United States should be able to get 85 percent of what it wanted. The Soviets, convinced that the Americans were bent on spreading capitalism to undermine their state-run economic system and fearing above all another attack from the West, maintained the massive Red Army and forced communist governments on their East European neighbors. The Russians extolled the glories of a communist future and encouraged left-wing movements in Europe, the Middle East, and Asia, while ruthlessly suppressing any opposition at home. Fearful that the fragile postwar environment would fuel the ambitions of the other, each superpower took actions that confirmed those fears.

The Truman administration exaggerated the threat of communism to rally public support for the policy of containment, which called for the use of American diplomatic, economic, and military power to block Soviet expansion. The situation prompting the announcement of containment in the Truman Doctrine of March 1947, however, was not Soviet aggression but the transition of power from the British Empire to the United States. Great Britain, struggling with its poor recovery from the war, announced that it could no longer afford to support pro-western governments in Greece and Turkey, two strategically important countries in the Mediterranean. It asked the United

States to take over its role. The Americans did not like to think of the United States as an imperial power. After granting independence to the Philippines in 1946, American officials tended to describe the decades of U.S. colonial rule there as a self-help opportunity for Filipinos. Nor, as policymakers had feared during World War II, did Americans embrace a vision of themselves as Santa Claus, giving away tax dollars to foreigners. So the administration faced the problem of persuading Congress and the public to spend $400 million to prop up authoritarian regimes in Greece and Turkey. Undersecretary of State Dean Acheson hit upon a convincing argument. Speaking to Congressional leaders, he said that the countries in question were like apples in a barrel. If Greece went rotten, the corruption would spread to the Middle East, North Africa, and Europe. An alarmed Senator Arthur Vandenberg (R-MI) advised the president to explain the danger to the country.[9]

Speaking before a joint session of Congress and on the radio on March 12, 1947, President Truman warned that in a world divided into two opposing forces, the United States had to defend free people from "totalitarian regimes." It was a stunningly clear formulation. There were only two sides: us (good) and them (bad). Now the Republican-dominated Congress had to decide which side to support. The *New York Times* headline the next day proclaimed, "Truman Acts to Save Nations From Red Rule." Critics challenged Truman's simplistic portrayal of a world divided into two "ways of life." They warned that the containment policy would commit Americans to an open-ended global conflict. Bernard Baruch, the financier who served the wartime administrations of Wilson, FDR, and Truman, said the speech was "tantamount to a declaration of . . . an ideological or religious war." The secretary of state, the esteemed General George Marshall, was startled. He wrote Truman that the speech "was overstating the case a bit," to which the president replied that it was "the only way" to get congressional support.[10]

Truman's speech successfully established the themes of Cold War propaganda. First, it defined the situation as an immediate crisis, which demanded quick action by the chief executive and allowed no time for investigation, domestic debate, or negotiation. Second, it blamed international problems, whether caused by postwar devastation, internal political struggles, nationalist movements, or actual Soviet aggression, on Soviet aggression. Third, it portrayed Americans as acting on behalf of human freedom, not out of economic self-interest. The Truman Doctrine established the framework that would justify the implementation of the Marshall Plan, the creation of the Central Intelligence Agency (CIA), the National Security Council (NSC), and the Federal Employee Loyalty Program, the rebuilding of West Germany, especially following the Russians' attempt to blockade Berlin, and, in 1949, the formation of the North Atlantic Treaty Organization (NATO). To mark its importance, the Truman Doctrine rode across the country on the Freedom Train. Americans in 322 cities could see it, along side the Declaration of Independence, the Constitution, and the Emancipation Proclamation. Organized by the newly created American Heritage Foundation and promoted by the Ad Council, the Freedom Train project urged citizens to "rededicate to Americanism."[11]

The Truman administration defined any gain for communists as a loss for the Free World. Such a global view assumed that all noncommunist areas were under U.S. protection. It distorted perceptions of indigenous anticolonial movements and civil wars. The victory of the communists in the Chinese civil war was a real blow. After years of supporting Chiang Kai-shek's Nationalists, the administration had decided to cut off aid to Chiang's corrupt government. In 1949, the Chinese Communists led by Mao Zedong defeated the Nationalists who fled to the island of Formosa, now Taiwan. Truman's critics, especially Republicans, charged the administration with "losing China." American policymakers, who since McKinley had eyed China as a potential economic partner, turned to its neighbors. In January 1950, Secretary of State Acheson famously defined the U.S. "defense perimeter" in the Pacific as running from the Aleutians to the Philippines. The people on the other side, he explained, would be protected by the "entire civilized world under the Charter of the United Nations."[12]

In early 1950, the administration decided to militarize containment following the addition of millions of Chinese to the communist world and the Soviet development of an atomic bomb the previous August. The National Security Council drew up a top-secret plan entitled NSC-68. Describing communists as fanatics who could be stopped only by force, NSC-68 called for a massive buildup of nuclear and conventional military forces at the cost of $50 billion a year in defense spending. Critics, including the State Department's Soviet expert George Kennan, who had authored the containment policy, pointed out that the Soviets had no immediate plans for using force outside of Eastern Europe. However, to Acheson, NSC-68 provided the justification the United States needed to assume global leadership in the "drama . . . now played on the world stage." The secretary viewed the communist threat to Western Europe as similar to the one posed by Islam centuries before, "with its combination of ideological zeal and fighting power." To reach the average American who, Acheson thought, might spend at the most ten minutes a day paying attention to international affairs, the message must be simple, blunt, and "clearer than truth."[13]

Confident that the government could "whip up sentiment" for the Cold War mobilization called for in NSC-68, Barrett, the assistant secretary of state for public affairs, had a plan. First, build "public awareness" with a "psychological 'scare campaign'" that would last anywhere from days to three months. Second, when the public was primed, the government then could sell an expensive military buildup against the Soviet Union. But policymakers did not want to stir up too much fear in case the public might demand a "dangerous escalation" of the Cold War. The president announced the "Campaign of Truth." He told the American Society of Newspaper Editors that against Soviet propaganda, the United States had "truth—plain, simple, unvarnished truth—presented by the newspapers, radio, newsreels, and other sources that the people trust." The United States was in danger, announced Acheson, as he called upon the news media to defend freedom around the world.[14] Then on June 25, 1950, North Korea attacked South Korea.

Containing Communism in Korea

DURING WORLD WAR II, the Allies had agreed to create a free and united Korea once they liberated it from Japan, which had controlled the 1300-year-old nation since 1905. As planned, the Soviets disarmed the Japanese north of the 38th parallel and the Americans the south. Dean Rusk, a young colonel at the War Department, had chosen the line because it placed Seoul, the capital, in the American zone. Once liberated, the Koreans, like the Greeks and the Chinese, plunged into a vicious civil war, fighting over whether a reunited Korea would have a left-wing or right-wing government. Throughout the country, Korean nationalists wanted to abolish Japanese landholding policies, redistribute land, and nationalize the major industries. In the South, the elderly Syngman Rhee, the longtime advocate of Korean independence who had lived in the United States for decades, opposed these policies. Backed by U.S. occupying authorities, Rhee suppressed worker and peasant uprisings, arrested thousands of political prisoners, and preserved the landholding policies that favored the traditional elite who had collaborated with the Japanese. In the North, the Soviets backed the thirty-three-year-old communist revolutionary leader, Kim Il Sung, who had resisted Japanese occupation since the early 1930s and had received military training in the Soviet Union during the war. Kim's regime pushed through land confiscation and the nationalization of industries. No opposition was allowed. Both the American and the Russian occupation forces pulled out in 1948 leaving behind two Koreas on the verge of turning guerrilla fighting into conventional war.[15]

The Korean War of 1950 was an international civil war in which the conflict between Koreans was intertwined with the superpowers' Cold War ambitions. After repeated requests for Soviet backing of an invasion, Kim received the go-ahead in early 1950. Joseph Stalin, the Soviet leader, hoped that a Soviet-sponsored communist victory in Korea would counter the prospect of a powerful capitalist Japan and check Mao's alternative Chinese communist brand of messy nationalist revolution from spreading through Asia. Kim also received approval from Mao, who detested American support for Chinese nationalists and feared a rebuilt Japan. From the American perspective, communist control of South Korea threatened U.S. plans for Japan, which depended on Korean rice and raw materials for its recovery. In addition, American policymakers believed that any failure to protect South Korea from communism would undermine the credibility of U.S. claims that it would protect Western Europe. Finally, Truman, already accused of "losing China," especially by conservative Republicans, felt a domestic political imperative to "win" Korea. Early press coverage in the United States referred to the war both as a "civil war" and "the beginning of World War III." UP reporter Jack Jones, who broke the story of the invasion, described the war as most Americans would see it: "The Russian-sponsored North Korean Communists invaded the American-supported Republic of South Korea today."[16]

President Truman announced, "The attack upon Korea makes it plain beyond all doubt" that the goal of communism was to "conquer independent nations." Without consulting the South Koreans, the administration defined its objective as restoring the division between North and South. Without consulting U.S. allies, Truman ordered American troops doing occupation duty in Japan to Korea. The administration organized an international coalition through the United Nations to carry out what Truman would call the "police action" in Korea. The U.N. Security Council adopted the U.S. resolution demanding that the North withdraw behind the 38th parallel. Since the Russian representative was boycotting in protest of U.S. insistence that China's seat go to Taiwan rather than the People's Republic and Yugoslavia abstained, the vote was 9 to 0. A second Security Council Resolution called for U.N. assistance to South Korea. Seventy-year-old General MacArthur, chief of the American Forces in the Far East and head of the U.S. occupation of Japan, took command of the sixteen nations in the U.N. forces. Referred to as "our father who art in Tokyo" by an irreverent army colonel on his staff, the imperious MacArthur led a force dominated by American naval and air power.[17]

Asserting his powers as commander-in-chief, Truman did not ask Congress to declare war. In the early weeks, the legislators rallied behind the president, giving him a standing ovation when he asked for an emergency defense appropriation of $10 billion. Congress extended the draft, gave Truman the authority to call up reserves, and granted him war powers similar to FDR's. Speaking at a meeting of Congressmen, Truman was specific about the enemy in Korea. He said, "This act was very obviously inspired by the Soviet Union." And he laid out the consequences: "If we let Korea down, the Soviets will keep right on going and swallow up one piece of Asia after another. We had to make a stand some time, or else let all of Asia go by the board. If we were to let Asia go, the Near East would collapse and no telling what would happen in Europe." Secretary of State Acheson pointed out to legislators that the president's public statement did not refer in any way to the Soviet Union and asked members of Congress to follow his lead. It simply referred to "communism." Acheson said the U.S. government was doing its best to leave a door wide open for the Soviet Union to "call off the North Koreans" and "back down without losing too much face."[18] This reticence on naming the Soviets as the real enemy did not last long, but the assumption that the Soviet Union pulled the strings in North Korea and elsewhere did. Barrett, who was in Los Angeles to talk to movie industry executives, was asked if he thought North Korea had invaded without the knowledge of the Russians or the Chinese communists. He answered, "I find it difficult to imagine Donald Duck going on a rampage without Walt Disney knowing about it."[19]

Truman explained to Congress and the public that to contain the spread of global communism he was expanding American commitments far beyond Korea. He declared that the United States must "draw the line at Indo-China, the Philippines, and Formosa." The president ordered the Seventh Fleet to prevent any attack by China on Taiwan. He announced that forces in the Philippines would be strengthened. A radical nationalist movement of socialists, communists, and peasants called the Huks, which had organized during World War II to fight the Japanese, now aimed to overthrow the American-sponsored government of the Filipino ruling class. Aware that the Filipinos were in desperate need of land reform and honest elections, the Truman administration nevertheless supplied the Manila government with economic aid, military advisors, and CIA counterinsurgency experts. Truman also sent aid and a military mission to help the French in their colonial war against the Vietnamese led by communist Ho Chi Minh. Thus, Truman committed the United States to intervening in three foreign conflicts that had much more to do with nationalist struggles than they did with Kremlin doctrines.

It is difficult to know exactly what the American public made of all this. "He was fighting against some kind of government," said the father of nineteen-year-old Kenneth Shadrick of Skin Forks, West Virginia, the first American soldier to be killed in Korea. *Life* sent reporters to do man-on-the-street interviews in Sycamore, Illinois, population 6000. Nearly everyone interviewed supported the decision to fight in Korea, seeing it as necessary to stop the Russians. The sole dissenter was a World War II veteran who felt that "Asiatic wars are not our business." Striking electrical workers in New Jersey heard that an aircraft carrier in the Pacific needed new pumps, went back to work to assemble the pumps, and then returned to the picket line. Many Americans, remembering shortages from the last war, rushed out to buy spare sets of tires and order new cars. Indeed, readers of *Life* in July 1950 saw a juxtaposition of consumer goods with the horrors of war. One page showed a haunting photograph of a dead American soldier tied up and lying on the side of a road in Korea. Another contained an ad for General Motors picturing a little girl and her well-dressed mother cradling a baby in the back seat. The ad read, "The peace that lulls your baby to sleep in a General Motors car came from a long war against discomforts."[20] In contrast to World War II ads counseling patriotic conservation, 1950 ads urged immediate gratification. As historian Lizabeth Cohen explains, the postwar "consumer's republic" identified the citizen as purchaser and patriot.[21]

The administration carefully monitored public opinion throughout the war. According to the Gallup poll, eight out of ten Americans approved the president's decision to send U.S. military aid to Korea. The wording of this question to describe American involvement as "military aid" may have led to the high approval. The State Department's analysis of polls and the press tended to be positive. Its Daily Opinion Summary of July 3, 1950, confidently claimed that the vote was nearly 2-to-1 that the stand in Korea would lead to peace rather than to another world war (57 percent peace; 29 percent war; 14 percent undecided). But another view of those poll results, showing that 57 percent saw peace ahead while 43 percent did not or were not sure, indicated that a sizable number were not convinced. As had emerged at the end of World War II, a noticeable gap existed between opinion leaders in the media who on the whole tended to be quicker to adopt the official view of the conflict and the public whose responses to polls indicated more ambivalence about U.S. policies. The State Department noted that press commentators expressed a sense of relief that the United States had at last decided to draw a firm line against communist expansion in Asia, but raised concerns about taking on the enormous task to "police the perimeter of the Soviet world."[22]

In order to construct "one official narrative," the administration had to define the communist threat, the purpose of the war in Korea, a new international role for the United States, and show that the president was up to the job. Caught by surprise when the North Koreans invaded, the administration had appeared unprepared, which it was. To correct this impression, the Democratic National Committee stressed Truman's competence in its newsletter: "With a quick, sure hand the President leads the way through decisions which have won the world's approval."[23] While numerous government agencies worked out complicated foreign policies behind the scenes, the president played the part of the decisive protagonist. Truman's slogan, "the buck stops here," added to his reputation as a stand-up guy who assumed responsibility and didn't back down from a crisis.

For soldiers who asked, "Why am I fighting in Korea?" the Defense Department had an answer: They fought to protect the American way of life from global communism. According to the "Armed Forces Talk" issued in August 1950, officers should tell their men that "if the Communists were successful, *you* would become the slave, body and soul, of as cruel a band of individuals as ever ranged the earth." Communism, it continued, "would deny you (if you were not a Party leader) the privilege of owning anything of importance— certainly not an automobile or a radio." To explain the first international police action, the Defense Department used an analogy right out of Hollywood Westerns, which went like this: In the old days on the frontier, every man was his own policeman. He carried a gun and used it, when necessary, to defend his life and guard his property. Eventually the people got together and named a sheriff to protect them. Similarly, the United Nations force in Korea "represents *the sheriff of the world*." The role of the United States was identified rather modestly as "a strong member of the U.N. sheriff's posse." The posse's job was to stop "the powerful and unprincipled forces running wild in the world."[24] According to the Defense Department, GIs had a personal stake in taming the globe. Of course officers in Korea put their own, often more vivid, interpretation before the troops. Marine Colonel Lewis "Chesty" Puller told his soldiers, "Our country won't go on forever, if we stay as soft as we are

Cpl. John W. Simons of Bradbury Heights, Maryland, says good-bye to his wife and son as he leaves for Korea, 1950. (National Archives, 306-PS-50-10792)

now. There won't be an America—because some foreign soldiers will invade us and take our women and breed a hardier race."[25] Communists, soldiers learned, threatened to take away what belonged to them.

President Truman's September 1, 1950, radio address insisted that the United States, while protecting civilization, was not pursuing Manifest Destiny. It was the communists who were imperialists. His speech, announced as a response to White House mail asking how the Korean War would affect American life, was the result of several drafts. The president's staff removed objectionable phrases such as "crafty and ruthless foe." The Free World, Truman asserted, had learned from the 1930s that "appeasement of dictators is the sure road to world war. If aggression were allowed to succeed in Korea, it would be an open invitation to new acts of aggression elsewhere." Truman defended America's record. "We helped the Philippines become independent," stated the president, "and we have supported the national aspirations to independence of other Asian countries." In a statement of aims, Truman affirmed the U.S. commitment to seek peace and security through the United Nations; the

U.S. belief that Koreans had a right to be free, independent, and united—as they want to be; that the United States did not want the fighting in Korea to expand into a general war; the hope that the people of China would not be misled or forced into fighting against the United Nations and against the American people, who have always been and still are their friends; that the United States was at war for freedom, not for territory in Asia; that the United States did not believe in preventive war, only defensive war; and finally, that the United States wanted "peace not only for its own sake but because we want all the peoples of the world, including ourselves, to be free to devote their full energies to making their lives richer and happier." According to the *Philadelphia Bulletin*, the speech was, in effect, "a formal acceptance of the world leadership which has been thrust upon this country."[26]

The administration took advantage of the new technology of television to deliver its explanation. Although most Americans still counted on their radios and newspapers for news coverage, by 1953 45 percent of American homes had television sets, up from 9 percent in 1950. Television's number one mission was to deliver viewers to sponsors who backed shows such as *The Milton Berle Show*, *I Love Lucy*, and *The Lone Ranger*. To attract as wide an audience as possible, the networks wanted their news programs to appear objective and their reporters independent and unbiased. The concern of sponsors, however, that the shows they supported be free of any views considered "un-American" or extreme meant that the programs tended to reinforce the Cold War consensus by marginalizing dissenting views. For example, NBC's *Meet the Press*, sponsored by the Revere Copper and Brass Corporation in the early 1950s, featured mostly government officials. When the United States went to war in Korea, the networks feared that the federal government might take over radio and television in order to prevent the enemy from using broadcast signals. To forestall any such move, they set up a system of close, voluntary cooperation with the government. This wartime collaboration did not seem strange to the people involved. Both William Paley, head of CBS, and David Sarnoff, head of NBC, had worked for the OWI during World War II, as had many others who used their expertise in media to serve the country. Ironically, Cold War era television touted American freedom and free enterprise as the "absence of government control."[27]

Working with the administration, the networks created current events programs to showcase government officials and policy. The White House approved the scripts for CBS's *The Facts We Face*, which displayed American military strength. NBC's *Battle Report—Washington* was produced in the

White House office of John B. Steelman, Truman's chief of staff, and reached an estimated audience of 1.8 million. On August 13, 1950, Steelman introduced the show, calling it "democracy in action." He said, "Through the magic of television, we hope we can bring millions of our citizens in close touch with official Washington. You will both *hear* and *see* the men who are working *for you*. We hope that, during these telecasts, you will feel as if you are attending a meeting in a conference room in Washington, where Cabinet Officers and other high-ranking officials are making their reports directly to you."[28] *TV Guide* encouraged viewers to tune in, "It doesn't indulge in flag-waving, but we guarantee you'll feel a new pride in your country—and your government." On these shows, the reporters stood in for the citizens, supposedly asking the questions the people wanted answered. In reality, the White House or the State Department wrote the questions for the network reporters, which explains why the right map would instantaneously appear in what was allegedly a spontaneous conversation. This type of program satisfied both government officials and the sponsors. For the many Americans who did not yet own a TV, newspapers covered the interview programs, quoting official statements. As for the citizens, their role as members of the television audience was to hear and see what government officials wished them to hear and see.[29]

On the September 10, 1950, episode of the CBS show *Diplomatic Pouch*, made in cooperation with the State Department, Acheson presented the Cold War as a conflict between civilization and barbarism. Pointing to a map, Acheson showed communist aggression threatening Europe, the Middle East, and Asia. Interviewer Griffin Bancroft asked, "Can you build up forces in the West powerful enough actually to resist an all-out aggression?" Acheson answered, "I believe we can and I believe with modern weapons and ingenuity we can do again exactly what was done for so many centuries at the time of the Roman Empire.... It depends on the strength of the organization, the superiority of your weapons. You can hold back all sorts of hordes if you have that." Bancroft asked about the chances of Communist China getting involved in Korea. "I should think it would be sheer madness on the part of the Chinese Communists to do that and I see no advantage to them in doing it," Acheson replied. Fellow interviewer Edward R. Murrow followed up, asking about stopping at the 38th Parallel in Korea. Acheson answered that the United Nations would decide. Throughout the program the secretary insisted that Americans must be steady, strong, and sensible. For government officials, television was becoming an ideal medium for scaring people and then telling them to remain calm.[30]

As in the past, the U.S. military attempted to manage the media's coverage of the war. The Armed Services Radio Division produced broadcasts, the Pictorial Division provided photographs and maps, the Signal Corps filmed footage, and the Press Division held two daily briefings. More than three hundred war correspondents from nineteen countries were accredited to cover the U.N. forces in Korea, compared to the 185 accredited to cover Allied forces in the European theater in World War II. Most were not at the front and therefore depended on what the military told them. They covered the war from General MacArthur's command post in Tokyo or Eighth Army headquarters. The military's public information officers (PIOs) took care of correspondents' travel arrangements and provided free transmission over the military communication system from Korea to Tokyo. In addition, the PIOs handed out communiqués illustrated with official photographs and quotations from soldiers. Described by one PIO as "factual, pertinent, informative," the reports were found by correspondents to be sometimes less than informative and occasionally unreliable. Robert Miller checked out an official photograph distributed by the Air Force claiming to show a Korean bridge destroyed by "pin point bombing," only to discover that it had been blown by Army engineers during a retreat south.[31]

Confident that the press would report the war as he saw it, MacArthur set up what turned out to be a confusing system of voluntary censorship. As always, correspondents were not to report anything that would endanger operations: no names and positions of units, no embarkation dates, and no numbers of reinforcements. Nor were they to report any "information as may be of aid and comfort to the enemy." This vague phrase frustrated correspondents because it seemed to include anything that would undermine the military's reputation. In the first few weeks, the military temporarily revoked the credentials of two wire service correspondents, Tom Lambert of the Associated Press (AP) and Peter Kalischer (UP), who had described the heavy sacrifices of unprepared and ill-equipped troops. "You don't fight two tank-equipped divisions with .30-caliber carbines," a soldier told Lambert. "I never saw such a useless damned war in all my life."[32] Correspondents Marguerite Higgins of the *New York Herald Tribune* and former marine Keyes Beech of the *Chicago Daily News*, who both won Pulitzer Prizes for their reporting, wrote stories that reflected their concern over the lack of American readiness to fight communism in Korea and elsewhere in Asia. In part to avoid losing their accreditation, in part because of the enormous confusion of the first weeks of the war, and in part because they took Ernie Pyle as their model, many reporters focused on human interest stories about American GIs. Most of the soldiers were younger (under twenty-one) and less educated (one-third had finished high school) than their World War II counterparts.

Few reporters paid much attention to Koreans. Those who did, such as *Time-Life* correspondent Robert Osborne, wrote about an "ugly story in an ugly war." U.S. troops fired as ordered on a crowd of civilian refugees, he reported, because the command feared that the people were shielding an enemy attack. The Americans, Osborne wrote, had committed acts of "utmost savagery." Another exception was Murrow, whose trip to Korea in August 1950 made him question U.S. policy, which he had initially supported. Foreshadowing the type of story that would challenge the government's official line in Vietnam, Murrow recorded a radio broadcast reporting that retreating American troops had torched Korean villages, leaving people who had so little with nothing. In it he raised the question of whether, given such destructive acts, America's return to occupy South Korea would lessen or increase the attraction of communism. He sent the recording back to CBS in New York where the top executives decided not to broadcast Murrow's critical report because, they said, it could give comfort to the enemy. Murrow objected, returned home where his reports were not subject to MacArthur's prohibition of "unwarranted" criticism, and did a broadcast suggesting that perhaps communists were better at understanding the desire of impoverished Asians for change and the end of foreign domination.[33]

Rollback and Retreat

THE SUCCESS OF U.N. ADVANCES following MacArthur's daring landing behind enemy lines at Inchon on September 15, 1950, inspired official and popular optimism about the war. The U.S. government decided to change its initial objective of defending South Korea to a new goal of creating a united, noncommunist Korea. Truman's decision to go beyond the 38th parallel was based in part on the assessment that the Soviets would not act and that they controlled the decisions of the Chinese. MacArthur, who liked to say that he understood the Oriental mind, declared that China would never enter the war. General Omar Bradley, the chair of the Joint Chiefs of Staff, was not so sure. Although he went along with the new objective, Bradley said that if the Chinese came in, the Americans should get out. Truman ordered MacArthur to destroy North Korea's armed forces. The orders also said that only South Korean troops were allowed to approach the Yalu River at the border between

When General Douglas MacArthur and President Harry Truman met on Wake Island in October 1950, they agreed on war aims in Korea. (National Archives, 111-SC-349615)

North Korea and China and that there would be no air or naval action against China.[34]

As though the war were over, the president announced in October, "We know now that the United Nations can create a system of international order with the authority to maintain peace."[35] Of course, Truman meant the United Nations acting in accordance with U.S. policy. Contrary to Acheson's statement that the U.N. would decide on going beyond the 38th parallel, the United States made the decision and the U.N. rubber-stamped it, some members with reluctance. Polls showed that most people thought the war would be over in a few months.[36] On the November 26 broadcast of *Battle Report—Washington*, a confident David Brinkley introduced the show, "Korea, where our troops are making a powerful bid against Old Man Winter to be out of the fox-holes by Christmas!"[37] On that day, over a quarter million soldiers of the People's Liberation Army of China crossed the Yalu River.

On the next *Battle Report—Washington* broadcast, the tone had changed. "Korea where the armies representing 53 United Nations are suddenly outnumbered and pushed back by the invading forces of one," announced Brinkley. "Communist China!... presenting an entirely new threat to world peace!" Despite China's warnings that it would respond if U.N. forces approached its border, the Americans were stunned. Mao was convinced that the United States, which occupied Japan and had now intervened in Korea, Taiwan, Indochina, and the Philippines, threatened China. Not only did the United States appear to be following in the footsteps of imperial Japan, it was challenging Mao's nationalist dream of restoring China's traditional dominance in Asia. In addition, Stalin had urged Mao on with promises of materiel and air support. Moreover, MacArthur had violated Truman's orders by sending American forces to the Chinese border at the Yalu River. China's entry into the war was a disaster and the Truman administration knew whom to blame. On *Battle Report—Washington*, Steelman announced, "The barbarous aggression of the Chinese hoards [*sic*] in Korea is not only an attack upon the forces of the United Nations—it is an attack upon civilization itself—it is an effort to destroy all the rights and privileges for which mankind has fought and bled since the dawn of time."[38]

In Korea, however, desperate American troops did not view the fight as a symbolic struggle between civilization and barbarism. Asked "What are you fighting for, son?" Corporal Frank Bifulk had an answer, "For my life, buddy. For my life." The Chinese, using human wave assaults, inflicted and suffered enormous losses. The U.S. Second Infantry Division was smashed, taking 80 percent casualties. Turkish and British troops tried and failed to relieve South Korean troops caught under heavy fire. Ten thousand men of the First Marine Division confronted 60,000 Chinese troops in ice, snow, and below zero temperatures. With losses of 700 dead and 3,500 wounded, they escaped from Chosin Reservoir to the coast where they could be evacuated. Private Paul Martin recalled that he couldn't hate their exhausted and frozen Chinese prisoners: "They were there for the same reasons we were there: orders."[39] By Christmas, battered U.N. forces had retreated more than three hundred miles back below the 38th parallel. In late December, MacArthur gave the command of the demoralized Eighth Army to the no-nonsense General Matthew Ridgway who began to turn things around.

The Truman administration faced the challenge of taking tough action to show the American public it was "doing something" in Korea and assuaging the fears of allies that this fight really was turning into World War III. Worried

Pfc. Preston McKnight, 19th Infantry Regiment, January 10, 1951, in the Yoju area.
(National Archives, 111-SC-356309)

that government leaders would respond to the crisis by hiding the truth and escalating the blustery rhetoric, Kennan urged candor and caution. He had good reason to advise calm. Truman had greatly heightened the level of alarm when he stated on and off camera that the United States would use every weapon it needed, including the atomic bomb. He also said that the military commander in the field had charge of the use of weapons. MacArthur already had told the Joint Chiefs that he favored using atomic bombs to create a radioactive barrier between China and Korea. The White House immediately organized a "damage-control party" to prepare a "clarifying statement," explaining that only the president could authorize the use of the atomic bomb and had not done so.[40]

Europeans, already alarmed over the possibility of another world war, responded with outrage. British Prime Minister Clement Attlee flew to Washington to protest. Truman told him that he hoped there would be no need to use the bomb and promised to keep the prime minister informed. Even so, international support for the United States diminished. Its allies began to view their role as one of restraining America's power rather than supporting it. As for Americans, the Gallup poll showed that if the United States went to war with China, 45 percent favored use of the bomb, 7 percent favored it "as a last resort," 38 percent opposed its use, and 10 percent had no opinion.[41] As historian Paul Boyer has shown, by 1950 American officials and the public continued to view the bomb with horror but showed growing acceptance of its necessity as a Cold War weapon. To mathematician Norbert Wiener of MIT, this acquiescence meant a high probability of atomic annihilation, "so long as we are dominated by a rigid propaganda which makes the destruction of Russia appear more important than our own survival."[42] Little wonder the world had the jitters.

Truman changed the war aim back to the original goal of containing communism from spreading to South Korea but, in doing so, focused on the threat to the United States. "If aggression is successful in Korea, we can expect it to spread through Asia and Europe to this hemisphere," he said on November 30. "We are fighting in Korea for our own national security and survival." He added that he hoped the Chinese people would not "continue to be forced or deceived into serving the ends of Russian colonial policy in Asia." Truman asked congressional leaders for a proclamation of national emergency. "There was only one thing to do," agreed Congressman Charles Eaton (R-NJ). "That was for us to strip off our peace clothes and to show our muscles to the world."[43] Truman received bipartisan support for expanding the military, increasing defense production, creating wage and price controls, and setting up an Office of Defense Mobilization.[44] On NBC's *Battle Report* in January 1951, Dean Rusk, assistant secretary of state for Far Eastern affairs, explained the goal of limited war: "We are in Korea because we are trying to prevent a world war."[45] A reunited Korea became a goal for the remote future, although the administration had not yet broken the news to Syngman Rhee or General MacArthur.

After months of tension between the military and the media in Korea, made worse by the chaotic retreat, war correspondents in December 1950 called for the establishment of a system of official censorship similar to the one used in World War II. Under his voluntary system, MacArthur already had tried to expel seventeen journalists for their unfavorable reporting. Now, in Korea or Tokyo, military officers would screen all reporting or photographs regarding operations. For correspondents, this system in which censors might block the publication of a particular story or photograph was preferable to the possibility of being expelled for ill-defined "unfavorable reporting."

Pictures of children often represented the Koreans to be rescued from communism in such government publications as the State Department's *The U. N. Guide to Korea*, which included this photograph of U.S. Air Force personnel evacuating Korean orphans from Seoul. The Defense Department entitled the photo "He Who Walks Alone" and released it in January 1951. (National Archives, 342-FH-4A 32649 + 78505 A.C.)

Official censorship continued to suppress criticism by declaring off limits any information that would undermine morale or embarrass the United States or its allies. The word "retreat," for example, was not allowed. The policies regarding photographs were similar to those in place at the end of World War II. Photographs of dead Americans and enemy troops appeared, but not the most gruesome.[46]

At home, the press was deeply pessimistic, noted the State Department. Commentators hoped that a settlement could be reached with the Chinese, so that the United States would not be "bled white" and rendered unable to build up its defense against the "real culprit," Russia. Although divided over whether to focus on the fight in Asia or in Europe, almost everyone favored increased mobilization for the United States. In January 1951 a Gallup poll showed growing public sentiment that the American entry into the Korean War was a mistake, up from 20 percent in August 1950 to 49 percent in

January 1951. Sixty-six percent favored pulling out the troops as soon as possible. In a February poll, 61 percent of the public thought the president should not be allowed to send troops overseas unless Congress approved first. Truman's approval rating dropped to 26 percent, a low from which it would never really recover.[47]

During the dark days of January 1951, Twentieth Century Fox released *Why Korea*. Made with the help of the Army and OWI veteran Ulric Bell, *Why Korea* followed in the tradition of Frank Capra's World War II *Why We Fight* films. Winner of the Oscar for best documentary, the 1951 film opened with scenes of casualties and asked why should American blood be spilled in Korea? Like Capra's *Prelude to War* (1942), *Why Korea* included a history lesson about invasions. Japan's invasion of Manchuria in 1931 was condemned by the League of Nations. Mussolini invaded Ethiopia, a country that "looked strange to us." A new addition to the invasion line-up not included in World War II films was Russia's 1939 invasion of Finland, illustrated with scenes of women and babies in bomb shelters. Maps showed the aggression of Nazi Germany and then Soviet Russia as a growing black mass. Thus, establishing the lesson of stopping aggression, the film turned to Korea. Scenes of the U.S. liberation of South Korea showed clapping and smiling Koreans. In South Korea, viewers were told misleadingly, the United States set up free democratic elections and the communists caused riots. Viewers saw Syngman Rhee, identified as the head of a legally elected government, shaking hands with General MacArthur. In Korea, narrator Joe King said, Americans defend a way of life and if they didn't fight there, they would have to fight here. From the White House, Steelman wrote to theater owners across the country asking them to show *Why Korea*. P. J. Wood of the Independent Theater Owners of Ohio responded that a lot of people disagreed with the administration's policy and would not appreciate having to pay to see this film. He wanted to know if the administration planned to make a film titled *Why We Should Get Out of Korea*.[48]

The doubts of an American marine named John Moullette provided the State Department with an opportunity to make the administration's case. Moullette had enlisted in 1944 at seventeen, served in the Pacific, and, as a reservist, was recalled to active duty in Korea. In January 1951, he wrote from Camp Pendleton in California to his father Clarence in New Jersey criticizing U.S. policy. Corporal Moullette's letter asked, "Don't you think that our 'foreign policy' is fouled up a bit?" He thought Red China had a right to voice its opinions in the United Nations. He favored a diplomatic solution, saying, "the needless waste of life in Korea, on both sides, is shameful.... Fighting won't settle anything." He questioned the president's authority to go to war, saying that he thought only Congress could declare war: "Why doesn't Congress either declare war against Red China or stop Truman from sending American troops throughout the world? Why should we take the brunt of it all?" He told his father that the morale of the troops was low because they felt the American people weren't behind them. "These men aren't afraid to fight, it's just that they have no cause to fight," he explained. "If ordered to, we will but only because of the obligation we have to each other." After the last war, Moullette believed that everyone, especially young men like himself, should demand peace. He wrote, "I believe that the people of our level want only peace but that the leaders (including Truman) are afraid to admit they are wrong and are ashamed to admit it for fear they will lose face." He signed off, "Love, Johnnie...P.S. I may be a rebel but these are my own thoughts and convictions."[49]

Clarence Moullette forwarded his son's letter along with his own to the secretary of state. Acheson directed his reply to the father who supported administration policies. Writing father to father about the difficulty for boys "brought up in the fundamental decency and rightness of American life," Acheson noted that just when they become men, they faced danger because of "some distant and shadowy figures in the Kremlin, controlling millions of people far from them, are setting out to make impossible such lives as they had every right and hope to have." Their hopes "for peace, and for a Good Life for all" have been disappointed. Acheson defined the problem as both ancient and new. Like our ancestors, he explained, some men must drill and keep watch while others till the fields. "Unless we are strong enough—we and the other free nations—to prevent the Soviet rulers from extending their control over the entire world," the Secretary stated, "then we shall never have the chance to help build the kind of a world we all want." Therefore the United States must stand firm against aggression in Korea or else start down the road to a third world war. Acheson assured Clarence Moullette that it was good that his son should question U.S. actions, as long as he remained steadfast in his faith of "the validity and the reality of the ideals on which this country was founded."[50]

The State Department released the letters to favorable front-page stories across the country. "Acheson Tells Bitter Marine to Have Faith in U.S. Ideals," Walter H. Waggoner reported in the *New York Times*, describing John Moullette as "a disturbed and questioning young Marine Corps corporal." Headlines read "Why Do I Have to Fight or Die in Korea, Corporal Asks;

According to the Defense Department's Office of Public Information, this 1950 poster showed that "we, as a people, highly cherish all of the things that we have in the American way of life, and that we intend to defend these rights even if we must fight to do so." Stanley Dersh, artist. (National Archives, Lot 18782 C-6093)

Acheson Points at Kremlin" in the *Waterloo Daily Courier* of Waterloo, Iowa, and "Why We Fight in Korea: 'Freedom vs. Tyranny' Acheson Tells Johnnie" in the *East Liverpool Review* of East Liverpool, Ohio. Tracked down by reporters, Corporal Moullette said that Acheson had convinced him that the United States had to fight in Korea with the argument that "maybe we could have avoided World War II if we had gone into Ethiopia." Months later, John told a reporter that he found first-hand experience of fighting communists more persuasive than Acheson's letter. Yet, the responses to Acheson's letter revealed that the secretary had not convinced everyone. Acheson and Clarence Moullette met in Washington to review 148 letters from members of the public to find that more than half agreed with John.[51] After all, Acheson's reply had not addressed John's specific criticisms of U.S. policy. It instead had called for young people to have faith in American ideals and, by extension, administration policies. As the war settled into a stalemate, people on the home front asked, why are we fighting in Korea, who is the real enemy, and what is the best way to fight communism? Disagreement over the answers to these questions broke out at the highest levels.

MacArthur and the Debate on Korea

THE OUTCRY OVER TRUMAN'S DECISION to fire General MacArthur in April 1951 led to a public debate over U.S. policy. By March, Ridgway's determined prosecution of Operation Killer had pushed communist forces back near the 38th parallel. American policymakers considered the possibility of negotiations with China in order to end the fighting. MacArthur, who disagreed with the reversal on rollback, had sabotaged Truman's plan to call for a ceasefire by demanding that the Chinese communists surrender immediately. He wanted to fight and win the Cold War in Asia. He called for an air attack, naval blockade, and land assault on the People's Republic of China using U.N. and Nationalist Chinese forces. He spoke about using atomic weapons, as had Truman earlier. And against orders, he expressed his views freely and repeatedly. He accused the administration of appeasement in a letter to Congressman Joe Martin (R-MA), which was read before the House of Representatives on April 5. The Joint Chiefs of Staff and American allies worried that the U.N. commander in Korea might provoke another world war.

On April 11, Truman relieved MacArthur on grounds of insubordination. The firing of the distinguished war hero prompted Senate hearings, partisan posturing, flags lowered in protest, and a deluge of press coverage. The general returned home to tickertape parades and declared, "There is no substitute for victory" before a televised joint session of Congress where he was welcomed with a standing ovation. MacArthur's speeches pronounced the Cold War a life or death struggle, just as Truman had for years. Television coverage of MacArthur's return helped to reinforce his heroic image. Two sociologists interviewed parade watchers in Chicago and found opinion on the streets to be divided for and against the general. The way the TV cameras framed the parade scene and the voice-over commentary gave viewers the impression of total adulation, however.[52]

Even though the recall of MacArthur was a crisis for Truman, it ultimately gave his administration the chance to persuade opinion leaders of the rightness of its policy. Well aware that it was losing the public relations battle over Korea, the administration launched its own offensive. The message: Truman stood for peace; MacArthur stood for war. Newsreel coverage illustrated this message. Film clips showed Truman being sworn in as president, reminding viewers of their civilian-led government. MacArthur, in contrast, was shown in the famous footage of his return to the Philippines in 1944. As the general waded ashore, the narrator stated that the nation owed him a debt of gratitude. Viewers might have unfavorably contrasted the unprepossessing president with the charismatic commander, but they could not help associating MacArthur with war.[53] The administration would now discuss Korea as a case of standing firm, as though rollback had never been attempted.

For officials dealing with the press and public, the State Department produced Information Policy Guidance or what would now be called "talking points." Regarding Korea, it asserted, spokesmen had two immediate major tasks. The first was "to restore perspective." For purposes of news management, "to restore perspective" meant to regain control over defining the issue. Korea must be seen as only one problem in the "collective global effort to ensure world security." The administration would link Korea to communist-inspired crises elsewhere in Indochina, Iran, Burma, Germany, Austria, Greece, and Azerbaijan. Such a global perspective would diminish Korea's importance. In addition, it presented an array of threats intended to raise fear and confirm the need for allies. Finally, it had the potential to overwhelm the public with a list of places about which they knew little. The implicit message was "trust the experts" to know what they are doing. As for the second task—"to underscore simply and clearly US and UN objectives in Korea"—the Guidance offered no guidance on what these objectives were. It had only an image of confidence to be projected. It didn't want U.S. policy in Korea to be seen as an "expedient half-measure," or a "compromise between appeasement or general war," but as a "bold collective step."[54]

The administration thought that it was slowly winning the public opinion battle against MacArthur among opinion leaders, if not among the general public. In Congress, the split for and against MacArthur was mainly partisan, with presidential hopeful Senator Robert Taft (R-OH) taking the lead in the pro-MacArthur camp. The press and radio, officials noted, supported the president in his decision to dismiss MacArthur, because many editors and commentators were concerned that the general's recommendations might lead to war with the Soviet Union and the loss of America's U.N. allies. In contrast, polls indicated that 62 percent of the public disapproved of the president's dismissal of MacArthur and 54 percent favored launching an all out fight to end the Korean War. Although opinion leaders in the media supported the limited war, they looked to the administration for a redefinition of aims in the conflict and an exercise of more positive leadership. The president, many charged, had not yet provided a "clear and logical" alternative to MacArthur's "forthright" position. Columnist James Reston summed up the administration's dilemma: it had "always been clearer about the disadvantages of an unlimited war in the Far East than about the advantages of the present limited war."[55] Truman's aide George Elsey warned that the White House could not "afford to slack off in our constant reiteration that MacArthur stood for war and the President stands for peace" because "this and this alone will sink in with the general public."[56]

In May 1951, the Senate Hearings on Korea addressed the question of who was the enemy. Top military and civilian leaders gave testimony. "Communism throughout the world was our main enemy," proclaimed MacArthur. Senator J. William Fulbright (D-AR) disagreed, saying he thought the enemy was imperialist Russia. "It seemed to me, you do not fight communism with a gun," he elaborated. "It is sort of like sin, we are all against sin; you don't fight sin with anything tangible. Communism is an idea, but what really bothers us is when people start to shoot." MacArthur answered, "I think you do fight sin with very practical weapons, and I think we are fighting communism with very practical weapons." About this exchange, the editors of the *Washington Post* observed that the designation of communism as the enemy implied that the United States intended to wipe it out by force. "Such a crusade would cost millions of lives and inestimable treasure," warned the editors, "and in the end would probably stimulate communism instead of suppressing it."[57] At the hearings, General Bradley scored the clearest rebuttal of MacArthur's position that failure to fight China meant appeasement. To take on China, declared Bradley, would "involve us in the wrong war, at the wrong place, at the wrong time and with the wrong enemy."[58] In their testimonies, Secretary of Defense George Marshall and Secretary Acheson emphasized the global nature of the Cold War, especially the Soviet threat to Europe. The U.S. war aim in Korea, stated Acheson, was to end aggression.[59]

For close observers, the Senate hearings revealed a significant problem for U.S. policy in Korea. None of the military leaders knew of any military solution that would work. "We must expect only to go on and on with a wretched war that the generals have admitted they cannot end," concluded prominent columnist Walter Lippmann.[60] At the crux of the matter, wrote *New York Times* columnist Anne O'Hare McCormick, was the foreign policy of the United States. Perhaps the United States should concentrate more on using its political rather than its military power in this world struggle, she suggested, even though an international system of collective security meant having allies and having allies meant having policies other nations would support.[61] The administration's projection of the world divided in two had not required building much support at home for the give and take of international cooperation. It had presumed that noncommunist nations would follow the United States wherever it led.

Truman and MacArthur agreed on the dominance of the United States in the Pacific; they disagreed over how to maintain it. As opposed to MacArthur's big war, Truman favored a limited war, working with allies in the United Nations, negotiating with the enemy, and building up U.S. forces throughout the world in the Cold War stand-off. MacArthur's popularity faded the more he spoke his mind. Much of the debate seemed mired in domestic politics and the Red Scare. Republicans seeking the White House in 1952 castigated the Democratic administration. The right wing of the party carried on MacArthur's call for victory in Asia, meaning war against China. Senator Joseph McCarthy (R-WI) blamed Korea on a communist conspiracy within the U.S. government. He and other communist hunters in Congress investigated the State Department by targeting "Red Dean" Acheson and the Asian specialists who were held responsible for "losing" China. Senator Patrick McCarran (D-NV) sponsored the Internal Security Act, which required Americans who were communists and others deemed "subversives" to register with the Attorney General and also authorized the detention of suspected spies. Truman pronounced the legislation a danger to civil liberties and vetoed it, but Congress overrode the veto. Journalist I. F. Stone published a leftist critique of the Korean policy, but most of the attacks came from the right. At the conclusion of seven weeks of Senate hearings, Americans like one Boston resident were left thinking, "The American people know just as little about how we get out of Korea, and what the end of it all is going to be, as they did a month and a half ago."[62]

Peace Talks

CALLING EACH OTHER BARBARIC AND IMPERIALIST, the belligerents in Korea sat down to peace talks in July 1951 with deep distrust, both sides determined to "win" the negotiations. The Truman administration tried to be both tough and conciliatory. Its vacillating policies created difficulties for the U.N. negotiating team in Korea, led by General Ridgway who had replaced General MacArthur in Tokyo. "The delegation and indeed General Ridgway never knew when a new directive would emanate from Washington," recalled Admiral C. Turner Joy, one of the negotiators. "It seemed to us that the United States Government did not know exactly what its political objectives in Korea were or should be."[63]

To many involved, Korea seemed less important than larger geopolitical issues. Truman concentrated on Moscow. The Chinese worried about Japan, which had enjoyed an economic resurgence as the U.S. base of operations. Europeans were wary of U.S. plans to rearm West Germany, especially France, whose military was bogged down in Indochina. The State Department's information policy guidance did not help explain Korea. In bureaucratic babble, it called upon officials to "utilize opportunity to recall consistent policy of US and other members of UN for honorable peaceful settlement in Korea, repeatedly expressed in public utterances by their leaders and in numerous concrete UN efforts." The press preferred to enliven its coverage of the peace talks by describing the communists as tricky, clumsy, devious, and maddening. Americans, by contrast, were described as firm, patient, and ready. Such characterization served the administration's desired image of the negotiations, if not the reality.[64] After displays of intransigence on both sides, it took the negotiators from July 1951 to May 1952 to agree that a demilitarized zone would follow existing battle lines and to hold a conference to discuss reunification.

Then the talks deadlocked over the issue of prisoners of war. The Truman administration used "the POW issue to instill a new moral purpose into the war effort," according to historian Steven Casey.[65] The Geneva Convention of 1949 called for the return of all POWs. In violation of the convention, the U.S. government declared its position to be a humanitarian effort to protect the prisoners it held from having to return to the communist world. Most of the POWs the administration portrayed as longing to stay in the Free World were actually people who simply wanted to go home. South Koreans who had chosen or been forced to fight for the North wanted to stay in the South. Nationalist Chinese who had been left behind in China after the Civil War wanted to go to Taiwan. Some of the Chinese POWS at U.N. camps who actually wanted to return to China were terrorized into changing their minds. The peace talks broke down when the United Nations announced that only 70,000 out of the 116,000 POWs who might be repatriated wished to be. In addition, communists accused the United Nations, primarily the United States, of using germ warfare in Korea, pointing to the high rate of typhoid, smallpox, and some unknown disease afflicting Chinese and North Korean troops. Historians have argued that given the available evidence, the claims of biological warfare remain inconclusive. At the time, however, the charges raised suspicions in Europe and the Middle East about America's moral authority.[66]

Meanwhile, U.S. leaders deflected attention from what was actually happening in South Korea because it conflicted with the portrayal of their ally as a would-be democracy. As the peace talks deadlocked, the war-ravaged country was coming apart. One in nine people had been killed. Millions were wounded and homeless. Syngman Rhee ordered mass executions of South Korean guerrilla forces who opposed his regime. Rhee, realizing that the National Assembly would not reelect him as president, declared martial law around Pusan and arrested his opponents. When the United States objected to Rhee's actions, the South Korean leader organized mass anti-American demonstrations. Washington considered a coup to remove Rhee from power. Before it took action, Rhee successfully compelled a change in the constitution that would allow popular elections, which he won overwhelmingly. Firmly in control, Rhee continued to demand unification of Korea. Correspondents, for the most part, did not report on Rhee's dictatorial abuses and lack of cooperation with U.S. policy. If they did, American officials warned, they would look procommunist.[67]

Throughout the two years of peace talks, the casualty rate in the war nearly doubled. Both sides dug in, fortified their lines, and brought in reinforcements. The Americans dominated the air, sea, and roads; the enemy held the hills. The U.N. Command carried out massive bombing raids on the north, which failed to compel the communists to accept peace terms. The air war escalated as the Chinese deployed Soviet MiG-15s and developed more effective anti-aircraft weapons. Little territory was gained, as the fighting on the ground consisted of ambushes, patrol engagements, and battles for hills. "I was attacked by two hordes and killed both of them," was a cynical joke told by American troops.[68]

With the support of the military, Hollywood produced Korean War films that illustrated official messages. "War films both reinforced and helped to create a martial spirit in the American people," believed Clayton Fritchey, Director of the Office of Public Information at the Defense Department. The military extended cooperation on approximately thirty full-length films every year. At the Pentagon, "cooperation" on films made for movie theaters or television included the review and approval of the script, the changing of scenes that violated policy, the use of equipment and personnel, and the assignment of technical advisors. The final product, according to the Defense Department, must be "accurate and authentic," while at the same time "be in the best interests of National defense and the Public good."[69]

Most war films made from 1950 to 1953 continued to be about World War II; those set in Korea frequently tacked on a United Nations theme to the conventional combat story. In RKO's *One Minute to Zero* (1952), Robert Mitchum, playing an American officer, pursues a romance with U.N. worker Ann Blyth. She learns to accept that Mitchum's tough tactics, which include shooting into crowds of refugees, are necessary because communists use civilians as human shields. Acknowledging the arrival of Australian forces, Mitchum says approvingly, "Wouldn't you know they'd be the first to help."[70] Also made with the assistance of the Defense Department, Twentieth Century Fox's *The Glory Brigade* (1953) told the story of a proud Greek American officer, played by Victor Mature, whose outfit teamed up with Greek troops who liked to play music and dance the night away before a reconnaissance mission. After overcoming their distrust, the Americans and the Greeks learn to respect each other and fight the reds together.[71]

Much more ambiguous was Sam Fuller's 1951 film *The Steel Helmet*, dedicated to the U.S. Infantry, but made without assistance from the Defense Department. In the story, a multiracial platoon adopts a South Korean boy whose family had been killed by communists. The boy tells the Americans, "I'm Korean, not gook." The sergeant explains how to tell the difference: "He's a South Korean when he's running with you and he's a North Korean when he's running after you." A captured North Korean taunts "Doc," the African

American medic, by pointing out that at home Doc has to sit at the back of the bus. Doc answers that maybe in another fifty years he'll be able to sit in the middle. The same prisoner reminds Sergeant Tanaka, called Buddha-head by one of his fellow Americans, that the United States put Japanese Americans in camps in the last war. Tanaka proudly answers that he fought in the Japanese American 442nd Combat Division, which was awarded more than 3,000 purple hearts. But they called you "a dirty Jap rat," insists the North Korean. Tanaka replies, "So they push us around at home—that's our business." In Cold War films, historian Lary May observed, "more often than not, good minorities mobilized to fight against bad minority characters."[72] Fuller, a World War II veteran who didn't flinch from pointing out the shortcomings of democracy on the home front, honored the soldiers facing a "million reds out there." The last title of *Steel Helmet* reads, "There is no end to the story."[73]

In the last year of the war, there were signs that television coverage could be critical of the conflict. For example, the CBS public affairs program *See It Now*, hosted by Murrow, broadcast a 1952 special, "Christmas in Korea." The program showed the "no-man's-land" between forces fighting for a hilltop, nurses at the 8055 Mobile Army Surgical Hospital (MASH), destroyed villages, the devastated capital of Seoul, which by that time had been lost, retaken, lost, and retaken, and troops at Christmas services held in the field. Soldiers sent home holiday greetings along with their views that the war was a bunch of nonsense. Although *See It Now* earned critical praise for its investigations of school segregation in Louisiana, poverty, and Senator McCarthy's pursuit of communists, it was not as popular as Murrow's celebrity show *Person to Person*, on which he interviewed Senator John Kennedy with his shy bride and married movie stars Humphrey Bogart and Lauren Bacall.[74]

The movie and television industry was under pressure to promote Cold War virtues while still making money. With funding from a wealthy lobbyist for Nationalist China, three former FBI agents published the book *Red Channels: The Report of Communist Influence in Radio and Television*. It named suspected "subversives." The lists included artists, entertainers, and reporters who had been communists, associated with communists, belonged to liberal organizations, or supported civil rights. Many of those named were eventually blacklisted by the industry, but not everyone. For instance, Lucille Ball, the most popular comedienne on television, briefly had joined the Communist Party in 1936, but she was too valuable to subject to the blacklist. The networks defended their use of blacklists as necessary to ensure profits, claiming that they still championed free speech. Contributing to television's promotion of consumer culture, presidential aide Steelman used *Battle Report—Washington* to condemn communism. "If we have any worldly possessions at all—a television set—an automobile—or even one savings bond, we are considered 'enemies of the people' and tools of Wall Street," he said. "Every one of us would be marked—to be robbed, enslaved, or slaughtered if the day ever came when the Soviet hoards [*sic*] overran our country. With God's help that will never happen." In Cold War popular culture, films about the "good war," Biblical epics, and Westerns along with consumer products and lovely wives lined up against subversives and communist hordes.[75]

The nomination of General Dwight Eisenhower as the Republican candidate for president in 1952 also recalled the relative clarity of World War II. Eisenhower, whose jobs since being the Supreme Commander of the Allied Forces in Europe had included commanding NATO, represented the internationalist wing of the Republican establishment. To appeal to voters' frustration with the war, Eisenhower promised to go and see it for himself. As president-elect, he went to Korea in December. His trip did not provide him with any answers. Once in office, he ordered a heavy bombing campaign against North Korea, but it did not seem to affect the stalled negotiations. Eisenhower and John Foster Dulles, his secretary of state, hinted about using the atomic bomb. Stalin's death in March 1953 raised hopes that diplomacy might have a better chance. The Chinese agreed to allow the POWs who refused repatriation to go to neutral states for further negotiation over their status. The last big roadblock was Syngman Rhee, who continued to insist on a united Korea and organized demonstrations against any armistice that divided the country. The Americans had to promise him a mutual security pact, a big military buildup, and economic aid. By standing up to the Americans, Rhee enhanced his prestige at home. In the last weeks of the war, a communist offensive resulted in about one thousand American casualties a week. The armistice was signed on July 27, 1953.[76]

"Die for a tie" was the bitter slogan in Korea for a war that never seemed limited to U.S. forces or the Koreans. Two million Americans served, 35,000 died, and 6000 remained missing in action. Allied deaths, mostly South Korean, reached 61,000. The North Koreans and the Chinese lost 1.5 to 2 million soldiers. The U.N. air force, over 90 percent American, dropped 635,000 tons of bombs and 32,557 tons of napalm on Korea. Civilian deaths were estimated at two million. Millions more were refugees.[77] Talks on reunification extended over months and failed. In the years that followed, the United States delivered billions of dollars worth of aid to South Korea, which

Keyes Beech of the *Chicago Daily News* and his wife, Linda Beech of the *Honolulu Advertiser*, cover the armistice negotiations at Kaesong. (National Archives, III-SC-376352)

developed a thriving economy. Washington backed authoritarian governments against increasingly anti-American opposition until 1987, when students and the middle class took to the streets to agitate successfully for democratic reforms. North Koreans, who remained under a totalitarian regime, suffered famines and severe repression. To this day, U.S. troops stand guard along the demilitarized zone.

The Forgotten War

THE KOREAN WAR BECAME KNOWN as the "forgotten war." It failed to live up to the official narrative, which projected the triumph of the Free World over savage communists. The Truman administration had only a mixed success in adjusting its propaganda messages to keep up with its changing war aims. It first presented a complicated civil war as a simplistic fight between good and evil Asians. When the administration decided to pursue rollback by pushing communist forces out of Korea, it disastrously misread China. Then the administration sought to "restore perspective" by returning to the aim of containment as the war settled into a stalemate. As opposed to Truman's shifting policy, MacArthur advocated all-out victory against communism in Asia. But Presidents Truman and Eisenhower did not want Korea to turn into World War III, so they negotiated an end to the fighting. Officials encouraged the "forgetting" of Korea by effectively directing attention to the global Cold War. The public, however dissatisfied, complied.

For all of its unpopularity, the Korean War had played a key role in stimulating support for the militarization of the Cold War. Before North Korea invaded South Korea in June 1950, the U.S. government already had decided on a massive military buildup. The Korean War proved a useful justification. On television in October 1951, Dean Acheson explained the buildup to ordinary Americans. Sheriff Glenn Jones of Clark County, Nevada, asked, "Secretary Acheson, when two outfits start packing guns, there is bound to be some shooting. Isn't that going to be the case with our arming of the Western world?" Acheson replied, "Well, Sheriff, what would happen in your county if the gangsters had the guns and you didn't.... These people on the other side are not only packing guns—they're shooting. That's what Korea is all about. And if Matt Ridgway and his boys didn't have something to shoot back with, we'd be in a...well, in whatever kind of a fix you call it in Clark County."[78] Clearly, Acheson, the embodiment of the eastern establishment, was not good at cowboy talk. But he cited Korea as evidence that the United States and its allies must rely on military power in its confrontation with the "other side." By 1955, the United States had developed the hydrogen bomb and set up 450 military bases in thirty-six countries around the world.

The administration designed a Cold War formula for news management by interpreting events to fit the "Free World vs. communist world" framework. Television news delivered the official position, serving more often as a vehicle of government information than as an independent agent in the tradition of a free press. As Lippmann observed, the propagandist required a monopoly on publicity. He pointed out that one dissenting voice—a general, a Congressman, or a Cabinet official—"can destroy the credibility of the official case."[79] Well aware of what happens when a general speaks out, the administration called for unity among opinion leaders. The result was largely supportive coverage of the Cold War. Dissenters risked being called "soft" on communism. More often than not, critics accused the administration of not being tough enough. Despite the construction of a Cold War consensus, the uncertainty about U.S. policies in Korea and increasing distrust of official information did hint at the possibility of a more adversarial relationship between the military and the press, which eventually developed during the Vietnam War.

The wartime relationship between the government and citizens had changed. Cold War policies called for constant mobilization but not the kind of total war that called on civilians to make sacrifices or an effort to follow closely the government's foreign policy. The administration preferred unquestioning support from a public that was neither complacent nor hysterical. To maintain that support, leaders sought to display conviction in their policies and show progress being made. And the public should, as Acheson had requested of John Moullette, have faith. As the United States assumed global leadership, government leaders did not want their hands tied by activist public opinion, especially if they needed to act quickly. They decided to lead by manipulation, first spreading fear and then projecting strength, justifying exaggeration of foreign threats as being in the public's best interests.

The oversimplified Cold War narrative of freedom versus communism had far-reaching consequences. It limited rather than fostered understanding of a sophisticated global policy that recognized limits on U.S. power, great as it was. The containment strategy relied on the calculated use of economic dominance, political influence, and military strength to check communist aggression and support allies. The idea behind the policy, observed political scientist Ian Shapiro, was "to refuse to be bullied, while at the same time declining to become a bully."[80] But to sell such a multifaceted policy to the American people, the Truman administration deliberately inflated the Soviet threat. Then it distorted its portrayal of the Korean War to fit the narrative. In doing so it presented a worldview that did not require a close investigation of civil wars or nationalist movements. Nor did it encourage an honest assessment of the authoritarian governments supported by U.S. policies. It assumed that allies would follow the U.S. lead and underestimated enemies such as the North Koreans and Chinese. The Cold War narrative that began as propaganda to promote policy ended up shaping policy. President Eisenhower turned Acheson's "rotten apples in a barrel" analogy into the Domino Theory when he asserted that if one country falls to communism, so will the next and the next. He and his successors would cite the Domino Theory to justify U.S. involvement in Vietnam.

As the "Forgotten War" faded from the Cold War narrative, Americans accepted the role of leader of the Free World, but differed over how to fulfill it. For some, the buildup of military power, U.S. intervention in global trouble spots, and the crackdown on civil liberties at home were all justified by fear of communism. Reformers argued that the United States should set an example for the rest of the world by living up to its ideals. That meant Americans should fix their own problems such as the persistence of poverty and racial segregation. All agreed on projecting the American way of life. The goal, as President Truman had explained, was to make everyone "richer and happier." While Americans enjoyed their affluence, however, they also practiced civil defense drills, learning to "duck and cover" in case of nuclear attack. President Eisenhower spoke of the importance of Christian faith and spiritual strength as "our matchless armor in our world-wide struggle against the forces of godless tyranny and oppression."[81] The slogan "better dead than red" said it all. Policymakers had made true their propaganda scare campaign.

5

Why Vietnam

More Questions Than Answers

If freedom is to survive in any American hometown it must be preserved in such places as South Viet Nam.

President Lyndon B. Johnson, 1965

War…what is it good for?

Edwin Starr, 1970

FROM THE BEGINNING, government leaders found it hard to explain to the American people why U.S. troops fought in Vietnam. As historian Marilyn Young observed, America's war in Southeast Asia was "war as performance."[1] U.S. leaders feared that failure to prevent Vietnam from going communist would damage America's image of strength considered to be vital in the stand-off with the Soviet Union. Policymakers relied on the Cold War official narrative to justify U.S. involvement. Their purpose, they said, was to contain the spread of communism from North Vietnam to U.S.-backed South Vietnam. As in the Korean War, "good Asians" fought with Americans against "bad Asians," who followed the doctrines of Moscow and Beijing. As U.S. policymakers knew, the narrative ignored the complicating reality that Vietnamese communists were also nationalists who sought to reunite their divided country and liberate it from foreign rule. But the Americans believed that an impressive demonstration of U.S. military strength and economic power would convince the enemy to quit. To quote U.S. Army officer John Paul Vann, U.S. leaders combined "massive self-delusion" with "bright shining lies."[2] In the end, the conflict would cost the lives of millions of Vietnamese civilians, between 500,000 to a million North Vietnamese troops, 350,000 South Vietnamese troops, and more than 58,000 Americans.

To the consternation of those officials charged with promoting the Vietnam War, the facts of the conflict did not fit the typical wartime narrative. There had been "no dramatic Pearl Harbor or *Lusitania* to cast us, willy nilly, in the public role of a victim of aggression," pointed out White House staffer Peter R. Rosenblatt. "You can't just 'kill Japs' in a war like this one," observed John Chancellor, former NBC broadcaster and, from 1965 to 1967, the head of Voice of America, the U.S. international radio service. "Our object is not so much to destroy an enemy as to win a people," summed up Chester Cooper of the National Security Council. Following the tradition set by McKinley, U.S. presidents from Truman through Nixon appealed to updated versions of the Christian mission and the "white man's burden" to justify U.S. policy. The Americans would bring the benefits of western civilization—democratic reforms and economic development—to the Vietnamese in order to win their "hearts and minds" while protecting them from communism. The contrast between these professed goals and the destruction of Vietnamese villages by American firepower was obvious to officials, however. Just months after U.S. ground forces went into combat, Chancellor concluded that this war seemed to be a "non-packageable commodity."³

To sell the unsellable, officials carried out what Walt W. Rostow at the State Department called in 1964 a "low-key campaign of public information" designed to generate enough home front support without mobilizing the population.⁴ Coordinated from the White House, the campaign, as in the Korean War, did not pursue a "strategy of truth" but sought to maintain credibility with the public. To manage the news, each administration concentrated on what it considered to be the most influential sources: the television networks, the *New York Times*, the *Washington Post, Time*, and *Newsweek. The New York Times*, considered to be the paper of record, had more foreign correspondents than any network or other daily newspaper. *Life* magazine still held sway as the foremost visual record but had difficulty competing with TV by the end of the 1960s. The newsmagazines—*Time, Newsweek*, and *U.S. News and World Report*—grew in importance and circulation, providing their readers with a weekly summary of domestic and foreign events. For the most part, Hollywood avoided Vietnam during the 1960s, preferring instead to produce epic movies about World War II. Twentieth Century Fox's blockbuster *The Sound of Music* (1965), a romantic musical about an Austrian family that escapes from the Nazis, made more money than the previous record-holder, *Gone with the Wind*.⁵

As radio had in World War II, television brought the war into the living rooms of America. In the 1960s, more than 90 percent of American homes had a television, which was watched an estimated average of six hours a day. Almost everyone watched in black and white; not until 1972 did more than half of American homes have a color television set. The three networks, CBS, NBC, and ABC, dominated television programming by producing shows carried by local affiliate stations. TV's primary purpose continued to be advertising products by attracting viewers with sports, dramas, and situation comedies, including *The Beverly Hillbillies*, the top-rated show from 1962 to 1964. Television also had proved to be the "national unifier" in time of crisis. For instance, it cancelled entertainment programs to provide four days of commercial-free coverage of President John F. Kennedy's funeral in 1963. News programs initially lost money for the networks but gained in profits and prestige over the decade. In part to prove to critics that television programming was not a wasteland, CBS and NBC increased their nightly news show from fifteen to thirty minutes in 1963. ABC followed in 1967. By the end of the decade, more than half of the population depended on television as their chief source of news.[6]

For many reasons, television's supportive or, at times, ambiguous coverage of the war in Vietnam tended to disguise the flaws in the administration's war aims. Television news accepted and validated the Cold War framework. In their reliance on government sources, the networks frequently allowed official Washington to deliver its message that the war in Vietnam was difficult and complicated for the average viewer to understand, but that the government's policy was thoughtful, measured, and effective. Less than 5 percent of television reports from Vietnam between August 1965 and August 1970 contained graphic violence. What tended to stand out in short reports filled with statistics and strange place names were interviews with appealing young Americans in uniform. Television news coverage, while ostensibly providing objective information, was communicating emotional messages of patriotism, trust, and reassurance. Not until events in Vietnam challenged the professed war aims did television coverage begin to reflect the public's growing doubts about the war. In March 1968, President Lyndon Johnson's former National Security Advisor, McGeorge Bundy, wrote to the president to say he thought it a miracle "that our people have stayed with the war as long as they have."[7]

The simplistic Cold War narrative, once constructed to build consensus for the containment of Soviet communism, shaped U.S. policy in Vietnam. Presidents Eisenhower and Kennedy cited the Domino Theory to justify

American involvement or else lose another Asian country to communism. The Johnson administration portrayed the decision to escalate the war as an exercise of U.S. leadership and military superiority. President Richard Nixon announced "peace with honor" as he withdrew U.S. forces and attacked the antiwar movement. Throughout, each administration preferred to direct public attention to World War II analogies, a Cold War worldview, and divisions on the home front, rather than Vietnam itself. The flawed policy and misleading propaganda left many questions unanswered. In the last years of the war, when General Douglas Kinnard, himself a veteran of two tours in Vietnam, surveyed 173 army generals who served in Vietnam as combat commanders, he found a shocking result. Almost 70 percent of the two-thirds who responded said they did not understand the war's overall objectives. "Why were we doing this?" they wondered.[8]

Vietnam as Domino

THE FUNDAMENTAL MISTAKE made by American policymakers was to define Vietnam as primarily a Cold War crisis. In the last years of World War II, President Franklin Roosevelt concluded that European imperialism in Asia was at an end. He criticized France's long rule over Indochina for leaving the people there worse off. At the same time, he did not believe that the Vietnamese were ready to govern themselves. He thought that they, like the Filipinos, needed to be educated. Shortly before he died, FDR stated that if France committed itself to preparing the people of Indochina for independence it should retain control over the colony. The Vietnamese members of the League for the Independence of Vietnam, or the Vietminh, would have disagreed with FDR's assessment had they been asked. Organized in 1941 when French colonial officials collaborated with the Japanese, the Vietminh recruited followers to resist both the French and the Japanese. It promised land reform and independence.[9]

In the mind of Vietminh leader Ho Chi Minh, the struggle of the Vietnamese against capitalist exploitation and the overthrow of imperial rule was the same revolution. After Ho had without success sought support for Vietnamese self-determination at the Versailles Peace Conference in 1919, he worked for the Comintern (Communist International) in the Soviet Union and China where he had a reputation for developing his own version of communism and nationalism. Back in Vietnam during World War II, he served as an agent of the U.S. Office of Strategic Services (OSS), the forerunner of the

Central Intelligence Agency (CIA), by helping to rescue downed American pilots. When Japan surrendered in August 1945, Ho declared Vietnam's independence in Hanoi before half a million people by quoting from the American Declaration of Independence. Then he appealed to the United States for aid. France, seeking to regain its great power status damaged by the 1940 surrender to Germany, wanted to retain its empire. It rejected Ho's attempts to negotiate independence and war broke out in 1946.

Ho was right when he assumed that U.S. officials felt uneasy about backing imperial France. Even though members of the Truman administration privately criticized France's colonial war, they decided that their priority was European recovery. A rebuilt France was more important to the West in its stand against Soviet communism than Vietnamese self-determination. The State Department asked U.S. officials in Vietnam more than once to report on "how communist" Ho Chi Minh was. The Americans who knew Vietnam best repeatedly replied that Ho was a communist, but, first and foremost, he was a nationalist dedicated to Vietnam's independence and the most respected leader in the country. There was no sign of Soviet presence, they asserted. Nevertheless Truman's secretary of state Dean Acheson decided to proclaim Ho an "outright Commie."[10] In that way, he could apply the acceptable Cold War justification for U.S. involvement. By the end of the Korean War in 1953, the United States funded up to 80 percent of France's war in Vietnam.

Vietnam and the other noncommunist nations of Asia stood like a row of dominoes, explained Truman's successor, President Dwight Eisenhower, in 1954; if one fell to communism, the rest would topple. The president linked the Domino Theory to American interests at stake. He pointed to the need to protect access to essential raw materials such as tin and tungsten as well as strategic military bases. Moreover, Eisenhower worried that if much more of the Asian mainland went communist, Japan would be compelled to trade with anti-capitalist enemies and, as a result, might slide over to the other side. Eisenhower did not want American troops in another land war in Asia, however. He refused to send manpower or use the atomic bomb to aid the French as they lost their fight in 1954. At the peace talks held in Geneva, Switzerland, the French and Vietnamese agreed to a temporary division of Vietnam at the 17th parallel. Ho Chi Minh's forces would withdraw to the north and pro-French forces would stay in the south. All agreed that the country would be reunited by nationwide elections in 1956, which Ho Chi Minh was certain he would win. So was the United States, which refused to back the agreement. The U.S. government declared that it would not interfere with the Geneva Accords but covertly moved to thwart the planned election. If the Vietnamese people voted for communists, American leaders believed, they weren't ready for self-determination.[11]

Pursuing a policy called nation-building, the United States decided to back an anticommunist regime in South Vietnam. As leader, it supported Vietnamese nationalist Ngo Dinh Diem, a dedicated anticommunist and devout Roman Catholic. The United States supplied millions of dollars in aid and hundreds of advisors to the Diem government, which had little support in the capital city of Saigon or in the countryside. The Navy and the CIA organized "Passage to Freedom" to the South for hundreds of thousands of Catholic refugees from the North who were expected to support the Diem government. From Saigon, the CIA conducted sabotage and psychological warfare operations against the Hanoi government. Although back in Washington a National Intelligence Estimate in 1954 predicted that the chances of constructing a viable, stable government in South Vietnam were "poor" and the Pentagon pronounced the situation "hopeless," Secretary of State John Foster Dulles concluded that even if the outlook was bad, doing something was better than doing nothing. Diem headed a corrupt government, which, while dependent on U.S. backing, frequently ignored American advice about reform. Rejecting the national election scheduled for 1956 under the Geneva Accords, Diem instead held a referendum on his rule. To the embarrassment of his U.S. advisors who cautioned that a 60 percent win would be respectable, Diem won 98.2 percent of the vote, receiving a suspicious tally of more than 605,000 votes from the 405,000 registered voters in Saigon alone.[12]

Diem was nevertheless identified in the United States as the George Washington of Southeast Asia. Speaking before a joint session of Congress in 1957, Diem echoed President Eisenhower by pledging that he would keep raw materials from falling into communist hands. He employed a New York public relations firm to improve his image and received support from the American Friends of Vietnam, founded by General William Donovan, former head of the OSS. Its Republican and Democratic members included Supreme Court Justice William O. Douglas, Cardinal Francis Spellman, historian Arthur Schlesinger, Jr., publisher Henry Luce, and Senators Mike Mansfield (D-MT), Hubert Humphrey (D-MN), and John F. Kennedy (D-MA). Describing Americans as the "godparents" of "little Vietnam," Senator Kennedy said the new republic was "a proving ground of democracy" and a "test of American responsibility and determination in Asia."[13]

President Eisenhower and Secretary of State John Foster Dulles greet South Vietnamese president Ngo Dinh Diem, Washington, 1957. (National Archives, 342-AF-18302AF)

By the time Senator Kennedy became president, Diem's unpopular regime was in serious trouble. Diem's repressive policies helped to recruit communists and noncommunists into the National Liberation Front (NLF), the successor of the revolutionary Vietminh, which used guerrilla operations and political agitation to attack the Saigon government. The South Vietnamese and U.S. governments called the insurgents of the NLF, communist or not, "Vietcong" or Vietnamese communists. American officials asserted that Hanoi controlled the Vietcong, while critics argued that the NLF was made up of southerners engaged in a civil war against a hated government. Both were right. Hanoi sent soldiers and supplies south along the hidden Ho Chi Minh trail running through neighboring Laos and Cambodia, while encouraging communists in the NLF to promote the goal of national unity. Yet, the critics were correct in pointing out that peasants, students, and religious leaders, as well as communists, opposed Diem who had outlawed Buddhist observances in a country where 80 percent of the people practiced Buddhism. The U.S. government urged Diem to expand civil liberties, allow village elections, and extend loans to small farmers. Diem did the opposite, cracking down on the press and arresting dissenting politicians. Reluctantly, Washington stuck by Diem, who was, in the words of Vice President Lyndon B. Johnson, "the only boy we got out there."[14]

To respond to the Vietcong, the United States shifted its policy from providing aid and training to engaging in offensive operations. It launched "Operation Beefup," which doubled U.S. military assistance and set up the Military Assistance Command, Vietnam (MACV). As Army officers went on combat missions with the South Vietnamese Army (ARVN for Army of the Republic of Vietnam) and Marines and Air Force helicopter pilots delivered troops to combat zones, the effectiveness of the South Vietnamese military soared temporarily until the Vietcong adapted. It seemed that as soon as ARVN troops returned from missions, the Vietcong would reclaim control over the countryside. Moreover, ARVN troops could not tell who was a communist guerrilla and who was a civilian peasant. Suffering heavy losses, they bombed villages, dropped U.S.-supplied napalm and defoliants, and shot people indiscriminately, thereby making it easier for the NLF to recruit support against the Saigon government. The Americans and the South Vietnamese implemented the Strategic Hamlet program. Its purpose was to relocate peasants in fortified hamlets, thereby separating the guerrillas from the Vietnamese people who supported them, whether willingly or unwillingly. Planners envisioned all sorts of political and land reforms taking place in the hamlets, even as they uprooted peasants from the sacred land of their ancestors.[15]

In Washington, the Kennedy administration skillfully practiced news management, using live press conferences at which the quick-witted president excelled. JFK explained that there were many problems in Vietnam but held to the Domino Theory. In September 1963 he signaled a move away from the Diem regime by pointing out that while it had been in power for ten years, civil unrest continued. In fact, the situation was deteriorating. NBC's David Brinkley asked, "With so much of our prestige, money, so on, committed in South Vietnam, why can't we exercise a little more influence there, Mr. President?" Kennedy answered, "We have some influence," but "we can't expect these countries to do everything the way we want to do them." He asked Americans to be patient.[16] The president's appearances had a number of purposes. He announced the "line" for officials, Congressmen, and supporters to follow. To elicit sympathy and support from the public, he projected the image of a hard-working president meeting crises in Berlin, Cuba, Laos, and Vietnam all the while projecting calm authority.[17]

By the early 1960s, experienced journalists had already registered their frustration with Cold War era official manipulation. They noted that the White House and State Department used background briefings, in which an official spoke to reporters under the condition that his or her identity would not be revealed, to test public reaction to a new policy or mobilize opinion. Veteran war correspondent Dickey Chappelle opposed the Defense Department's policy of prohibiting reporters from speaking to an official without a public information officer present unless that official delivered a written report of the conversation to his superiors the same day. On overseas trips, she observed, the U.S. government provided reporters with transportation, lodging, press kits, and tour directors of the rank of major or above who decided what reporters would and would not see. Most important, she felt that the government's management of the news interfered with the reporter's role as an eyewitness of history. She had covered the marines on Iwo Jima and Okinawa in 1945 and objected to the administration's policy of preventing reporters from covering U.S. armed forces during the Cuban Missile Crisis in October 1962. When a member of the White House press staff defended the policy, telling the Overseas Press Club that no one could expect to have an eyewitness to an atomic bombing, Chappelle wryly noted the presence of William Laurence, the Pulitzer Prize–winning science reporter from the *New York Times* who had been on the plane that dropped the bomb on Nagasaki.[18] Significantly, Chappelle, like most members of the press, objected to what she considered heavy-handed news management but not to Cold War foreign policy.

In its effort to carry out news management in South Vietnam, the administration faced a dilemma. It wanted to enhance South Vietnam's image as an independent nation, so it ostensibly left press policy up to the Diem regime. Since the Saigon government had no respect for the tradition of a free press it threatened and deported news reporters from the *New York Times* and *Newsweek* who filed unflattering stories. Such actions embarrassed Washington, which wanted to maintain good relations with influential news organizations. U.S. officials instructed Diem not to crack down too heavily on American reporters and placed restrictions on its own spokesmen. Washington did not want reporters to know that U.S. "military advisors" led combat missions nor did it want correspondents to go on missions that might result in unfavorable reports. It banned stories on civilian casualties and the use of napalm.

Yet, despite all the restrictions, American correspondents traveled fairly freely. They witnessed events such as the protest against the Diem regime of Thich Quang Duc, a sixty-six-year-old Buddhist monk, who sat in the middle of a Saigon intersection and burned himself to death.[19]

Although General Earle G. Wheeler, the U.S. Army Chief of Staff, announced in February 1963 "we have made measurable progress in Vietnam," the press began to challenge such an assessment.[20] Reporters did not question Wheeler's fundamental premise that Americans stood for freedom against communist slavery in a strategically important part of the world. Instead they pointed to the corruption of the Diem government and the ineffectiveness of the South Vietnamese Army after years of American training and millions of dollars of equipment. When U.S. officials in Saigon announced another victory against the Vietcong at the village of Ap Bac (40 miles southwest of Saigon), reporter Neil Sheehan was unconvinced. He had witnessed the heavy damage done by a lightly armed NLF force of 350 guerrillas against 2,000 reluctant ARVN troops backed by American helicopters, fighter bombers, and armored personnel carriers. Correspondents heard U.S. military advisors, fed up with South Vietnamese incompetence, vent their anger. Although the U.S. command knew Ap Bac was a disaster, it ordered advisors to leave assessments of operations to higher-ups. In dealing with reporters, instructed the U.S. Army, the job of information officers was, in the words of the popular Johnny Mercer song, to "accentuate the positive and eliminate the negative."[21]

The Kennedy administration was divided on how to proceed. It wanted the South Vietnamese government to clean up corruption, win the support of the people, and follow instructions from Washington. Instead Diem and his powerful family opposed the increased presence of the U.S. military, pursued their self-interests, and in the spring of 1963 reached out to Ho Chi Minh about a possible cease-fire. Kennedy's ambassador to South Vietnam, Henry Cabot Lodge, Jr., the Republican grandson of Woodrow Wilson's nemesis, urged a coup. In late October, Washington gave the CIA the go-ahead. After the coup succeeded, South Vietnamese military officers, without Kennedy's approval, assassinated Diem. In his place, a series of military dictators, dependent on the United States, would run South Vietnam. At his last press conference on November 14, 1963, Kennedy defined the objective in Vietnam: "to bring Americans home, permit the South Vietnamese to maintain themselves as a free and independent country, and permit democratic forces within the country to operate."[22]

Johnson: Escalation

FOLLOWING PRESIDENT KENNEDY'S ASSASSINATION in November 1963, President Johnson inherited a confused situation as American policymakers struggled among themselves to define America's purpose in Vietnam. Fifteen years had passed since Acheson had proclaimed Ho Chi Minh an "outright commie." Johnson believed that communism had to be contained in Vietnam but was unsure about how to do it. He responded to conflicting advice from military and civilian advisors by choosing the middle course of a gradual escalation. The Joint Chiefs of Staff advocated national mobilization, the commitment of a million men for seven years and all-out bombing of the North, but Johnson feared that a major expansion of the war might provoke Soviet or Chinese intervention as it had in Korea. Nor did he want to be the first president to lose a war, and so he rejected the option of withdrawal. He decided to use military means to convince Vietnamese communists that they could not win and should therefore negotiate, by which he meant accept the U.S. goal of a noncommunist South Vietnam.[23] Determined to demonstrate his strength and confidence, LBJ thought it best to delay escalation until after the November 1964 presidential election.

Aware that according to the polls 63 percent of Americans paid little or no attention to Vietnam, the administration wanted to keep it that way. "For most Americans this is an easy war," said the president: "Prosperity rises, abundance increases, the Nation flourishes."[24] He worried that if the Republicans charged him with being soft on communism he would not be able to muster the political support needed for his expensive and ambitious reforms on civil rights, education, and health care known as the Great Society. He thought the United States was rich enough to afford both his domestic programs and the war. For the fiscal year 1965 (July 1964 through June 1965), the government budgeted $100 million for military action in Southeast Asia. Although it ended up spending $800 million, the administration did not want to raise taxes because it would mean rallying support for war in Congress and among the public.[25]

To promote a war without calling a lot of attention to it was a tricky assignment for officials in the White House Press Office, the National Security Council (NSC), the United States Information Agency, the Public Affairs Offices of the State and Defense Departments, and the public information offices of the armed services. At various times, they organized themselves under such innocuous names as the Public Affairs Policy Committee and the

Vietnam Information Group. They concluded that a "quick reaction team" at the White House would be more flexible than the public affairs offices at the State and Defense Departments. Urging discretion, Harold Kaplan, head of the Vietnam Information Group, warned that some reporters considered it a "miniature Office of War Information."[26] These officials preferred to stay behind the scenes while they provided background to reporters, editors, publishers, Congressional leaders, and influential citizens. Following the method used by the Truman administration during the Korean War, these information teams employed a "trickle down" method of persuasion, which relied on the support of opinion leaders to sway the public at large.[27]

To improve relations between the press and the military in South Vietnam, the administration and the Pentagon launched Operation Maximum Candor. From 1964 to 1967, three thousand U.S. military and civilian personnel in South Vietnam provided information to the 600 accredited journalists who covered the war. Johnson named Barry Zorthian as the chief public relations officer of the U.S. mission. Zorthian worked closely with General William C. Westmoreland, the new U.S. military commander, who arrived in Vietnam with a heroic reputation for his service in World War II and Korea. They made the MACV Office of Information, based in Saigon, the one and only source of official news. Reporters agreed not to release information that would harm military operations. Westmoreland held weekly off-the-record briefings and took reporters with him on visits to the field, guiding their attention to favorable stories. Westmoreland and Zorthian arranged for politicians and celebrities to tour South Vietnam, witness U.S. accomplishments, and return home to give interviews about what they had seen. Officials preferred to provide the media with a massive amount of selected news rather than leave it up to reporters to find out what was happening for themselves.[28]

The major flaw in Operation Maximum Candor was that its objective of projecting positive news conflicted with its commitment to openness and accuracy. Back in Washington, the administration maintained that its efforts to build up South Vietnam were succeeding. So when news reports from Saigon cited the low opinion the U.S. military advisors held of their ARVN counterparts, the Defense Department expressed its concern to Westmoreland, who could reply only that the reports were true. Members of the White House information team debated the value of candor. James Greenfield, assistant secretary of state for public affairs, pointed out that the American people and the press will "accept our involvement in this problem—if they are told what is going on. But they deeply resent—and properly—an[y] hint of cover-up." He insisted that keeping the press informed worked to the administration's advantage. Besides, he noted, by using "the background device," officials could put out a lot of information on Vietnam without unnecessarily committing U.S. policy or putting the U.S. government formally on record. Aware that the number of "inaccuracies" reported by government spokesmen in Saigon and in Washington affected their credibility, the White House believed it could recover with a presidential speech, the right briefing, or well-placed leak. *Los Angeles Times* correspondent William Tuohy summed up the consequences of Operation Maximum Candor: "We're drowning in facts here, but we're starved for information."[29]

To gain congressional approval for the planned escalation the administration intentionally misrepresented a confrontation in August 1964 between the U.S. Navy and the North Vietnamese in the Gulf of Tonkin. The destroyer *Maddox*, while engaged in covert operations close to the North Vietnamese coast, exchanged fire with North Vietnamese torpedo boats. A few days later, both the *Maddox* and the destroyer *C. Turner Joy* reported they were again under attack. Later the captain of the *Maddox* admitted their reports of the second confrontation, which occurred at night, were based on unreliable sonar and radar readings and that there was no definite evidence of hostile activity from the North Vietnamese. Although there was uncertainty at the Pentagon about exactly what had happened, Secretary of Defense Robert McNamara chose to announce that an attack had occurred and that it justified retaliation against the North. President Johnson asked for a congressional resolution giving him the authority to "take all necessary measures to repel any armed attacks against the forces of the United States and to prevent further aggression." McNamara misled Congress by saying that the North Vietnamese had without provocation attacked the *Maddox* while it was on "a routine patrol in international waters."[30]

The Gulf of Tonkin resolution said that the unprovoked attack was part of a "deliberate and systematic campaign of aggression" by the communists in the north and that the United States, without any territorial, military, or political ambitions for itself, desired that the people of Southeast Asia "be left in peace to work out their own destinies in their own way."[31] In the House the vote for the resolution was unanimous and in the Senate only two voted against it. One of the dissenting senators, Wayne Morse (D-OR), tried to interest fellow senators in what he had heard from a source in the Pentagon who told him that the attack was not unprovoked. "Hell Wayne, you can't get into a fight with the president when all the flags are waving and we're about to go to a national convention," one warned him. "All Lyndon wants is a piece of paper telling him we did right out there, and we support him." Senator J. William Fulbright (D-AR), who pushed through the resolution, later explained that he didn't think the president would lie and, after all, he accepted the basic premise of the policy. "These people would give up if we would just bomb them in a serious way," he believed. The Gulf of Tonkin Resolution gave Johnson what he wanted, a demonstration of national unity to show North Vietnam that it should back down before U.S. resolve and a display of action that boosted his approval rating from 42 to 72 percent while countering Republican presidential candidate Barry Goldwater's call for more military force. At the same time LBJ assured voters, "We don't want our American boys to do the fighting for Asian boys."[32]

Few allies backed U.S. policy. Greenfield observed that one of the administration's justifications—"Our friends won't trust us if we desert the Vietnamese"—gave them trouble when "foreigners say publicly that they want us out of Vietnam." The State Department initiated the "more flags" campaign, intended to show international support for the Free World stand against communism in Southeast Asia. But America's allies—Britain, France, West Germany, Japan, and Canada—did not consider Vietnam to be strategically vital nor did they did think that South Vietnam had much of a future. They preferred a political solution to an expanded war. Britain, the most eagerly sought ally, refused to send ground troops. "A platoon of bagpipers would be sufficient," LBJ told British Prime Minister Harold Wilson to no avail. The "more flags" campaign failed. In the end, only Australia, New Zealand, and, for substantial U.S. payment, South Korea, the Philippines, and Thailand sent troops and advisors. Their assistance was needed more for symbolic than military purposes.[33]

Johnson's Vietnam policy attracted a small but articulate opposition. In the summer of 1964, five thousand scholars published a petition advocating a neutral Vietnam. Their spokesman, University of Chicago political scientist Hans Morgenthau, an advocate of a realist U.S. foreign policy based on national self-interest, explained that the best outcome would see Vietnam on its own, dominated by neither China nor the United States. General David M. Shoup, the recently retired Commandant of the Marine Corps, echoed General Smedley Butler's critique of U.S. interventions in the 1920s and 1930s. Americans, he said, should "keep our dirty bloody dollar crooked fingers out of the business of these nations so full of depressed exploited people." Marines were trained to fight, believed the Medal of Honor recipient, not to win hearts and minds.[34] The president, however, was more worried about criticism from the right than the left. For example, conservative columnist Joseph Alsop branded the policy of withdrawal as appeasement. The loss of South Vietnam, he warned, would mean the loss of everything the United States fought for in World War II and Korea. Trumping critics at home and abroad, Johnson had the support of Congress, the media, the military, and the Wise Men, a bipartisan advisory group of elder statesmen, which included former secretary of state Acheson.[35]

Reelected by a landslide in November 1964, LBJ went ahead with escalation. In early 1965, he ordered Operation Rolling Thunder, a controlled bombing attack on North Vietnam's industry and infrastructure. The Navy supported amphibious operations and prevented the shipment of enemy supplies by sea and inland waterways. On the ground, the gradual buildup of combat forces began with the Defense Department's announcement that the 3000 marines sent to Da Nang were there to defend the U.S. air base. That was partly true, but the marines also were ordered to conduct offensive operations in the region. Infantry troops, called "grunts," engaged in "search and destroy" operations against the Victcong in the South by using superior mobility and firepower to carry out a strategy of attrition. The U.S. troops measured their success with numbers of enemy dead or the "body count." These numbers tended to be exaggerated because they included civilians as well as enemy dead. "If it's dead and it's Vietnamese, it's VC," was a familiar saying. Wayne Smith, a combat medic in the 9th Infantry Division, remembered, "if we came across four different body parts we called in four kills." Over the next three years, ground forces grew to 800,000 South Vietnamese troops, 68,000 Allied troops, and half a million American soldiers.[36]

The American forces performed well, but the Vietnamese did not respond as expected. Under the leadership of General Vo Nguyen Giap, the North Vietnamese and the NLF adopted a defensive strategy. Avoiding direct confrontations with the heavily armed U.S. military, the Vietnamese enemy relied on ambushes, sniper fire, sabotage, and night attacks, making the most of their lightly armed fighters and knowledge of the terrain, including sanctuaries in neighboring Laos and Cambodia. Aware of the importance the Americans placed on claims that their bombs hit only military targets, the Hanoi government placed schools and hospitals next to military installations. The North suffered enormous damage from bombing but managed to conceal much of its limited industrial base and made up some of the losses with two billion dollars worth of planes and weapons from the Russians and the Chinese. In the South, American firepower destroyed villages, turning millions of Vietnamese into refugees. In addition, the flow of dollars into the Saigon government created more corruption. Without a unified command structure, the U.S. and South Vietnamese military effort lacked coordination. The Americans trained ARVN units to rely on U.S. air power and tended to give their allies "simple tasks," which the Vietnamese, long familiar with the condescension of colonial rulers, resented. Weary of war, many South Vietnamese adopted a "let the Americans do it" attitude. The North Vietnamese meanwhile matched the U.S. escalation of manpower. It was "the duty of my generation to die for our country," said a North Vietnamese officer.[37]

The American public greeted the escalation in 1965 with approval but seemed confused about its purpose. The solution was to place the cumbersome explanation of U.S. policy in Vietnam within the Cold War framework of a showdown between freedom and communism.[38] President Johnson's April 1965 "Why Vietnam" speech, delivered at Johns Hopkins University, exemplifies this effort. Echoing his predecessors, Johnson portrayed the United States as generous, steady, and patient with revolution in impoverished, backward Southeast Asia. He was confident that peace would bring development to rice-producing regions, build a beneficial balance between industrial Japan and its agricultural neighbors, and create mutually advantageous trade. The president promised massive aid in the tradition of the New Deal's Tennessee Valley Authority to develop the Mekong delta if North Vietnam withdrew its troops from the South. The North would reject this offer, saying it refused to negotiate until the United States pulled out its troops.

The much more dramatic part of LBJ's "Why Vietnam" speech linked Cold War themes to images from World War II. The president's speech was turned into a film called *Why Vietnam*, in the tradition of Frank Capra's *Why We Fight* series. The administration made sure that troops on their way to Southeast Asia saw *Why Vietnam*; it also distributed 10,000 prints of the film to schools and universities across the country. The film opens with LBJ reading a letter from a mother in the midwest who says she doesn't understand the war. The president asks why Vietnam? The answer is film footage of Adolf Hitler. "Aggression unchallenged is aggression unleashed," says Johnson, applying the lesson of Munich to the containment of communism. American objectives of "freedom," "hope," and "prosperity," Johnson declared, were threatened by a war of aggression to extend Asiatic communism, described with the words "terror," "infiltration," and "subversion." The ruthless enemy, backed by Communist China, assassinated "simple farmers," strangled women and

children, and ravaged "helpless villages." He warned, "If freedom is to survive
in any American home town it must be preserved in such places as South Viet
Nam."[39]

A year later, the president asserted that the United States would accomplish in Asia what it had accomplished in Europe and Latin America. Citing
Theodore Roosevelt, the president defined the era as the Pacific era. He
answered critics such as George Kennan, known as the father of containment, Senator Fulbright, who had learned that he had been lied to about
the Tonkin Gulf incident, and leading columnist Walter Lippmann, who
claimed that Vietnam was outside the sphere of U.S. interests, by saying that
the United States had learned the mistake of isolationism and must accept
Asia as either "our partner or our problem." The editors of the *Washington
Post* praised the president for boldly committing the United States to a great
power role in Asia, even if many Americans were not prepared for it.[40] LBJ's
speeches reflected his own uncritical embrace of the official narrative of the
Cold War. Appeasement and isolation were wrong; the United States must
demonstrate its leadership with force if necessary. On the twentieth anniversary of the Truman Doctrine, Johnson wrote in a public letter to the
eighty-three-year-old Harry Truman, "Today America is again engaged in
helping to turn back armed terrorists."[41]

The administration's news management and the media's war coverage for a
time masked the contrast between the grand vision of an American-led Free
World and what was happening on the ground in Vietnam. The White House
relied on top military and civilian officials to toe the policy line. LBJ, who
watched the network news on three monitors in the Oval Office, personally
and energetically cultivated reporters. Johnson liked to cite favorable opinion
polls, which discouraged other politicians from expressing criticism. "Popular
support and sound policy are obviously not the same thing," pointed out *New
York Times* columnist James Reston, as he reminded readers that isolationism
in the years before World War II had been a popular policy at the time.[42]
Because U.S. war aims in Vietnam were so hard to explain, the information
team concluded that in addition to the president only three people could
deliver the administration's policy effectively—McNamara, Secretary of State
Dean Rusk, and National Security Advisor McGeorge Bundy. "Bundy is probably not good for the housewife in the back yard," observed John Chancellor.
"Unfortunately, Bundy appeals to the sophisticated and the sophisticated are
already rigid in their confusion."[43] McNamara, he felt, was probably less able
than Rusk. In the end, President Johnson bore the brunt of explaining his

own policy to the extent that his advisors feared that he had become overexposed on television and appeared obsessed with Vietnam.

Operation Maximum Candor continued to work for the administration. Known by reporters as the "Five O'Clock Follies," official briefings in Saigon became more likely to misinform than to inform. Officials sanitized language, using terms such as "soft ordnance" for napalm, "surgical precision" to describe bombing, and "collateral damage" for killed and wounded civilians. They announced the body count as well as stories of road construction and food handouts. For the most part, correspondents cooperated but became frustrated with what was becoming known as the "credibility gap." Visiting Saigon, Arthur Sylvester, the assistant secretary of defense for public affairs, had little patience with their complaints. "Look," he said, "if you think any American official is going to tell the truth you're stupid." The job of the media in time of war was to serve the government, he asserted, as angry correspondents walked out.[44] Correspondent Ward Just recalled how difficult it was to report from Vietnam because reporters inhabited "four zones of reality"—the U.S. government version, the South Vietnamese government version, the North Vietnamese government version, taken least seriously by reporters, and the fourth and most elusive version, which was the situation as it actually was. No one knew that version, he concluded.[45]

TV as a Tool

THE ADMINISTRATION EXPECTED TELEVISION COVERAGE to put across its version of the war. TV news tended to reinforce the good versus evil drama of the Cold War. On CBS, news anchors sat in front of a map of Southeast Asia that seemed to have been drawn by the Domino Theory mapmaking company. It had only three place names on it—China, Hanoi, and Haiphong—making Hanoi look like a provincial capital of its giant communist neighbor. Broadcasters reserved the name Vietnamese for the government and civilians of South Vietnam, referring to Vietnamese enemies as communists or "reds" in the early war years. Television coverage focused on American forces, but because of network policies and military strategy it tended to show a sympathetic, if uneventful, war. Citing concerns about taste and decency, network policy prohibited showing identifiable American casualties, dead and wounded, unless the Defense Department had already notified the family. In Saigon, Barry Zorthian warned network executives that if there were complaints about film footage showing American dead or wounded, television cameras would probably be denied access. Under the circumstances, the networks often limited coverage of casualties to scenes of the wounded being carried to assistance.[46]

Until 1968, there was not a lot of gruesome footage to show because of the difficulty TV crews faced in covering actual combat operations. The correspondent, the cameraman, and the soundman carried about one hundred pounds of equipment connected by cables. Their film footage usually was flown from Saigon to New York; only rarely would the networks pay to have footage flown to Tokyo, developed, and transmitted by satellite to New York. Most reports, therefore, did not involve fast-breaking stories. Indeed, as TV crews accompanied troops on search and destroy missions, they might or might not witness any contact with the enemy. The few film reports that showed combat might include air strikes, incoming mortar rounds, or the sound of sniper fire. Typically their reports would consist of interviews with soldiers who would talk about an enemy action after it happened.[47]

At a 1965 White House meeting on the "information problem," John Chancellor was optimistic that more press in Vietnam would mean more "poignant Ernie Pyle-type stories," which in turn would generate more public support.[48] War correspondents frequently did "citizen soldier" interviews with articulate young officers who would be identified by name, rank, and home town. The soldier would talk about being "here to do a job" and express confidence in eventually getting it done. These short exchanges seemed to echo coming of age stories out of an ancient warrior tradition. Viewers saw a youthful body in military posture exuding physical competence. Then the camera would focus on the close-cropped head with its clean-shaven jaw and unlined face, showing a compelling combination of strength and vulnerability. The young American appeared sincere, and while he and the viewers knew he might die, his bearing and confidence belied the danger. Sometimes the soldier, when asked about his feelings on the war, would echo the president's "Why Vietnam" speech with an answer such as "Better to be fighting the Communists here than fighting them back in San Diego."[49] Based on the responses to the survey question, "Has the television coverage of the war made you feel more like you ought to back up the boys fighting in Vietnam or not?" the Harris poll reported in July 1967 that 83 percent of Americans felt more prowar after they watched television.[50]

In contrast, the enemy was routinely dehumanized in news coverage. American troops referred to the enemy as "gooks," "slopes," or "dinks." For example, an NBC reporter interviewed a soldier who referred to "dinks" as

Lance Corporal W. E. McDonald of the 1st Marine Division is interviewed by a CBS reporter, August 11, 1966. (National Archives, 127GVB-306-A369577)

he burned his personal effects so they would not fall into enemy hands. The reporter asked if "dinks" were NVA. The soldier smiled and replied, "Dinks were NVA, North Vietnamese, Communists, Charlies." On ABC, anchor Peter Jennings reported that U.S. marines near Da Nang had tightened the noose around a North Vietnamese battalion, turning the conflict into what an officer called a "turkey shoot." Jennings said the enemy's inability to escape was a rare occurrence because "like a fox when there is no place to go, the Viet Cong goes to ground." Correspondent Don North, with the U.S. 1st Cavalry Air Mobile Division, showed how a lone soldier carried on "a cat and mouse game" under sniper fire. Wrapping up, North said, "after a day of chasing Charlie in and out of his tunnels, the men of Abel Company relax."[51]

Occasionally network news reports challenged the image of brave Americans helping the innocent Vietnamese fend off ruthless communists. In August 1965, CBS correspondent Morley Safer reported on the destruction of the South Vietnamese village of Cam Ne by U.S. marines, as villagers pleaded with them to stop. Military officials stated that Vietcong guerrillas, who had mixed in with the civilian population in a region long dominated by communists, had fired upon the marines. Safer said that the marines acted in retaliation, but the accompanying film showing a marine using a cigarette lighter to ignite a hut challenged the military's announcement that homes burned because of an exchange of fire. In his report, Safer said, "Today's operation shows the frustration of Vietnam in miniature." American fire power can win a military victory, he predicted, but it will be tough to convince a Vietnamese peasant who has lost everything he has worked so hard for that "we are on his side."[52]

Safer's report set off a White House debate over what Barry Zorthian called "the village-burning problem." Zorthian and Sylvester blamed the problem on the ineffectiveness of U.S. military spokesmen in Vietnam, the absence of impressive representatives of the South Vietnamese government and military, and the lack of good war correspondents. Sylvester viewed the thirty-three-year-old Safer, identified as a Canadian, with suspicion and White House Press Secretary Bill Moyers suggested that more mature war correspondents who were U.S. nationals might provide more balanced reporting. With some longing, presidential aide Douglass Cater looked back to World War II when Edward R. Murrow and Elmer Davis provided calm and perspective. Notably, he looked back to the Murrow who reported from 1940s Europe, not the Murrow who reported from 1950s Korea with a warning about losing civilian support that sounded similar to Safer's. They observed that their task of public relations would be easier if U.S. troops conformed to the accepted standards of warfare. "It might be best," Zorthian noted, "to have orders issued that no villages should be attacked except under very exceptional circumstances." Greenfield looked beyond military conduct to question the fundamental policy, pointing out, "You can't win the people in Viet-Nam by burning their villages." He insisted, "We have to take steps to prevent these things from happening, not just to make sure reporters don't see them." Others agreed, noting that if burning a village inspired a hundred people to join the communists it was counterproductive.[53]

Of the three options discussed—improve manipulation of news coverage, ask the military to change its conduct, or rethink U.S. policy—the first two were acted upon. Under pressure from the Joint Chiefs of Staff, Westmoreland ordered that villagers must be warned of air or ground assaults "wherever security allowed," that there must be no indiscriminate killing of civilians and destruction of their property, and that South Vietnamese units should accompany U.S. forces to serve as intermediaries. In addition, upon learning that an Associated Press (AP) photographer had pictures of American marines observing South Vietnamese troops torturing Vietcong prisoners,

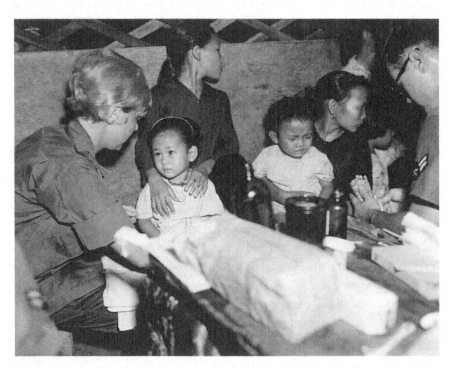

As part of the nation-building effort, U.S. military teams visited villages "to treat the sick and teach villagers the basics of sanitation and cleanliness." In this photograph, Second Lieutenant Kathleen M. Sullivan treats a Vietnamese child during Operation MED CAP, a U.S. Air Force civic action program in 1967. (National Archives, 342-C-K28429)

Westmoreland ordered, "try to keep Americans out of the picture." And the information team recommended that bad news be countered by stories of Vietcong atrocities, better PR from the South Vietnamese government, and supportive statements from prestigious citizens. "We may not know how to fight the war in Vietnam," concluded Chester Cooper, "but the correspondents don't know how to report it either."[54]

In many ways television news coverage reflected the confusion about the war but reported it as though it made sense. Without detailed maps and organizational charts, viewers would have a hard time following the details of Vietnamese place names, U.S. military units, and policy statements. For example, on February 15, 1967, network news broadcasts included four Vietnam-related stories. On NBC, news anchor Chet Huntley announced how many communists had been killed. Second, he cited reports from TASS, the Soviet press agency, saying that the United States bombed economic and civilian targets in the north. So did ABC and CBS, although CBS followed it up with a Pentagon statement saying that its reports show no basis for the claim. All three reported on a statement by McNamara, who said that he doubted that bombing alone would induce North Vietnam to change its ways, but that it had reduced North Vietnamese infiltration and bolstered South Vietnamese morale. NBC and ABC showed clips of the Women's Strike for Peace demonstration at the Pentagon. A large crowd of middle-class women chanted, "Stop the war in Vietnam. Bring the boys home. Stop burning children." ABC's final story covered Operation Pershing and the use of napalm and high explosives on a Vietnamese village. The film footage showed U.S. troops walking around huddled Vietnamese peasants. Don North interviewed a soldier who said that the women, children, and old men could be Vietcong or could be just trying to get away. The young American said he couldn't communicate with the people and added that it would be helpful to have someone who spoke Vietnamese.[55]

A viewer might or might not have time before the next news story or commercial break to wonder why the likable soldier didn't have someone who spoke Vietnamese. Would he or she consider the implications of his statement? American troops could not tell who was an enemy and who was a civilian. The news reports provided little analysis or interpretation. Viewers of ABC might have registered the broadcast's tone of condescension for the women's march, deference to the secretary of defense, and sympathy for the young serviceman. Certainly, the authority of McNamara contrasted sharply with the baffled air of the soldier surrounded by miserable villagers. But

McNamara was not telling the truth. The bombing had not reduced North Vietnamese infiltration.

The peace movement countered official pronouncements on the war with its claim that by prosecuting the war the United States was violating democratic principles. Raising concerns about the moral implications of the bombing, church leaders called for negotiations. Reinhold Niebuhr, the highly respected theologian who had long supported Cold War policies, admitted, "For the first time I fear I am ashamed of our beloved nation." Middle-class women joined Another Mother for Peace, co-chaired by actress Donna Reed, who played the ideal homemaker on her long-running television show. Their slogan, "War is not healthy for children and other living things," appeared on posters, bumper stickers, and Mother's Day cards. Initially, African American activists, caught up in the struggle for racial equality, did not participate in the antiwar movement. In 1967, however, Martin Luther King, Jr. connected the two when he declared, "We were taking the black young men . . . and sending them eight thousand miles away to guarantee liberties in Southeast Asia which they had not found in Southwest Georgia or East Harlem." Prominent black leaders condemned King for criticizing the foreign policy of an administration that had accomplished so much for civil rights. However, advocates of the Black Power movement saw racism as a fundamental component of both foreign and domestic policy. African American activist Stokely Carmichael condemned a war about "white people sending black people to make war on yellow people in order to defend the land they stole from red people."[56]

Unlike the administration, antiwar activists advocated citizen mobilization. In public places, they plastered posters that transformed traditional prowar symbols. One featured a Vietnamese Paul Revere on horseback alerting villagers, "The Americans Are Coming." Another showed soldiers in the Iwo Jima pose, raising a flag bearing the peace symbol. In October 1967, the National Mobilization Committee organized Stop the Draft week. Protests took place around the country while 100,000 people demonstrated in Washington. The slogan was "Support Our GI's, Bring Them Home Now!" University students demonstrated against U.S. support for an undemocratic government in South Vietnam and condemned what they saw as undemocratic practices at home, such as the absence of a declaration of war, official lying, and the drafting of young men under twenty-one years who couldn't vote to fight a war they might not support. In addition, the antiwar movement supported acts of civil disobedience such as the public burning of draft cards. Following in the footsteps of the civil rights movement, most protesters practiced nonviolent dissent. Some activists, inspired by teach-ins held on university campuses, identified themselves as part of an international revolutionary movement against U.S.-led imperialism. A few admitted that they attended demonstrations for the parties, the girls, and the music. Yet, for most protesters, bringing home the troops was their number one goal.[57]

The television cameras focused on the more colorful hippies who rejected mainstream society's views on proper dress, hygiene, and manners. At the Pentagon during the 1967 protest, clean-cut troops from the 82nd Airborne confronted longhaired demonstrators wearing their own uniform of ragged jeans. Some protesters carried Vietcong flags or posters honoring Ho Chi Minh. Encouraged by the White House, the media featured stories about radicals who had thrown flowers, eggs, and bags of excrement at the soldiers, couples who had sex on the Pentagon grounds, Abby Hoffman's attempt to levitate the building, and Jerry Rubin's arrest for urinating on it. Press coverage ignored the main peaceful demonstration at the Lincoln Memorial and the excessive force used by the soldiers against the protesters when they cleared the area after the media had left for the night.[58]

In addition to directing media attention to the behavior of a minority of the protesters sure to disgust most Americans, the White House tried to combat the antiwar movement in a number of ways. It sent what it called "truth squads," groups of government officials, to college and university campuses to counter antiwar critics. It helped behind the scenes to stage a "Support Our Boys in Vietnam" parade of 70,000 in New York City, a parade advertised by contrasting images of hippie demonstrators with dead soldiers. Also behind the scenes, the White House set up the National Committee for Peace and Freedom in Vietnam, headed by honorary chairmen Harry Truman and Dwight Eisenhower, to express the bipartisan support of moderates for a "sensible" U.S. policy.[59]

Still, the president and his advisors decided they had to tell a better story. "We must get off the defensive in the propaganda battle," urged LBJ's friend, Supreme Court Justice Abe Fortas.[60] Public uncertainty about U.S. war aims in Vietnam was articulated in July 1967 by Eric Sevareid on CBS. The eminent commentator asked viewers in honor of Independence Day to remember fallen soldiers. "Exactly what their deaths accomplished," he said, "we do not know." By the summer of 1967, Americans increasingly believed that the war was a mistake, including some members of the Johnson administration who had worked so hard to build public support for it. McNamara, for one, wanted out and in November was appointed president of the World Bank.

A Louis Harris poll of August 1967 revealed that 24 percent of Americans thought the United States should pursue total military victory, 37 percent wanted the United States to fight to get a negotiated peace (the administration position), and 34 percent thought the United States should get out as quickly as possible. From within the administration, the State Department's Philip Habib offered a devastating critique of its information campaign. The "data do not explain away dismay at our own casualty figures," he noted. "They do not answer those who doubt that it is in our national interest to do what we are doing at the price we are paying." But his only solution was to do more of the same. He wrote, "People need to be told again and again why we are there."[61]

The Progress Campaign

THE ADMINISTRATION LAUNCHED the "Progress Campaign" in September 1967. Although General Wheeler admitted, "We are not sure who has the initiative in South Vietnam," the White House wanted briefings and statistics to show success. Officials reported that 67 percent of South Vietnamese lived in secure areas, that the South Vietnamese performed well in battle, and that the communists suffered heavy casualties and were faltering. General Westmoreland returned home in November to tell Congressmen, the press, and the public that progress meant that within two years they would be able to leave the South Vietnamese in charge. General William Sidle, the new head of the MACV Office of Information, saw that the press corps was growing difficult to manage. The few veteran reporters distrusted official briefings and hundreds of others arrived fresh with little experience and less knowledge. Aware that the troops themselves either in interviews or through their actions often provided correspondents with stories that contradicted the message of progress, he made sure that officers accompanied reporters and cameramen in the field so that soldiers would censor themselves, a practice that would be repeated in the 1991 Persian Gulf War.[62]

Television reporting from Vietnam was ambiguous on the official message of progress. For example, Wilson Hall of NBC took a dim view of U.S. involvement but on his own edited out from his scripts his more pointed comments. NBC's editors also shortened and simplified a Hall report about Phuoc Vinh village broadcast on October 3, 1967, perhaps to make it run a certain length, but with the result that it appeared more neutral. Hall reported that Phuoc Vinh was called a "new life hamlet" because the enemy no longer controlled it. When Huntley introduced the report he did not quote Hall's script, which raised a question regarding claims of progress. "New life hamlets are often pointed to as evidence that the allies are slowly, but surely, winning over villages," Hall had written. "Seldom talked about is how costly it is to keep the villages won over." Kept in the report was Hall's voice-over narration that the village had been a Vietcong stronghold and would still be one if not for the 5000 American troops stationed just down the road on an old French rubber plantation. As viewers saw bar signs reading "Playboy" and "Suzy," Hall stated that most of the villagers worked at the 48 bars, the laundries, and the barber shops. The American officers, he said, claimed that the village was safe enough for the district chief to stay there. The chief, however, did not agree and lived in the middle of the U.S. base. Hall closed, "The problem of Phouc Vinh is the problem of South Vietnam. There are not enough American troops to keep villages pacified, provide protection for the base camp, and go out to hunt and destroy large units of Viet Cong."[63]

As broadcast, this report could be interpreted to mean that more troops might be the answer. Removed from Hall's script was his summary of fundamental problems. Americans patrolled the countryside during the day and the Vietcong controlled it at night, U.S. officers described the South Vietnamese troops stationed around the village as "passive at best," the base itself was not safe from incoming artillery, and hundreds of villages like Phouc Vinh were really American enclaves rather than viable South Vietnamese communities. As for the civilians, American TV viewers may have seen them as bar girls and barbers who were not worth fighting for or as the victims of a corrupting American influence. For whatever reason, nation-building did not appear to be working. Other news reports reinforced this conclusion. On NBC, Howard Tuckner reported from Vietnam that while eighteen-year-old Americans risked everything to fight communists, tens of thousands of Vietnamese teens did not. He interviewed a sixteen-year-old Vietnamese who calmly explained that he would be willing to fight Cambodians but refused to fight other Vietnamese.[64]

The networks reported the official version of progress along with stories from Vietnam in a way that sometimes exposed the credibility gap. On CBS, correspondent Robert Shackne opened a report from Con Thien showing wounded Americans being carried on stretchers. Shackne asked a corporal how many men were left, adding "I'd be scared stiff." The soldier answered, "I'm not scared stiff, but I'm scared." A major assured Shackne that they were dug in and in a good position. As the footage showed two soldiers supporting a wounded man between them walking toward the helicopter, Shackne said that the wounded wait two hours for evacuation and signed off saying, "This is the way it is, this is the way it's been, and the way it's going to be for quite a while in Con Thien." Then news anchor Walter Cronkite appeared, apparently staring off at the disheartening image of the wounded American that he and the viewers had just seen, before turning to the camera to say, "Newsmen returning from Con Thien say that the North Vietnamese barrages and marine casualties are much heavier than reported by the military and today the U.S. Command ordered sharp restrictions on information that is given out about communist shelling." Closing the report, Cronkite said, "General Westmoreland today issued one of his most optimistic appraisals of the war, saying that . . . the picture of ultimate military success may be viewed with increasing clarity." Skeptical viewers might have found some confirmation for their doubts about the war in Cronkite's short pause following Shackne's bleak sign off and the juxtaposition of his report raising questions about the military's truthfulness followed by quoting Westmoreland's upbeat claim.[65]

The Progress Campaign was the administration's last effort to explain the strategy of fighting a war of attrition dedicated to convincing the enemy to surrender. By the end of 1967, the campaign seemed to be working. Polls showed that half of the American people thought the United States was making progress. In an interview with Steve Rowan on CBS on November 17, General Westmoreland used the words "progress," "improve," or "confidence" in almost every answer. At the end of the interview, however, when Rowan asked, "Is there any chance of total military victory before the election in 1968?" the general answered, "By us? Very unlikely." This stunning answer was a moment of actual candor in the Progress Campaign. Then Westmoreland tried to maintain the message while explaining that Americans were not fighting for total military victory. He said, "This is not the name of the game. . . . I think the next couple of years, and progressively from now on, we will weaken the enemy by virtue of the pressure that hopefully we will continue to apply."[66] By the end of the year, 16,000 Americans had been killed since the start of the war.

The Tet Offensive, launched on the Vietnamese New Year, January 30, 1968, by 84,000 Vietcong and North Vietnamese, quashed the Progress Campaign and confirmed public doubts about the policy of limited war in Vietnam. The assault on South Vietnam's cities from Hue to Saigon caught the Americans by surprise. Tet, a sacred holiday, was a time of cease-fire, when half of the South Vietnamese forces were on leave to celebrate with

During the "Progress Campaign," General William Westmoreland gave a briefing at the Pentagon on November 22, 1967. In this photograph he points to a chart on the monthly average of those from the GVN (South Vietnam or ARVN), VC/NVA (Vietcong and North Vietnamese), U.S., and Other Free World who were killed in action (KIA) from April to October in 1965, 1966, and 1967. As a sign of progress, the chart shows a significant increase in enemy forces killed. (Library of Congress, LC-U9-18322)

their families. Hoping to take advantage of the tension between the Americans and their Vietnamese allies, Giap thought a coordinated attack in the South would inspire a Vietnamese uprising against the United States. It did not. Indeed, the effectiveness of the South Vietnamese military encouraged Americans who wanted to replace U.S. troops with Vietnamese soldiers. Both sides claimed victory. The American and South Vietnamese forces pointed to the punishing defeat of communist forces on the battlefield; the communists claimed a political victory by exposing the weakness of the South Vietnamese regime. According to historian Ronald Spector, Tet proved both sides wrong by showing the war to be what it was—a stalemate.[67]

The news coverage reflected this conclusion. At Ben Tre, an American officer told AP reporter Peter Arnett, "It became necessary to destroy the town to save it." Widely quoted, the officer's statement seemed to sum up the self-defeating consequences of American policy. Also shocking was the shooting on a Saigon street of a suspected Vietcong prisoner by General Nguyen Ngoc Loan, the chief of the South Vietnamese National police, captured on film by AP photographer Eddie Adams and an NBC camera crew. The marines should be honored for their superb achievement in recapturing Hue, but it was the "wrong victory," wrote Joseph C. Harsch in the *Christian Science Monitor*. A win would be South Vietnamese troops raising their flag over the battered Citadel, he observed, not U.S. marines raising the Stars and Stripes. From President Johnson's point of view, the most damaging report came from Cronkite who returned from a tour of South Vietnam to announce on national TV that "we are mired in stalemate" and "the only rational way out would be to negotiate—not as victims, but as an honorable people who...did the best they could."[68]

When the *New York Times* reported in early March 1968 that West-moreland requested 205,000 more troops, Congressional critics lashed out. Senator Mansfield echoed General Omar Bradley's 1951 pronouncement on Korea when he declared, "We are in the wrong place and we are fighting the wrong kind of war."[69] McNamara's successor, Clark Clifford, learned from civilian analysts at the Pentagon that under the current strategy 200,000 more troops would not change Hanoi's determination to fight or inspire the South Vietnamese government to defend itself. He recommended a negotiated settlement. For LBJ, the worst blow was when the Wise Men counseled disen-gagement. After all, Acheson and others had defined the conflict in Vietnam as a crucial stand against communism. Now they concluded that the United States could not achieve victory nor could it afford to fight much longer. The war, at a cost of two billion dollars a month, contributed to inflation and a growing federal deficit. The most serious international economic crisis since the Great Depression threatened the United States as uncertainty about the value of the dollar prompted a panic on the gold market. In an election year, Congress voted to raise taxes and cut six billion dollars from Great Society programs.[70] With a 36 percent approval rating and facing Democratic chal-lengers Senators Eugene McCarthy of Minnesota and Robert F. Kennedy of New York, LBJ made the surprise announcement on March 31, 1968, that he would not run for reelection.

The war invaded politics and popular culture. The Democratic nominee, Vice President Hubert Humphrey, vowed to continue the war while pursuing negotiations. He consequently lost a lot of support in his own party. Third party candidate George Wallace, who made his national reputation by opposing racial desegregation, would win ten million votes in November. His fervently anticommunist running mate, retired Air Force General Curtis LeMay, made headlines by saying that if necessary he would use nuclear weapons to end the war in Vietnam. Between the struggling Humphrey and the alarming LeMay, the Republican nominee Richard Nixon positioned himself as an experienced and reasonable anticommunist.[71] Hollywood icon John Wayne tried to promote the war with his film *The Green Berets* (1968). Not a critical or popular success, the film showed valiant Americans and their Vietnamese allies defending their fort named "Dodge City" from savage communist attackers who raped women and brutalized children. *The Green Berets* revived the World War II conversion narrative by showing the transformation of a liberal journalist played by David Janssen from skeptic to believer in U.S. policy in Vietnam. Even so the film showed no victory, just more fighting. An alternative conversion narrative, which called upon people to oppose war and challenge authority, rang out in the rock and folk anthems of the peace movement.[72]

Although peace talks began in Paris in May 1968, Johnson did little to revise U.S. policy dedicated to establishing a noncommunist South Vietnam.

Legendary movie star John Wayne signs the helmet of Pfc. Fonsell Wofford during a visit to the 3rd Battalion, 7th Marines, at Chu Lai in 1966. (National Archives, NWDNS-127-N-A187201)

He ordered a halt to the bombing of North Vietnam but stepped up the air war in the South. One hundred thousand U.S. and ARVN troops embarked on the largest search and destroy operation of the war. Before he was replaced by General Creighton W. Abrams, Westmoreland tried to improve the military's image by changing official terminology. Instead of "search and destroy," which was understood to include civilians, he used "spoiling attack" and "reconnaissance in force." TV coverage shifted to Paris where the North and South Vietnamese refused to cooperate. Hanoi wanted the Americans out and a coalition government created, terms that the United States would not accept. The South Vietnamese government, fearing American withdrawal, stalled with objections to sitting at a round table.[73]

Sgt. Barry Sadler's 1965 hit, "The Ballad of the Green Berets," celebrated "fearless men...who mean just what they say." The maintenance of credibility had been the foundation of the Johnson administration's low-key propaganda campaign. It had sought to construct generalized support for its Vietnam policy, which allowed Johnson freedom of action to conduct the war without attracting much congressional oversight or public attention. Encouraging the World War II analogy and Cold War themes had worked for, but also against, the administration. Reporters looking for conventional fronts and battles could not find them. The line between the good guys and the bad guys became blurred. The Ernie Pyle stories could backfire when individual soldiers questioned their role. As one GI told a reporter, "I don't like mowing the people's gardens down."[74] Television reported on a continuing fight whose purpose seemed less clear. Meanwhile on the home front, reformers and radicals challenged tradition by demanding equal rights for women and racial minorities, condemning consumer capitalism, and rejecting conventional morals. Between April and August 1968, Americans witnessed the traumatic assassinations of Martin Luther King, Jr. and Robert Kennedy, race riots, and violence between demonstrators and the Chicago police outside the Democratic National Convention. Civilians experienced decline rather than economic growth. President Johnson's declaration that our "brave young men have to fight to ensure others their freedom" failed to explain how this war furthered America's own prosperity and stability.

"Peace with Honor"

THROUGHOUT THE TURMOIL OF 1968, Richard Nixon campaigned on the pledge to restore law and order. Appealing to Americans who wanted out of

A Sky Trooper from the 1st Cavalry Division (Airmobile) keeps track of the time he has left in Vietnam on his helmet while participating in "Operation Pershing," 1968. (National Archives, 111-SC-647323)

Vietnam, but did not want to lose the war, he promised to win "peace with honor." Nixon, who had lost the presidency to JFK in 1960, had worked hard to improve his poor public image. His problem, summed up his astute public relations advisor Roger Ailes, was that he came across like the boy at school who always had "his homework done and never let you copy."[75] Concluding that voters based their decision on image over reality, his advisors made sure that the candidate appeared on television only in circumstances when he would feel confident. Nixon promised to step up support to South Vietnam so it could take over the fighting (called Vietnamization), pull out American troops, end the draft, and be honest with the American people. He won the election by defeating Vice President Humphrey with a slim margin of 500,000 votes.

Although Nixon publicly announced that he would not be the first president to lose a war, he privately concluded that Americans had to get out of Vietnam. To maintain the global prestige of the United States, he wanted to put off losing, or the appearance of losing, as long as he could. Just as he had repackaged himself, he attempted to repackage the Vietnam War. He and his National Security Advisor Henry Kissinger believed that communism remained the number one enemy, but they decided that the United States had to find a less expensive method of containment. Nixon thought that a policy of détente or easing of tensions with Moscow and Beijing would benefit the United States economically and strategically. The superpowers would be able to negotiate nuclear arms reductions and establish favorable trade relations. The communists, the president assumed, would put pressure on North Vietnam to accept U.S. terms. Above all, as the United States withdrew, Nixon wanted to convey the image of American power. To do so, he would expand the war with massive bombing campaigns in North Vietnam and neutral Cambodia. A "fourth-rate power like North Vietnam" had to have a "breaking point," said Kissinger.[76]

Nixon applied the "us versus them" dichotomy not only to the war, but also to the home front. According to polling, six out of ten Americans by 1969 thought the war in Vietnam was a mistake. The Harris poll showed that while 81 percent of Americans thought the antiwar demonstrators raised legitimate questions, 51 percent disapproved of their methods of protest. For his part, Nixon viewed Americans who supported the administration as patriotic and Americans who opposed the war or criticized government policies as enemies. The president especially wanted to counter the growing mainstream opposition to the war illustrated by the widespread participation in the national Moratorium on October 15, 1969. Millions of citizens in 200 cities across the country stopped conducting business as usual to respectfully protest the war. They listened to speeches, held candlelight vigils, attended special church services, honked car horns, and held marches. Organizers built on their success with a second Moratorium in November. During the "March against Death," protesters carried the names of the 45,000 Americans who by then had died in Vietnam. As had LBJ, Nixon believed that international communism backed the antiwar movement. The CIA could not find evidence for this, but Nixon, acting on his belief, used the CIA, FBI, National Security Agency, and Internal Revenue Service to harass antiwar activists and those members of the media that he designated as enemies.[77]

The Nixon administration's news management strategy called for attacking the media while simultaneously using it to construct the image of a strong president standing firm against enemies overseas and critics at home. Nixon wanted his staff to "build a mythology" of the president. Dissatisfied with the limitations of the Press Office, he created the White House Office of Communications to better "sell" himself and his policies. Its first chief, Herb Klein, a former San Diego newspaper editor, announced, "Truth will become the hallmark of the Nixon administration" as he pledged to eliminate the credibility gap. The Office of Communications developed a long-range media strategy and, in the tradition of the World War I era Committee on Public Information, coordinated the information campaigns of the executive branch. It designed slogans and sound-bites, lobbied columnists, generated letters to the editor, and scheduled appearances for administration spokespeople in person and on television. Target shows included Johnny Carson's *Tonight Show* and *The Dick Cavett Show*, the popular new morning shows, NBC's *Today* and ABC's *Good Morning America*, as well as the Sunday interview shows *Meet the Press, Face the Nation*, and *Issues and Answers*. White House task forces met twice a day to create favorable news stories in time for broadcast media deadlines. Nixon's aide Patrick Buchanan compiled news summaries so that the administration could reward favorable reporters with more access and shun the others. In January 1971, the White House Television Office was created to produce the president's TV appearances, attending to backdrops, lighting, makeup, and wardrobe. After all, noted Nixon privately, "millions of dollars...go into one lousy 30-second television spot advertising a deodorant."[78]

President Nixon preferred to communicate directly to the public. While in office he held 39 press conferences, far fewer than the 998 under FDR, 193 under Eisenhower, and 132 under Johnson. He avoided an open question and answer format in favor of controlled television speeches. As had Johnson, Nixon took advantage of the networks' policy of providing free airtime to the president upon request to make prime-time speeches. His press secretary, Ron

Ziegler, who had worked for chief of staff H. R. Haldeman when both were admen at the J. Walter Thompson agency, promoted the president's image. Reporters, who were used to press secretaries with backgrounds in journalism, were uneasy with the changing nature of White House press relations. They objected to Ziegler's use of advertising jargon such as "photo opportunity." The press corps liked to recall Ziegler's former summer job as a Disneyland tour guide—"welcome to the world of make-believe, folks."[79]

The administration's management of the media coincided with a decrease in investigative reporting. Television coverage of the Vietnamization policy was one example. In 1969, television executives decided to shift their coverage of Vietnam from stories about the battlefield to stories about American troops on their way home and pacification, the programs designed to put the South Vietnamese government in control by securing rural populations, instituting political reforms, and fostering economic development. Instead of showing combat footage three or four times a week, they broadcast it only three or four times a month. "So straightaway people got the impression the war was less important," concluded the executive producer of NBC's Huntley–Brinkley news program. Based on his survey of media coverage of the president in 1972, critic Ben Bagdikian observed that the news media had moved closer to becoming a "propaganda arm of the administration in power."[80]

Manipulating American public opinion, observed historian George Herring, turned out to be easier than making Vietnamization work. U.S. forces kept up an attack on communist bases and supply lines, while American military and economic aid turned the South Vietnamese Army into one of the biggest and best-equipped military forces in the world. Yet, senior U.S. officers, noting the high desertion rate and the degree of corruption and incompetence among ARVN officers, had their doubts about whether the South Vietnamese military could stand on its own against the North. Pacification policies, which prompted both sides to harass and assassinate village leaders, failed to win support for the government in Saigon. Washington tried to convince President Nguyen Van Thieu, a former ARVN officer, to reform the South Vietnamese government and military. Thieu allowed some reforms but preferred rigged elections or none at all. At the same time the administration sought to convince the North that the United States would fight as long as it took to negotiate an honorable peace. Nixon presented Hanoi with an ultimatum calling for mutual withdrawal, which Ho Chi Minh rejected in the weeks before his death in September 1969. To signal the U.S. commitment to the fight, Nixon, following the advice of the Pentagon, ordered bombing raids against communist sanctuaries in neutral Cambodia. During "Operation Menu," B-52s dropped 100,000 tons of bombs on Cambodia; the raids were kept secret from the American public.[81]

Despite the military's reservations regarding the president's Vietnamization policy, the information officers undertook, in the words of Admiral John L. McCain, Jr., commander-in-chief, Pacific, "a coordinated program...to ensure maximum political and psychological benefit from this reduction."[82] To show progress, they adopted two themes. One celebrated the accomplishment of the U.S. troops and the other extolled the capabilities of the South Vietnamese military as it took on greater responsibilities. Most of the withdrawn American units went to Okinawa or Hawaii, but at Nixon's insistence, one returned to the United States for publicity purposes. The homecoming arrangements called for the Second Brigade of the Ninth Division, accompanied by 1,200 reservists recalled to active duty during the Tet Offensive, to parade through Seattle, a city chosen for its moderation both in size and antiwar activism. All seemed to go well, reported *Newsweek*. The crowd shouted "Thank you! Thank You!" as pretty girls handed red roses to the troops. General Westmoreland attended. Most of the returning soldiers "felt they had gone to Vietnam to do a job and had done it." Several, however, registered dismay with the celebration. One said the welcoming ceremonies were "just a gimmick"; others expressed consternation that they were honored as victors before the war had been won. The press reported on the presence of fifty demonstrators who carried signs saying "It's a Trick Dick" and "Bring the Other 500,000 Home." The *Washington Post* noted that bystanders "jeered" the veterans. As these men came home, the *New York Times* pointed out, a thousand others left for duty in Vietnam. Viewing such coverage as a public relations failure, the Defense Department decided to hold no more parades for returning troops.[83]

In November 1969, Nixon outlined his Vietnam policy in a major address known as the "Silent Majority" speech. In response to congressional critics who supported Clark Clifford's call for a pullout of American troops by the end of 1970, Nixon asserted that a complete withdrawal would lead to a bloodbath in South Vietnam and create a crisis of confidence in American leadership. He appealed to the "great silent majority" for support. Then he blamed the protesters for "sabotaging" his diplomacy, saying, "North Vietnam cannot humiliate the United States. Only Americans can do that." Nixon defined his supporters as loyal Americans who by their silence endorsed his policies, which were dedicated to bringing home U.S. troops without suffering a defeat. The president and his followers donned flag lapel pins to show their patriotism.[84]

The White House launched an effort to make it look as though a "silent majority" existed. When network commentators followed his speech with critical analysis, the president decided that the commentators should be discredited. He gave the job to Vice President Spiro Agnew. "The President of the United States has a right to communicate directly with the people who elected him," declared Agnew in a televised speech, "and the people of this country have the right to make up their own minds and form their own opinions about a Presidential address without having the President's words and thoughts characterized through the prejudices of hostile critics before they can even be digested." He described the press as a small, unelected fraternity of privileged snobs in New York and Washington whose views "do not represent the views of America." Although NBC president Julian Goodman viewed the speech as an attack on the freedom of the press, Agnew received a largely favorable response in letters from the public to the networks and his office. According to historian Melvin Small, the administration effectively intimidated the media by accusing it of liberal bias and then asking the Federal Communications Commission to investigate the network coverage. Through this attack on the "elite" media, the administration positioned itself as respecting the people's right to think for themselves, while at the same time defining what they thought. Behind the scenes the White House set up a Tell It to Hanoi Committee and a Committee to Support the President for Peace in Vietnam, which posed as independent grass roots organizations in favor of the president's policies.[85]

Concerned that his Vietnamization policy made him appear soft in Southeast Asia and at home, Nixon expanded the war and stepped up the attack on Americans who opposed it. He used a speech at the Air Force Academy in April 1970 to announce the invasion of Cambodia by ground forces. "If when the chips are down, the world's most powerful nation acts like a pitiful helpless giant, the forces of totalitarianism and anarchy will threaten free nations and free institutions throughout the world," declared the president. At the White House, the senior staff met to receive talking points, such as "Only the president has all the facts on this situation. He must act in what he considers to be the best interests of our country and our troops." Kissinger lost his temper when Donald Rumsfeld, the head of the Office of Economic Opportunity, pointed out that it was not credible to say that the Cambodian invasion was not an expansion of the war. Then Kissinger rushed off to brief his own staff remarking, "I can't have them running loose saying what they think." The president himself delivered a "pep talk" to "the people who talk with people." He said, "Don't play a soft line…The big game is to pull this off.…It's a bold move, imaginative." He instructed the Cabinet to get out this message: "Don't stab our men in the back while *they are fighting for this country* in Vietnam."[86]

Nixon justified the invasion of Cambodia as an attack on the "nerve center" of North Vietnam's military operations, even though the Pentagon had told him it was not sure if this headquarters existed or where it was. The invasion, which did not locate the command center, resulted in the capture of 2000 enemy troops and large stashes of weapons. It also expanded the theater of operations at a time when the United States was attempting to limit its role in Vietnam. The consequences for Cambodia turned tragic when civil war erupted between North Vietnamese-backed Khmer Rouge insurgents and the U.S.-backed government. Nor was the February 1971 expansion of the war by American and South Vietnamese forces into neighboring Laos a success. Looking back, Kissinger pronounced the invasion into Laos "a splendid project on paper. Its chief drawback, as events showed, was that it in no way accorded with Vietnamese realities."[87]

For Americans at home, there was tragedy as well. Demonstrations against the expansion of war into Cambodia broke out on college campuses across the country. National guardsmen and police killed four students at Kent State University in Ohio and two at Jackson State College in Mississippi. Hundreds of university campuses closed down for several days. Members of Nixon's cabinet defended the demonstrations, but the majority of Americans blamed the Kent State shootings not on the National Guard, but on the students. Such antagonism toward protesters was enhanced by news reports in the summer of 1970 of antiwar radicals like the Weathermen who bombed a police department and the Bank of America in New York and the four who bombed the Army Math Research Center at the University of Wisconsin, which killed a student. Two hundred New York City construction workers— referred to as the twin tower guys because they worked on the new World Trade Center—attacked student demonstrators, chanting, "All the way USA!" and "America: Love It or Leave It!" Nixon praised what he called "hard-hat patriotism." On July 4th, the White House sponsored "Honor America Day" starring Bob Hope and the Mormon Tabernacle Choir. On the issue of the war, nonetheless, the president's approval rating sank to 31 percent. Nixon pulled U.S. troops out of Cambodia, but to retaliate against his domestic opponents, he authorized intelligence agencies to spy on American citizens by opening mail and bugging phones.[88]

Polls showed that 71 percent of the public thought that the United States had made a mistake when it sent troops to Vietnam. Angry senators, who had not been consulted about the Cambodian escalation, voted to terminate the Gulf of Tonkin Resolution in June 1971. The *New York Times* began to publish a secret history of U.S. involvement in Vietnam prepared by the Defense Department and leaked by analyst Daniel Ellsberg. Called the Pentagon Papers, the 7,000-page study revealed a flawed decision-making process. It also showed that the Kennedy and Johnson administrations repeatedly had misled Congress and the public about the war. Citing issues of national security, President Nixon tried to block the publication of the Pentagon Papers, but the Supreme Court ruled that the papers did not pose a threat to national security and that the *Times* had the right to publish under the First Amendment's protection of freedom of the press. The administration had Ellsberg arrested, but the charges were later dismissed because of government misconduct. It was discovered that a secret White House group known as the "plumbers" had broken into the office of Ellsberg's psychiatrist to steal damaging information about the man the administration wanted to convict for acts of conspiracy, espionage, and the theft of government property. In June 1972, the arrest of the "plumbers" during their break-in of the Democratic National Party headquarters at the Watergate complex in Washington triggered an investigation by journalists and Congress into the illegal activities of the Nixon White House known as the Watergate Scandal.

Prisoners of War (POWs) and Propaganda

THE ADMINISTRATION MEANWHILE CAPITALIZED on the one Vietnam issue that seemed to unite everyone: POWs. Of the 2,273 Americans who were listed as prisoners of war or missing in action (MIA), about half were known to be killed in action, but their bodies were never recovered. This sad reality of war held true for 78,750 Americans who had fought in World War II and were still unaccounted for, although remains were uncovered every year in Europe. Most of the 587 POWs held by North Vietnam were downed airmen. They endured torture by the North Vietnamese, who paraded their captives as symbols of American vulnerability. In May 1969, Secretary of Defense Melvin Laird opened the "Go Public" campaign when he charged the North Vietnamese and the Vietcong with violating the Geneva Convention on the humane treatment of POWs. In North Vietnam, captured navy pilot John S. McCain III, son of Admiral McCain, experienced improved treatment after two-and-a-half years of abuse, which he believed was the result of all the attention on POWs.[89]

In administration statements, the POWs, rather than the apparently corrupt and incompetent South Vietnamese, now represented what Americans fought to save. Public affairs officials from the Defense and State departments organized the POW families, who held press conferences with political leaders. The "United We Stand" organization led by Texas millionaire H. Ross Perot (a director of the Richard M. Nixon Foundation) set up gala events featuring the families, politicians, and celebrities. The most successful promotion of the POW/MIA campaign was the sale of bracelets, engraved with the name of an American POW or MIA. By 1973, between four million and ten million Americans, including President Nixon, General Westmoreland, Bob Hope, Charlton Heston, Bill Cosby, Johnny Cash, and Sonny and Cher Bono, were wearing bracelets that they promised not to remove until their POW/MIA was returned home or found to be dead. Not all Americans accepted the administration's use of the POW issue to justify continuing the war. Antiwar activists and some POW families argued that ending the war was the way to bring everyone home. "The truth of the matter is that all our sons in Vietnam are POWs," wrote one POW mother to Another Mother for Peace.[90]

Among Americans still fighting in Vietnam, discipline declined as morale plummeted. Soldiers questioned why they should risk their lives. "The dinks are just playin' with us, waiting for us to go home, then they'll beat the ___ out of the ARVN," a rifleman told reporter Donald Kirk for his *New York Times Magazine* story, "Who Wants to Be the Last American Killed in Vietnam?"[91] Small units "sandbagged" missions by calling in fake reports while staying in safe places. Outright mutinies increased. Enlisted men carried out assaults called "fraggings" on officers who ordered dangerous operations. "Officers are afraid to lead their men into battle, and the men won't follow," said General Abrams in 1971. "Jesus Christ! What happened?"[92] Drug abuse and racial conflicts among American servicemen in rear areas increased. Combat troops experienced powerful bonds of trust regardless of racial and ethnic differences, recalled Charley Trujillo, a Chicano from California, and Lt. Vincent Okamoto, a Japanese American who had been born in a World War II internment camp. But they both recognized the pervasive racism directed by Americans at the Vietnamese people they were supposed to be helping.[93]

By the time the draft ended in January 1972, many U.S. soldiers did not support the war they were fighting. Medic Wayne Smith recalled seeing a peace ring on the hand of a dead soldier lying in a body bag. On a trip home to Rhode Island, he found himself hating America where his friends talked about dating and going to the beach while in Vietnam people were fighting and dying. "I hated our materialistic superficiality and our indifference," he remembered. Smith reenlisted so he could provide medical treatment to the Vietnamese. Twenty thousand veterans joined Vietnam Veterans Against the War. The antiwar veterans organized a demonstration in Washington in April 1971, where several hundred gathered on the steps of the Capitol and one by one threw away their medals. With their long hair and sloppy fatigues, the vets, some on crutches and in wheel chairs, did not fit the traditional image of U.S. soldiers home from war. "Son, I don't think what you are doing is good for the troops," a delegate attending the Daughters of the American Revolution convention told one vet. "Lady, we are the troops," he answered. To the administration's frustration, the television networks featured moving interviews with antiwar veterans whose voices cracked as they spoke of dead buddies.[94]

More devastating was the story of the most notorious atrocity committed by Americans in Vietnam, the My Lai massacre. In the summer of 1971, Lt. William Calley of Waynesville, North Carolina, was found guilty of twenty-two murders committed in March 1968. Charlie Company, First Battalion, Twentieth Infantry Brigade of the Americal Division had landed at 8:00 in the morning outside of the village known to Americans as My Lai. The area, declared a free-fire zone, had been leafleted with warnings that all non-Vietcong should flee. Expecting resistance, Charlie Company entered the village firing and by noon had killed every living thing, pigs, chickens, and 504 people. The only U.S. casualty was one self-inflicted gunshot wound in the foot. The Army covered up the incident. Handed out at the Five O'Clock Follies, a press release announced, "In an action today, Americal Division forces killed 128 enemy near Quang Ngai City."[95] A recently discharged helicopter gunner named Ron Ridenhour, who heard men of Charlie Company describe what they had done, challenged the cover-up by writing to the Army and several members of Congress asking for an investigation. The Army Inspector General's investigation led to Lt. Calley's arrest in September 1969.[96]

People's responses to the reports of the My Lai massacre varied. The peace movement cited the killing of civilians as proof of a bad war. The massacre confirmed the fear of some Americans that their troops had become amoral murderers. Others insisted that My Lai was a regrettable exception and resented the application of the label "babykiller" to all soldiers. The incident so challenged the predominant view of American fighting men that many looked for excuses. Nixon told Kissinger that the massacre took place because "these boys" were "being killed by women carrying that stuff in their satchels." Calley's lawyer defended him by saying it was a case of shot or be shot in a fight against communists. Those who felt the real responsibility rested with the higher-ups who gave the orders viewed Calley as a scapegoat.[97]

During the year of Calley's trial, antiwar moderates teamed up with advertising professionals to mount a campaign called "Unsell the War." They designed approximately a million dollars worth of first-rate print ads, radio spots, and TV commercials urging citizens to write their congressman to demand that the troops come home by December 31, 1971. In 1972, the campaign featured television commercials narrated by actors Henry Fonda and James Whitmore calling upon Americans to act responsibly and end the destruction of Vietnam. Fonda, a World War II veteran praised for

Army Photographer Ronald Haeberle's picture taken at the village known to Americans as My Lai in March 1968 appeared in the *Cleveland Plain Dealer* in November 1969 before it was turned into an antiwar poster. The quotation "And Babies" comes from Private Paul Meadlo, who in an interview with Mike Wallace on CBS, said that, as a member of Charlie Company, he killed women, children, and babies at My Lai. (Library of Congress, LC-USZ62-130601)

his performances as Abraham Lincoln, Tom Joad, Wyatt Earp, and Mister Roberts, spoke directly into the camera:

> When I was a kid, I used to be really proud of this country. I thought that this was a country that cared about people, no matter who they were or where they came from. But now, when I see my country engaged in an endless war, a pushbutton war in which American pilots and electronic technicians are killing thousands of Asians, without even seeing who they kill... when I see us each week stepping up the tonnage of bombs dropped on Indochina... then I don't feel so proud any more. Because I thought that was what bad countries did... not my country. What can you do about it? Well, this is still a democracy, isn't it?[98]

Fonda's "citizen" ad ranked near the top of all commercials ever tested for day-after recall, with a 43 percent favorable and 21 percent negative response.

The Committee to Unsell the War produced a series of posters, including this revised version of James Montgomery Flagg's famous World War I poster of Uncle Sam. (Library of Congress, LC-USZC4-3860)

In contrast to World War II when movie stars, advertisers, university professors, athletes, and the media all teamed up with the government to boost morale, the Vietnam War saw division. Outrageous in the eyes of many Americans was the visit of actress Jane Fonda, Henry's daughter, to Vietnam. With actor Donald Sutherland, she had formed the Anti-War Troupe, which toured U.S. military camps as an alternative to the Pentagon-approved USO performances. In July 1972, she visited Hanoi where she was photographed with an anti-aircraft gun that had shot down American airmen who, she said, were being treated well. In addition to being wrong about the POWs, Fonda had violated all sorts of traditions, epitomized by Betty Grable, about the role of attractive movie stars in wartime. Nor did boxing heavyweight champion Muhammad Ali follow in the footsteps of World War II-era champ Joe Louis. When Ali refused to be drafted in 1967, he was stripped of his championship and sentenced to jail. In 1971, the Supreme Court overturned his conviction for draft evasion and he returned to boxing, a hero to some and a villain to others. Also controversial was the number of professional athletes in the National Guard or reserve units, a way for "fortunate sons" and those with connections to avoid going to Vietnam.[99]

Nixon's approval rating went up as the administration encouraged attention on its foreign policy successes rather than Vietnam. In February 1972, Nixon became the first president to visit China and, in May, he went to the Soviet Union. To showcase these achievements, Nixon and Kissinger combined secret travel with surprise announcements, staging diplomatic ceremonies with stunning backdrops. In March North Vietnam launched a major offensive to demonstrate that Vietnamization was not working; the only alternatives were serious negotiation or more war. Ninety-five thousand American forces were still in Vietnam but only 6000 were combat troops. The decrease in the American presence on the ground was countered by an increase at sea and in the air. The United States carried out heavy bombing, the mining of Haiphong harbor, and a naval blockade. At the same time, reporting from Vietnam diminished without ground troops to cover. The air offensive was conducted in secrecy from carriers or bases in Guam and the Philippines. In the past, officials had tried to persuade newsmen, observed correspondent Malcolm Browne. "Now they don't bother. They just freeze us out."[100]

After months of negotiation, the Americans and the North Vietnamese seemed to reach a compromise in 1972. Under its terms, U.S. troops would withdraw, the North would return American POWs, North Vietnamese troops would be allowed to stay in the South, and a political settlement would be worked out by the Vietcong, the South Vietnamese government, and representatives of neutral nations. Washington did not count on the objections of Thieu's government, which had the most to lose. Nixon sent one billion dollars worth of military equipment to the South and pledged that if North Vietnam violated the agreement, the United States would retaliate. In addition, the Americans bombed the North by dropping more tons in a few weeks than they had from 1969 to 1971. The so-called Christmas bombing of 1972 was controversial at home and overseas. Although Nixon and Kissinger claimed that the bombing had compelled Hanoi to give in, they were the ones who accepted the terms they had rejected before Christmas. Kissinger's aide, John Negroponte, put it this way: "We bombed the North Vietnamese into accepting our concessions."[101]

Aware that the peace treaty of January 1973 was not what the White House had projected, officials sought to make it appear that it was. White House aide Patrick Buchanan drafted the four-part message, which summarized the themes of the repackaged conflict. First, Nixon, with the support of the silent majority, had shown the "courage, toughness, and wisdom to make the hard decisions and see them through." Second, the critics in Congress, the universities, and the media, along with the peace activists on the streets, had prolonged the war by advocating that the United States cut and run, a dishonorable solution that would have instead led to a longer war in which the Vietnamese would be left to fight on without American assistance. Third, the United States had achieved the major goals of the war: the return of U.S. POWs, independence for South Vietnam, and the preservation of American credibility, "which is essential not only to our national self-respect but to our continuing role as a force for peace in the world." Fourth, the January agreement was an improvement over the October peace agreement, the Thieu government had not been abandoned, and the December bombing over Hanoi had forced the other side back to the negotiating table and won concessions from them. The goal of the White House was to assure Americans that President Nixon and the United States stood for honor, strength, and peace.[102]

After more than 20,000 Americans had been killed in Vietnam during the Nixon presidency, the United States was out of the war. The peace treaty had not resolved the conflict however; the Vietnamese kept fighting. In Saigon, the Five O'Clock Follies gave its final performance with an American cast, reported *Time* in February 1973. "Well, we may not have been perfect," Army Major Jere Forbus admitted, "but we outlasted *Fiddler on the Roof.*"

Looking back, Barry Zorthian, who had become a vice president at Time, Inc., admitted that the briefings had provided incomplete or inaccurate information. Reporters observed that their access to the field often had made it possible to challenge the official briefings. With the South Vietnamese now in full control of the press and willing to suspend credentials, attack reporters, and destroy their equipment, they noted, it would be more difficult to cover the war.[103]

The administration launched Operation Homecoming, announcing that it was bringing home every one of the 587 POWs. Fifty-five of the Pentagon's PR officers prepared the men for their return to life in 1970s America, explaining male fashions of flared trousers and pastel shirts, women's liberation, and the Super Bowl. When POWs asked who won the war, the officers were to answer, "South Vietnam didn't lose and North Vietnam didn't win." Noting that officers prepped the POWs on what to say in public, *Newsweek* columnist Shana Alexander found it ironic that after years of captivity the POWs had "become hostages of propaganda."[104] For their reports on Operation Homecoming, the networks featured special logos: CBS had an American flag woven with barbed wire, ABC showed a POW dove with a flag, and NBC had a waving soldier. The arrivals home were moving rituals. The red carpet was rolled out, the color guard paraded, and the crowd waved flags. The returning prisoner appeared in uniform at the door of the plane, saluted, and walked down the stairs. Parents, wives, and children ran forward and viewers saw the former POW shed his stiff military posture and turn back into a son, husband, and father as everyone tearfully embraced. Everett Alveraz, returning after eight years and six months of captivity, said "God Bless the President and God Bless You Mr. and Mrs. America." Another officer said, "We went to Vietnam to do a job that had to be done. President Nixon brought us home with honor." *Time* called their return "a needed tonic for America" and a "reaffirmation of faith." As NBC reporter Jeff Perkins put it, "The prisoners coming back seems to be the one thing about Vietnam that has made all Americans finally, indisputably, feel good."[105]

And there was not a lot to feel good about. Following the 1973 Yom Kippur War between Israel and Egypt, the oil-producing countries raised the price of oil 400 percent before placing an embargo on shipments. Rising prices, high unemployment, and the cost of the war contributed to economic decline in the 1970s. As the televised Watergate hearings attracted more viewers than daytime soap operas, Congress asserted its foreign policy powers by making drastic cuts in aid to South Vietnam. In November, legislators passed the

War Powers Act, which required the president to notify Congress within forty-eight hours of the deployment of troops and to withdraw them in sixty days if he did not have congressional endorsement. When Nixon resigned to avoid impeachment proceedings in August 1974, the new president, Gerald R. Ford, attempted to restore decency to the office, but he was unable to heal the country. In that year's Academy Award winner for best documentary, an antiwar film called *Hearts and Minds* (1974), wheelchair-bound veteran Robert Muller explained what hurt the most was that his pride in being a marine and an American was gone.[106]

In Vietnam, the end of the war came sooner than expected as South Vietnam fell to communist forces. In April 1975, the U.S. military evacuated the U.S. embassy in Saigon by helicopter. One of the last to get out was sixty-one-year-old Keyes Beech of the *Chicago Daily News*. Beech reported that he was among the frantic crowd begging to be admitted to the safety of the embassy compound. He was pulled over the embassy wall by marines under orders to grab the Americans first, third-country nationals second, and the Vietnamese last. Beech pronounced the fall of South Vietnam the end of "the most humiliating chapter in American history." Aboard the *U.S.S. Okinawa*, Captain Stuart Herrington and Lt. Col. H. G. Summers felt betrayed. Ordered to assist the evacuation, they told the Vietnamese, as they themselves had been told, that everyone in the compound would be flown out. Instead they left behind 500 people. "We let this country down to the very end," an exhausted Summers concluded. U.S. forces had evacuated 70,000 people on the last day, but left behind millions of South Vietnamese who fled. Some died, some ended up in refugee camps, and thousands came to the United States.[107]

War...Nothing But a Heartbreak

THE EXTENSIVE RESEARCH conducted by U.S. military and civilian scholars into what went wrong in Southeast Asia concluded that American policy, as Kissinger had put it, failed to take into account the realities on the ground. The Cold War official narrative had served to inspire support for war in Vietnam, but it had misled policymakers. The Domino Theory, which explained that Americans must fight communists in Vietnam so they would not have to fight them at home, turned out to be wrong. Nor did the assumption hold up that a show of American military power would persuade Vietnamese communists to back down. The administrations of Eisenhower, Kennedy, Johnson, and

Nixon declared that they aimed to establish an independent South Vietnam. What Washington really wanted was an obedient South Vietnam that would follow U.S. policy. As Thieu observed after the Paris peace talks, "When the Americans wanted to enter, we had no choice, and now [when] they are ready to leave, we have no choice."[108] Throughout, American leaders had been concerned primarily with the image of the United States. At first, U.S. leaders said that the United States must intervene in Vietnam to fulfill its role as leader of the Free World. As more Americans became convinced that the war was a mistake, leaders said the United States could not withdraw without losing its global reputation. In the end, the "war as performance" did not enhance U.S. prestige, but the nation remained a superpower.

At home, war propaganda contributed to the legacy of confusion. Preferring not to attract too much public attention to the conflict in Southeast Asia, the White House information team knew early on that close scrutiny of the Saigon government and civilian losses would not inspire home front support. Instead they practiced news management with Operation Maximum Candor and the Progress Campaign. TV coverage initially presented the conflict as a Cold War contest between freedom and communism. It featured sympathetic interviews with young soldiers and General Westmoreland's optimistic assurances. Officials accentuated the positive and eliminated the negative until events proved otherwise and they lost credibility. As the Cold War consensus fell apart, President Nixon's solution was to redefine the war with slogans such as "peace with honor" and "silent majority." Nixon played up the home front divisions by presenting himself as the tough-minded Cold War expert who must be trusted to know what's best for the country. Although Nixon deflected attention away from Vietnam itself, he could not justify continued U.S. involvement there. His declaration that U.S. troops were engaged in "one of the most selfless enterprises in the history of nations" did not explain why.

Johnson and Nixon used the media to promote their policies and then blamed it for turning people against the war. In doing so, they avoided acknowledgment of U.S. policy failures and the growing disbelief regarding official statements. This blame also ignored how much of the media's war coverage had been supportive. Even so, polls showed that the public had serious misgivings about the war before the Tet Offensive when Cronkite pronounced it a stalemate and viewers saw rows of body bags on their television screens. The credibility gap resulted because, in their news management strategy, officials had relied on communicating to Americans the way they were supposed to feel about the war, not what was actually happening.

Television reporting had for much of the time complemented such a strategy. "The main thing is not the event, and the need to describe it," pointed out critic Michael Arlen, "but to describe it in such a way that people feel the way you would like them to feel about it."[109]

The lesson, according to Nixon, was that the president must master the art of manipulating the media without appearing to do so. By setting up the White House Office of Communications and increasing the numbers of people with backgrounds in public relations and advertising on his staff, he had enhanced the ability of the executive to transmit its message through dramatic images. At the same time, he used secrecy as had Kennedy and Johnson to hide policies from the public. His successors would rely even more on emotional visuals and media restrictions to shape the way war news was perceived by civilians. In this effort, they would have the cooperation of viewers, observed Malcolm Browne. "Honest reporting is the last thing most people want when the subject is war," asserted the veteran correspondent. "War is thundering good theater, in which cheering the home team is half the fun."[110]

When the performance in Vietnam ended badly, President Ford and Secretary of State Kissinger urged Americans to move on and not dwell on it. As historian David Anderson points out, for some that was hard to do. The Vietnam Veterans Memorial, also known as the Wall, dedicated in Washington in 1982, served as a place to acknowledge loss and pain. Architect Maya Lin designed a wound in the earth with 58,000 names etched into black granite, polished like a healed scar. Ross Perot, who opposed Lin's untraditional design, asked the architect whether she thought the veterans might prefer something happier like a homecoming parade. Lin concluded that veterans needed acknowledgement in both ways. Just as soldiers had served as symbols for those who supported and opposed the war, so would veterans, often in ways that denied their individuality and range of opinion. Because of official manipulation, popular movies, and a prevailing spirit of distrust, as many as 69 percent of Americans in 1991 believed that American POWs were still held captive in Vietnam. Two veterans, Senator and former POW John McCain (R-AZ) and Senator and former spokesman for Vietnam Veterans Against the War, John Kerry (D-MA), led a year-and-a-half-long bipartisan investigation that concluded that no POWs remained in Southeast Asia.[111]

The Vietnam War challenged Americans' beliefs about their identity and purpose. Those who were unwilling to accept that the United States had been fought to a stalemate by the Vietnamese placed the blame for failure on the antiwar movement, Congress, civilian leadership, military planners, or the media. In the 1980s, President Ronald Reagan referred to the war as the self-inflicted defeat of a "noble cause." In the 1985 movie *Rambo: First Blood Part II*, Vietnam veteran John Rambo, played by Sylvester Stallone, bitterly demands "Do we get to win this time?" In contrast, the television hit *M*A*S*H*, set in Korea, showed war to be an absurd and deadly waste. While Hawkeye and Trapper dismissed war as futile, Reagan and Rambo glorified victory and home front unity. Neither version addressed General Kinnard's observation: "There was not enough civilian participation in terms of asking the big questions about what we were really doing in Vietnam."[112] Yet, from the perspective of U.S. leaders, there had been too much civilian participation—by students, mothers, religious leaders, veterans, actors, athletes, and others who opposed the war.

As John Chancellor noted in 1965, Vietnam was a hard sell. "Perhaps, therefore, we should try to emulate the 19th century British and try to get a sort of general commitment and support by the American people rather than a specific commitment and support for Vietnam," proposed Chancellor. "The 'This is a long-term proposition—we are a world power and are stuck with this sort of thing' psychology may in fact bring greater comfort to the American people than the definition of the struggle as one of sharp confrontation."[113] To get a "general commitment" for "this sort of thing," leaders would confront at least two problems. First, in emulating imperial Britain as a world power, they would have to revise the traditional view of Americans that the side of empire was the wrong side. In his memoir, *A Rumor of War*, Vietnam veteran Philip Caputo recalled the uneasy feeling that as they searched people's huts he and his men were behaving like "bullying Redcoats" rather than "all-American good-guy G.I. Joes." Second, officials would have to address the public's disillusion with war and propaganda. "The biggest lesson I learned from Vietnam is not to trust government statements," said Senator Fulbright. The attitude that war was good for "absolutely nothing" became known as the Vietnam syndrome. To apply Chancellor's solution, government leaders would have to overcome the public reluctance for war.[114]

6

Operation Iraqi Freedom

War and Infoganda

We will not allow any terrorist or tyrant to threaten civilization with weapons of mass destruction.

George W. Bush, 2002

I wish I could have some real answers to why we're here, but I don't think I'll ever have them.

U.S. soldier in Iraq, 2005

WHEN HE LAUNCHED OPERATION IRAQI FREEDOM in March 2003, President George W. Bush declared that war would make Americans safer and the Iraqis free. Such assertions masked the real purpose: the expansion of U.S. influence in the Middle East. In the months following the terrorist attack by Islamic extremists in September 2001, the president decided to invade Iraq in order to remove dictator Saddam Hussein from power and transform the Persian Gulf nation into a reliable ally. Officials came up with many reasons why Americans must fight, designed to rally support for a war of choice. Their masterful promotion of Operation Iraqi Freedom initially disguised flawed intelligence and inept planning for the occupation. The disastrous results left many Americans wishing for real answers about why they were fighting in Iraq.

Following in the footsteps of McKinley, Wilson, Roosevelt, Truman, and Johnson, Bush described a clash between civilization and barbarism. As had his predecessors, the president extolled the American mission. "The United States will use this moment of opportunity to extend the benefits of freedom across the globe," Bush announced in September 2002. "We will actively work to bring the hope of democracy, development, free markets, and free trade to every corner of the world." To accomplish this goal, he declared, the Americans must confront an enemy on scattered battlefields from the Philippines to North Africa. Terrorists sought to build a radical Islamic empire from Spain to Indonesia, he explained in 2005. "And we must recognize Iraq as the central front in our war on terror."[1]

The promotion of the Iraq War built on the successes of the Persian Gulf War of 1991. Following Iraq's invasion of Kuwait in August 1990, President George H. W. Bush, the father of George W. Bush, skillfully organized an international coalition dedicated to the liberation of Kuwait. He built support at home for Operation Desert Storm by comparing Saddam Hussein to Adolf Hitler, which deflected descriptions of the Iraqi leader as a beneficiary of U.S. policies during the Iraq–Iran War of the 1980s, and using the atrocity story, later discredited, of Iraqi soldiers removing Kuwaiti babies from incubators. With the call to "support the troops," civilian and military officials kept the focus on American fighting men and women as human interest stories rather than instruments of a foreign policy dedicated to maintaining order in the Persian Gulf. Determined not to lose another war on television, the Pentagon used extensive controls to make sure that viewers saw positive images of a clean, high-tech war, although the precision weapons shown at military briefings accounted for only 10 percent of the bombs dropped. John Rendon, who called himself an "information warrior and perception manager" for the CIA and the Pentagon, arranged for Kuwaitis to wave hundreds of small American flags as they greeted their U.S. liberators. At the end of the quick and victorious conflict, the president celebrated the demise of the "Vietnam syndrome," the term for American reluctance to go to war. The wrong lesson had been learned from Vietnam, concluded Barry Zorthian, the former U.S. government spokesman in Saigon. "The lesson of Vietnam," he told a Senate committee in 1991, "is a critical need for accurate and credible coverage by both the government and media which together present a complete picture for the public, not reliance on the presentation essentially of only one side."[2]

The George W. Bush administration coordinated its propaganda campaign by expanding on the news management techniques used in the past. According to Scott McClellan, who served as press secretary from 2003 to 2006, the White House communications staff fought to "seize the media offensive" and "win every news cycle." Proud of their "iron message discipline," officials used facts, lies, and patriotic symbols as well as censorship to conduct "perception management." In a time of bitter rivalry between Republicans

This Operation Desert Storm T-shirt illustrated the "new world order" in the Persian Gulf by placing British, American, and French soldiers at the top of an allied coalition backed by the U.S. flag. The slogan "mission accomplished" contrasted the quick victory in the desert with the drawn-out failure in Vietnam.

and Democrats, they did not benefit from the bipartisan consensus of the Cold War era, but instead manufactured the appearance of consensus. The White House disseminated talking points to Cabinet secretaries, members of Congress, retired generals, think tank experts, lobbyists, journalists, radio talk show hosts, and internet bloggers. "To get everyone on the same song sheet" was the goal of Dan Bartlett, the director of the White House Office of Communications who oversaw a staff of fifty-two.[3]

The administration produced its own combination of propaganda and information, dubbed "infoganda" by comedian Rob Corddry on Comedy Central's fake news show *The Daily Show*.[4] Using dramatic visuals and emotional appeals, officials employed a strategy of credulity, asking people to believe in them and their policies. For example, the White House produced dramatic events such as the ceremonial declaration of the end of combat operations on the U.S.S. *Abraham Lincoln* in May 2003. In the world of public relations, wrote scholar Robert Jackall, "creating the impression of truth displaces the search for truth."[5] The administration made the most convincing case it could by choosing evidence that supported its version and rejecting evidence that did not. A "judicious study of discernible reality" was "not the way the world really works any more," explained a presidential aide. "We're an empire now, and when we act, we create our own reality."[6] In creating their own reality, as persuasive as it was, American leaders neglected the one on the ground in the Middle East. As their predecessors had learned in Southeast Asia, they did so at great cost.

The mainstream media, for the most part, cooperated with the official management of perceptions. During the first months of Operation Iraqi Freedom, 70 percent of Americans turned to the three cable news networks, CNN, MSNBC and Fox, which provided live and continuous coverage. According to market research, television audiences preferred news that directly affected their lives, validated their beliefs, and was fun to watch. Competition for viewers and corporate pressure for ratings caused many news programs to limit foreign affairs coverage. Only ten out of 800 foreign correspondents working for U.S. news organizations could conduct interviews in Arabic. The average "sound bite" had shrunk from forty-two seconds long in 1968 to ten seconds by 1988, making attitude easier to communicate than analysis. Moreover, the format of "objective" reporting on any story required the broadcast only of unexamined pronouncements from two sides of the debate, which allowed each to deliver unchallenged and uninvestigated its spin on the issue. The notion that there were only two sides already simplified the story; typically one side would be the administration's version. To cultivate more specific audiences, news programs began to use aggressive, opinionated personalities to hold viewers' attention and tell them what they wanted to hear. Called the "Fox Effect" after the popular Fox Television News, broadcasters in 2003 delivered an assertive and entertaining mix of prowar bombast with their news reports. As had yellow journalism in the 1890s, such sensational news overshadowed more nuanced reporting.[7]

In the lead-up to the invasion of Iraq, not many Americans paid attention to Iraq itself. While they heaped condemnation on Saddam Hussein, few commentators or officials addressed the long-standing ethnic and religious divisions in Iraqi society. In addition, what Americans typically saw about the people of the Middle East helped to dehumanize them. Classic Hollywood's desert epics had contrasted the modern, masculine civilizers of the west with exotic, villainous Arabs. In action movies *Delta Force* (1986) and *True Lies* (1994), Chuck Norris and Arnold Schwartzenegger rescued Americans from Arabs, who, it seemed, had replaced communists as the routine bad guys. Since the late 1970s, news stories from the Middle East had featured chanting mobs burning American flags, hostage takers, and terrorists. U.S. soldiers, as in the past, drew on racial and religious prejudice to refer to enemy fighters as "sand niggers," "ragheads," and "hajis." While officials described Iraqis as freedom-loving victims who wanted to be like Americans, media coverage usually showed the people of the Middle East as poor, violent, and fanatically religious.[8]

The blurring of news, propaganda, and entertainment helped the administration to sell Operation Iraqi Freedom. The war seemed like a new reality show in which the entire country had been given a part to play. With its logos and theme music, media coverage featured decisive leaders, authoritative anchors, courageous war correspondents, ramrod straight military briefers, can-do troops, and the folks at home displaying flags and yellow ribbons. As a result, two wars were fought simultaneously: the staged war as seen on television and the actual war as fought in Iraq. Official propaganda contributed to this "two wars" phenomenon, first developed during the Persian Gulf War in 1991. The George W. Bush administration, in waging the global War on Terror, promulgated a "culture of fear," which provided the emotional framework for preemptive war against Iraq.[9] As it prosecuted Operation Iraqi Freedom, the administration made progress its daily message. The staged version of the war was a success as long as everyone stayed on script. But the actual war did not unfold as predicted. The Iraqis, in particular, failed to play their assigned parts. When the fighting did not end as announced, the public became disillusioned.

The Case for Iraq

THE PUBLIC CASE FOR THE INVASION OF IRAQ rested on the terrorist attacks of September 11, 2001. Nineteen radical Islamic terrorists hijacked four American airliners and crashed two into the World Trade Center in New York and a third into the Pentagon in Washington, DC. The fourth went down in Pennsylvania because the passengers, who knew the fate of the other planes, fought the hijackers for control. One passenger ended her phone call, "Everyone's running up to first class. I've got to go. Bye."[10] In eighty-four minutes over 3,000 people from more than eighty countries died. Scenes of the collapse of the twin towers, the heroism of the rescuers, the trauma of the survivors, and the horror of the bystanders were broadcast around the world.

From Saudi Arabia, Egypt, the United Arab Emirates, and Lebanon, the hijackers were members of Al Qaeda, the extremist Islamic organization led by Osama bin Laden. The United States and bin Laden once had been on the same side in support of the Islamic fundamentalists who fought against the Soviet army when it invaded Afghanistan in 1979. After the 1991 Persian Gulf War, bin Laden directed his wrath at the United States for keeping troops in Saudi Arabia, which he believed violated the sacred ground of Islamic holy sites. Al Qaeda had attacked a U.S. base there in 1996, bombed U.S. embassies in Kenya and Tanzania in 1998, and attacked the destroyer U.S.S. *Cole* in Yemen in 2000.

The White House defined the crisis in terms of American righteousness, not in terms of U.S. involvement in the Middle East. "This will be a monumental struggle of good versus evil. But good will prevail," declared the president before Congress on September 20. He referred to the World Trade Center and the Pentagon as symbols of freedom and democracy, not American economic and military power. He described the terrorists as heirs to the Nazis and totalitarians. He said, "Either you are with us, or you are with the terrorists" as he announced that the United States would make no distinction between terrorists and those who harbored them. President Bush referred to the war on terrorism as a crusade once in front of the television cameras but quickly dropped it. Although the term crusade along with images of chivalric soldiers was used widely in World War I, when applied to the Middle East, it recalled centuries of Christians invading and slaughtering Muslims in an effort to gain control over the Holy Land. President Bush reached out to American Muslims by visiting an Islamic Center in Washington, D.C., on September 17 and asking Americans to respect each other. Nevertheless, the president, a born-again Christian, continued to use religious terms and apocalyptic rhetoric to claim God's blessings on a worldwide struggle against "evildoers."[11]

The Texan in the White House seemed just as comfortable with cowboy and action-hero imagery. Of Osama bin Laden, he said, "I want him—I want justice. And there's an old poster out West, as I recall, that said 'Wanted: Dead or Alive.'" First Lady Laura Bush told her husband to tone down the dead-or-alive rhetoric, but he didn't. Consciously or not, the president borrowed from the movies. "Make no mistake," asserted the president. "The United States will hunt down and punish those responsible for these cowardly acts." In doing so, he echoed actor Bruce Willis playing a general who declared martial law in New York City as he searched for Arab terrorists in the 1998 film *The Siege*. "Make no mistake," declared Willis. "We will hunt down the enemy, we will find the enemy, we will kill the enemy." Such tough talk was popular at home, but it also raised expectations for dramatic action in a war that the president warned would be long, difficult, and unsatisfying. America's goal, according to the National Security Presidential Directive 9, was "the elimination of terrorism as a threat to our way of life."[12]

To project the president as resolute and in charge was an important goal of the Bush White House. Vice President Richard Cheney and Secretary of Defense Donald Rumsfeld, who had served in the Nixon White House, believed in unchallenged executive power. "The most powerful tool you have," said Cheney, "is the ability to use the symbolic aspects of the presidency to promote your goals and objectives."[13] Before 9/11, President George W. Bush's approval ratings had been mediocre. Comedians had joked about his intelligence, his mangled speech, his controversial record as a Vietnam-era pilot in the Texas National Guard, and the legitimacy of his presidency since he had lost the popular vote in the 2000 presidential election. On September 12, news articles and television commentary featured the president's friends and rivals all asserting that he was up to the job. A Republican advisor thought, "They're overselling a product that's selling itself." Those who worked closely with Bush felt that he came into his own as a wartime president where he could exercise his strength—the ability to make quick and aggressive decisions relying on his gut instincts and beliefs.[14]

Reluctant to provide much in the way of real news, the administration stressed that patriotism and loyalty were expected from the media and the

In honor of the victims and heroes of the terrorist attacks three days earlier, Americans held a National Day of Prayer on September 14, 2001. At the University of Wisconsin–Stevens Point, participants expressed their grief and patriotism. Tom Charlesworth, photographer.

public. For their reporting in the hours following the September 11 attacks, the news media earned praise for stating what they did and did not know. Soon, however, television reverted to speculation from retired military officers, health experts on the terrifying case of mail deliveries of anthrax which killed five Americans, and conditions at ground zero where the World Trade Center had stood. "You can't tell the pundits from the Psychic Friends Network," observed critic Caryn James. Officials asked the networks not to air videos of bin Laden without editing them first. Ari Fleischer, the White House press secretary, said it was possible but not likely that bin Laden used his videos to send coded messages. His remarks turned up on news crawls as "White House fears Osama bin Laden is sending coded messages." When comedian Bill Maher questioned the designation by officials of the terrorists as cowards on his show *Politically Incorrect*, Fleischer, who had not seen the show, said that Americans "need to watch what they say, watch what they do." The crisis inspired self-appointed censors in the media and politics to monitor and condemn any deviation from the official line. Broadcasters adopted the first person plural, saying "our foreign policy" and "to protect us." The White House ordered $23,000 worth of flag lapel pins to boost national morale; as in the Nixon administration, the pins also signaled that the "with us or against us" distinction would apply on the home front as well.[15]

The White House announced almost daily that "we're making very good progress" at home and abroad. Congress enacted the USA Patriot Act, which expanded law enforcement powers and weakened civil liberties by allowing the indefinite detention of immigrants, searches without court orders, and easier government access to personal records. The Department of Justice set up the short-lived Terrorist Information and Prevention System (TIPS), in which postal workers were expected to report strange behavior, and the Total Information Awareness Office for collecting personal information in cyberspace. These policies inspired the satirical *Onion* headline: "Freedoms Curtailed in the Defense of Liberty." Attorney General John Ashcroft held press conferences stating that terrorists planned to hit the United States and asked Americans to be vigilant. The new Department of Homeland Security announced color-coded terror alert levels and staged mock terror attacks reminiscent of Cold War civil defense drills across the country. It advised Americans to purchase canned goods and have at the ready plastic and duct tape to secure their homes. President and Mrs. Bush made TV ads encouraging Americans to "live their lives" by going shopping and taking vacations. Recalling that everyone wanted to help, author Toni Morrison despaired, "We were not to be called on as citizens, only as consumers."[16]

The administration admitted it had more trouble maintaining a "crisper message" on the home front, because, as Dan Bartlett put it, "we don't control when new facts come to light." He meant in contrast to the presentation of military action. In that case, the message and its makers were "all under one roof at the Pentagon," said Bartlett, "and we control it." In October 2001, Bush announced Operation Enduring Freedom against Afghanistan, the current known base of Al Qaeda, by borrowing from Winston Churchill, "We will not waver, we will not tire, we will not falter, and we will not fail." For the first time since its creation in 1949, NATO invoked the mutual defense provision of Article V to declare that the attack on the United States was an attack on all of its members. Fearing that formal NATO involvement would infringe on U.S. freedom of action, Bush sent Deputy Defense Secretary Paul Wolfowitz to Europe to reject the offer of assistance. On its own terms, the United States led an international coalition joined by Britain, Russia, Germany, and France. The president's claim, "We will rally the world," was celebrated by the Enduring Freedom trading card collection produced by the Topps Company, which featured New York City firefighters, German police, and French president Jacques Chirac. "They provide kids with a feeling of assurance that the president and his folks are going to get the bad guys," said Topps Company executive Arthur T. Shorin.[17]

In Afghanistan, the administration managed news coverage by adopting more restrictive press policies than those used in the 1991 Gulf War. The powerful military force of the U.S.-led coalition carried out "asymmetrical warfare" against the governing body of Afghanistan, the Taliban, which had little army and no navy or air force, and Al Qaeda, the stateless organization hiding out in caves. The United States collaborated with the Afghanis of the Northern Alliance who did most of the ground fighting in what was called "proxy war." U.S. Central Command (Centcom) allowed reporters no contact with American troops deployed in the Gulf States, Pakistan, Uzbekistan, and northern Afghanistan. Nor were reporters allowed to cover special forces units that played a key role in the fighting. Centcom placed correspondents with other troops for short periods lasting four or five days. Although effective, the administration's media strategy ran into some trouble. The press began to question contradictions when one week officials announced that the Taliban was finished and the next week they called the Taliban tough adversaries. When the Pentagon announced a victorious raid against the Taliban north of Kandahar, television news reported the story as received. Not until correspondents in Afghanistan challenged the Pentagon's version did Rumsfeld admit that U.S. forces had killed fourteen Afghan villagers, not Taliban members. The military effort stalled in December 2001 after the Pentagon decided not to send troops into the mountains against the Al Qaeda stronghold at Tora Bora and bin Laden got away. When the United States failed to take Osama bin Laden, Rumsfeld assured Americans that it didn't matter, saying, "you can be certain he's having one dickens of a time operating his apparatus."[18]

While Rumsfeld practiced "expectations management," the administration embarked upon a global propaganda campaign that included the home front. First, it set up a domestic news management operation at the White House, led by top communications directors from the White House, and the departments of State, Defense, and Homeland Security. These veterans of political campaigns and public relations jobs at Hill and Knowlton and Disney met every morning to coordinate the message to be delivered to the news media day by day and week by week. Described as a successor to the Office of War Information (OWI), the White House group had power over the daily message and a level of presidential cooperation far beyond anything that OWI chief Elmer Davis could ever have imagined. The administration portrayed the Taliban as "hijackers" of the peaceful religion of Islam and Americans as liberators of oppressed Afghani women. This portrayal, notes historian Emily Rosenberg, cast the United States again in the role of manly rescuer on a mission to protect brutalized women and girls.[19]

In recognition of Osama bin Laden's success in portraying the War on Terror as a war against Islam, the State Department launched a public diplomacy campaign to reach out to foreign audiences, especially in the Islamic world. It conducted polling in Muslim countries in order to find out what people thought, not to help Americans learn more about them, but so that the United States could more effectively target its message. The campaign essentially was a one-way street, projecting the American lifestyle. It did not address the issues that concerned Muslims such as U.S. support for Israel or the growing U.S. presence in the Middle East. For distribution in Islamic countries, the "Shared Values" videos featured happy Muslim-Americans at work and home praising American values. After watching one of these ads, Ahmad Imron, a student in Indonesia, said "We know that there's religious freedom in America, and we like that. What we're angry about is the arrogant behavior of the U.S. in the rest of the world."[20]

The Defense Department announced a new Office of Strategic Influence "to more directly influence foreign public opinion about U.S. military operations." Coinciding with news stories of the Pentagon's false reports from Afghanistan, this announcement sparked concern. Within the military, public affairs officials and the relatively new group of "information warriors" disagreed over the plan. "The problem," said a former head of the Air Force's press desk, was that the information warriors "don't see anything wrong with not telling the truth." In response to criticism, the White House disavowed any plan for disinformation. On NBC, Rumsfeld declared, "The Pentagon does not lie to the American people." He announced that the Office of Strategic Influence would be closed, but the campaign to influence foreign opinion would continue.[21]

In the summer of 2002, the administration announced that it would adopt major new foreign policies of preemptive war and unilateralism "to help make the world not just safer but better." Its National Security Strategy contained a revised version of Franklin Roosevelt's Four Freedoms. It maintained FDR's freedoms of speech and worship, but replaced freedom from fear and freedom from want with democracy and free enterprise, more specific goals that reflected American political and economic preferences. Identifying "free trade" as a "moral principle," the strategy explained, "If you can make something that others value, you should be able to sell it to them." Such an explanation was a direct descendent of William McKinley's assertion that expansion overseas meant midwestern farmers would be able to sell more of their good broom-corn.[22] To justify replacing the Cold War policy of containment with preemption, Bush asserted, "If we wait for threats to fully materialize we will have waited too long." When House Majority Leader Dick Armey (R-TX) told reporters, "We Americans don't make unprovoked attacks," the White House asked him to withhold public comment. "America has, and intends to keep, military strengths beyond challenge," declared the president at West Point on June 1. The U.S. military budget of nearly $400 billion was larger than the military budgets of the next twenty-five nations combined. The United States only needed allies, it assumed, to provide bases and take care of peacekeeping. The Bush Doctrine, as the strategies of unilateralism and preemption became known, suggested that the Americans could go to war when and where they wanted.[23]

The administration's bold strategy prompted criticism abroad and at home. News stories reported that the United States had squandered the world's goodwill following 9/11. European critics observed that the United States preached democracy, human rights, and free enterprise, but didn't practice them, pointing to the suspension of rights for arrested terrorism suspects and corporate corruption scandals. Nor did foreign leaders welcome the pressure to support U.S. policies. "This sort of Dallas syndrome—with us or against us—is not helpful," said Egyptian Foreign Minister Admed Maher. Bush asserted that in the War on Terror he had the power to act without restraint from the United Nations or Congress. Not according to the Constitution, pointed out Yale University law professor Bruce Ackerman in a *Washington Post* article. Treaties ratified by the Senate, including the U.N. Charter, are the "supreme law of the Land," said Ackerman, which the president was required to faithfully execute. Senior Republicans, former national security advisor Brent Scowcroft, former secretary of state James Baker, and former secretary of state Henry Kissinger advised against unilateralism, encouraging the administration to build up international support for its policies. No need, replied Congressman Tom Delay (R-TX). "We're no longer a superpower. We're a super-duper-power," said Delay on Fox News. "We are the leader that defends freedom and democracy around the world. We are the leader in the war on terrorism. When we lead, others will follow."[24]

Although the Bush administration justified the invasion of Iraq as a response to the 9/11 attack, its policy had deeper roots. Since the 1991 Persian Gulf War, the goal of "finishing the job" or removing Saddam Hussein from power had been promoted by prominent neo-conservatives such as Cheney, Rumsfeld, and Wolfowitz. To push for a larger military and urge a tougher line against Iraq, they had in 1997 organized the Project for the New American Century. It lobbied Congress to approve the Iraqi Liberation Act, which stated that it "should be the policy of the United States to support efforts to remove the regime headed by Saddam Hussein from power." Signed by President Bill Clinton, the act authorized ninety-seven million dollars for U.S. military equipment and the training of Iraqi opposition groups. Twelve million dollars went to the chief opposition group, the Iraqi National Congress (INC), which had been established in 1992 with covert CIA funding. The INC advocated U.S. intervention in Iraq. So did the Committee for the Liberation of Iraq, a Washington-based group set up in November 2002. Chaired by Bruce Jackson, a former vice president of Lockheed Martin Corporation, a company that in 2002 received seventeen billion dollars in contracts from the Pentagon, the committee worked closely with the Bush White House. Its members included the organizers of the Project for the New American Century along with Senators John McCain (R-AZ) and Joseph Lieberman (D-CT), who appeared as experts on news shows.[25]

Appeals to fear and patriotism served as the emotional core of the White House campaign. In the summer of 2002, the White House Iraq Group (WHIG) was set up to design the promotion of war. Unlike the largely reactive Vietnam Information Group, also based in the White House, WHIG intended to control the message. Nor would this task be left to behind-the-scenes staffers. Headed by chief of staff Andrew Card, WHIG included deputy chief of staff Karl Rove, the vice president's chief of staff Lewis "Scooter" Libby, the head of all White House communications, Karen Hughes, national security advisor Condoleezza Rice, and her deputy, Stephen Hadley. It opened the campaign on the first anniversary of 9/11. "From a marketing point of view you don't introduce new products in August," said Card. The timetable would not be based on events in the Persian Gulf but on the upcoming November congressional elections; its activities would be aimed at pressuring politicians to back the president or risk charges of weakness and disloyalty. WHIG used the term "death squads" in place of Iraqi military forces and "liberation" rather than occupation. The press readily adopted the phrase "regime change," essentially the overthrow of a foreign government through military invasion.[26]

The administration's case for war rested on three principal aims. First, eliminate the urgent threat presented by Saddam Hussein's weapons of mass destruction. It was the one justification for war on which everyone could agree, Wolfowitz later explained. Iraq, President Bush declared, was capable of striking Western targets "on any given day." Defending preemption, he said, "Facing clear evidence of peril, we cannot wait for the final proof— the smoking gun—that could come in the form of a mushroom cloud." In his 2003 State of the Union address, the president claimed that Niger had signed a deal to sell Iraq yellow cake uranium, a necessary ingredient in the uranium enrichment process that could lead to the development of a bomb. WHIG repeatedly used this story because unlike most highly technical reports on nuclear weapons development it simply linked "uranium" and "bomb" to Iraq. In doing so, WHIG ignored the fact that the U.S. intelligence community had discredited the Niger report; CIA Director George Tenet already had interceded once before to remove this claim from a presidential speech in October. In what became known as a "feedback loop," the U.S. government funded the INC, which produced Iraqi defectors who said that Iraq had mobile biological weapons laboratories and was trying to reconstitute its nuclear weapons program; the INC passed on the unreliable defector reports to journalists such as Judith Miller of the *New York Times*, which printed her reports on the front page; during television interviews Vice President Cheney then cited Miller's stories as evidence of the Iraqi threat.[27]

Another declared aim was the elimination of the threat that Saddam Hussein and Al Qaeda would unite against the United States. The administration produced little evidence to show that this threat existed. To suggest a connection, officials repeatedly linked the "tyrant" Hussein with terrorists in statements describing the on-going danger to America. In his 2003 State of the Union address, Bush announced that Iraq had ties to Al Qaeda, a more direct claim than his usual references to "Al Qaeda-type organizations" or "a terrorist network like Al Qaeda." The vice president announced that it was "pretty well confirmed" that one of the 9/11 hijackers had met with Iraqi intelligence officials in Prague, a claim later found to be false. At a press conference on March 6, the president conflated 9/11 with the war in Iraq eight times. He insisted that the United States should take care of the threat now so "we don't meet it later with firefighters and police in our cities." Critics complained that most American media outlets paid little attention to reports that the administration had cited unconfirmed or erroneous information. By March 2003 many Americans believed what was not true—that Iraq was responsible for the September 11 attacks. Polls showed that 53 to 70 percent of Americans thought that Saddam Hussein was personally behind the attacks and that 50 percent thought that some of the hijackers had been Iraqis. Administration officials did not make an effort to correct these widespread misperceptions.[28]

The most far-reaching war aim proclaimed by the administration was spreading democracy to Iraq and strengthening peace in the Middle East. By liberating the Iraqis from their "nightmare world" of "torture chambers and poison labs," Bush asserted before the American Enterprise Institute in February 2003, the United States would create a democratic and free Iraq that would serve as a "dramatic and inspiring example of freedom" to other Arabs. To those who said an invasion would destabilize the region and interfere with the war on terrorism, Cheney rejoined: "The opposite is true.... Extremists in the region would have to rethink their strategy of jihad. Moderates... would take heart, and our ability to advance the Israeli–Palestinian peace process would be enhanced." Officials predicted that the Iraqis would welcome the U.S. military as liberators. Therefore the Pentagon did not expect much resistance, as General Richard B. Myers, the chair of the Joint Chiefs of Staff, explained on the *Today* show.[29]

The administration drew attention to Saddam Hussein's villainy rather than to U.S. interests in the Persian Gulf. President Bush and his top aides stressed that the Iraqi dictator had used chemical weapons against Iranians and Iraqi Kurds but did not explain that Hussein had done so while benefiting from U.S. support during the Iran–Iraq War in the 1980s. Nor were they comfortable discussing the issue of oil, which had long been the key to U.S. economic and strategic interest in the region. Although the top secret national security directive signed by the president in August 2002 listed "minimize disruption in international oil markets" as one of the U.S. objectives in Iraq, Rumsfeld declared that the war had nothing to do with oil. Cheney, however, said it was likely that Saddam Hussein would acquire nuclear weapons "fairly soon" and that once he had them, he would seek to dominate the Middle East and its oil supplies through nuclear blackmail. Wolfowitz announced that Iraqi oil profits would finance postwar reconstruction, although experts questioned the feasibility of this plan.[30]

Although President Bush had decided to go to war, he publicly pursued a diplomatic solution while moving troops into the Persian Gulf. According to a September 2002 poll, 64 percent of Americans favored military action against Iraq, but only 33 percent approved military action without allies. British Prime Minister Tony Blair persuaded Bush that for reasons of "political viability" he needed to show he had tried to obtain U.N. support. Secretary of State Colin Powell persuaded the Security Council that the best way to avoid war was to support a resolution demanding that Iraq cooperate with U.N. weapons inspectors and reveal whether it possessed weapons of mass destruction (WMD) or else face "serious consequences." The Council passed the resolution on November 8 by a vote of 15 to 0. Saddam Hussein allowed inspectors to return to Iraq. From the administration's perspective, the outcome was already determined. For policymakers convinced that the inspectors might take months to locate WMD, it was better to strike soon before it got too hot in the desert. When the United States signaled it was prepared to end inspections only weeks after they commenced, the French and German foreign ministers objected.[31]

The White House selected Powell, who was, according to polls, the most trusted member of the administration, to make the definitive case before the United Nations on February 5, 2003. The target audience of this speech was not just the international community, but also doubtful Americans. Behind the administration's unified facade, officials disagreed over the evidence. State Department staffers dismissed a draft written by the vice president's office because it relied on information taken out of context, newspaper stories written by journalists known to rely on Pentagon sources, and the dismissed report that one of the 9/11 hijackers had met with Iraqi officials in Prague. In the end, the secretary used the flawed but more credible CIA intelligence. At the United Nations, Powell detailed Iraq's nuclear ambitions, biological and chemical weapons, and ties to Al Qaeda. Later it would be revealed that the facts he cited were known to be false or unreliable, under dispute at the CIA, the Defense Intelligence Agency, the Energy Department, and the International Atomic Energy Agency. Despite the secretary's assertion that U.S. evidence was backed by "solid sources," France, Germany, Russia, and China successfully led the opposition joined by Mexico and Chile against a second U.N. resolution condemning Saddam Hussein for failing to comply. But Powell's speech hit its domestic mark. A CNN/USA Today/Gallup poll found that 79 percent of Americans thought that the secretary of state had made a "strong" case for invading Iraq.[32]

The president found Congress to be more cooperative than the United Nations. In October, the Senate debated a resolution empowering Bush to use force against Iraq. An amendment offered by Senator Richard Durbin (D-IL), which required the president to "demonstrate that Iraq poses an imminent military threat to the United States before he could order an invasion," went nowhere. Asserting that Saddam had stockpiles of poisons to kill the entire population on the planet several times over, Senator McCain said the vote "will reveal whether we are brave and wise or reluctant, self-doubting." Before the November election and before Bush failed to get U.N. support, Congress, by a vote of 77 to 23 in the Senate and 296 to 133 in the House, granted the president the authority to use force against Iraq. The president announced that the resolution told the world that "America speaks with one voice." Congress "decided to let Bush decide," explained Louis Fisher, an expert on constitutional war powers. "So there was kind of an abdication."[33]

In the weeks before the war, the administration kept supporters and critics busy debating its versions of the present, past, and the future. News stories reported that officials from the State Department and the CIA believed that administration hawks had exaggerated the evidence of the Iraqi threat. A few reports noted the use of shaky facts. For example, Bush cited as evidence an International Atomic Energy Agency (IAEA) report that said Iraq was six months away from developing a nuclear weapon even though the report said this was the case before the 1991 war when U.S. bombing had destroyed Iraq's nuclear facilities. The White House later admitted that Bush was "imprecise."[34] When the president used the 1962 Cuban missile crisis as an example of preemptive action against an enemy, Senator Edward Kennedy (D-MA) pointed out that JFK had avoided a preemptive assault against Cuba and used a naval blockade instead. General Eric Shinseki, the Army Chief of Staff, told a Senate panel that based on U.S. experience in Germany and Japan following World War II, and Bosnia in the 1990s, it would take several hundred thousand soldiers to effectively occupy postwar Iraq. Two days later, Wolfowitz dismissed Shinseki's estimate. He had heard from Iraqi Americans that U.S. forces would be greeted as liberators, which meant that far fewer troops would be necessary to keep order. Commentators turned to the question of whether the United States should embrace its role as a global empire. Proponents argued that the United States was a benevolent force on its way to rescue the Iraqi people from a brutal dictatorship. Former U.S. diplomat Joseph Wilson disagreed. The "underlying objective of this war," he asserted, "is the imposition of a Pax Americana on the region and the installation of vassal regimes that will control restive populations."[35]

Prowar politicians and pundits competed to see who could heap the most scorn upon Americans who questioned administration policies. They joined Senate Minority Leader Trent Lott (R-MS) in his outrage over Majority Leader Tom Daschle's (D-SD) request that President Bush clarify the plans for the next stages of the war. Lott demanded, "How dare Senator Daschle criticize President Bush while we are fighting our war on terrorism, especially when we have troops in the field!" Antiwar protests at home and overseas received less than flattering coverage. On February 15, ten million people around the world, including people in 150 American cities, demonstrated against launching a war against Iraq. National Public Radio led its report by announcing that "Iraq is gloating over" the protests. Little media attention was given to the antiwar positions of the National Council of Churches, the National Conference of Catholic Bishops, college groups, 9/11 families against the war, and numerous Operation Desert Storm veterans. Entertainers who took antiwar positions were chastised. When Natalie Maines of the Dixie Chicks said at a London concert that she was embarrassed to be from the same state as George W. Bush, radio stations banned the group. Appearing on CNN, antiwar actress Janeane Garofalo pointed out that prowar celebrities were honored, not ridiculed. She said she would prefer it if television shows asked experts and professors to represent antiwar views, but instead they asked actors and then condescendingly questioned their competence to know what they were talking about.[36]

The issue of Iraq was pushed aside as officials and supporters of the war unleashed anger at France, America's oldest and least loved ally, for its refusal to back U.S. policy. Rumsfeld dismissed France and Germany as "old Europe," while Fox commentators expressed outrage that in contrast to the United States' moral approach to foreign policy, France based its on crass economic self-interest. Recalling the World War I effort to rename all things German, French fries became freedom fries and French toast became freedom toast. On Capitol Hill, House cafeteria workers put red, white, and blue freedom stickers on packets of French dressing. People in West Palm Beach, Florida, poured French champagne in the street. Former Office of Strategic Services operative and chef Julia Child mourned "a waste of good wine." Bumper stickers promised, "First Iraq, then France." Dismissing "Euroweenies" and "EU-nuchs," prowar Americans proclaimed their toughness.[37]

As commentators debated historical analogies, imperial ambitions, and unworthy allies, the president and his advisors stuck to their simple message that war against Iraq would make Americans safe and Iraqis free. Referring to

Saddam Hussein and his sons as killers and deviants, they described the rape rooms where women and girls were at the mercy of Iraq's rulers. They warned that Hussein would use the Iraqi people as human shields as he had in 1991 but asserted that the precision of American weapons would minimize civilian casualties. From September 2002 to February 2003, more than 90 percent of the stories on the rationale for war on ABC, NBC, and CBS originated from the White House. "The president uses his public appearances very artfully to advance his message; he says the same thing over and over," said Bill Plante, CBS News White House correspondent. On March 6, Bush dismissed the report of Hans Blix, the U.N. chief weapons inspector, who said that Iraq was not actively attempting to manufacture nuclear weapons. Saddam Hussein, interviewed by Dan Rather on CBS, talked about the "huge lie that was being waged against Iraq about chemical, biological, and nuclear weapons." No one believed the Iraqi leader, a lesson in what happens when liars tell the truth.[38]

By March 2003, many Americans suffered from "justification fatigue." The impatience to get on with it was felt by troops in the desert, primed to fight. The country expressed regard for the all-volunteer military, which as of 2000 drew 42 percent of its members from minority populations. Television covered the farewells between the men and women in the armed services and their families. The *Today Show* interviewed military men who, because of reports of infertility among veterans of the 1991 war, were leaving part of themselves behind in sperm banks. On the same show, a business expert explained that employers were not hiring until the uncertainty over the war was settled. Most Americans thought that Iraq had WMD whether they supported the war or thought continued inspections should be given a chance to work. The claim that Iraq had ties to Al Qaeda encouraged the mistaken belief that Saddam Hussein was behind 9/11. The goal of spreading democracy to the Middle East appealed to many, although some expressed doubts about whether a military invasion was the best method of achieving it. Critics argued that war could further inflame the Arab world and diminish confidence in American leadership. "We are stronger than anyone else, but we are not capable of simply dictating to the entire world," warned former national security advisor Zbigniew Brzezinski; "We don't know what we're doing."[39] Polls showed Americans were divided and concerned. In contrast, the administration betrayed no misgivings. Announcing that Saddam and his sons had forty-eight hours to "get out of town," the president stuck to the script of the Western.

Operation Iraqi Freedom

"THE PURPOSE OF THIS OPERATION is to force the collapse of the Iraqi regime and deny it the use of WMD to threaten its neighbors and U.S. interests," stated the classified U.S. war plan. The opening assault, labeled "shock and awe," was intended to demonstrate the enormous might of American military power, which would persuade the enemy to surrender. The goal had been the same in Vietnam, although this time there would be no gradual escalation. To inspire his top officers, General Tommy Franks of Centcom showed the opening of the movie *Gladiator* (2000) when actor Russell Crowe, playing a Roman general, orders his legions to "unleash hell" on rebellious Germanic tribes resisting the empire. The actual initial assault against Iraq on March 20 was not a success. Acting on intelligence regarding Saddam Hussein's location, the U.S. Air Force carried out "decapitating strikes" by dropping "bunker-busting" bombs on what turned out to be an empty field. Incorrect intelligence would continue to be a problem. Although American forces excelled at using superior speed and innovative technology, they did not understand their enemy. Washington had not provided them with sufficient troops or adequate planning for the occupation. In contrast, the campaign to manage perception on the home front was carried out with precision.[40]

From the beginning, the message was progress. At the White House, the newly formed Coalition Information Center (CIC) joined WHIG in coordinating the official line of the White House with the Pentagon, the departments of Justice, State, and Treasury, the Voice of America, the U.S. Agency for International Development, and participating allies, especially Great Britain. At a 9:30 AM conference call, the CIC defined the theme for the day to be delivered every few hours at briefings and television appearances. Each weekday, four senior officials from the State Department and the Pentagon went to Capitol Hill to deliver top-secret briefings to members of Congress. "If you keep them informed, they're happy," said the Pentagon's head liaison to Congress.[41] The White House posted aides to Centcom in Doha, Qatar, to manage the military side of the message for the 700 journalists who would cover the war from headquarters. James Wilkinson, the thirty-two-year-old deputy White House communications director with a lieutenant's rank in the naval reserve, wore full desert-battle dress and held a civilian rank equal to that of a two-star general. Wilkinson prepared Centcom spokesman, General Vincent K. Brooks, for his 7 AM briefing timed for the morning television shows and delivered from a $250,000 stage set. Daily

General Brooks announced a version of "Our plan is working, and we're one day closer to achieving our objectives."[42]

The chief news source about military action, the administration decided, would be the confident secretary of defense, nicknamed "Rumstud" by the president. On March 22, Rumsfeld announced the objectives of the war: eliminate weapons of mass destruction, end the regime of Saddam Hussein, "search for, capture, drive out terrorists who have found safe harbor in Iraq," deliver humanitarian relief, "secure Iraq's oil fields and resources, which belong to the Iraqi people, and which they will need to develop their country," and help the Iraqis make a rapid transition to "representative self-government." Secretary Powell kept a low profile. As Americans would learn later, the Pentagon ignored the State Department's plans for occupation, which correctly had predicted looting and insurgency once Saddam Hussein was removed from

Secretary of Defense Donald Rumsfeld and Joint Chiefs of Staff Chair General Richard Myers held a briefing about the opening hours of Operation Iraqi Freedom at the Pentagon on March 20, 2003. They displayed a World War II poster of a little girl holding a picture of her father in uniform that says, "Don't kill her Daddy with Careless Talk." Lawrence Jackson, photographer. (Associated Press)

power. Powell's chief job appeared to be to lend dignity to the idea of the "coalition of the willing."[43]

Aware that Americans were uneasy about the policy of unilateralism, the Bush administration announced the existence of major international support for Operation Iraqi Freedom. It celebrated the "coalition of the willing" even though only Britain and Australia committed sizable forces in 2003. In contrast to the Johnson administration, which dropped the "more flags" campaign when it failed to attract allies during the Vietnam War, President Bush pronounced the "coalition of the willing" to be "huge." The administration listed forty-three nations, including Micronesia, Panama, and Uganda, "willing to be identified as coalition members," even if they provided only moral support. In the end, private security firms, at the cost of one billion dollars by 2006, provided approximately the same amount of combat forces, about 25,000, as the coalition nations.[44]

President Bush, it was reported, was a calm and cool commander-in-chief. To show that his boss was neither micromanaging the war nor obsessed with news coverage like LBJ, Fleischer announced that the president was not even watching television. This claim suggested, however, that the president might be a little too detached from the war. Later, the press secretary announced that the president did watch television coverage. Throughout the spring of 2003, Bush's public appearances at military bases reinforced his commander-in-chief image. Wearing a U.S. Coast Guard jacket, the president spoke to Coast Guard employees in Philadelphia about how Iraqi "death squads" killed civilians who did not fight coalition forces. At Camp Lejeune, North Carolina, the president, with Laura Bush beside him, told cheering marines that "Saddam's thugs" who had "shielded themselves with women and children" would be considered war criminals.[45]

As the war began, news reports announced that Americans rallied around the president, and the price of stocks soared as uncertainty came to an end. Senator Daschle, who had been condemned as a traitor by his colleague from Mississippi two weeks earlier, said in a radio address, "Our nation is united in gratitude and respect for [the troops] and in support for our commander in chief." Daschle displayed more bipartisan unity than the polls. Republicans gave the president an approval rating of 95 percent and Democrats gave an approval rating of 37 percent. At a similar point in the Persian Gulf War, the president's father enjoyed a 94 percent approval rating from Republicans and an 83 percent approval rating from Democrats. Americans were not certain about the president's aims despite his declaration, "We will stay on task until we've achieved our objective, which is to rid Iraq of weapons of mass destruction." Fifty percent said he wanted to remove Saddam Hussein from power, 20 percent said he was trying to halt the spread of weapons, and 16 percent believed his chief reason was to protect America's oil supply. As to be expected, the troops in the field had their own assessment. On the way to Baghdad under artillery fire, a marine lieutenant heard a corporal sing, "One, two, three, four, what the fuck are we fighting for?"

"You'll have to answer that for yourself."
"Well, sir, I guess I'm fighting for cheap gas and a world without ragheads blowing up our fucking buildings."
"Good to know you're such an idealist."
"That world sounds pretty ideal to me right about now."[46]

Media attention focused on the military forces being covered by journalists who accompanied them. Although presented as new, the Pentagon's policy of embedding would have felt familiar to Frederick Palmer in the Philippines or Ernie Pyle in Italy. About 600 reporters, chosen by the Pentagon, were assigned to military units and reported from the front lines. In addition to the major news organizations, the Pentagon selected reporters from MTV, *People, Rolling Stone*, and *Business Week*. Each reached a different audience, explained a Pentagon spokesman, who said, "Our goal is to dominate the information market." Bryan G. Whitman, deputy assistant secretary of defense for media operations, explained that "objective third-party accounts from professional observers" would counter Saddam's lies and deceptions. At the same time, the Pentagon was confident that embedding reporters with their soldiers would erase objectivity. As one commanding general put it, "These guys are going to be a band of brothers with our troops." The reporters agreed to the usual restrictions not to divulge troop locations or operations. Nor could they report on the identities of Americans wounded or killed until the next of kin were notified. Instituting strict controls, the military ordered that reporters could not travel independently and interviews with the troops had to be on the record. Public Affairs officers supplied soldiers with messages for the media: "We are here to help Iraq restore its independence" and "We will remain in Iraq until told our mission is complete." Pamela Hess, United Press correspondent, said the military favored embedding because it wanted better coverage and because reporters "turn to mush" around gung-ho, polite eighteen-year-olds.[47]

As the Pentagon expected, embedded reporters became more than objective witnesses. Embedded reporters "have been very user friendly," said Second Brigade's Commanding Officer, Col. David Perkins. "They do what we say, stay out of the way and keep their heads down." Acknowledging the relationship between the reporter whose survival depends on the troops he is covering to be "professionally treacherous," *New York Times* reporter Jim Dwyer observed that the soldiers wanted people back home to know what was happening to them and were "willing to talk around the clock until it is time to go and kill people." Veteran correspondent George Wilson observed that the military had more control over news coverage than ever. Reporters could not cover villages and the people who lived there as they had in Vietnam. Being embedded, he concluded, was "like being the second dog in a dogsled team."[48] Nevertheless, by using videophones, portable satellites, laptop computers, digital cameras, and night-sight scopes, embedded reporters provided twenty-four hours a day of riveting coverage. The Project for Excellence in Journalism later concluded that 94 percent of the embedded reports were accurate. Reports that proved to be false—such as the discovery of a chemical factory or the morgue of torture victims that turned out to be corpses from the Iraq–Iran War—sounded true because they fulfilled expectations.[49]

News reports from Iraq were themselves embedded in TV entertainment formulas of heroes triumphant and villains vanquished. Cable networks titled their war coverage "Showdown: Iraq," "Strike on Iraq," and "Target: Iraq." Reporters, news anchors, and retired generals adopted the official language that sanitized American actions and dehumanized the enemy. Americans "cleaned up," "mopped up pockets of resistance," launched "surgical strikes," hit "targets of opportunity," and "secured" the airport. They "hunted," "flushed out," or "drained the swamp" of "enemy thugs," "death squads," and "terrorists." Television also reported the war as it did sports, which reinforced the official message that the war would follow a predictable game plan. Military officers, embedded correspondents, and pundits talked about "read our offense," "red zone," and "blue on blue," the term substituted for "friendly fire." When MSNBC anchor Lester Holt asked its expert commentator, former Navy SEAL, professional wrestler, and Minnesota governor Jesse Ventura, "Have we made war glamorous?" he answered, "It reminds me a lot of the Super Bowl."[50]

Occasionally television stories included off-message exchanges that had a haunting quality. On CBS, correspondent David Chater approached a soldier in Baghdad who was crouching by a curb and looking through binoculars. Chater bent down with his mike and asked, "What are you doing?" and then, cheerfully, "It's all worth it, right?" as though the only answer could be yes. The soldier kept looking ahead and did not turn to face Chater. He took his hands off his binoculars, spreading them out a little, and almost shook his head as if to indicate no or that he did not know if it was all worth it. Chater said, "Well, you're still in the middle of it. I'll let you get on with your work."[51]

News programs used images of soldiers and their families—a serviceman bidding farewell to his crying daughter, a soldier carrying a wounded buddy, a woman tying a yellow ribbon around a tree—as they cut to commercials. Critic Nancy Franklin observed that during the delay caused by sandstorms, instead of reporting on Iraqi society or global politics, television filled the time with stories on "the mood of America," emphasizing themes of service and sacrifice. When sacrifice occurred, television programs conducted emotional interviews with family members. On the *Today Show*, Katie Couric in New York would gravely ask some grieving person sitting in her living room how she felt when her son or husband was killed in action. Tears all around, followed by Al and the weather, summed up critic Charles McGrath.[52]

In many ways these exchanges with the families were the closest viewers came to seeing that people were being killed. In the twenty-four hour coverage, little blood appeared. One reason was the lack of detail present in the low-resolution video images. Another was the reliance of U.S. troops on long-range weapons, which prevented them and the embedded reporters from seeing the results of their hits. Of course, cameramen and photographers did film death, but news editors often chose not to broadcast or print gory images in the name of taste and decency. For example, the deputy managing editor of *Time* decided not to publish a picture of the bloodied head of a dead Iraqi with an American soldier standing in the background. "You want a little picture with your blood," he said. One editor told independent photojournalist Kael Alford, who documented the awful scene of an Iraqi boy sitting on a filthy hospital floor next to his wounded mother as he waited for her to die, "Please don't send any more wounded civilian pictures." On ABC, Charles Gibson said he thought it would be disrespectful to show the dead from either side. The embedded Ted Koppel disagreed: "We need to remind people in the most graphic way that war is a dreadful thing." It was graphic enough for some American mothers. They restricted television watching because their children were worried about relatives in the service or what was happening to the kids in Iraq. As in 1991, the administration banned cameras from filming the arrival of caskets at Dover Air Force base in Delaware.[53]

The administration's management of expectations ran into difficulties when the war did not proceed as projected. As the president's aides called for patience, recalling that the advance was slow after D-Day in 1944, a retired Air Force general expressed his frustration with the repeated World War II references by saying, "Someone ought to tell these guys that we're taking out a failing, rogue regime, not the conqueror of all Europe." No weapons of mass destruction had been found. After eighty of the top hundred sites thought to have contained such weapons turned out to be empty, Fleischer announced that the president "believed" the weapons would yet be located, while the administration began to downplay the topic. Cheney's prediction that "the streets in Basra and Baghdad are sure to erupt in joy" did not take place. Expecting mass surrenders, U.S. forces instead faced stiff resistance. When field commander Lt. Gen. William Wallace told reporters that the enemy was "a bit different from the one we'd wargamed against," Centcom hustled to deny such a challenge to their planning. Wallace's candor cost him his career. Rescued Iraqis displayed ambivalence about American intentions. Hamid Neama, liberated from the Iraqi police who had tortured him, said, "Of course I'm grateful that the Americans saved me. But I'm only one of 28 million people in this country. We would not like it if the Americans try to stay here for long."[54]

Reporters at Centcom's daily briefings began to suspect that they would hear actual news only if someone slipped up. Repeated showings of "precision" bombing aroused skeptical memories of the Persian Gulf War. Correspondents depended upon Centcom briefings to explain the overall operation so that the thousands of stories covered by embedded reporters made sense. After all, as Vincent Morris of the *New York Post*, embedded with a helicopter unit, remarked, "The war is whatever piece of dirt you are sitting on." If people read only his reports, they would think the whole war was about helicopters. Centcom, however, failed to provide the big picture beyond reiterating the theme of progress. Moreover, reporters pressed to deliver something on the spot to fill air time could describe only what was immediately in front of them. "Back in the Middle Ages when I covered wars," remarked CBS veteran Morley Safer, "you had reflection time—you weren't winging it."[55] Without context, the amount of information became overwhelming. Weary and confused, many viewers changed their habits. People checked their sets only a few times a day, switched to radio, or tuned out altogether. Even Rumsfeld announced his longing for the upbeat newsreels of World War II that summed up the week's events.[56]

Viewers could seek out alternative sources such as international coverage available by satellite or the internet. "The Arabs are watching a different war than we are in the US," wrote Middle East specialist, Dr. Mamoun Fandy. While Western journalists stayed with coalition forces, Arab TV reporters covered towns and villages and, to the dismay of U.S. officials, focused on horrific civilian casualties—"armless children, crushed babies, stunned mothers." Rumsfeld charged the Al Jazeera network based in Qatar with violating the Geneva Convention when it broadcast pictures of American dead and prisoners of war. U.S. networks, in part, followed Al Jazeera's lead and released portions of the POW footage after editing out the dead and disturbing shots of wounds. News websites offered viewers less repetition and more perspectives. On its website, the *Dallas Morning News* decided to put up a warning regarding the military's graphic photographs of Saddam Hussein's sons killed in a fight with American forces; one-half of the site's viewers chose not to see them. When the Defense Department released video footage of the cleaned-up bodies of Qusay and Uday, the networks showed them all day long. Internet sites, which featured messages and photographs from the troops, blogs from embedded reporters, and e-mails from viewers, provided an interactive exchange at odds with the administration's efforts to manage the news from the top down.[57]

Criticism of the media's coverage became a war story itself. Military authorities asked Fox's Geraldo Rivera to leave Iraq when, on camera, he drew a map in the sand, which showed the position of the 101st Airborne Division as he announced where it was going. After receiving angry e-mails, NBC and the National Geographic Society dismissed correspondent Peter Arnett, who had stayed in Baghdad, for making remarks critical of U.S. war plans on Iraqi television. According to Erik Sorenson, the president of MSNBC, owned by Microsoft and General Electric, what Americans wanted after 9/11 was "more optimism and benefit of the doubt. It's about being positive as opposed to being negative."[58] What were the implications of telling Americans only what they wanted to hear about themselves and the world, critics from across the political spectrum wondered.

The story of Private Jessica Lynch exemplified "being positive." General Brooks announced the rescue under fire of a U.S. army POW, a nineteen-year-old supply clerk who had been reported missing on March 25 when the 507th Maintenance Company was ambushed outside Nasiriyah. Expecting an "awesome story" and "good visuals," Centcom had supplied the rescuers with cameras. The Army's video showed commandos carrying Lynch out to a Black Hawk helicopter. Public Affairs Officer Lt. Col. John Robinson said, "We knew it would be the hottest thing of the day." Although some news organizations handled the story cautiously, others, citing unnamed official sources, reported that Lynch had fought back before her capture and that the rescue team faced a "blaze of gunfire." Corrections began to appear in the weeks that followed. Lynch had been injured when her Humvee crashed into a tractor trailer, killing four. Her gun had jammed; she had not fired at anyone. Although U.S. soldiers exchanged fire on the perimeter, the rescue commandos did not meet any resistance at the hospital. One Iraqi doctor who witnessed the rescue said that it was like Hollywood: "They make a show... action moves like Sylvester Stallone or Jackie Chan... with jumping and shouting, breaking the door." The Pentagon and the White House did not dispel the media's dramatic version of the rescue. Many Americans, it seemed, preferred the romanticized story to the truth. When ABC broadcast a report from the perspective of the Iraqi hospital staff, which contended with 200 casualties from bombing a day and had been trying to return Lynch to the Americans, it received hundreds of calls accusing the network of "undercutting the military."[59]

To symbolize victory, officials and broadcasters used the pulling down of a twenty-foot statue of Saddam Hussein in Baghdad on April 9. Although fighting continued throughout the city, live coverage and careful camera angles focused on cheering Iraqi men filling Firdos Square as chains were hooked up to American tanks. Spectators in the square and commentators in news studios briefly fell silent as a marine draped the Stars and Stripes over the statue's head. This image undermined the message that the war was about the liberation of Iraqis, not the takeover of Iraq by the United States. To avoid the appearance of occupation, Lt. General David McKiernan, the commander of allied ground forces, already had rejected a CIA plan to provide Iraqis with American flags to wave at the liberators, which would then be filmed and shown around the Arab world. In Firdos Square, an Iraqi flag quickly replaced the U.S. flag. Eyewitness reporter Anne Garrels, pressed by her bosses at National Public Radio to glorify her report, refused, insisting instead on broadcasting the conflicted responses of Iraqis present who hated Saddam but asked, "Why couldn't we do this ourselves?" On Fox and CNN, anchors pronounced the event to be historic as they showed scenes of the statue falling amidst jubilant Iraqis every six minutes on average throughout the day. On

A U.S. marine and an Iraqi man look on as Cpl. Edward Chin briefly covers the face of a statue of Saddam Hussein with an American flag before hauling down the statue in Baghdad on April 9, 2003. Jerome Delay, photographer. (Associated Press)

Arab TV, the flag incident, which confirmed widespread suspicion regarding U.S. intentions in the Middle East, was shown repeatedly.[60]

As the American military swept into Baghdad, the administration attempted to maintain what it called a "No Gloat Zone," an indication that it deserved to gloat but was above that sort of thing. Fleischer said, "Slowly but surely the hearts and minds of the Iraqi people are being won." On April 11 the president, whose approval rating soared to 92 percent, announced that Saddam Hussein's rule had ended, but the war would not be over until Iraq had been cleared of banned weapons. He explained that his decision to remove Hussein was part of his plan "not to sit and wait, leaving enemies free to plot another September 11." Although the United States had justified its preemptive war as necessary to fulfill U.N. resolutions, the administration made it clear that it intended the United Nations to play a minor role in shaping the new government in Iraq. Rice told reporters that only the nations that shed "life and blood to liberate Iraq" would take a lead in remaking the nation. Bush announced that the Iraqi people would decide on an interim authority "until a real government shows up." The president said, "The position of the United States is the Iraqis are plenty capable of running Iraq."[61]

Instead of stability, chaos broke out in Iraq, characterized by looting at an estimated cost of twelve billion dollars, murder, and destruction. "Freedom's untidy," said Rumsfeld. In Baghdad, middle class Iraqis contrasted the U.S. military's expert guarding of the Oil Ministry with the lack of protection of hospitals, universities, and the world famous National Museum of Iraq. When looters carried away ancient artifacts, archeologist Raid Abdul Ridhar Muhammad said, "This is not a liberation, this is a humiliation."[62] The administration, as had its predecessors, started to change its tone regarding the victims of oppression they had come to liberate. Wolfowitz made several television appearances to explain that it could take more than six months to turn authority over to Iraqis and that it was necessary to act quickly. "It's like the problem if you leave the training wheels on a bicycle too long, the kid never learns to ride," said Wolfowitz. On the satirical *Daily Show*, Jon Stewart showed excerpts from Bush's televised speech to the Iraqi people in which the president said, "You're a good and gifted people, the heirs of a great civilization that contributes to all humanity. You deserve better than tyranny and corruption and torture chambers." Then Stewart pretended to chuck an infant under the chin and cooed, "Yes you do, yes you do, you're a very good country, ga, ga, ga, goo goo."[63]

On its advance to Baghdad, the Third Infantry Division already had faced serious resistance. With 20,000 soldiers, 250 M1-A1 tanks, more than 280 Bradley fighting vehicles, and more than 150 helicopters and helicopter gunships, the division preferred open terrain, taking on enemy tanks or bunkers at a distance. "We don't want to go to the cities," said Colonel William F. Grimsley, the First Brigade Commander who nevertheless ended up in Najaf, one of the holiest Shiite sites. Senior commanders had not anticipated the ambushes, the snipers, and the suicidal assaults by lightly armed men dressed as civilians. "They're not playing by the rules," soldiers told CNN. The violence escalated. A suicide bomber killed four American soldiers of the First Brigade at a checkpoint. Days later soldiers from the Second Brigade fired on a minivan that failed to stop as warned, killing seven women and children. The Iraqis would never like us, concluded Lt. Col. Bryan McCoy of the Third Battalion, Fourth Marines. "All we can do is make them respect us and then make sure that they know we're here on their behalf."[64]

The administration, aware that its stated goal of bringing democracy to the Middle East was not widely believed by Arabs, launched a public relations campaign called "Iraq: From Fear to Freedom." Appearing on Al Arabiya television, Bush said, "Iraqis are sick of foreign people coming in their country and trying to destabilize their country, and we will help them rid Iraq of these killers." The U.S. government disseminated images to Middle Eastern media outlets of soldiers handing out candy to children, putting out oil fires, and passing out food and medicine. The campaign did not address the invasion of Iraq by American forces. Khaled Abdelkariem, a Washington-based correspondent for the Middle East News Agency, thought the effort patronizing. "This feed and kill policy—throwing bombs in Baghdad and throwing food at people—is not winning hearts and minds," he said. Worse than that, charged Egyptian president Hosni Mubarak, photographs of Iraqi women and children accidentally killed by American soldiers inspired more Osama bin Ladens. Acknowledging the difficulties, Dan Bartlett said he believed the administration was making progress. "At the end of the day," he stated, "our actions will speak louder than words."[65]

By declaring regime change accomplished, the administration lost some of its ability to manage the news. To the dismay of the Pentagon, news organizations pulled out many of their embedded reporters who would now report free of military oversight. Critics, who had been closemouthed as troops advanced, spoke out. Former national security advisor Scowcroft argued that the Iraq War was an unwise distraction from the war against terrorism. Less able to manage the news, the administration made its own. On the day it was reported that ten suspected members of Al Qaeda, including two suspects in the bombing of the *Cole*, had escaped from a high-security Yemeni prison by drilling through a bathroom, President Bush declared Saddam Hussein's rule over. Homeland Security lowered the terrorism alert level to yellow. The administration delivered "good news" stories about Iraqi-Americans, Afghani women, and U.S. soldiers to local television stations, which were broadcast to millions of viewers without any acknowledgment that they were produced by the State Department's Office of Broadcasting Services and the Army and Air Force Hometown News Service.[66]

The American public registered mixed feelings. Polls showed that most Americans thought the war was a success even though the whereabouts of weapons of mass destruction or Saddam Hussein remained unknown. Many seemed ready to accept losses of American lives, which by early April 2003 had not yet reached one hundred. Some compared that number to the 3000 lost on September 11, 2001, as did the thousands of union workers who held a support-the-troops rally in New York at ground zero. Polls also showed that

51 percent of Americans opposed the policy of preemption and two-thirds thought that the United Nations rather than the United States should lead the rebuilding of Iraq. "We have definitely sent a John Wayne message to the world," said Alan Reid, Jr. of San Mateo, California. "We're the good guys. We're the big guns in town." But can we build relationships, he wondered.[67]

Rejecting such ambivalence, the administration celebrated on May 1, 2003, with a made-for-television jet landing on the aircraft carrier U.S.S. *Abraham Lincoln*. Exuberant in a green flight suit, the president said he had helped to fly the jet and posed for pictures. Later, surrounded by cheering sailors, he stood before a "Mission Accomplished" banner to announce that "major combat operations have ended." He said, "The battle of Iraq is one victory in a war on terror that began on September the 11th, 2001." The scene, bathed in late afternoon sunlight, was stunning. Democrats complained that the taxpayers had just forked over a million dollars to make a campaign commercial.

Under the banner "Mission Accomplished," President Bush flashed a "thumbs-up" after he declared the end of major combat in Iraq before the cheering crew of the U.S.S. *Abraham Lincoln* on May 1, 2003. J. Scott Applewhite, photographer. (Associated Press)

Although the White House at first said the jet landing was necessary, it later admitted that a helicopter could have delivered the president. Indeed, the *Lincoln*, which had delayed its crossing to arrive during primetime, had to keep shifting so the TV cameras would not show how close it was to the San Diego shoreline.[68] Six months later Bush said that the White House had nothing to do with the "Mission Accomplished" banner. But when questioned, staffers admitted that the White House had made it and ordered it displayed. Unsatisfied with what had been accomplished in the 1991 Persian Gulf War, officials brandished the slogan used in the Operation Desert Storm to show that they had finished the job.

Staying the Course

IN THE YEARS THAT FOLLOWED, the administration's definition of the mission declared accomplished kept shifting. With no WMD in sight, officials minimized their importance. They preferred to focus on Saddam Hussein's brutality. Of that there was plenty of evidence in mass graves and mourning families. The Iraqi leader's removal from power had not led to peace and stability, however. In the summer of 2003, the president dismissed the ongoing violence. "My answer is: Bring 'em on," said Bush. "We've got the force necessary to deal with the security situation." Washington announced it would keep 138,000 troops in Iraq, extending tours of National Guard and Reserve soldiers. Seventy-four percent of Americans approved of the war, but polls revealed growing concerns about the occupation. As the administration was well aware, people's concerns were justified. Nevertheless, it would continue to project progress, regularly announcing new slogans: "stay the course," "finish the job," "plan for victory," "way forward," and "as the Iraqis stand up, we will stand down."[69]

Within a year, more than half the American public concluded that they had been misled or lied to about war aims. After an extensive search, the Iraq Survey Group, created by the Pentagon in June following the invasion to find WMD, reported that it uncovered no evidence that Iraq had any WMD in 2003. Assured by Wolfowitz that Iraq could finance its own reconstruction, Americans were shocked by the administration's request in September for eighty-seven billion dollars to fund the occupation after already spending seventy-nine billion dollars in Iraq and in Afghanistan, where 20,000 American troops continued to look for Al Qaeda. And there was controversy over where some of those billions of dollars were going. News reports that

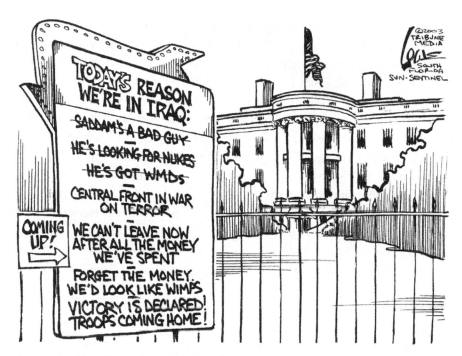

Cartoonist Chan Lowe illustrated the White House's changing justifications for Operation Iraqi Freedom. (© Tribune Media Services, Inc. All Rights Reserved. Reprinted with permission)

Halliburton and its subsidiary KBR had received government contracts worth billions of dollars prompted an outcry since Vice President Cheney had been CEO of the oil field services and construction company from 1995 to 2000. In July 2004, the Senate Intelligence Committee determined that the CIA had relied on discredited sources in its assessment of WMD and the alleged link between Iraq and Al Qaeda. The 9/11 Commission, the bipartisan group created by President Bush and Congress to investigate the September 11th attack, reported that no connection existed between the 9/11 terrorist attacks and Saddam Hussein. The numbers of American soldiers killed increased, even after Hussein was captured in December 2003. ABC's *World News Tonight* showed a military medic attending American wounded who quoted the president, "All major combat operations have ceased." Then he rolled his eyes and said sarcastically, "Right!"[70]

With two out of its three chief reasons for war discredited, the administration talked up the spread of democracy. Its claims of progress regarding that goal were challenged by reports of a troubled occupation. Initially the White House put the Defense Department in charge. The Pentagon ignored studies from the State Department and the CIA, which had warned that the construction of a new government would be the most difficult part of the regime change. Rumsfeld sent retired Lt. General Jay Garner to head the Office of Reconstruction and Humanitarian Assistance with the expectation that Garner would finish up by the end of the summer. Within weeks, Washington replaced Garner's ill-prepared outfit with the Coalition Provisional Authority (CPA) led by former diplomat L. Paul Bremer III. The CPA was staffed by administration loyalists who knew little to nothing about Iraq and spoke no Arabic. Hundreds of U.S. military and civilian personnel settled into the former palaces of Saddam Hussein and his sons in an area of Baghdad known as the Green Zone.[71]

Assuming that there was nothing of value in existing Iraqi institutions, the CPA wanted to start with a clean slate. Committing what has been widely viewed as the worst mistake, Bremer disbanded the Iraqi military. Some 400,000 armed men were left without jobs. The CPA removed tens of thousands of Saddam Hussein's Ba'ath party members from their positions running government ministries, maintaining the nation's infrastructure, and operating hospitals and universities. The American authorities shut down state-run factories, eliminating more jobs, as they prepared to set up a free-market economy. Instead of holding elections, the CPA created the Iraqi Governing Council made up of people without much of a following in Iraq and headed by Iyad Allawi, a former Ba'athist who worked for the CIA. On a more mundane level, it suspended the Iraqi traffic code, which contributed to the chaos in the streets. Following a car crash, an Iraqi yelled, "What kind of driving is that?" Another replied, "This is a democracy now, and I can drive as I please," revealing the depth of misunderstanding all around.[72]

Although the CPA oversaw two constitutions, two elections, and a referendum held with much fanfare, it feared real democracy. Its actual goal was an Iraqi government friendly to the United States. Out of the $300 million the Pentagon supplied to public relations firms to promote U.S. policies in Iraq, it paid over $25 million to the Lincoln Group, a Washington, DC-based PR firm, to place more than a thousand positive stories secretly written by American military personnel in the Iraqi press. Critics of this effort pointed out that the United States should be seen in Iraq as a supporter of a free press, not one that was bought and paid for. Although officials cited growing numbers of reliable Iraqi forces ready to take over, they knew these numbers existed only on paper. There was widespread corruption in the new Iraqi army and Civil Defense Corps where soldiers were paid sixty dollars a month and taught to say "drop your weapon" in English. To whom would these troops be loyal, wondered observers. The CPA's fears were realized in the December 2005 election when the vote fell along sectarian and ethnic lines of Kurds, Shiites, and Sunnis. Within months, Iraq disintegrated into civil war with Iraqis killing more Iraqis than they killed Americans. The White House denied it, saying instead that if U.S. forces left, Iraq would fall into civil war. Neither the United States nor the Iraqi government appeared capable of providing the Iraqi people with what they wanted: electricity, jobs, and law and order.[73]

The Iraqi insurgency bombed, kidnapped, and executed American military personnel and civilians, U.N. officials, coalition partners, and Iraqis who worked with the Americans or belonged to rival religious sects or ethnic groups. Administration spokesmen routinely referred to the insurgents as terrorists, but as Deputy Secretary of State Richard Armitage admitted, "We can't even agree on who we are fighting." The CIA thought the insurgents were nationalists who wanted foreigners out. The Pentagon said they were former Ba'athists who had run Saddam Hussein's regime and wanted to regain their power, aided by foreign Sunni extremists. Rumsfeld said they were criminals, Iranian agents, and foreign terrorists who wanted to make Iraq the front line in a global religious struggle. An Iraq expert at the State Department said they were "pissed off Iraqis" who resented the destruction of property and the deaths of family members. Such confusion over who was fighting and why made it difficult to determine how to fight them.[74]

"I don't know who I'm fighting most of the time," said a U.S. sergeant based in Baghdad. For the troops, pride in their accomplishments mixed with frustration and confusion. The administration's misleading war aims and optimistic predictions had a negative effect on the military's strategy and tactics. By putting their resources and manpower into the search for WMD, American forces failed to destroy stockpiles of conventional weapons, which ended up in the hands of insurgents. Home-made bombs called improvised explosive devices or IEDs proved especially deadly. Because they expected to be greeted as liberators, military leaders were not prepared for carrying out an occupation or meeting resistance. One officer pronounced the lack of Arabic speakers to be "the biggest limiting factor on the battlefield." Like many Americans, 85 percent of the troops believed that they were in Iraq to retaliate for Saddam Hussein's role in the 9/11 attacks. A U.S. Army report found that less than half of the soldiers and marines believed that civilians "should be treated with dignity and respect." The effort to win the "hearts and minds" of Iraqis was hampered by the military's practices of "recon by fire" and "movement to contact"—terms that had replaced "search and destroy"—as well as raids on civilians and the imprisonment of thousands of Iraqis without trial. In November 2005, troops of the 1st Marine Regiment killed twenty-four civilians, including women and children, in Haditha. Most shocking of all was the May 2004 release of photographs of Americans torturing Iraqi prisoners at Abu Ghraib prison. The picture of a hooded man hooked up to electrodes became an anti-American icon worldwide, representing the hypocrisy of U.S. war aims. The national press coverage, however, followed the White House lead by treating the incident as a case of "isolated abuse" by a few "bad apple" troops rather than the violation of the Geneva Convention on torture approved at the highest levels.[75]

To the administration and its supporters, the oft-repeated phrase "support the troops" meant no criticism of U.S. policy in order to maintain morale. Those who refused to play their parts became controversial figures. Cindy Sheehan, whose son was killed in Sadr City in April 2004, set up a vigil outside the president's Texas ranch. When she failed to conform to the expected behavior of a grieving parent, commentators debated her actions, with some denouncing her as a crackpot and a liar. To the cheers of his fellow troops, Specialist Thomas Wilson of the Tennessee Army National Guard asked the secretary of defense during a "town hall" meeting in Kuwait why they lacked sufficient armor for vehicles. "You go to war with the Army you have, not the Army you might want or wish to have at a later time," answered Rumsfeld. Later it was found that 80 percent of the marines killed in Iraq could have survived with extra body armor available since 2003 and that such armor had been requested by field commanders but had not been supplied by the Pentagon. At the time, however, prowar commentators, who learned that Wilson had consulted a reporter about how to word his question, referred to the Tennessean as insubordinate and a media plant. Wilson's detractors implied that if troops weren't silent or appreciative when they appeared in photo opportunities they must be manipulated by someone else. When the military's most famous volunteer, pro-football star Pat Tillman, was killed in Afghanistan during the Abu Ghraib scandal, the command lied and covered up the fact that his death was by friendly fire until after the nationally televised memorial service. His furious family demanded an investigation.[76]

In preparation for the 2004 presidential election, the White House emphasized the process of turning over control in Iraq to the Iraqis as though the
United States had control to turn over. The "transfer of sovereignty" from
the CPA to the Iraqi Interim Government took place in June. Bush consis-
tently recalled 9/11. Matthew Dowd, the president's campaign strategist, said
of his boss, "He shows resolve, and the public wants resolve." The Democratic candidate, Senator John Kerry (D-MA), recalled his record of service
in Vietnam but did not articulate a clear policy on Iraq. Bush won the election by a small margin of 500,000 votes. In his 2005 inaugural address, the
president used the word freedom twenty-seven times in twenty minutes.
Maintaining the progress theme, Cheney declared in May that the insurgents
were "in their last throes."[77]

The Office of Media Outreach at the Defense Department, working with
a public relations firm, used taxpayer dollars to arrange tours to Iraq for radio
talk show hosts. The purpose of the week-long "Operation Truth" was to
allow broadcasters to hear about "positive developments" from the troops.
In addition, the Pentagon recruited more than seventy-five retired military
officers, who appeared as expert analysts on news shows, for special briefings
and guided tours organized to show progress in Iraq. Armed with talking
points, these officers, referred to by the Pentagon as "message force multipliers," appeared as independent authorities and often received more airtime
than reporters. Nor were their extensive ties to defense industries and military
contractors disclosed on the air. The administration relied on the retired officers to counter reports that there were not enough American troops in Iraq,
that morale among U.S. forces was low, that the Iraqi security forces were
poorly trained and equipped, and that detainees were badly treated.[78]

As in the past, the military sought to influence Hollywood's portrayal of
war. In return for access to military bases, planes, ships, and Humvees, movie
makers accepted script advice and addressed any problems noted by military
officers. Stationed in Los Angeles, Army Lt. Col. J. Todd Breasseale described
his job as helping "filmmakers tell an accurate story and help the American
people understand their Army." Phil Haggis, the writer and director of *In the
Valley of Elah* (2007), starring Tommy Lee Jones, submitted his script to the
military and received twenty-one pages of objections to parts of the film. He
did not make the changes and made his film without the military's assistance.
"Of course they want to publicize what is good," said Haggis. "But that doesn't
mean that it is true."[79] Most films about Iraq did not do well at the box office.
One that did was Michael Moore's controversial documentary *Fahrenheit 9/11*,

which broke attendance records when it opened in 2004. From the White House, Bartlett condemned the highly partisan film as "outrageously false," while the president's supporters declared that seeing the movie was unpatriotic. Film historian Robert Brent Toplin concluded that Moore's facts were for the most part correct; it was his scathing and humorous interpretation of them that inspired a conservative effort to discredit him and the film. In the tradition of antiwar documentaries, *Fahrenheit 9/11* showed the impact of war on ordinary Iraqis and Americans. An American soldier in Iraq says, "You cannot kill someone without killing a part of yourself."[80]

Criticism of the war increased in 2005 as oil prices rose, an investigation was launched into the administration leak that blew the cover of CIA operative Valerie Plame, wife of war critic and former U.S. Ambassador Joseph Wilson, and the Downing Street memo was published. In the memo the head of British intelligence reported that in July 2002 the U.S. government had decided to go to war against Iraq and that the "intelligence and the facts were being fixed around the policy." Concerns regarding civil liberties grew as the government claimed the right to imprison Americans and foreigners without habeas corpus hearings required by law and carried out domestic spying, which bypassed the Fourth Amendment protection against unreasonable searches and seizures. When Congress outlawed torture, the president signed the bill, but added a "signing statement" indicating that he would ignore the law if he thought it interfered with his executive powers. The White House claim that the invasion of Iraq would weaken terrorism was overturned by a CIA report describing war-torn Iraq as a terrorist training ground. "We're taking the fight to the terrorists abroad so we don't have to face them at home," said the president. Terrorists who claimed affiliation with Al Qaeda struck at U.S. allies with bomb attacks in Madrid and London killing 248 and injuring 2,750. As the news reported that 2,000 U.S. soldiers had died in Iraq, polls showed that 65 percent of the American people disapproved of the president's handling of the war. Officials tried to blame the negative perceptions of the war on the media coverage and the policy failures on the Iraqis. One exception was Zalmay Khalilzad, the U.S. Ambassador to Iraq, who admitted, "I think the American people lose confidence when they think either the war is not important or we don't know what the hell we're doing."[81]

This assessment was shared by Dr. Peter Feaver, a political scientist at Duke University, who joined the National Security Council staff in June 2005. If Americans believed that the war was for a worthy cause and would succeed, Feaver posited, they would support rising casualties. Accordingly, the White

In an unusual live radio address on December 17, 2005, President Bush was backed by a portrait of Theodore Roosevelt on horseback as Bush defended a domestic spying operation in the United States as "a vital tool in our war against the terrorists." Manuel Balce Ceneta, photographer. (Associated Press)

House released a thirty-five-page document, "National Strategy for Victory in Iraq," which the president outlined in a speech before midshipmen at the U.S. Naval Academy in November 2005. With the slogan "Plan for Victory" plastered over the backdrop, the president used the word "victory" fifteen times. The National Strategy document explained that victory would be achieved when "Iraq is peaceful, united, stable and secure" and "a full partner in the global war on terrorism." The White House's public relations offensive was not a success. Only 25 percent of Americans, according to a December *New York Times*–CBS poll, thought the president had a "clear plan for victory in Iraq."[82]

Nor did the "Plan for Victory" change the deteriorating situation in Iraq. To the astonishment of veteran White House reporter Helen Thomas, press secretary Scott McClellan continued to stick to the staged version of the war at a briefing in March 2006 when he announced, "There are democratically elected governments now in Iraq and Afghanistan, and we are there at their invitation."[83] Yet when Iraqi Prime Minister Nuri al-Maliki asked the United States to lower its profile in Iraq later that year, the administration responded with an increase of 30,000 American forces. Even many of the war's supporters felt the "surge" was "too little too late." The bipartisan report of the Iraq Study Group, headed by James Baker and former Democratic Congressman Lee Hamilton, pronounced the invasion a failure and urged withdrawal. In November, frustrated voters returned control of Congress to the Democrats. Before he resigned following the election, Rumsfeld conceded in a memo to the White House that the current strategy in Iraq was not working. He suggested that the administration should not "lose," but recast the way it talked about the U.S mission.[84]

The flexibility with which the administration could recast the mission contrasted with the permanence of the sacrifices made by the American men and women in military service. When twenty-one-year-old Kurt Frosheiser of Des Moines, Iowa, enlisted in the army, he told his father that he wanted "to be part of something bigger than myself." After Kurt was killed in Baghdad, his father said, "We need to see the coffins, the flag-draped coffins."[85] In February 2007, Bob Woodruff of ABC did a special report on the 23,000 wounded veterans, following his own recovery from injuries sustained as an embedded correspondent. He raised questions about the physical and psychological health of the 200,000 returning personnel who were treated by the Veterans Administration, including 73,000 treated for mental disorders and 61,000 treated for diseases of the nervous system. Other reports exposed the poor treatment of casualties at Walter Reed Army Hospital and the trauma of sexual abuse experienced by female soldiers, who made up 15 percent of the troops. One of the 16,000 single mothers serving in Iraq and Afghanistan slept on a pillow with a photo of her three children that said, "This is why I fight."[86] With military forces stretched to the breaking point in 2007, Defense Secretary Robert M. Gates, Rumsfeld's replacement, approved the longest overseas deployments since World War II. He admitted that U.S. troops would probably have to stay in Iraq "through several presidencies."[87]

Policymakers had misunderstood how to use military power to achieve their political goal of a stable, friendly Iraq. If the Americans were in Iraq as liberators they were welcome as guests, explained Sheikh Munthr Abood to U.S. officials in 2003. If they were there as occupiers, he declared, then he and his descendents would "die resisting." The surge of five additional combat brigades in 2007 achieved limited military success, but soldiers of the

82nd Airborne in Baghdad noted that U.S. forces, while militarily superior, "have failed on every promise."[88] Two million Iraqis had fled the country; two million more were refugees within their own borders. No one knew how many had died as a result of the conflict, but estimates ranged from 100,000 to 600,000. War-torn Iraq had become a breeding ground for terrorists. Ironically, American soldiers now fought against insurgents calling themselves Al Qaeda in Iraq, turning a false argument for going to war into a reason to continue it. In 2008, U.S. forces had assistance from tens of thousands of Sunnis paid ten dollars a day by the United States to help drive out Al Qaeda in Iraq. As violence declined, some analysts pronounced the surge a success while others worried about the stability of a society with a majority Shiite government and an armed Sunni minority. According to the Joint Campaign Plan, written by Commanding General David Petraeus and U.S. Ambassador Ryan Crocker and approved by President Bush in November 2007, the ultimate aim was to move U.S. forces from combat to the role of "overwatch" of the Iraqi Army and police. Five years after the March 2003 invasion, U.S. leaders were still trying to figure out how to achieve what they, not the Iraqis, wanted in Iraq.[89]

President Bush's "forward strategy of freedom in the Middle East" focused on terrorism, access to oil, and the rise of China, which had the potential to rival U.S. dominance in the region. In 2003 the United States quietly pulled its troops out of Saudi Arabia, home to most of the 9/11 hijackers, but had established new bases in Central Asia, the Persian Gulf, and Iraq. The United States continued its long-standing policy of backing authoritarian governments in Saudi Arabia, Kuwait, Jordan, Egypt, and Pakistan. As a State Department study warned, those in the Middle East allowed to vote were more likely to elect anti-American and promilitant Islamic leaders. In response, the Iraq Study Group called for more diplomacy overseas to promote U.S. objectives in the Middle East. But the military had the greater resources. U.S. forces, as the Project for a New American Century had asserted in 2000, served as the "cavalry on the new American frontier."[90]

War without Peace

PORTRAYED AS A WAR to make Americans secure and Iraqis free, Operation Iraqi Freedom was intended to expand U.S. power in a vital region. Although presented to the public as a response to the 9/11 attacks, the war continued a decades-long strategy of policing the Middle East. In promoting it, the Bush administration constructed an apocalyptic narrative to persuade Americans to fight a war of choice. In Bush's version, the Hitler-like Saddam Hussein threatened the United States and all free peoples with WMD. To protect civilization, the War on Terror had to be fought against the Iraqi leader and his terrorist allies, the "Islamo-fascists." Regime change would result in a democratic Iraq and a peaceful Middle East. Once the war was underway, officials daily declared progress and projected success through staged events. During the occupation, the administration defined numerous events as victories, including the deaths of Uday and Qusay Hussein, the capture of Saddam Hussein, the transfer of sovereignty, the Iraqi elections, and the Plan for Victory. This highly charged portrayal combined dramatic made-for-TV moments with the message of progress. It was, noted an American general, an "illusionist version."[91]

By claiming that the U.S. invasion would bring democracy and free enterprise to Iraq and the Middle East, officials assured Americans that their aims united U.S. values and interests. Although the Bush administration had drawn heavily on references to the "good war" to sell Operation Iraqi Freedom, its propaganda strategy recalled World War I and the Vietnam War. Surrounding themselves with flags and uniformed troops, the president and his top advisors called for urgent action to defend civilization from a savage and exaggerated threat. Like the Committee on Public Information, they succeeded in exploiting fear and patriotism to rally support for war but failed to build a consensus for any long-term commitment. They drew on the Vietnam era by launching their own, more attractively produced, version of the 1967 "Progress Campaign." As in Vietnam, reality caught up with the upbeat version.

"Message discipline" was the way the White House and the military ensured that their version of the staged war dominated the news media. Officials crafted the message of the day and orchestrated its delivery through "message force multipliers." In the lead-up to the invasion, they supplied such a steady stream of reasons for the war that by the time critics addressed one, a new talking point changed the subject. The "feedback loop" of officials citing news stories based on government sources reinforced the appearance that the administration had inside intelligence and knew what it was doing. The White House and its supporters equated being "on-message" about WMD, preventing another 9/11, and spreading democracy with patriotism. Lawmakers and critics who raised questions were accused of disloyalty and ridiculed. Within the government, many career military, intelligence, and foreign affairs experts who had reservations about the policy decided to remain team players. Those who objected were marginalized. Army chief of staff General Eric Shinseki spoke his mind about the need for more troops and retired; others resigned. Managing perceptions was more important than critical analysis. When asked at a press conference in April 2004 what his biggest mistake had been since 9/11, President Bush could not come up with one. For the president's communications staff, the worst had happened. Not only had the president's statement been off script from the message of the day, it had created actual news.[92]

The administration's "infoganda" was delivered by the news media, which had also concluded that viewers preferred good news and patriotic fanfare. The result, wrote critic Andrew Hoskins, was a "growing reality gap." Vice President Cheney said that he spent a lot of time watching Fox News "because they're more accurate in my experience." A University of Maryland study found that 80 percent of those who mostly watched Fox News believed at least one of three false conclusions: that weapons of mass destruction had been found, that Iraq had ties to Al Qaeda, or that world opinion supported the U.S. war in Iraq. The same held true for 55 percent of CNN viewers and 23 percent of the PBS/NPR audience.[93] The military's embedding policy gave correspondents a thrilling role. "For a month, I got to watch—not from the front row, but from center stage—what happens when the most powerful country in the history of the world decides to flex its full force of muscle," said Jim Axelrod of CBS.[94] As a companion to the display of "shock and awe," viewers saw reassuring scenes of U.S. soldiers sharing dance moves with Iraqi children. "Television reports soften war and allow it to penetrate even deeper into the living rooms and minds of America," concluded Persian Gulf War veteran Anthony Swofford. "War can't be that bad if they let us watch it."[95] But the lack of success affected media coverage. By 2008, prominent news stories on Iraq were down by 80 percent from what they had been the year before. According to the Pew Research Center, only 6 percent of Americans cited Iraq as the news story they followed most closely; only 28 percent of Americans knew that, as of March, 4000 U.S. troops had been killed in the conflict. "If the war were a TV show," remarked one critic, "it would be canceled."[96]

The treatment of war news as a commodity to be sold and the citizen as a customer to be cajoled into buying it meant less attention for events that were complicated, depressing, or about other people. In many ways, the staging of the war seemed to fulfill John Chancellor's Vietnam-era suggestion "to get a sort of general commitment and support" from the American people for military operations around the world. In the 1991 Persian Gulf War, the George H. W. Bush administration had been determined to overcome the Vietnam syndrome by showing Americans that powerful technology assured a quick victory. Both father and son combined the appealing narrative of liberation with the imperative that everyone must unite in support of the troops once the commander-in-chief had ordered them overseas. And once U.S. forces were in position, they were expected to fight, not to withdraw following some diplomatic solution because fighting showed strength; withdrawal meant weakness. In 2003, the George W. Bush administration cast the Iraq conflict as a fight between civilization and terrorism. Once the war was underway, pulling out without victory insulted those who fought and died, went a powerful argument applicable to any military intervention. As historian Walter LaFeber warned, Bush's open-ended commitment to fighting terrorism called "for a continual war required to 'lead the world' to continual peace."[97]

The strategy of credulity had its successes and failures. To describe the strategy, satirist Stephen Colbert coined the term "truthiness": what feels like the truth is more persuasive than facts.[98] Following the trauma of 9/11, the appeals to fear and faith were compelling. In addition, the Bush administration downplayed U.S. strategic interests and the costs of the war, not demanding that most Americans make sacrifices. In May 2007, the War on Terror at $750 billion became the second most expensive conflict in U.S. history after World War II. Fought on credit, not increased taxes or spending cuts, it was "designed to be a war the American people don't feel," concluded economist Joseph E. Stiglitz.[99] Although many Americans were unsure about the Iraq war, they had given the president the "benefit of the doubt." For the troops and their families, there was added incentive to trust in the mission. "I believed in what we are doing. You know, we kind of have to think that," said Iraq War veteran Steve Reighard, pointing to his missing arm. "Otherwise, this is in vain."[100] At the same time, the manipulation of the truth by officials resulted in record levels of anger and distrust directed at the federal government. Some turned to conspiracy theories for explanation. A 2006 Scripps Howard poll found that a third of Americans believed that federal officials assisted in the 9/11 terror attacks or took no action to stop them so they could lead the United States into war in the Middle East.[101]

The consequences of such a "reality gap" between the staged war and the actual war were severe. The administration put more effort into producing the staged war than planning and carrying out the real one. Overly confident of

U.S. military power and disdainful of warnings about the difficulties of regime change, civilian leaders had concentrated on what they excelled at, whether it was bureaucratic infighting or public relations campaigns. Officials, like the best salesmen who believe in their product, fooled themselves with their own lies and exaggerations. Only some of the president's supporters argued that mistakes and lies about war aims did not matter because the goal of removing the fiendish Saddam Hussein from power was accomplished. Many Americans had grave concerns about the damaged reputation of the United States, the strain on the U.S. military as it struggled to carry out flawed objectives, and the corrosive effect of wartime policies on civil liberties and the democratic process. Meanwhile it appeared that leaders would continue to rely on perception management. "We lost control of the context," said information warrior John Rendon as he explained the decline in popular support for Operation Iraqi Freedom. "That has to be fixed for the next war."[102]

CONCLUSION

You can't handle the truth.

        Jack Nicholson as Col. Nathan R. Jessep, *A Few Good Men*, 1992

SPEAKING BEFORE THE PHILIPPINE CONGRESS in October 2003, President George W. Bush announced, "A new totalitarian threat has risen against civilization." In the fight between civilization and terrorism, he declared the Philippines to be an important ally. "America is proud of its part in the great story of the Filipino people," said the president. "Together our soldiers liberated the Philippines from colonial rule." Bush asserted that the Middle East, like Asia, could become democratic as illustrated by the Republic of the Philippines six decades ago. Bush's use of the Philippines as a model for Iraq raised concern among those who knew that the islands had remained a colony of the United States for almost half a century. Nor did the president draw a connection between the growing Iraqi insurgency and the fierce opposition of Filipinos to U.S. rule in the Philippine War.[1]

Not only did the president gloss over the inconvenient facts of the past, but he also put a positive face on the present. Uneasy about the stability of the Philippines, where military officers had recently attempted a coup and the U.S. Secret Service would not allow him to stay overnight, Bush announced a joint American–Filipino five-year plan to "modernize and reform" the Philippine military. Policymakers were worried about Abu Sayyaf, a terror group thought to have links to Al Qaeda and Islamic extremism. A few thousand U.S. marines were already in the southern Philippines assisting local forces in fighting an Islamic separatist movement with roots going back to the resistance against the Americans a century before. A more forthright statement about the Philippine model came from Jay Garner, the general who led the initial reconstruction team in Iraq. The islands, he said, "were a coaling station for the navy, and that allowed us to keep a great presence in the Pacific. That's what Iraq is for the next few decades: our coaling station that gives us great presence in the Middle East."[2]

Throughout the twentieth century, American leaders presented war aims dedicated to the spread of democracy and freedom rather than the expansion of U.S. power. Officials have assured Americans that they fought for both their ideals and interests with slogans such as "to make the world safe for democracy," the "Four Freedoms," and the "American way of life." Rarely have leaders failed to point out the economic interests at stake, pointing to trade opportunities, acquisition of raw materials, or the ability to own a car and a washing machine. When explaining the interests at stake, they have, however, placed more emphasis on enemy threats to U.S. security. From World War I to the Iraq War, Americans were told that they must fight "over there" so they would not have to fight at home. Although the United States repeatedly denied that it sought more territory, it steadily acquired naval and military bases. As of 2008 the United States had more than seven hundred bases in 132 countries. In addition, its priority was the maintenance of governments, whether democratic or not, that allowed the Americans economic and strategic access to their countries. Leaders typically have not ignored the self-interested aspects of what Presidents Woodrow Wilson and George H. W. Bush called the new world order, but they have not highlighted them.

Wartime administrations produced official narratives dramatizing the clash between civilization and barbarism. These narratives emphasized what the United States claimed it stood for rather than what it was doing. They pitted the West led by the United States against the East—Asiatics, Huns, Orientals, Islamo-fascists—dehumanized as savages, fanatics, and hordes. To arouse anger, they cited enemy atrocities, some true and some false, committed against women and children. On the side of civilization stood the allies, such as the British and French in World War I or the Russians and the Chinese in World War II, shown as grateful partners who shared U.S. goals. The backward and the oppressed, propaganda assured the public, welcomed American leadership. When the Americans arrived to help, however, the Filipinos, Koreans, Vietnamese, and Iraqis failed to behave as predicted. From the perspective of many of these people, the Americans looked more like invaders than humanitarians. In turn, U.S. officials described the people they had come to liberate

as misguided and unfit. In the official narratives, such unworthiness justified the use of force and reinforced the portrayal of Americans as civilizers,
spreading not an empire but a better way of life. In these stories, Americans
remained on the side of good, while the identity of friend or foe could shift if
yesterday's freedom fighter became tomorrow's enemy.

On the home front, propaganda presented war as ennobling. It celebrated
unity, showing racial and ethnic minorities doing their part, workers and bosses
cooperating with each other, and courageous men backed by faithful women.
Americans saw themselves portrayed as idealistic, generous, and proud of their
can-do spirit. Typically propagandists assured citizens who feared change that
war restored traditional values, while promising those who wanted reform that
war meant opportunity for a better life. Messages that at first glance seemed
to have nothing to do with the battle at hand such as William McKinley's talk
of healing Civil War wounds or George H. W. Bush's celebration of kicking
the Vietnam syndrome claimed that Americans could put a bad war behind
them by fighting a good one. Such justifications disguised the real goal, which
was to win popular approval for the use of force at the president's discretion.
Even so, the portrayal of war as ennobling has been challenged repeatedly.
Assuming that they were supposed to be the good guys, not bullies, soldiers
and civilians have wondered how Americans live up to their ideals when they
use force against the weak. As one general reported to his higher-ups during
the Korean War, it went against the grain of U.S. troops to burn out poor
farmers as ordered.[3]

To deliver official narratives that overshadowed such contradictions, leaders
have relied on managing the news. McKinley made the president in time of
war the chief source and interpreter of events. During the world wars, Wilson
and Franklin Roosevelt used temporary propaganda agencies to inspire and
instruct the public about total mobilization. Working with the entertainment
and advertising industries, they had the assistance of Mary Pickford, Donald
Duck, Humphrey Bogart, and General Electric. Their successors coordinated
the official message from the White House, relying on a greatly expanded
communications staff and permanent public affairs departments throughout
the executive branch. From the Johnson administration's Operation Maximum
Candor to the George W. Bush administration's "iron-message discipline,"
officials provided the media with briefings and photo opportunities to deliver
the official line or image of the day. Overall, they preferred to spotlight events
that enhanced their promotion and remain silent about those that did not.
For the most part, the media cooperated voluntarily. Its attempt to maintain

a role as eyewitness of war was complicated by its own patriotic cheerleading, self-censorship, deference to power, and pressure to appeal to commercial sponsors. The media shared with government propagandists a desire to show the audience what it wanted to see. Overall, wartime presidents effectively used the media to deliver their messages, which perhaps explains why they have complained bitterly when the media fail to do so.

To enhance their promotion of war, government leaders have relied on censorship. In addition to restrictions designed to protect military operations, officials banned stories and images that would hurt morale or raise doubts about war aims. In the era of live and continuous news coverage, the George W. Bush administration favored extensive influence over news from the battlefield. At briefings, military and civilian leaders showed scenes of precision weapons hitting military targets, minimized reports of civilian casualties, and prohibited scenes of dead Americans. The media contributed to the cleaned-up presentation of war with their own standards of taste and decency. Such "sugar-coated" versions of war have been controversial, with some citizens wanting more honest and complete coverage of what was happening and others demanding upbeat, one-sided reporting. Despite official censorship and cover-ups, challenging stories have come out. News of atrocities committed by Americans in the Philippines, Korea, Vietnam, and Iraq offered a harsh contrast to images of troops doing good works, which muddied the message of uplift and progress. Such reports took on symbolic importance for civilians who had doubts about the justifications for war. As soldiers on the front lines have observed again and again, only those who were there know what real war is like. The combination of propaganda and censorship has made that distance between those who fight and those back home even greater.

Over time, the strategies of persuasion have resulted in a diminished role for citizens. The portrayal of the nation in crisis with its warrior president, deferential allies, fanatical enemies, patriotic media, and valiant troops included the loyal folks at home. McKinley reinforced the desired behavior when he praised the children for waving flags at train stops. Faced with mobilizing the country, officials during World War II concluded that flag-waving would not be enough to defeat the Axis. As they called on Americans to do their part, they encouraged citizens to adopt a global perspective in order to understand the need for allies in a tough fight. They honored the skeptical individual who weighed the pros and cons before making the right decision to help defeat the Axis powers. In contrast, during the Cold War and the War on

Terror, civilians were told to have faith in their leaders and carry on with their daily lives without questioning or dissent. Following the Persian Gulf War of 1991, veteran newsman Walter Cronkite turned to World War II for a somber warning about what happens when people accept restrictions on freedoms of speech and the press. He recalled that the German people claimed they did not know about concentration camps, but their ignorance did not absolve them from blame. He concluded that Americans, who after all elected their leaders, "had better darned well know what they are doing in our name."[4]

Truths or Consequences

AMERICANS DO NOT EXPECT TO KNOW the whole truth during wartime, but they do not want to be lied to about why they are fighting. What happens when people learn they have been misled deliberately by wartime propaganda? The reaction after World War I gives us one example. The Committee on Public Information presented the war as a noble crusade fought for democracy against demonized Germans. Such a portrayal was overturned by unfulfilled war aims overseas, the abuse of civil liberties at home, and revelations of false atrocity propaganda. In the years that followed, Americans expressed distrust of government propaganda and military intervention in what they considered to be other people's wars. It took the Japanese attack in 1941 to convince the majority of Americans that it was time to fight. The propagandists of the Roosevelt administration adopted the "strategy of truth" to regain the trust of a skeptical public. In contrast to World War I, when censorship shielded Americans from the trauma on the front lines, they eventually allowed more graphic depictions of death to counter home front complacency. Acting on the premise that the public would have a say over foreign policy, propagandists sought to correct the failure of their predecessors to pave the way for international commitments. At the same time, FDR and the State Department preferred to be vague about postwar plans, suggesting that as the United States reached superpower status the "strategy of truth" would go only so far. Nevertheless, by taking the long-term view that winning the war and the peace required a public consensus in favor of internationalism, they built support for American global leadership that their successors have relied on ever since.

The aftermath of the Vietnam War provides a contrasting example of how leaders have dealt with a disillusioned public. The Johnson administration cited the Domino Theory to justify U.S. intervention, but the "Free

"This is a people's war, and to win it the people should know as much about it as they can. This Office will do its best to tell the truth and nothing but the truth, both at home and abroad. Military information that will aid the enemy must be withheld; but within that limitation we shall try to give the people a clear, complete and accurate picture."

Elmer Davis

July 10, 1942   *Director*

Office of War Information director Elmer Davis announced the "strategy of truth" on a World War II poster. (National Archives, NWDNS-44-PA-2030)

World versus the communist world" framework did not fit the realities on the ground. The "credibility gap" resulted when officials misled the public about the Tonkin Gulf incident, the body count, and the "Progress Campaign." After the Vietnam War, Americans felt divided and distrustful as they had after World War I. To rally support for Operation Iraqi Freedom, the Bush administration did not follow in the footsteps of their World War II–era predecessors by adopting a "strategy of truth." Instead it relied heavily on censorship, exaggeration, and lies. It built on the George H. W. Bush administration's production of a "clean," high-tech war in 1991 to cure the Vietnam syndrome. To promote a war of choice against Iraq, the George W. Bush administration manipulated intelligence to appeal to fear and patriotism. To avoid the discrepancies between the official version and the actual war that led to a "credibility gap" in Vietnam, the authorities restricted correspondents from covering civilians under attack and provided the troops with scripted statements for the press. Although it justified invading Iraq because it was supposedly the front line in the Global War on Terror, the administration promised a quick and easy victory in what was projected to be a long and unsatisfying war. Unlike their World War II counterparts, officials did not treat public skepticism with respect and seek to regain trust as the first step to building a long-term bipartisan consensus. Instead they ridiculed or condemned as disloyal any deviation from their position. Their disdain for the democratic process at home contrasted with their idealistic talk of spreading democracy overseas.

Why America Fights shows that as necessary as the manipulation of public opinion may be in time of crisis, propaganda remains controversial. The question of whether the manipulation is tolerable depends in large part on the legitimacy of the policy being promoted. As much as World War II era citizens griped about or made fun of the multitude of official messages they received daily, they endured them as part of a war effort they supported. Some even believed that in the late 1930s the Roosevelt administration should have engaged in more propaganda than it did to promote U.S. intervention against Nazi Germany. Years later, many citizens who concluded that the Vietnam War was a mistake considered Lyndon Johnson's manipulation of the Tonkin Gulf incident to be an abuse of the president's power to persuade.

As we have seen, the more flawed the policy, the more heavily officials have relied on lies and exaggerations to manipulate opinion. Indeed, government officials have found that despite their efforts, Americans continue to think for themselves, expressing their disapproval of wars that go wrong through votes and protests. In response, officials in recent decades have turned to more misleading manipulation to preserve their freedom of action. In the extreme case of the Iraq War, the Bush administration threw off numerous constraints, dismissing allies and the United Nations, marginalizing career military, diplomatic, and intelligence personnel who questioned its policies, and misleading Congress and the public, all the while practicing expectations management and promising progress. As Mark Twain had said about the Philippine conflict a century earlier, people were "sold a bill of goods."

Propaganda and History

THE POLITICIANS, JOURNALISTS, POETS, screenwriters, artists, and historians who have served as government propagandists were good storytellers. They knew how to draw on a romanticized past and to project an idealized future. At the same time, they relied on interpreting events as they happened, fitting them into the framework of the official narrative. In recent years, the officials charged with constructing and delivering persuasive messages were more likely to have backgrounds in politics, public relations and marketing, media, and entertainment than to have expertise in foreign relations. Their concern was the successful selling of war aims rather than the quality of the policy being sold. This phenomenon was not altogether new, but the trend has led to a greater disconnect between the war aims being promoted and the policy being conducted. For instance, in creating their own reality, Bush administration officials told the entire story of the war ahead of time. Relying on speed and high-tech weapons, U.S. forces would liberate Iraq from the brutish Saddam Hussein, capture stockpiles of weapons of mass destruction in order to make everyone safer, and be greeted by grateful Iraqis who would embrace democracy and free enterprise. To tell this story, they recalled cowboy heroes facing down wanted men, epic World War II battles, and liberated Kuwaitis waving American flags. Such a projection of the war had a lot to do with winning over the U.S. public but little to do with Iraq.

Yet, because the official narrative of the clash between civilization and barbarism makes such a good story, it has been told again and again by wartime leaders. Even when such portrayals of war prove to be misleading, they survive to serve again. As historian Emily Rosenberg noted, the dramatic propaganda disseminated by the Roosevelt administration during World War II continues to shape the public memory of that war.[5] It makes sense that officials reprise such vivid and immediately recognizable images rather than nuanced histories to claim the blessings of tradition. In doing so, they take those images out of the context of their times, showing them as representations of what happened rather than objects of persuasion. The poster "Americans will always fight for liberty" links Revolutionary war soldiers with GIs and ignores the reluctance with which World War II era Americans viewed any call to spread democracy. Moreover, such portrayals of the past, illustrating as they do a clear and straightforward direction, distract from the current messy realities. When George W. Bush asked on September 11, 2006, "Do we have the confidence to do in the Middle East what our fathers and grandfathers accomplished in Europe and Asia?" he connected the propaganda-inspired memory of "good war" confidence to Operation Iraqi Freedom. Like McKinley standing in front of portraits of Washington, Lincoln, and himself labeled as "liberators," Bush called upon Americans to believe in their "divine mission."[6]

The compelling narratives that serve as propaganda for one generation can affect policymaking in the next. Wilson made the case that when Americans fight for their ideals and interests they will be rewarded with a world ordered as they want it. FDR echoed that vision as he built support for an internationalist foreign policy. Harry Truman argued that in order to uphold that world order, called the Free World, the United States needed a global military presence. By exaggerating the enemy threat, he and his successors justified a permanent war footing in the Cold War and War on Terror. Relying on the framework of "the Free World versus the communist world" and "civilization versus terrorism," they went to war with the expectation that their military would prevail without a clear understanding of who they were fighting or how to achieve their objectives. Notably, even as officials exaggerated the enemy threat, they also underestimated enemy forces. When things went wrong in Korea and Vietnam, Truman and Nixon repackaged their war aims. The George W. Bush administration went even further by selling a prepackaged war against Iraq in 2003. Even though much has happened to call into question the story of America's civilizing mission, administration after administration has labored to preserve it, blaming failures on disappointing allies, liberated peoples, the media, or the lack of home front support. Their goal has been to maintain popular approval for the assertion of U.S. global dominance.

Over the past century, wartime propaganda declared, the United States fought for liberty. That along the way it happened to become the most powerful country in the world was no accident. When leaders announced that Americans used force to make the world a better and safer place to live, they did not go into detail about the consequences of their policies. Although the United States has won a number of victories, its war aims as proclaimed were seldom achieved. People became disillusioned when leaders who promised happy endings failed to deliver them. The purpose of propaganda in the next war was to restore a sense of clarity and national purpose. Americans, who desired to live up to their ideals even if they did not agree on how to go about it, continued to find appealing these messages about spreading freedom and democracy. Propaganda did not provide them with an honest appraisal of the costs of protecting what leaders call the American way of life. The official narratives seldom portrayed real war fought by real human beings who were not symbols of good or evil. As long as propaganda assumes that people cannot handle the truth, it leaves Americans to wonder why they fight.

NOTES

Introduction

1. George W. Bush, "Remarks to the Nation," September 11, 2002, www.whitehouse
   .gov/news/Releases/2002/09/20020911–3.html, see www.georgewbushlibrary.gov;
   Michael Isikoff and David Corn, *Hubris: The Inside Story of Spin, Scandal, and the
   Selling of the Iraq War* (New York: Crown, 2006), 42; Frank Rich, *The Greatest Story
   Ever Sold: The Decline and Fall of Truth from 9/11 to Katrina* (New York: Penguin,
   2006), 57.
2. Dean Acheson, *Present at the Creation: My Years in the State Department* (New York:
   W. W. Norton, 1969), 414.
3. Tony Judt, "What Have We Learned, If Anything?" *New York Review of Books*,
   May 1, 2008, 18.
4. Joan Hoff, *A Faustian Foreign Policy: From Woodrow Wilson to George W. Bush:
   Dreams of Perfectibility* (New York: Cambridge University Press, 2008), 1–21.
5. Philip M. Taylor, *Munitions of the Mind: A History of Propaganda from the Ancient
   World to the Present Day* (Manchester, UK: Manchester University Press, 2003),
   19–24; Drew Gilpin Faust, " 'We Should Grow Too Fond of It': Why We Love the
   Civil War," *Civil War History* 50, no. 4 (2004): 380–81; Randolph Bourne, *The
   History of a Literary Radical* (New York: S. A. Russell, 1956), 188–89; Chris Hedges,
   War Is a Force That Gives Us Meaning (New York: Public Affairs Press, 2002).
6. Edward L. Bernays, *Propaganda* (1928; reprinted, Port Washington, NY: Kennikat
   Press, 1972), 159.
7. Bernays, *Propaganda*, 20; Philip M. Taylor, *War and the Media: Propaganda and
   Persuasion in the Gulf War* (Manchester, UK: Manchester University Press, 1992), 27.
8. Jeff Gerth, "Military's Information War Is a Vast and Secret Mission," *New York
   Times*, December 11, 2005; Richard Alan Nelson, *A Chronology and Glossary of
   Propaganda in the United States* (Westport, CT: Greenwood Press, 1996), vii.
9. Mike McCurry and Liz Rosenberg, "When It's O.K. to Lie," *New York Times
   Magazine*, February 21, 1999, 28; Propaganda targeted at the enemy is called
   psychological warfare or psyops; propaganda directed at allied and neutral nations is
   called information or public diplomacy. For definitions of overt (white) and covert
   (black) propaganda, see *Propaganda and Mass Persuasion: A Historical Encyclopedia,*

1500 to the Present, ed. Nicholas J. Cull, David Culbert, and David Welch (Santa Barbara, CA: ABC-CLIO, 2003), 41, 317, 425.

10. *NewsHour* (PBS, November 6, 1998).

11. Nancy E. Bernhard, *U.S. Television News and Cold War Propaganda, 1945–1960* (Cambridge: Cambridge University Press, 1999), 128.

12. John Steinbeck, *Once There Was a War* (New York: Viking Press, 1958), xviii; James L. Baughman, *The Republic of Mass Culture: Journalism, Filmmaking, and Broadcasting in America since 1941* (Baltimore: Johns Hopkins University Press, 1992), 1–8; Richard L. Kaplan, "American Journalism Goes to War, 1898–2001: A Manifesto on Media and Empire," *Media History* 9, no. 3 (2003): 209–19; Robert M. Entman, *Projections of Power: Framing News, Public Opinion, and U.S. Foreign Policy* (Chicago: University of Chicago Press, 2004), 4–5.

13. Marguerite Higgins, *War in Korea: The Report of a Woman Combat Correspondent* (Garden City, NY: Doubleday, 1951), 84.

14. Ulysses S. Grant, *Personal Memoirs*, vol. I (New York: Century Company, 1895), 32; Mary Ann Heiss, "The Evolution of the Imperial Idea and U.S. National Identity," *Diplomatic History* 26 (Fall 2002): 511–40.

15. Cecilia Elizabeth O'Leary, *To Die For: The Paradox of American Patriotism* (Princeton, NJ: Princeton University Press, 1999), 236.

16. Office of War Information, "The Coordinated Distribution of Government War Graphics," June 1, 1942, OWI, Record Group (RG) 208, Entry 6A, Box 2; "Design of the Post-War World as a Weapon in Fighting the War," April 16, 1942, Office of Government Reports, RG 44, Box 888, National Archives and Records Administration (NARA), Archives II, College Park, Maryland.

17. O'Leary, *To Die For*, 160–62.

Chapter 1

1. "He is evidently going to make unity—a re-united country—the central thought." Diary of George B. Cortelyou, December 9, 1898, Box 52, George B. Cortelyou Papers, Library of Congress, Washington, DC.

2. Ida Tarbell, "President McKinley in War Times," *McClure's Magazine*, July 1898, 209–24; Stephen Ponder, "The President Makes News: William McKinley and the First Presidential Press Corps, 1897–1901," *Presidential Studies Quarterly* 24 (Fall 1994): 823–37.

3. James Bryce, *The American Commonwealth*, vol. 2, 3rd ed. (New York: Macmillan, 1899), 252–54; Henry Adams, *The Education of Henry Adams* (Boston: Houghton Mifflin, 1961), 374.

4. Paul M. Kennedy, *The Rise and Fall of the Great Powers: Economic Change and Military Conflict from 1500–2000* (New York: Random House, 1987), 150.

5. Walter LaFeber, *The American Search for Opportunity, 1865–1913* (New York: Cambridge University Press, 1993), 133, 138.

6. Robert Hannigan, *The New World Power: American Foreign Policy, 1898–1917* (Philadelphia: University of Pennsylvania Press, 2002), 1–16; Thomas Schoonover, *Uncle Sam's War of 1898 and the Origins of Globalization* (Lexington: University Press of Kentucky, 2003), 98.

7. Robert Hilderbrand, *Power and the People: Executive Management of Public Opinion in Foreign Affairs, 1897–1921* (Chapel Hill: University of North Carolina Press, 1981), 27–28.

8. Margaret Leech, *In the Days of McKinley* (New York: Harper & Brothers, 1959), 167–68.

9. Allan R. Millett and Peter Malowski, *For the Common Defense: A Military History of the United States of America* (New York: Free Press, 1994), 287–88.

10. LaFeber, *American Search*, 142–43; Lewis L. Gould, *The Presidency of William McKinley* (Lawrence: University Press of Kansas, 1980), 77.

11. Louis A. Pérez, Jr., *The War of 1898: The United States and Cuba in History and Historiography* (Chapel Hill: University of North Carolina Press, 1998), 10–12.

12. Hilderbrand, *Power and the People*, 32.

13. William Allen White, "When Johnny Went Marching Out," *McClure's Magazine*, June 1898, 198–205.

14. Leech, *Days of McKinley*, 209.

15. Leech, *Days of McKinley*, 238; Gould, *Presidency of William McKinley*, 101.

16. Gould, *Presidency of William McKinley*, 50.

17. Charles Belmont Davis, ed., *Adventures and Letters of Richard Harding Davis* (New York: Charles Scribner's Sons, 1918), 243-44; John Seelye, *War Games: Richard Harding Davis and the New Imperialism* (Amherst: University of Massachusetts Press, 2003), 275.

18. Walter Millis, *The Martial Spirit* (1931; reprinted, Chicago: Ivan R. Dee, 1989), 334.

19. Paul A. Kramer, "Race-Making and Colonial Violence in the U.S. Empire: The Philippine-American War as Race War," *Diplomatic History* 30 (April 2006): 190; Paul A. Kramer, *The Blood of Government: Race, Empire, the United States and the Philippines* (Chapel Hill: University of North Carolina Press, 2006), 102–5.

20. Seelye, *War Games*, 275; F. W. Hewes, "The Fighting Strength of the United States," *McClure's Magazine*, July 1898, 280–87; Edna Woolman Chase and Ilka Chase, *Always in Vogue* (Garden City, NY: Doubleday, 1954), 47.

21. Hilderbrand, *Power and the People*, 36, 41.

22. William McKinley, *Speeches and Addresses of William McKinley: From March 1, 1897 to May 30, 1900* (New York: Doubleday & McClure Co., 1900), 85, 97, 109, 113–14, 124.

23. Gould, *Presidency of William McKinley*, 132, 139; George B. Waldron, "The Commercial Promise of Cuba, Porto Rico, and the Philippines," *McClure's Magazine*, September 1898, 481–84.

24. H. Wayne Morgan, ed., *Making Peace with Spain: The Diary of Whitelaw Reid, September–December 1898* (Austin: University of Texas Press, 1965), 215.

25. McKinley to Secretary of War, transmitted to General Otis, December 21, 1898; Adjutant General to Otis, December 21, 1898; Alger to Otis, December 30, 1898, Box 70, Cortelyou Papers; H. W. Brands, *Bound to Empire: The United States and the Philippines* (New York: Oxford University Press, 1992), 48.

26. Robert L. Beisner, *Twelve Against Empire: The Anti-Imperialists, 1898–1900* (Chicago: University of Chicago Press, 1985); Roger J. Bresnahan, *In Time of Hesitation: American Anti-Imperialists and the Philippine-American War* (Quezon City, Philippines: New Day, 1981).

27. Leech, *Days of McKinley*, 353; McKinley, "Speech at Banquet of Board of Trade and Associated Citizens," Savannah, December 17, 1898, in *Speeches*, 174.

28. Diary, February 5, 1899, Box 52, Cortelyou Papers; McKinley, "Address Before the Tenth Pennsylvania Regiment," Pittsburgh, August 28, 1899, in *Speeches*, 215.

29. Brian McAllister Linn, *The Philippine War, 1899–1902* (Lawrence: University Press of Kansas, 2000), 34, 325; Glenn Anthony May, *A Past Recovered* (Quezon City, Philippines: New Day, 1987), 133.

30. Kramer, *Blood of Government*, 112–13.
31. Charles Musser, *The Emergence of Cinema: The American Screen to 1907* (New York: Charles Scribner's Sons, 1990), 225–61; *Advance of Kansas Volunteers at Caloocan* (Thomas A. Edison, Inc., 1899), http://memory.loc.gov; Nick Deocampo, "Imperialist Fiction: The Filipino in the Imperialist Imagery," in *The Philippine-American War and the Aftermath of an Imperial Dream, 1899–1999*, ed. Angel Velasco Shaw and Luis H. Francia (New York: New York University Press, 2002), 224–36; Amy Kaplan, *The Anarchy of Empire in the Making of U.S. Culture* (Cambridge, MA: Harvard University Press, 2002), 146–60.
32. Linn, *Philippine War*, 132–36; Frederick Palmer, "The Campaign in Luzon," *Collier's Weekly*, November 4, 1899, 3.
33. Otis to Adjutant General, January 17, 1899, Box 71, Cortelyou Papers; Linn, *Philippine War*, 135, 325; Hilderbrand, *Power and the People*, 49.
34. Brands, *Bound to Empire*, 58; Palmer, "Campaign in Luzon," 3.
35. William Oliver Trafton, *We Thought We Could Whip Them in Two Weeks*, ed. William Henry Scott (Quezon City, Philippines: New Day, 1990), 65–66.
36. McKinley, "Speech at Dinner of the Home Market Club," Boston, February 16, 1899, in *Speeches*, 185–93; *Nation*, February 23, 1899, 140.
37. McKinley, "Address Before the Tenth Pennsylvania Regiment," in *Speeches*, 211–17.
38. Diary, September 17, 1899, Box 52, Cortelyou Papers; Henry Cabot Lodge, "Shall We Retain the Philippines?" *Collier's Weekly*, February 10, 1900, 4.
39. "Albert J. Beveridge's Salute to Imperialism," in *Major Problems in American Foreign Relations*, vol. I, 4th ed., ed. Thomas G. Paterson and Dennis Merrill (Lexington, MA: D. C. Heath, 1995), 425.
40. Lodge, "Shall We Retain," 3; Walter L. Williams, "American Imperialism and the Indians," in *Indians in American History: An Introduction*, ed. Frederick E. Hoxie and Peter Iverson (Wheeling, IL: Harlan Davidson, 1998), 244; John F. Bass, "Jolo and the Moros," *Harper's Weekly*, November 18, 1899, 1159.
41. Kristin L. Hoganson, *Fighting for American Manhood: How Gender Politics Provoked the Spanish-American and Philippine-American Wars* (New Haven, CT: Yale University Press, 1998), 152–53; McKinley, "Speech at Madison, Wisconsin," October 16, 1899, in *Speeches*, 318; Dean C. Worcester, "Some Aspects of the Philippine Question," November 15, 1899, Hamilton Club of Chicago, Serial Publications. No. 13.
42. William McKinley, "William McKinley's Imperial Gospel," 1899, in *Major Problems*, ed. Paterson and Merrill, 424.
43. George F. Hoar, "Shall We Retain the Philippines?" *Collier's Weekly*, February 3, 1900, 2–3; Alan McPherson, "Americanism against American Empire," in *Americanism: New Perspectives on the History of an Ideal*, ed. Michael Kazin and Joseph A. McCartin (Chapel Hill: University of North Carolina Press, 2006), 176.
44. William McKinley, "Annual Message," December 5, 1899, www.presidency.ucsb.edu/ws/index.php?pid=29540; Speech of Hon. George Turner, U.S. Senate, January 22–23, 1900, Washington, DC; Editorial, "The Country and Its War," *Harper's Weekly*, June 3, 1899, 540.
45. Hoar, "Shall We Retain," 3; "Anti-Imperialist League Pamphlets," Box 7, Moorfield Storey Papers, Library of Congress, Washington, DC; Mark Twain, "To the Person Sitting in Darkness," February 1901, in *Mark Twain's Weapons of Satire: Anti-Imperialist Writings on the Philippine-American War*, ed. Jim Zwick (Syracuse, NY: Syracuse University Press, 1992), 22–39.

46. William Howard Taft to Elihu Root, August 11, 1900, Series 21, Reel 640, William Howard Taft Papers, Library of Congress, Washington, DC; Kramer, *Blood of Government*, 133.

47. McPherson, "Americanism," 175; William McKinley, "Second Inaugural Address," March 4, 1901, www.presidency.ucsb.edu/ws/index.php?pid=25828.

48. Linn, *Philippine War*, 221.

49. Taft to Root, July 14, 1900, Series 21, Reel 640, Taft Papers; Taft to Root, October 14, 1901, Container 164, Elihu Root Papers, Library of Congress, Washington, DC.

50. Root to Taft, January 15, 1901, Taft to Root, January 17, 1901, Root to Taft, January 21, 1901, and Root to McKinley, January 24, 1901, Series 21, Reel 640, Taft Papers; Hoganson, *Fighting for American Manhood*, 180, 191.

51. "Extracts from President McKinley's Last Speech," September 5, 1901, Joseph Tumulty to Woodrow Wilson, September 20, 1919, Container 50, Joseph Tumulty Papers, Library of Congress, Washington, DC; Robert W. Rydell, *All the World's a Fair: Visions of Empire at American International Expositions, 1876–1916* (Chicago: University of Chicago Press, 1984), 4, 126–53.

52. Kramer, *Blood of Government*, 145–56; Roosevelt to the Secretary of War, February 18, 1902, Container 162, Root Papers.

53. Kramer, *Blood of Government*, 155.

54. Brands, *Bound to Empire*, 79; LaFeber, *American Search*, 177.

55. Leech, *Days of McKinley*, 384.

56. Theodore Roosevelt, "Annual Message," December 3, 1901, www.presidency.ucsb .edu/ws/index.php?pid=29542; Theodore Roosevelt, "Annual Message," December 2, 1902, www.presidency.ucsb.edu/ws/index.php?pid=29543.

Chapter 2

1. David M. Kennedy, *Over Here: The First World War and American Society* (New York: Oxford University Press, 1980), 178.

2. James Kerney to Joseph Tumulty, October 2, 1918, Container 45, Joseph Tumulty Papers, Library of Congress, Washington, DC.

3. Robert C. Hilderbrand, *Power and the People: Executive Management of Public Opinion in Foreign Affairs, 1897–1921* (Chapel Hill: University of North Carolina Press, 1981), 117.

4. "Lansing Gags State Department," undated, probably May 1917, Box 3, Arthur Sweetser Papers, Library of Congress, Washington, DC.

5. Wilson quoted in Albert H. Sanford, "Why the United States is at War," March 1918, Bulletin of the State Normal School, La Crosse, Wisconsin, Committee on Public Information (CPI), Record Group (RG) 63, Entry 13, Box 1, National Archives and Records Administration (NARA), Archives II, College Park, Maryland.

6. Tumulty to Wilson, May 8, 1917, Container 48, Tumulty Papers.

7. Larry Wayne Ward, *The Motion Picture Goes to War: The U.S. Government Film Effort during World War I* (Ann Arbor, MI: UMI Research Press, 1985), 24; Hilderbrand, *Power and the People*, 104.

8. Woodrow Wilson, "Address at the Salesmanship Congress," July 10, 1916, in *President Wilson's State Papers and Addresses* (New York: Review of Reviews Company, 1918), 279- 83; Robert H. Zieger, *America's Great War: World War I and the American Experience* (Lanham, MD: Rowman & Littlefield, 2001), 41.

9. Reinhard R. Doerries, *Imperial Challenge: Ambassador Count Bernstorff and German-American Relations, 1908–1917* (Chapel Hill: University of North Carolina Press, 1989), 141–90; Harold Lasswell, *Propaganda Technique in World War I* (1927; reprinted, Cambridge, MA: MIT Press, 1971), 149–51; Michael Sanders and Philip Taylor, *British Propaganda in the First World War, 1914–1918* (London: Macmillan, 1982), 170.

10. Zieger, *America's Great War*, 22–25.

11. John Horne and Alan Kramer, *German Atrocities, 1914: A History of Denial* (New Haven, CT: Yale University Press, 2001), 232–37, 249–56, 422; Nicoletta F. Gullace, "Sexual Violence and Family Honor: British Propaganda and International Law during the First World War," *American Historical Review* 102 (June 1997): 714 47.

12. Richard J. Barnet, *The Rockets' Red Glare: When America Goes to War: The Presidents and the People* (New York: Simon & Schuster, 1990), 154; Randolph Bourne, *The History of a Literary Radical* (New York: S. A. Russell, 1956), 215; Notes, February 4, 1917, Box 3, Sweetser Papers; Walter Karp, *The Politics of War* (New York: Franklin Square Press, 2003), 238.

13. Cecilia Elizabeth O'Leary, *To Die For: The Paradox of American Patriotism* (Princeton, NJ: Princeton University Press, 1999), 225.

14. Tumulty to Wilson, January 17, 1916, Container 47, Tumulty Papers.

15. Hilderbrand, *Power and the People*, 136 37.

16. "Interview with Lansing," November 10, 1916, Box 3, Sweetser Papers.

17. Notes, March 28 (probably 1917), Box 3, Sweetser Papers.

18. Thomas J. Knock, *To End All Wars: Woodrow Wilson and the Quest for a New World Order* (Princeton, NJ: Princeton University Press, 1992), 125.

19. Stephen Vaughn, *Holding Fast the Inner Lines: Democracy, Nationalism, and the Committee on Public Information* (Chapel Hill: University of North Carolina Press, 1980), 4.

20. Jennifer D. Keene, *Doughboys, the Great War, and the Remaking of America* (Baltimore: Johns Hopkins University Press, 2001), 1–34.

21. Zieger, *America's Great War*, 79.

22. George Creel, *How We Advertised America* (1920; reprinted, New York: Arno Press, 1972), 4; Vaughn, *Holding Fast the Inner Lines*, 24.

23. Creel, *How We Advertised*, xiv.

24. Tumulty to Wilson, May 31, 1917, Container 48, Tumulty Papers.

25. Vaughn, *Holding Fast the Inner Lines*, 193.

26. July 27 (probably 1917), Box 3, Sweetser Papers.

27. Editorial, *New Republic*, May 12, 1917; "Lansing Gags State Department," Sweetser Papers; Hilderbrand, *Power and the People*, 146–47.

28. "Bulletin for Cartoonists," June 21, July 13, August 24, August 27, September 28, and October 26, 1918, CPI, RG 63, Entry 19, Box 2, NARA; "Report of the Bureau of Cartoons," September 9, 1918, CPI, RG 63, Entry 13, Box 1, NARA.

29. CPI, *German War Practices*, ed. Dana C. Munro of Princeton University, George C. Sellery of the University of Wisconsin, and August C. Krey of the University of Minnesota, November 15, 1917.

30. Sanford, "Why the United States is at War."

31. Vaughn, *Holding Fast the Inner Lines*, 150; Knock, *To End All Wars*, 130.

32. Walton Rawls, *Wake Up America! World War I and the American Poster* (New York: Abbeville Press, 1988), 12; Susan Zeiger, *In Uncle Sam's Service: Women Workers with*

the American Expeditionary Force, 1917–1919 (Ithaca, NY: Cornell University Press, 1999), 145.

33. Vaughn, *Holding Fast the Inner Lines*, 165.
34. CPI Division of Advertising, "The German Idea," RG 63, Entry 13, Box 1, NARA.
35. CPI Division of Advertising, November 1917–June 1918, RG 63, Entry 13, Box 1 and Entry 20, Box 1, NARA.
36. Zieger, *America's Great War*, 124.
37. Richard M. Fried, *The Russians Are Coming! The Russians Are Coming!: Pageantry and Patriotism in Cold-War America* (New York: Oxford University Press, 1998), 6–7.
38. CPI Division of Four Minute Men, "Danger to America," Bulletin No. 31, May 27, 1918, RG 63, Entry 62, Box 2, NARA.
39. Vaughn, *Holding Fast the Inner Lines*, 126.
40. Hilderbrand, *Power and the People*, 159.
41. Arthur Sweetser to Kendall Banning, undated reply to letter dated May 22, 1917, Box 3, Sweetser Papers.
42. Ward, *Motion Picture Goes to War*, 25–26.
43. *Pershing's Crusaders* (1918), Records of the Office of the Chief Signal Officer, RG 111-H-1213, NARA; Hart, Director of CPI Division of Films to August P. Lindlar and Hart to Augustus Thomas, May 10, 1918, CPI, RG 63, Entry 62, Box 2, NARA; Creel, *How We Advertised*, 121–23.
44. *The Training of Colored Troops* (1918), RG 111-H-1211, NARA; Thomas Winter, "The Training of Colored Troops: A Cinematic Effort to Promote National Cohesion," in *Hollywood's World War I: Motion Picture Images*, ed. Peter C. Rollins and John E. O'Connor (Bowling Green, OH: Bowling Green State University Popular Press, 1997), 13–25.
45. Rufus Steele, "Progress Report of the Department of Scenarios and Outside Production," August 10, 1918, CPI, RG 63, Entry 13, Box 1, NARA; According to Larry Wayne Ward, none of these newsreel-style films survives under the original titles in the Signal Corps collection at the National Archives. The Signal Corps reedited most of these films in the 1930s. Ward, *Motion Picture Goes to War*, 103.
46. *The Unbeliever* (Alan Crosland, 1918); *Shoulder Arms* (Charles Chaplin, 1918).
47. *The Birth of a Nation* (D. W. Griffith, 1915); Ward, *Motion Picture Goes to War*, 54; Russell Merritt, "D. W. Griffith Directs the Great War: The Making of Hearts of the World," *Quarterly Review of Film Studies* (Winter 1981): 50.
48. *Hearts of the World* (D. W. Griffith, 1918); Leslie Midkiff DeBauche, "Melodrama and the World War I Film," in *The Bounds of Representation: Censorship, the Visible, Modes of Representation in Film*, ed. Leonardo Quaresima, Alessandra Raengo, and Laura Vichi (Udine, Italy: VI International Film Studies Conference, University of Udine, 1999), 177–86.
49. Merritt, "D. W. Griffith Directs the Great War," 55-56.
50. Liberty Loan Drive Films, RG 111-H-1133, NARA; Leslie Midkiff DeBauche, *Reel Patriotism: The Movies and World War I* (Madison: University of Wisconsin Press, 1997), 71–136.
51. O'Leary, *To Die For*, 235, 241.
52. Wilson to Creel, February 28, 1918, Container 3, George Creel Papers, Library of Congress, Washington, DC; Christopher Capozzola, *Uncle Sam Wants You: World War I and the Making of the Modern American Citizen* (New York: Oxford University Press, 2008), 181–85.

53. Zieger, *America's Great War*, 78.

54. The War Department oversaw telephone and telegraph censorship, the navy cable censorship, and the post office mail censorship. Vaughn, *Holding Fast the Inner Lines*, 219–21; John D. Stevens, "When Sedition Laws Were Enforced: Wisconsin in World War I," *Transactions of the Wisconsin Academy of Sciences, Arts, and Letters* 58 (1970): 39–60.

55. President Wilson later commuted the sentence of *Spirit of '76* producer Robert Goldstein. Ward, *Motion Picture Goes to War*, 118–19; Capozzola, *Uncle Sam Wants You*, 144–60; Stevens, "When Sedition Laws Were Enforced," 43.

56. Phillip Knightley, *The First Casualty: The War Correspondent as Hero and Myth-Maker from the Crimea to Kosovo* (Baltimore: Johns Hopkins University Press, 2002), 116–17.

57. Vaughn, *Holding Fast the Inner Lines*, 9; Arthur Bullard, "Democracy and Diplomacy," *Atlantic Monthly*, April 1917, 491–99.

58. The President to Foreign Correspondents, April 8, 1918, Container 48, Tumulty Papers.

59. Knightley, *First Casualty*, 133, 139; Michael S. Sweeney, *The Military and the Press: An Uneasy Truce* (Evanston, IL: Northwestern University Press, 2006), 59.

60. For more on the wartime practices of posing, cropping, retouching, and faking photographs see Susan D. Moeller, *Shooting War: Photography and the American Experience of Combat* (New York: Basic Books, 1989), 130–52.

61. Heywood Broun, *The A.E.F.: With General Pershing and the American Forces* (New York: D. Appleton and Company, 1918), 295–96; Keene, *Doughboys*, 77.

62. Kennedy, *Over Here*, 212.

63. Will Judy, *A Soldier's Diary* (Chicago: Judy Publishing Company, 1930), 35, 125.

64. Keene, *Doughboys*, 46–51; Zieger, *America's Great War*, 105–7.

65. "He Will Come Back a Better Man!," *Collier's Weekly*, November 30, 1918, 22.

66. Ronald Schaffer, *America in the Great War: The Rise of the War Welfare State* (New York: Oxford University Press, 1991), 208–11.

67. Judy, *Soldier's Diary*, 211–12.

68. Merritt, "D. W. Griffith Directs the War," 51, 59.

69. Woodrow Wilson, "Address of the President," January 8, 1918, www.presidency.ucsb.edu/ws/index.php?pid=65405&st=&st1=.

70. James R. Mock and Cedric Larson, *Words That Won the War: The Story of the Committee on Public Information, 1917–1919* (Princeton, NJ: Princeton University Press, 1939), 247.

71. Wilson quoted in Lloyd C. Gardner, *Safe for Democracy: The Anglo-American Response to Revolution, 1913–1923* (New York: Oxford University Press, 1984), 1.

72. Zieger, *America's Great War*, 188–94.

73. CPI Division of Four Minute Men, "Instructions to Four Minute Men," May 27, 1918, RG 63. Entry 62, Box 2, NARA.

74. Kerney to Tumulty, October 2, 1918.

75. Ronald Steel, *Walter Lippmann and the American Century* (Boston: Little, Brown & Company, 1980), 157.

76. Erez Manela, *The Wilsonian Moment: Self-Determination and the International Origins of Anticolonial Nationalism* (New York: Oxford University Press, 2007), 3, 201; Margaret MacMillan, *Paris 1919: Six Months That Changed the World* (New York: Random House, 2001), 381–408; Newton D. Baker to Arthur Sweetser, July 22, 1920, Box 30, Sweetser Papers.

77. Hilderbrand, *Power and the People*, 177; Sweetser to Newton D. Baker, February 4, 1919, Box 30, Sweetser Papers.
78. Admiral Cary T. Grayson to Tumulty, April 10, 1919, Container 44, Tumulty Papers.
79. Tumulty to Grayson, December 16, 1918, Container 44; President to Tumulty, cable from Paris received December 19, 1918, Container 48, Tumulty Papers.
80. Diary, March 5, 1919, Sweetser Papers.
81. Knock, *To End All Wars*, 237, 241; Kennedy, *Over Here*, 360; Kerney to Tumulty, January 9, 1919, Box 45, Tumulty Papers.
82. Tumulty to Wilson, September 20, 1919, Container 50, Tumulty Papers.
83. Arthur Link, ed., *The Papers of Woodrow Wilson*, vol. 63 (Princeton, NJ: Princeton University Press, 1990), 23, 47, 115, 279, 318–19, 325.
84. Jonathan Rosenberg, "For Democracy, Not Hypocrisy: World War and Race Relations in the United States, 1914–1919," *International History Review* 21 (September 1999): 618–20.
85. Edward L. Bernays, *Biography of an Idea: Memoirs of a Public Relations Counsel* (New York: Simon & Schuster, 1965), 287–95.
86. Bourne, *History of a Literary Radical*, 225–35; Walter Lippmann, *Public Opinion* (1922; reprinted, New York: Free Press, 1965), 257.
87. Kennedy, *Over Here*, 218; Frederick Palmer, *America in France* (New York; Dodd, Mead, 1919), 4; Judy, *Soldier's Diary*, 214.

Chapter 3

1. Office of War Information (OWI) Bureau of Intelligence, "Public Attitudes Toward the Post-War World," September 15, 1942, Office of Government Reports (OGR) Record Group (RG) 44, Entry 171, Box 1842, National Archives and Records Administration (NARA), Archives II, College Park, Maryland.
2. "Aide Memoire to A. MacLeish," April 6, 1942, Box 52, Papers of Archibald MacLeish, Library of Congress, Washington, DC; "Operating Policies to be observed by Domestic Branch OWI," May 1943, OWI, RG 208, Entry 1, Box 3, NARA.
3. James L. Baughman, *The Republic of Mass Culture: Journalism, Filmmaking, and Broadcasting in America since 1941* (Baltimore: Johns Hopkins University Press, 1992), 1.
4. Lary May, *The Big Tomorrow: Hollywood and the Politics of the American Way* (Chicago: University of Chicago Press, 2000), 139–74.
5. *This Is the Army* (Michael Curtiz, 1943).
6. Thomas B. Wenner, "People's Fears and Hopes About the Post-War World," November 30, 1942, OWI Bureau of Intelligence, Box 37, Arthur Sweetser Papers, Library of Congress, Washington, DC.
7. Steven Casey, *Cautious Crusade: Franklin D. Roosevelt, American Public Opinion, and the War against Nazi Germany* (New York: Oxford University Press, 2001), 214–15.
8. William A. Lydgate, *What Our People Think* (New York: Thomas Y. Crowell, 1944), 41.
9. Smedley D. Butler, *War Is a Racket* (New York: Round Table Press, 1935), 26–36.
10. Eric Sevareid, *Not So Wild a Dream* (New York: Atheneum, 1976), 60–63.
11. Joan Hoff, "The American Century: From Sarajevo to Sarajevo," *Diplomatic History* 23 (Spring 1999): 286.
12. Henry Luce, *The American Century* (New York: Farrar and Rinehart, 1941); James L. Baughman, *Henry R. Luce and the Rise of the American News Media* (Boston: Twayne Publishers, 1987), 131.

13. *Sergeant York* (Howard Hawks, 1941); Robert Brent Toplin, *History By Hollywood: The Use and Abuse of the American Past* (Urbana: University of Illinois Press, 1996), 82–101; Clayton R. Koppes and Gregory D. Black, *Hollywood Goes to War: How Politics, Profits and Propaganda Shaped World War II Movies* (Berkeley: University of California Press, 1987), 39–46.

14. Frederick S. Voss, *Reporting the War: The Journalistic Coverage of World War II* (Washington, DC: Smithsonian Institution Press, 1994), 123–33.

15. Richard W. Steele, *Propaganda in an Open Society: The Roosevelt Administration and the Media, 1933–1941* (Westport, CT: Greenwood Press, 1985), 143–44.

16. Koppes and Black, *Hollywood Goes to War*, 56; Steele, *Propaganda in an Open Society*, 73–77.

17. Steele, *Propaganda in an Open Society*, 69–73.

18. "Home from the Sea," *Time*, August 25, 1941, 11.

19. Gerhard L. Weinberg, *A World At Arms: A Global History of World War II* (New York: Cambridge University Press, 1994), 86.

20. Most studies conclude that 2,400 men were killed at Pearl Harbor. The controversy over what happened and who was responsible prompted seven inquiries from 1942 to 1945. Emily S. Rosenberg, *A Date Which Will Live: Pearl Harbor in American Memory* (Durham, NC: Duke University Press, 2003), 34–52; Phillip Knightley, *The First Casualty: The War Correspondent as Hero and Myth Maker from the Crimea to Kosovo* (Baltimore: Johns Hopkins University Press, 2002), 297; Franklin D. Roosevelt, "Fireside Chat," February 23, 1942, www.presidency.ucsb.edu/ws/php?pid=16224.

21. Sidney Stewart, *Give Us This Day* (New York: W. W. Norton, 1986), 12.

22. Williamson Murray and Allan R. Millett, *A War To Be Won: Fighting the Second World War* (Cambridge, MA: Belknap Press, 2000), 182–86.

23. Steele, *Propaganda in an Open Society*, 172.

24. OWI, "Functions of the OWI," and "Government Campaigns of Information," October 28, 1942, RG 208, Entry 39, Box 140, NARA; "Operating Policies to be observed by the Domestic Branch."

25. "Bureau of Graphics—Function," June 1942, OWI, RG 208, Entry 6A, Box 2, NARA.

26. Committee on War Information, "Minutes," January 26, 1942, OGR, RG 44, Entry 78, Box 888, NARA; OWI, "Functions of the OWI."

27. Allan M. Winkler, *The Politics of Propaganda: The Office of War Information, 1942–1945* (New Haven, CT: Yale University Press, 1978), 71; Elmer Davis to All Staff Members, March 17, 1943, OWI Bureau of Intelligence, OGR, RG 44, Entry 170, Box 1828, NARA.

28. "Truth and Trouble," *Time*, March 15, 1943, 14; Michael Darrock and Joseph P. Dorn, "Davis and Goliath: The OWI and Its Gigantic Assignment," *Harper's*, February 1943, 225–37; "Notes of 16 June 1942," Box 10, and George Creel to Elmer Davis, August 4, 1942, Box 1, Elmer Davis Papers, Library of Congress, Washington, DC.

29. Voss, *Reporting the War*, 24.

30. Arthur Krock, "In Wartime What News Shall the Nation Have?" *New York Times Magazine*, August 16, 1942.

31. "Notes of 16 June 1942," Davis Papers; Winkler, *Politics of Propaganda*, 47–50.

32. Harry Alpert to Clyde Hart, "War, War Aims, and Postwar World," March 25, 1943, OGR, RG 44, Entry 170, Box 1828, NARA.

33. "Mr. Sweetser's Notes," May 29, 1942, Box 38, Sweetser Papers.

34. "Memo, Interview with Hull," August 6, 1942, Box 37 and "Interview with Undersecretary of State Sumner Welles," May 27, 1942, Box 1, Sweetser Papers.

35. OWI Intelligence Report #66, "Popular Reactions," March 12, 1943, Official Files (OF) 5015, Box 3, Franklin D. Roosevelt Papers, Franklin D. Roosevelt Library, Hyde Park, New York; "The Government's War Information Policy," May 25, 1942, Box 4, Philleo Nash Papers, Harry S. Truman Library, Independence, Missouri; "Priority Rating for Radio Campaigns," undated, OWI, RG 208, Entry E-103, Box 641, NARA; Gerd Horton, *Radio Goes to War: The Cultural Politics of Propaganda during World War II* (Berkeley: University of California Press, 2002), 117–18.

36. Thomas Doherty, *Projections of War: Hollywood, American Culture and World War II* (New York: Columbia University Press, 1993), 5; "Government Information Manual for the Motion Picture Industry," [1942], OWI, RG 208, Entry 6A, Box 2, NARA; "Newsreel Analysis," May 1942, OGR, RG 44, Box 888, NARA; "Desperate Dorothy," *Life*, December 7, 1942, 132–139; OWI Bureau of Publications and Graphics, July 1, 1942, RG 208, Entry 6A, Box 2, NARA.

37. J. Michael Sproule, *Propaganda and Persuasion: The American Experience of Media and Mass Persuasion* (Cambridge: Cambridge University Press, 1997), 184–85.

38. OWI Bureau of Intelligence, "Public Attitudes Toward the Post-War World," "Aide Memoire," April 6, 1942 and Minutes of Board Meeting, April 22, 1942, Box 52, MacLeish Papers; Keith Kane to Arthur Sweetser, "American Opinion and Post-War Problems," January 26, 1943, OWI Bureau of Intelligence, Box 37, Sweetser Papers.

39. M. S. Eisenhower to Archibald MacLeish, December 1, 1942, OWI, RG 208, Entry 1, Box 5, NARA.

40. Henry Wallace, Speech of May 8, 1942, quoted in "War Aims," OGR, RG 44, Box 888, NARA; *Why We Fight: Prelude to War* (Frank Capra, 1942). The same themes were broadcast in Norman Corwin's radio series "This is War!" Made at the request of OFF, the series was paid for and broadcast by the radio networks (NBC, CBS, Blue, Mutual) from February to May 1942 reaching an estimated 20 million people. See James Spiller, "This is War! Network Radio and World War II Propaganda in America," *Journal of Radio Studies* 11 (June 2004): 55–72.

41. OWI Intelligence Report, "American Estimates of the Enemy," September 2, 1942, Box 53, MacLeish Papers; Archibald MacLeish, "Basic Policy Directive: The Nature of the Enemy," October 5, 1942, OWI, RG 208, Entry 6A, Box 1, NARA.

42. Horton, *Radio Goes to War*, 57–59.

43. OFF, Bureau of Intelligence, Division of Information Channels, Special Intelligence Report No. 45, "Newspaper Comic Strips," June 17, 1942, OGR, RG 44, Entry 171, Box 1844, NARA; In *Tarzan Triumphs*, the natives, like Tarzan, are white; *Tarzan Triumphs* (Wilhelm Thiele, 1943).

44. Dick Dorrance and Joseph Liss (Domestic Radio Bureau of OWI), "When Radio Goes to War," February 20, 1943, Container 114, Raymond Clapper Papers, Library of Congress, Washington, DC.

45. John Morton Blum, *V Was For Victory: Politics and American Culture During World War II* (New York: Harcourt, Brace Jovanovich, 1976), 52.

46. "Design of the Post-War World as a Weapon in Fighting the War," April 16, 1942, OGR, RG 44, Box 888, NARA.

47. *Four Freedoms*, OWI, RG 208, Entry 94, Box 621, NARA.

48. *Spirit of '43* (Walt Disney, 1943).

49. "Notes of June 16, 1942," Davis Papers.

50. "Transcript of Short Wave Broadcast (Radio Tokyo)," July 3, 1942, OWI, RG 208, Entry 27, Box 33, NARA; "Five Months of Axis Propaganda on the Negro Question," December 7, 1941–May 7, 1942, OGR, RG 44, Entry 171, Box 1849, NARA.

51. OFF, "Newspaper Comic Strips."

52. *Star Spangled Rhythm* (George Marshall, 1942); Winkler, *Politics of Propaganda*, 67–68.

53. Roger Daniels, *Prisoners Without Trial: Japanese Americans in World War II* (New York: Hill & Wang, 1993), 23–48; Dorrance and Liss, "When Radio Goes to War."

54. *Bataan* (Tay Garnett, 1943); George H. Roeder, Jr., *The Censored War: American Visual Experience During World War Two* (New Haven, CT: Yale University Press, 1993), 88.

55. "War Advertising Council Press Release," October 8, 1943, OWI, RG 208, Entry 27, Box 42, NARA; Maureen Honey, *Creating Rosie the Riveter: Class, Gender, and Propaganda during World War II* (Amherst: University of Massachusetts Press, 1984), 215–16.

56. Robert B. Westbrook, *Why We Fought: Forging American Obligations in World War II* (Washington, DC: Smithsonian Books, 2004), 67–91.

57. Lizabeth Cohen, *A Consumers' Republic: The Politics of Mass Consumption in Postwar America* (New York: Vintage Books, 2004), 74.

58. Anthony Hyde to Palmer Hoyt and Arthur Sweetser, "Report on United Nations Flag Day, June 14, 1943," July 5, 1943, OWI, RG 208, Entry 43, Box 1, NARA.

59. Leo Rosten to Harold Jacobs, "Newsreel Coverage of OFF's Posters," May 7, 1942, OGR, RG 44, Box 888, NARA; Kane to Sweetser, "American Opinion and Post-War Problems"; Koppes and Black, *Hollywood Goes to War*, 185–247; *Mission to Moscow* (Michael Curtiz, 1943); Todd Bennett, "Culture, Power, and *Mission to Moscow*: Film and Soviet-American Relations during World War II," *Journal of American History* 88 (September 2001): 489–518.

60. Robert A. Taft, "American Foreign Policy," August 26, 1943, Container 613, Robert A. Taft Papers, Library of Congress, Washington, DC.

61. *Casablanca* (Michael Curtiz, 1942).

62. OWI Bureau of Intelligence, Media Division, "Feature Films and OWI Campaigns and Programs: January 1943," February 10, 1943, Box 4, Nash Papers; Bureau of Motion Pictures Report, "Feature Review of *Casablanca*," in *Hollywood's America: United States History Through Its Films*, ed. Steven Mintz and Randy Roberts (St. James, NY: Brandywine Press, 1993), 178–79.

63. Lydgate, *What Our People Think*, 60–63.

64. Kane to Sweetser, "American Opinion and Post-war Problems." In Casablanca, aid societies persuaded the military to carry refugees who had visas and quota numbers on empty ships returning to the United States, but this plan broke down when the State Department refused to give quota numbers to refugees without guaranteed transport—which the military would not promise to refugees without quota numbers. David S. Wyman, *The Abandonment of the Jews: America and the Holocaust, 1941–1945* (New York: Pantheon Books, 1984), 127–29; Bureau of Motion Pictures Report, "Feature Review of *Casablanca*"; OWI, "Looking Forward to a Global Peace," Special Services Division Report No. 102, January 13, 1943, OGR, RG 44, Entry 171, Box 1844, NARA.

65. "Specimen Day in Washington," January 5, 1943, Container 10, Davis Papers; Frank Costigliola, *France and the United States: The Cold Alliance, 1941–1990* (New York: Twayne Publishers, 1992), 18–22.

66. Winkler, *Politics of Propaganda*, 89; OWI, "Looking Forward to a Global Peace"; Kane to Sweetser, "American Opinion and Post-War Problems."

67. Warren Kimball, *The Juggler: Franklin Roosevelt as Wartime Statesman* (Princeton, NJ: Princeton University Press, 1991), 63–81.

68. Joe Louis quoted in Lawrence R. Samuel, *Pledging Allegiance: American Identity and the Bond Drive of World War II* (Washington, DC: Smithsonian Institution Press, 1997), 183.

69. Stephen Holden, "Wartime Dreams Revisited," *New York Times*, July 23, 1995.

70. Lt. Sherwood M. Snyder to the Federal Communications Commission, May 29, 1943, forwarded to the OWI, RG 208, Entry 1, Box 6, NARA.

71. Lt. Col. Paul M. Jacobs to General Marshall and Paramount Pictures, January 2, 1943, OGR, RG 44, Entry 78, Box 890, NARA.

72. Dorothy Johnstone to Katherine Blackburn, April 3, 1943, OGR, RG 44, Box 1659, Entry 138, NARA.

73. James J. Kimble, *Mobilizing the Home Front: War Bonds and Domestic Propaganda* (College Station: Texas A&M University Press, 2006), 5–7.

74. Alpert to Hart, "War, War Aims, and Postwar World."

75. Winkler, *Politics of Propaganda*, 64.

76. Chester LaRoche to Gardner Cowles, Jr., April 16, 1943, OWI, RG 208, Entry 20, Box 12, NARA; "War Advertising Council Press Release," October 8, 1943, OWI, RG 208, Entry 27, Box 42, NARA.

77. Cohen, *Consumer's Republic*, 72; Mark H. Neff, "The Politics of Sacrifice on the American Home Front in World War II," *Journal of American History* 77 (March 1991): 1297; Charles F. McGovern, *Sold American: Consumption and Citizenship, 1890–1945* (Chapel Hill: University of North Carolina Press, 2006), 361–62.

78. Milton Mayer's "The Case Against the Jew," which appeared in the March 28, 1942, issue, was the last of three articles on what the *Saturday Evening Post* editor called "the Jewish question." An editorial page apology appeared a month later following the cancellation of subscriptions and advertising. Stuart Murray and James McCabe, *Norman Rockwell's Four Freedoms* (New York: Gramercy Books, 1993), 72–73; Westbrook, *Why We Fought*, 46.

79. Murray and McCabe, *Norman Rockwell's Four Freedoms*, 60–61.

80. Murray and McCabe, *Norman Rockwell's Four Freedoms*, 79–92.

81. Murray and McCabe, *Norman Rockwell's Four Freedoms*, 79–92.

82. Horton, *When Radio Goes to War*, 96; Bernard DeVoto to Elmer Davis, August 26, 1943, Container 1, Davis Papers.

83. John Steinbeck, *Once There Was a War* (New York: Viking Press, 1958), 25–29.

84. Roeder, *Censored War*, 19; *Life*, July 5, 1943.

85. Roeder, *Censored War*, 11–12.

86. "Realism for Breakfast," *Newsweek*, September 20, 1943, 98.

87. James J. Lorence, *Screening America: United States History Through Film Since 1900* (New York: Pearson, 2006), 114; *Every 2 ½ Minutes* (1944).

88. James Agee, "These Terrible Records of War," *Nation*, March 24, 1945, reprinted in Library of America, *Reporting World War II, Part II: American Journalism, 1944–1946* (New York: Library of America, 1995), 660–61; Bosley Crowther, "The Movies," in *While You Were Gone: A Report on Wartime Life in the United States*, ed. Jack Goodman (New York: Simon & Schuster, 1946), 522–23.

89. Edward Klauber to the Secretary of the Treasury, April 5, 1945, OWI, RG 208, Entry 1, Box 5, NARA; Board of War Information, "Minutes," January 28, 1944, OWI, RG 208, Entry 16, Box 1, NARA; Clifton Fadiman to Leo Rosten, "Memorandum of Meeting with Commentators," March 19, 1943, Box 11, Nash Papers; Samuel, *Pledging Allegiance*, 56–57; John W. Dower, *War Without Mercy: Race and Power in the Pacific War* (New York: Pantheon Books, 1986), 51–52.

90. Deborah Lipstadt, *Beyond Belief: The American Press and the Coming of the Holocaust* (New York: Free Press, 1986), 243, 252; Richard Breitman, *Official Secrets: What the Nazis Planned, What the British and Americans Knew* (New York: Hill & Wang, 1998), 122–36.

91. Voss, *Reporting the War*, 126–27.

92. Susan D. Moeller, *Shooting War: Photography and the American Experience of Combat* (New York: Basic Books, 1989), 191.

93. Roeder, *Censored War*, 24, 57; Michael S. Sweeney, *The Military and the Press: An Uneasy Truce* (Evanston, IL: Northwestern University Press, 2006), 104–6, 111.

94. Moeller, *Shooting War*, 183, 197; Lester Markel, "The Newspapers," in *While You Were Gone*, ed. Goodman, 341; Susan A. Brewer, *To Win the Peace: British Propaganda in the United States during World War II* (Ithaca, NY: Cornell University Press, 1997), 117.

95. Karal Ann Marling and John Wetenhall, *Iwo Jima: Monuments, Memories, and the American Hero* (Cambridge, MA: Harvard University Press, 1991), 39–67.

96. Marling and Wetenhall, *Iwo Jima*, 75–121.

97. James Tobin, *Ernie Pyle's War: America's Eyewitness to World War II* (New York: Free Press, 1997).

98. Bill Mauldin, *Up Front* (1945; reproduced W. W. Norton, 1995), 16.

99. Brendan Gill, "Young Man Behind Plexiglass," August 12, 1944, in *The New Yorker Book of War Pieces* (New York: Reynal & Hitchcock, 1947), 280.

100. OWI, "Looking Forward to a Global Peace," January 13, 1943; OWI Bureau of Intelligence, "Attitudes Toward Postwar Problems," February 1, 1943, Special Services Division, Report No. 106, OGR, RG 44, Entry 171, Box 1844, NARA; Kane to Sweetser, "American Opinion and Post-War Problems"; Public Opinion News Service Release, June 5, 1943, Box 69, Sweetser Papers; "Presenting Postwar Planning to the Public," Office of Public Opinion Research, March 1943, Container 211, John Winant Papers, Franklin D. Roosevelt Library, Hyde Park, New York.

101. Jerry Brooks to George Ludlam, "Spots for International Cooperation Campaign," April 10, 1945, OWI, RG 208, Entry 94, Box 621, NARA; OWI Domestic Radio Bureau, "To Prevent Future Wars—The United Nations," undated (probably late 1944), RG 208, Entry 6A, Box 5, NARA.

102. Dorrance and Liss, "When Radio Goes to War."

103. In the fall of 1943, Congress overwhelmingly approved the Fulbright and Connelly resolutions in favor of an international security organization. Members of Hull's committee included Sumner Welles, Adolf A. Berle, Stanley Hornbeck, Harley Notter, Leo Pasvolsky, Myron Taylor, Professors James T. Shotwell and Isaiah Bowman, *Foreign Affairs* editor Hamilton Fish Armstrong, columnist Anne O'Hare McCormick, Senators Tom Connelly, Walter George, Warren Austin, Elbert Thomas, and Wallace White, Jr., and Representatives Sol Bloom, Luther Johnson, and Charles Eaton. "Minutes of April 24, 1943 State Department Meeting," Box 53, MacLeish

Papers; MacLeish to Secretary of State, December 29, 1944 and January 13, 1945, Department of State, RG 59, Lot 52–249, Entry 1245, Box 1, National Archives and Record Administration (NARA) Archives II, College Park, Maryland.

104. "Minutes of April 24, 1943 State Department Meeting," Box 53, MacLeish Papers.
105. "Minutes of May 8, 1943 State Department Meeting," Box 53, MacLeish Papers; Forrest Davis, "Roosevelt's World Blueprint," *Saturday Evening Post*, April 10, 1943, 110.
106. Forrest Davis, "What Really Happened at Teheran," *Saturday Evening Post*, May 20, 1944, 22+.
107. "Controversial Trends of Opinion: Japan," July 1–31, 1944, prepared for the United Nations Information Board, Box 38, Sweetser Papers; Marling and Wettenhal, *Iwo Jima*, 120.
108. Joseph H. Ball, "How We Planned for the Postwar World," in *While You Were Gone*, ed. Goodman, 564–65.
109. Daniel Yergin, *The Prize: The Epic Quest for Oil, Money and Power* (New York: Touchstone, 1992), 395.
110. Minutes of the Board of War Information, February 17, 1944, OWI, RG 208, Entry 16, Box 1, NARA.
111. Dorrance and Liss, "When Radio Goes to War."
112. Address by the Secretary of the Treasury, "The United Nations Monetary and Financial Conference," July 22, 1944, and Press Release from the Secretary of State, July 24, 1944, *The Department of State Bulletin*, vol. 11, no. 266, July 30, 1944; Dean Acheson, Assistant Secretary of State, "The Place of Bretton Woods in Economic Collective Security," March 23, 1945, Department of State Publication 2306.
113. C. P. Trussell, "Atlantic Charter Unsigned But Intact, Roosevelt Says," December 20, 1944, and "Roosevelt Urges Homefolks to Back Soldiers at Front," December 23, 1944, *New York Times*; Ernest K. Lindley, "The State of the Atlantic Charter," *Newsweek*, January 1, 1945.
114. Joseph Grew to the President, "Latest Opinion Trends in the US," February 24, 1945, President's Secretary's File (PSF) Departmental Correspondence, State Department, Box 91, Franklin D. Roosevelt Papers, Roosevelt Library.
115. Lloyd C. Gardner, *Spheres of Influence: The Great Powers Partition Europe, from Munich to Yalta* (Chicago: Ivan R. Dee, 1993), 229.
116. Hadley Cantril, "How Real is America's 'Internationalism'?" *New York Times Magazine*, April 29, 1945, 9.
117. "Memorandum of Conversation on Services to Feature Writers," March 9, 1945, RG 59, Entry 1245, Box 1; Francis H. Russell to Mr. Morin and Mr. Dickey, "Immediate Objectives of PL (Public Liaison)," December 8, 1944, and H. Schuyler Foster to Frances Russell, "Domestic Information Activities of the State Department," April 8, 1946, RG 59, Entry 5052, Box 1; "Dumbarton Oaks Proposals: Current Developments and Comment," Report No. 14 for the week ending March 6, 1945, RG 59, Entry 568, Box 23, NARA.
118. Anne O'Hare McCormick, "His 'Unfinished Business'—And Ours," *New York Times Magazine*, April 22, 1945, 43.
119. E. B. White, "Beautiful Upon a Hill," *New Yorker*, May 12, 1945, reprinted in Library of America, *Reporting World War II: Part II*, 750–51.
120. Lester Markel, "The Newspapers," 353.

121. Kai Bird, *The Chairman: John J. McCloy and the Making of the American Establishment* (New York: Simon & Schuster, 1992), 239; "Daily Summary of Opinion Developments," U.S. Delegation, United Nations Conference, May 5 to June 7, 1945, RG 59, Entry 568, Box 23, NARA. Noted on the May 7, 1945 report, this survey of the U.S. civilian public did not include "Southern Negroes."

122. Knightley, *First Casualty*, 328–29.

123. Paul Boyer, *By the Bomb's Early Light: American Thought and Culture at the Dawn of the Atomic Age* (Chapel Hill: University of North Carolina Press, 1994), 6; Murray and Millett, *A War To Be Won*, 526.

124. Brooks to Ludlam, "Spots for International Cooperation Campaign."

125. OWI, "Looking Forward to a Global Peace"; Lydgate, *What Our People Think*, 42.

126. *Gone With the Wind* (Victor Fleming, 1939).

127. Moeller, *Shooting War*, 214.

128. Bernard DeVoto to Elmer Davis, March 28, 1944, Container 1, Davis Papers.

129. Edward R. Murrow to Elmer Davis, December 15, 1943, Container 1, Davis Papers.

130. Captain Horace R. Hansen, December 8, 1945, Papers of John Regnier. In private hands.

131. Elmer Davis, "Report to the President, 13 June 1942–15 September 1945," Container 10, Davis Papers.

132. David M. Kennedy, *Freedom from Fear: The American People in Depression and War, 1919–1945* (New York: Oxford University Press, 1999), 855–57.

Chapter 4

1. Dean Acheson, *Present at the Creation: My Years in the State Department* (New York: W. W. Norton Company, 1969), 414.

2. "President Truman's Address," September 1, 1950, Box 46, George M. Elsey Papers, Harry S. Truman Library, Independence, Missouri.

3. Michael Emery, *On the Front Lines: Following America's Foreign Correspondents across the Twentieth Century* (Washington, DC: American University Press, 1995), 105.

4. U.S. Army, General Staff, *Korea Handbook*, September 1950, Washington, DC, 95.

5. John Dower, *War Without Mercy: Race and Power in the Pacific War* (New York: Pantheon Books, 1986), 309–11.

6. Nancy E. Bernhard, *U.S. Television News and Cold War Propaganda, 1947–1960* (Cambridge: Cambridge University Press, 1999), 75; John Tebbel and Sarah Miles Watts, *The Press and the Presidency: From George Washington to Ronald Reagan* (New York: Oxford University Press, 1985), 455–63.

7. The Committee on the Present Danger included leading members Dwight Eisenhower, president of Columbia University, James B. Conant, president of Harvard University, and Harold Stassen, president of the University of Pennsylvania. Steven Casey, *Selling the Korean War: Propaganda, Politics and Public Opinion, 1950–1953* (New York: Oxford University Press, 2008), 104; Thomas G. Paterson, *Meeting the Communist Threat: Truman to Reagan* (New York: Oxford University Press, 1988), 80–81; Daniel L. Lykins, *From Total War to Total Diplomacy: The Advertising Council and the Construction of the Cold War Consensus* (Westport, CT: Praeger, 2003), 57–71; Gabriel A. Almond, *The American People and Foreign Policy* (1950; reprinted, New York: Frederick A. Praeger, 1960), 88.

8. Marshall Shulman to Ed Barrett, "Secretary's Speech to Newspaper Guild," June 28, 1950, Box 71, Elsey Papers; Nancy E. Bernhard, "Ready, Willing, Able: Network

Television News and the Federal Government, 1948–1953," in *Ruthless Criticism: New Perspectives in U.S. Communication History*, ed. William S. Solomon and Robert W. McChesney (Minneapolis: University of Minnesota Press, 1993), 297.

9. Acheson, *Present at the Creation*, 219.

10. Harry S. Truman, "Special Message to the Congress on Greece and Turkey: The Truman Doctrine," March 12, 1947, www.presidency.ucsb.edu/ws/index. php?pid+12846&st=&st1; Richard M. Freeland, *The Truman Doctrine and the Origins of McCarthyism: Foreign Policy, Domestic Politics, and Internal Security, 1946–1948* (New York: New York University Press, 1985), 100–101.

11. The motion picture industry, the news media, the Chamber of Commerce, the National Association of Manufacturers, and the advertising industry set up the American Heritage Foundation as a nonprofit in 1947 to run The Freedom Train project. Richard M. Fried, *The Russians Are Coming! The Russians Are Coming!: Pageantry and Patriotism in Cold-War America* (New York: Oxford University Press, 1998), 29–49; Robert Griffith, "The Selling of America: The Advertising Council and American Politics, 1942–1960," *Business History Review* 57 (Autumn 1983): 398.

12. Walter LaFeber, *America, Russia, and the Cold War, 1945–2006*, 10th ed. (New York: McGraw-Hill, 2008), 99–100.

13. Acheson, *Present at the Creation*, 375–76.

14. Bernhard, *U.S. Television News*, 83–85.

15. Jon Halliday and Bruce Cumings, *Korea: The Unknown War* (New York: Pantheon, 1988), 51–61.

16. William Stueck, *Rethinking the Korean War: A New Diplomatic and Strategic History* (Princeton, NJ: Princeton University Press, 2002), 61–82; "War is Declared by North Koreans," *New York Times*, June 25, 1950.

17. "Statement by the President," June 27, 1950, Box 71, Subject File: J-Korea, July 19, 1950, Elsey Papers; LaFeber, *America, Russia, and the Cold War*, 112–13; James Quirk to Darling, February 24, 1951, Box 1, James T. Quirk Papers, Harry S. Truman Library, Independence, Missouri.

18. Memo of June 27th meeting, Box 71, Elsey Papers.

19. Edward W. Barrett, Oral History Interview, July 9, 1974, www.trumanlibrary.org/oralhist/barrette.htm.

20. "Sycamore Backs the President," *Life*, July 10, 1950, 30; "Pvt. Kenneth Shadrick," *Life*, July 17, 1950, 47; Carl Mydans, "Why Are We Taking A Beating?" *Life*, July 24, 1950, 21.

21. Lizabeth Cohen, *A Consumer's Republic: The Politics of Mass Consumption in Postwar America* (New York: Vintage Books, 2004), 8.

22. Department of State, Daily Opinion Summary, June 28, July 3, and July 13, 1950, Box 76, Elsey Papers.

23. Democratic National Committee, "Capital Comment," July 8, 1950, Box 77, Elsey Papers.

24. Office of the Secretary of Defense, Armed Forces Talk 340, "The Issues at Stake in Korea," August 18, 1950, Box 77, Elsey Papers.

25. Joseph C. Goulden, *Korea: The Untold Story of the War* (New York: Times Books, 1982), 336.

26. "Fourth Draft," August 28, 1950; President Truman's Address, September 1, 1950; Department of State, Daily Opinion Summary, September 5 and 6, 1950, Box 46, Elsey Papers.

27. Bernhard, *U.S. Television News*, 2, 94–114, 162–65.

28. *Battle Report—Washington* was produced in Steelman's White House office until the spring of 1952 when NBC feared increased Republican complaints during the presidential election campaign. "Battle Report, Washington," NBC, August 13, 1950, Staff Member and Office Files (SMOF): Charles W. Jackson Files, Box 18, Harry Truman Papers, Harry S. Truman Library, Independence, Missouri.

29. Bernhard, *U. S. Television News*, 88–89, 117–31.

30. "Department of State Press Release of Text of CBS *Diplomatic Pouch*," September 8, 1950, Box 77, Elsey Papers.

31. Emery, *On the Front Lines*, 101; Susan D. Moeller, *Shooting War: Photography and the American Experience of Combat* (New York: Basic Books, 1989), 274–76.

32. Casey, *Selling the Korean War*, 47; Moeller, *Shooting War*, 256.

33. Sahr Conway-Lanz, "Beyond No Gun Ri: Refugees and the United States Military in the Korean War," *Diplomatic History* 29 (January 2005), 63; A. M. Sperber, *Murrow: His Life and Times* (New York: Freundlich Books, 1986), 346–49; "Situation Not Normal," *Newsweek*, September 25, 1950, 61.

34. Burton I. Kaufman, *The Korean War: Challenges in Crisis, Credibility, and Command* (New York: McGraw-Hill, 1997), 64.

35. "Address by President Truman," October 17, 1950, Box 12, Folder-White House Press Releases, Papers of Charles G. Ross, Harry S. Truman Library, Independence, Missouri.

36. George Gallup, Public Opinion News Service, "Speed of U.S. Advances in Korea Came as Big Surprise to U.S. Public," October 4, 1950.

37. *Battle Report—Washington*, November 26, 1950, SMOF: Charles W. Jackson, Box 19, Truman Papers.

38. *Battle Report—Washington*, December 3 and December 10, 1950, SMOF: Charles W. Jackson, Box 19, Truman Papers; Stueck, *Rethinking the Korean War*, 107–8.

39. Donald Knox, *The Korean War: Pusan to Chosin: Oral History* (New York: Harcourt, Brace Jovanovich, 1985), 603; Kaufman, *Korean War*, 68.

40. Acheson, *Present at the Creation*, 476–79.

41. Miss Ruckh to Mr. Elsey, "Analysis of Public Comment contained in communications to the President," received December 4 to 8, 1950, December 12, 1950, Box 73, Elsey Papers; Department of State, "Daily Opinion Summary," December 1, 1950, Box 72, Elsey Papers.

42. Paul S. Boyer, *By the Bomb's Early Light: American Thought and Culture at the Dawn of the Atomic Age* (New York: Pantheon, 1985), 340.

43. "Text of Truman Statement," *New York Herald Tribune*, December 1, 1950; "Meeting of the President with Congressional Leaders in the Cabinet Room," December 13, 1950, Box 73, Elsey Papers.

44. Paul G. Pierpaoli, Jr., *Truman and Korea: The Political Culture of the Early Cold War* (Columbia: University of Missouri Press, 1999), 225–30.

45. Department of State, "Text of Remarks by Dean Rusk, Assistant Secretary for Far Eastern Affairs, on NBC show, *Battle Report*," January 28, 1951, Box 77, Elsey Papers.

46. Moeller, *Shooting War*, 305–7; Bernhard, *U.S. Television News*, 108–9.

47. Department of State, Daily Opinion Summary, November 29 and December 1, 1950, Box 72, and December 4, Box 77, Elsey Papers; George Gallup, Public Opinion News Service, January 21, 24, and February 9, 1951; Casey, *Selling the Korean War*, 215.

48. *Why Korea* (Twentieth Century Fox, 1951); P. J. Wood to John R. Steelman, January 22, 1951, Box 1356, Official File, Harry S. Truman Papers, Truman Library.

49. John Moullette to Clarence Moullette, January 16, 1951, Box 1, Papers of John Moullette, Harry S. Truman Library, Independence, Missouri.

50. Clarence Moullette to Dean Acheson, January 19, 1951; Dean Acheson to Clarence Moullette, February 23, 1951, Box 1, Moullette Papers.

51. Walter H. Waggoner, "Acheson Tells Bitter Marine to Have Faith in U.S. Ideals," *New York Times*, March 4, 1951; "Why Do I Have to Fight or Die in Korea, Corporal Asks; Acheson Points at Kremlin," *Waterloo Daily Courier*, March 4, 1951; "Why We Fight in Korea: 'Freedom vs. Tyranny' Acheson Tells Johnnie," *East Liverpool Review*, March 5, 1951; Miss Ruckh to Mr. McDermott, "Analysis of the 148 letters received by Mr. Clarence Moullette," March 15, 1951, Box 1, Moullette Papers.

52. James L. Baughman, *The Republic of Mass Culture: Journalism, Filmmaking, and Broadcasting in America since 1941* (Baltimore: Johns Hopkins University Press, 1992), 57.

53. "Truman Album," 1950 and 1951, Warner Pathe, Reel 1, MP 72–63, Truman Library Motion Picture Archives, Independence, Missouri.

54. Department of State, "Weekly Information Policy Guidance," No. 55, April 18, 1951, Box 75, Elsey Papers.

55. Department of State Division of Public Studies, "Monthly Survey of American Opinion on International Affairs, Developments of April 1951," Ross Papers; Department of State Daily Surveys, Box 75, Elsey Papers; James Reston, "MacArthur Affair Is Found to Have Positive Effects, Too," *New York Times*, April 26, 1951.

56. George Elsey, "Memorandum for Mr. Harriman, Mr. Murphy, and Company," May 29, 1951, Box 75, Elsey Papers.

57. Editorial, "Who Is the Enemy?" *Washington Post*, May 7, 1951.

58. Kaufman, *Korean War*, 107–8.

59. Acheson, *Present at the Creation*, 531.

60. Walter Lippmann, "What the Generals Told Us," *Washington Post*, June 4, 1951.

61. Anne O'Hare McCormick, "Coming to the Point of the Argument," *New York Times*, June 4, 1951.

62. "A Report from the Nation: Views on MacArthur Now," June 17, 1951, *New York Times*.

63. Kaufman, *Korean War*, 129.

64. Department of State, "Overnight Information Policy Guidance No. 742," June 25, 1951; Department of State Daily Opinion Summary, July 9 and August 24, 1951; Department of State "Weekly Foreign Information Policy Guidance," No. 66, July 5, 1951, Box 76, Elsey Papers.

65. Casey, *Selling the Korean War*, 289.

66. Kaufman, *Korean War*, 154–57.

67. Kaufman, *Korean War*, 158–60; Casey, *Selling the Korean War*, 349–51.

68. "Letter from Korea," *New Yorker*, April 21, 1951, 111.

69. Lawrence Suid interview with Clayton Fritchey, December 18, 1974, Document 73; Lt. Col. Clair E. Towne, Motion Picture Section, to Julius Cahn, December 11, 1952, Document 74; "A Guide for Obtaining National Military Establishment Cooperation in the Production of Motion Pictures for Television, n.d. [1949], Document 71; Clayton Fritchey to the Secretaries of the Military Departments, "Military Cooperation or Collaboration on the Production of Commercial Motion Pictures for either Theatrical or Television Release," March 20, 1951, Document 72 in *Film*

and Propaganda in America: A Documentary History, Volume IV: 1945 and After, ed. Lawrence H. Suid and David Culbert (Westport, CT: Greenwood Press, 1991).

70. *One Minute to Zero* (Tay Garnett, 1952).

71. *The Glory Brigade* (Robert D. Webb, 1953).

72. Lary May, *The Big Tomorrow: Hollywood and the Politics of the American Way* (Chicago: University of Chicago Press, 2000), 209.

73. *The Steel Helmet* (Sam Fuller, 1951).

74. Sperber, *Murrow*, 392–95, 424.

75. Bernhard, *U.S. Television News*, 128; Thomas Doherty, *Cold War, Cool Medium: Television, McCarthyism, and American Culture* (New York: Columbia University Press, 2003), 58; Stephen J. Whitfield, *The Culture of the Cold War* (Baltimore: Johns Hopkins University Press, 1996), 166–69.

76. Kaufman, *Korean War*, 184–86.

77. Conway-Lanz, "Beyond No Gun Ri," 79–80.

78. *Battle Report—Washington*, October 21, 1951, SMOF: Charles W. Jackson Files, Box 18, Truman Papers.

79. Walter Lippmann, "The Many Voices of America," *Washington Post*, December 27, 1951.

80. Ian Shapiro quoted in Samantha Power, "Our War on Terror," *New York Times Book Review*, July 29, 2007, 9.

81. Ira Chernus, "Operation Candor: Fear, Faith, and Flexibility," *Diplomatic History* 29 (November 2005): 800.

Chapter 5

1. Marilyn Young, *The Vietnam Wars 1945–1990* (New York: HarperPerennial, 1991), 113.

2. Neil Sheehan, *A Bright Shining Lie: John Paul Vann and America in Vietnam* (New York: Random House, 1988), 695.

3. Peter R. Rosenblatt to Mr. Komer, "A Bright Light From the Boob Tube?" April 22, 1967, Official Files of George Christian, Vietnam—Unclassified, in *Vietnam, the Media and Public Support for the War: Selections from the Lyndon B. Johnson Library* ed. Robert E. Lester (Bethesda, MD: University Publications of America, 1986), Reel 9 (hereafter cited by reel number); Gordon Chase, "Memorandum for the Record—August 3 Dinner Meeting on the Information Problem," August 4, 1965, and "Memorandum of Discussion on Meeting in Mr. Moyer's Office," The White House, August 10, 1965, National Security Council (NSC) Country File, Vietnam, Public Affairs Policy Committee, Vietnam, Reel 6.

4. W. W. Rostow to Secretary of State, "The Public View of Vietnam," May 6, 1964, Box 24, James C. Thomson Papers, John F. Kennedy Library, Boston, Massachusetts.

5. James L. Baughman, *The Republic of Mass Culture: Journalism, Filmmaking, and Broadcasting in America since 1941* (Baltimore: Johns Hopkins University Press, 1992), 91–142.

6. Baughman, *Republic of Mass Culture*, 91–142; Mitchell K. Hall, *Crossroads: American Popular Culture and the Vietnam Generation* (Lanham, MD: Rowman & Littlefield, 2005), 91–95.

7. William M. Hammond, *Reporting Vietnam: Media and Military at War* (Lawrence: University Press of Kansas, 1998), 75; Daniel C. Hallin, *The Uncensored War: The Media and Vietnam* (New York: Oxford University Press, 1986), 129–30; McGeorge Bundy to President Johnson, March 21, 1968, Reel 8.

8. Douglas Kinnard, *The War Managers* (Hanover, NH: University Press of New England, 1977), 25; Christian Appy, *Patriots: The Vietnam War Remembered from All Sides* (New York: Penguin, 2003), 321.

9. David F. Schmitz, *The Tet Offensive: Politics, War, and Public Opinion* (Lanham, MD: Rowman & Littlefield, 2005), 9.

10. Young, *Vietnam Wars*, 22–23.

11. Schmitz, *Tet Offensive*, 17–20.

12. George C. Herring, *America's Longest War: The United States and Vietnam, 1950–1975*, 2nd ed. (New York: Alfred A. Knopf, 1986), 47–55.

13. Young, *Vietnam Wars*, 58; James T. Fisher, "A World Made Safe for Diversity: The Vietnam Lobby and the Politics of Pluralism, 1945–1963," in *Cold War Constructions: The Political Culture of United States Imperialism, 1945–1966*, ed. Christian G. Appy (Amherst: University of Massachusetts Press, 2000), 217–37.

14. David Halberstam, *The Best and the Brightest* (New York: Random House, 1972), 135.

15. Herring, *America's Longest War*, 86–90.

16. John Kennedy, "Press Conferences of July 17, November 8, and NBC Interview on September 9, 1963," in *Kennedy and the Press: The News Conferences*, ed. Harold W. Chase and Allen H. Lerman (New York: Thomas Y. Crowell, 1965), 461, 487, 488.

17. Theodore C. Sorensen to the President, "A TV Report on Viet Nam and Southeast Asia," November 24, 1961, Box 55, Theodore Sorensen Papers, John F. Kennedy Library, Boston, Massachusetts.

18. Dickey Chappelle was killed by a land mine while on patrol with marines in Vietnam in 1965. Alan L. Otten, "Blurred 'Backgrounders': How Washington Uses Press Briefings to Manage News," *Wall Street Journal*, January 11, 1963; Dickey Chappelle to Hobart Lewis, March 9, 1963, and Dickey Chappelle, Draft of "The Government, the Press and the News Management Effort," April 1, 1963, U.S. Mss. 87AF, Box 7, Dickey Chappelle Papers, Wisconsin Historical Society, Madison, Wisconsin.

19. Hammond, *Reporting Vietnam*, 2–10; Malcolm W. Browne, *Muddy Boots and Red Socks: A Reporter's Life* (New York: Times Books, 1993), 98–99.

20. General Earle G. Wheeler, "Statement of Vietnam," February 4, 1963, News Release, Department of Defense Office of Public Affairs, Box 3, Roger Hilsman Papers, John F. Kennedy Library, Boston, Massachusetts.

21. Hammond, *Reporting Vietnam*, 8–11.

22. Kennedy, "Press Conference of November 14, 1963," in *Kennedy and the Press*, ed. Chase and Lerman, 516.

23. George C. Herring, ed. *The Pentagon Papers: Abridged Version* (New York: McGraw-Hill, 1993), 100, 115, 129; Herring, *America's Longest War*, 116.

24. LBJ quoted in Walter LaFeber, "Johnson, Vietnam, and Tocqueville," in *Johnson Confronts the World: American Foreign Policy, 1963–1968*, ed. Warren I. Cohen and Nancy Bernkopf Tucker (New York: Cambridge University Press, 1994), 35; Hammond, *Reporting Vietnam*, 19.

25. Diane B. Kunz, "The American Economic Consequences of 1968," in *1968: The World Transformed*, ed. Carole Fink, Phillipp Gassert, and Detlef Junker (New York: Cambridge University Press, 1999), 93.

26. For example, the Vietnam Information Group was set up to "provide background material to leak to correspondents regularly," prepare "speeches and filter them to the Congress regularly," and achieve "higher quality information flow results." George

Christian to the President, August 22, 1967, Office Files of Fred Panzer, "Viet-nam Information Group," Reel 9; Chester Cooper to Mr. Bundy, "Coordination of Information Policy," August 18, 1965, NSC Country File, Vietnam, Public Policy Affairs Committee, Reel 6; Harold Kaplan to Walt Rostow, October 9, 1967, National Security File, Country File, Vietnam, 7E (1) a, 9/67–10/67, Public Relations Activities, Reel 2.

27. "Inventory: Department of State's Public Affairs Activities on Viet-Nam," August 13, 1965, Public Affairs Policy Committee, NSC Country File, Vietnam, Reel 6.

28. Clarence Wyatt, *Paper Soldiers: The American Press and The Vietnam War* (New York: W. W. Norton, 1993), 129, 158, 163; Hammond, *Reporting Vietnam*, 23–24.

29. James P. Greenfield, "Recent Public Affairs Handling of Viet-Nam," December 8, 1964, Box 24, Thomson Papers; Wyatt, *Paper Soldiers*, 164.

30. Young, *Vietnam Wars*, 117–20.

31. Young, *Vietnam Wars*, 119.

32. Young, *Vietnam Wars*, 120–21; Herring, *America's Longest War*, 123.

33. Chase, "August 3 Dinner Meeting on the Information Problem;" Fredrik Logevall, *Choosing War: The Lost Chance for Peace and the Escalation of War in Vietnam* (Berkeley: University of California Press, 1999) 133, 181; Alex Danchev, "'I'm With You': Tony Blair and The Obligations of Alliance: Anglo-American Relations in Historical Perspective," in *Iraq and the Lessons of Vietnam*, ed. Lloyd C. Gardner and Marilyn B. Young (New York: New Press, 2007), 56.

34. Howard Jablon, *David M. Shoup: A Warrior against War* (Lanham, MD: Rowman & Littlefield, 2005), 101, 113.

35. The Wise Men included former Secretary of State Dean Acheson; Generals Omar Bradley, Matthew Ridgway, and Maxwell Taylor; Abe Fortas; John J. McCloy; Henry Cabot Lodge, Jr.; and former Secretary of the Treasury Douglas Dillon. Logevall, *Choosing War*, 167, 288.

36. Appy, *Patriots*, 365.

37. Allan R. Millett and Peter Malowski, *For the Common Defense: A Military History of the United States* (New York: Free Press, 1994), 571; George C. Herring, "'Peoples Quite Apart': Americans, South Vietnamese, and the War in Vietnam," in *The United States and the Vietnam War*, ed. Walter L. Hixson (New York: Garland Publishing, 2000), 29–51; Herring, *America's Longest War*, 148–49.

38. Chester L. Cooper and James C. Thomson, Jr. to Mr. Bundy, "The Week That Was," January 22, 1965, Box 11, and James C. Thomson, Jr. and Chester L. Cooper to Mr. Bundy, "Proposed Speech by the President," February 16, 1965, Box 12, Thomson Papers.

39. Script of Final Revision for "Why Vietnam," Hearst Metrotone News, Inc., September 24, 1965, Reel 11; *Why Vietnam* (1965); Tony Shaw, *Hollywood's Cold War* (Amherst: University of Massachusetts Press, 2007), 210.

40. "Text of the Remarks of the President to the American Alumni Council at the Greenbrier, White Sulpher Springs, West Virginia," Office of the White House Press Secretary, July 12, 1966, Box 11, Thomson Papers; Editorial, "Our Great Power Role," *Washington Post*, July 13, 1966.

41. Waldo Heinrichs, "Lyndon B. Johnson: Change and Continuity" and Walter LaFeber, "Johnson, Vietnam, and Tocqueville," in *Lyndon Johnson Confronts the World*, ed. Cohen and Tucker, 28–30, 55.

42. LaFeber, "Johnson, Vietnam, and Tocqueville," 47.

43. Gordon Chase, "August 3 Dinner Meeting on the Information Problem," August 4, 1965 and "Memorandum for Mr. Cater—The Information Problem," August 23, 1965, NSC Country File, Vietnam, Public Policy Affairs Committee, Reel 6; Heinrichs, "Lyndon B. Johnson," 20–21.
44. Hammond, *Reporting Vietnam*, 57, 74–76.
45. Ward Just, "Why I Was In Vietnam," *New York Times Magazine*, March 19, 2000, 85.
46. CBS, February 15, 1967, Weekly News Summary, Assistant Secretary of Defense for Public Affairs, Record Group (RG) 330, A-82, National Archives and Record Administration (NARA), Archives II, College Park, Maryland; Hallin, *Uncensored War*, 129–30.
47. Wyatt, *Paper Soldiers*, 145–46.
48. Chase, "August 3 Dinner Meeting on the Information Problem."
49. Michael Arlen, *The Living Room War* (New York: Penguin Books, 1968), 88.
50. John E. Mueller, *War, Presidents and Public Opinion* (New York: John Wiley & Sons, 1973), 167.
51. NBC and ABC, February 21, 1967, RG 330, A-82, NARA.
52. Hammond, *Reporting Vietnam*, 58–59. In September 1965, CBS commentator Charles Collingwood returned from Vietnam with a similar assessment: more U.S. military power made the United States more politically vulnerable. CBS, September 1, 1965, RG 330, A-4, NARA.
53. The White House ordered an investigation of Morley Safer and an infuriated LBJ complained to CBS president Frank Stanton. Wyatt, *Paper Soldiers*, 144–45; "Memorandum of Discussion on Meeting in Mr. Moyer's Office"; Chase, "August 3 Dinner Meeting on the Information Problem."
54. James L. Greenfield, Assistant Secretary, and William J. Jorden, Deputy Assistant Secretary, Department of State to Mr. Moyers, "Public Affairs Problems in the Viet-Nam Conflict," August 13, 1965, NSC Country File, Vietnam, Public Affairs Policy Committee, Reel 6; Hammond, *Reporting Vietnam*, 60; Chase, "August 3 Dinner Meeting on the Information Problem."
55. NBC, CBS, ABC, February 15, 1967, RG 330, A-82, NARA.
56. Melvin Small, *Antiwarriors: The Vietnam War and the Battle for America's Hearts and Minds* (Wilmington, DE: Scholarly Resources, 2002), 51–60.
57. Small, *Antiwarriors*, 36, 45.
58. Small, *Antiwarriors*, 78.
59. "Douglas Committee and Vietnam Information Group PR Activity," National Security File, Vietnam 7E(1)a 9/67–10/67, Public Relations Activities, Reel 2.
60. Abe Fortas to LBJ, "Re: Vietnam," 1967, National Security File, Vietnam, 7E (1)a, 9/67–10/67, Reel 2.
61. Eric Sevareid quoted in Chester Pach, "Lyndon Johnson's Living-Room War: The Johnson Administration, Vietnam, and Making War in the Television Age" (paper presented at the Annual Meeting of the Society for Historians of American Foreign Relations, Lawrence, Kansas, June 25, 2006); Philip Habib to Harold Kaplan, "Statistical Defense of Progress in the War," September 26, 1967, National Security File, Vietnam, 7E (1) a, 9/67–10/67, Public Relations Activities, Reel 2; Louis Harris, Harris Survey, August 28, 1967, Reel 9.
62. Hammond, *Reporting Vietnam*, 97–107.
63. Wilson Hall, "Evening Circuit," Radio Scripts, November 26, 1967, January 24, 1968, and "Phouc Vinh, TV Script," September 27, 1967, Box 2, U.S. Mss 184 AF, Wilson

Hall Papers, Wisconsin Historical Society, Madison, Wisconsin; NBC, October 3, 1967, RG 330 A-115, NARA.

64. NBC, December 27, 1967–January 4, 1968, RG330, A-128, NARA.

65. CBS, September 22–29, 1967, RG 330, A-114, NARA.

66. "Interview with General William C. Westmoreland and Steve Rowan, CBS," November 17, 1967, Official Files of George Christian, "Vietnam—Unclassified," Reel 9; Chester J. Pach, "Tet on TV: U.S. Nightly News Reporting and Presidential Policy Making," in *1968*, ed. Fink, Gassert, and Junker, 61.

67. Ronald H. Spector, *After Tet: The Bloodiest Year in Vietnam* (New York: Free Press, 1993), 311–15.

68. Hammond, *Reporting Vietnam*, 115; Pach, "Tet on TV," 55–81; Joseph C. Harsch, "The Wrong Victory," *Christian Science Monitor*, February 6, 1968.

69. Hammond, *Reporting Vietnam*, 124.

70. Schmitz, *Tet Offensive*, 113–16.

71. Walter LaFeber, *The Deadly Bet: LBJ, Vietnam, and the 1968 Election* (Lanham, MD: Rowman & Littlefield, 2005), 139–42.

72. *The Green Berets* (Ray Kellogg, John Wayne, 1968).

73. Hammond, *Reporting Vietnam*, 128; Herring, *America's Longest War*, 207–20.

74. Arlen, *Living Room War*, 63.

75. LaFeber, *Deadly Bet*, 107.

76. Herring, *America's Longest War*, 221–25.

77. Hammond, *Reporting Vietnam*, 173–75; Small, *Antiwarriors*, 61.

78. Chester Pach, " 'Our Worst Enemy Seems To Be the Press': The Nixon Administration, Television News, and the Vietnam War (1971)" (paper presented at the American Historical Association, Pacific Coast Branch, Vancouver, Canada, August 9, 2001); John Anthony Maltese, *Spin Control: The White House Office of Communications and the Management of Presidential News* (Chapel Hill: University of North Carolina Press, 1992), 28–74.

79. Maltese, *Spin Control*, 30, 44.

80. Baughman, *Republic of Mass Culture*, 177; Young, *Vietnam Wars*, 245.

81. Herring, *America's Longest War*, 230.

82. Hammond, *Reporting Vietnam*, 154.

83. Hammond, *Reporting Vietnam*, 154.

84. Richard Nixon, "Address to the Nation on the War in Vietnam," November 3, 1969, www.presidency.ucsb.edu/ws/index.php?pid=2303&st=&st1=.

85. Maltese, *Spin Control*, 52–58; Small, *Antiwarriors*, 113; Melvin Small, "Containing Domestic Enemies: Richard M. Nixon and the War at Home," in *Shadow on the White House: Presidents and the Vietnam War, 1945–1975*, ed. David L. Anderson (Lawrence: University Press of Kansas, 1993), 143.

86. William Safire, *Before the Fall: An Inside View of the Pre-Watergate White House* (Garden City, NY: Doubleday, 1975), 185–94.

87. Young, *Vietnam Wars*, 253.

88. Small, *Antiwarriors*, 128–29.

89. H. Bruce Franklin, "The POW/MIA Myth," in *The United States and Vietnam*, ed. Hixson, 189–209; John S. McCain III, "How the POWs Fought Back," *U.S. News and World Report*, May 14, 1973, reprinted in Library of America, *Reporting Vietnam: Part II: American Journalism 1969–1975* (New York: Library of America, 1998), 451.

90. Franklin, "The POW/MIA Myth;" Michael J. Allen, "'Help Us Tell the Truth about Vietnam': POW/MIA Politics and the End of the Vietnam War," in *Making Sense of the Vietnam Wars: Local, National, and Transnational Perspectives*, ed. Mark Philip Bradley and Marilyn B. Young (New York: Oxford University Press, 2008), 268.

91. Donald Kirk, "Who Wants To Be the Last American Killed in Vietnam?" *New York Times Magazine*, September 19, 1971, reprinted in Library of America, *Reporting Vietnam: Part II*, 217.

92. Appy, *Patriots*, 395.

93. Appy, *Patriots*, 357–62, 366–70.

94. Small, *Antiwarriors*, 140–41; Appy, *Patriots*, 366.

95. "Farewell to the Follies," *Time*, February 12, 1973, 36.

96. David L. Anderson, ed., *Facing My Lai: Moving Beyond the Massacre* (Lawrence: University Press of Kansas, 1998), 1–16.

97. Anderson, ed., *Facing My Lai*, 1–16, 54–56; Hammond, *Reporting Vietnam*, 191–92; Telephone Conversation between Nixon and Kissinger, March 17, 1970, quoted in "Grumbling and Rumbling Over an Unraveling War," *New York Times*, April 30, 2000.

98. Three hundred people from fifty advertising agencies donated their expertise to Unsell the War. The ads were reviewed by a panel that included Yale University president Kingman Brewster, retired Marine General David Shoup, former Defense Department official Morton Halperin, and the former U.S. ambassador to Japan, Edwin Reischauer. Mitchell K. Hall, "Vietnam and Antiwar Advertising: The Unsell the War Campaign" (paper presented at the Annual Meeting of the Society for Historians of American Foreign Relations, Waltham, Massachusetts, June 1994).

99. Small, *Antiwarriors*, 155; Hall, *Crossroads*, 107.

100. Sydney H. Schanberg, "The Saigon Follies, or, Trying to Head Them Off at Credibility Gap," *New York Times Magazine*, November 12, 1972, reprinted in Library of America, *Reporting Vietnam, Part II*, 404.

101. Young, *Vietnam Wars*, 279.

102. Jeffrey P. Kimball, "'Peace with Honor': Richard M. Nixon and the Diplomacy of Threat and Symbolism," in *Shadow on the White House*, ed. Anderson, 176–77.

103. "Farewell to the Follies."

104. Shana Alexander, "Prisoners of Peace," *Newsweek*, March 5, 1973, 32; "Home At Last!" *Newsweek*, February 26, 1973, 16–24.

105. "A Needed Tonic for America," *Time*, March 19, 1973, 19; NBC, ABC, CBS News, February–March 1973, RG 330, A-396, A-397, A-398, NARA.

106. *Hearts and Minds* (Peter Davis, 1974).

107. Keyes Beech, "We Clawed for Our Lives!" *Chicago Daily News*, May 1, 1975, and Bob Tamarkin, "Diary of S. Viet's Last Hours," *Chicago Daily News*, May 6, 1975, reprinted in Library of America, *Reporting Vietnam: Part II*, 534, 537.

108. Herring, "Peoples Quite Apart," 47.

109. Arlen, *Living Room War*, 143.

110. Richard Nixon, *The Memoirs of Richard Nixon* (New York: Grosset & Dunlap, 1978), 354; Browne, *Muddy Boots*, 349.

111. Anderson, *Facing My Lai*, 12; Maya Lin, *Boundaries* (New York: Simon & Schuster, 2000), 4:08–4:17; Franklin, "The POW/MIA Myth," 189.

112. *Rambo: First Blood Part II* (George P. Cosmatos, 1985).

113. Chase, "August 3 Dinner Meeting on the Information Problem."
114. Philip Caputo, *A Rumor of War* (New York: Ballantine Books, 1977), 83–84; Melvin Small, *At the Water's Edge: American Politics and the Vietnam War* (Chicago: Ivan R. Dee, 2005), 4.

Chapter 6

1. "National Security Strategy of the United States," September 2002, www.whitehouse.gov/nsc/nss; George W. Bush, "President discusses War on Terror at National Endowment for Democracy," October 6, 2005, www.whitehouse.gov/news/releases/2005/10/20051006-3.html, see www.georgewbushlibrary.gov.
2. Sheldon Rampton and John Stauber, *Weapons of Mass Deception: The Uses of Propaganda in Bush's War on Iraq* (New York: Tarcher/Penguin, 2003), 5; John R. MacArthur, *Second Front: Censorship and Propaganda in the Gulf War* (Berkeley: University of California Press, 1993), 194; see also W. Lance Bennett and David L. Paletz, eds., *Taken by Storm: The Media, Public Opinion, and U.S. Foreign Policy in the Gulf War* (Chicago: University of Chicago Press, 1994) and John Mueller, *Policy and Opinion in the Gulf War* (Chicago: University of Chicago Press, 1994).
3. Scott McClellan, *What Happened: Inside the Bush White House and Washington's Culture of Deception* (New York: PublicAffairs, 2008), 174–75; Ken Auletta, "Fortress Bush," *New Yorker*, January 19, 2004, 53–65.
4. Frank Rich, "Operation Iraqi Infoganda," *New York Times*, March 28, 2004.
5. Robert Jackell, "The Magic Lantern: The World of Public Relations," in *Propaganda*, ed. Robert Jackall (New York: New York University Press, 1995), 365.
6. Ron Suskind, "Faith, Certainty and the Presidency of George W. Bush," *New York Times Magazine*, October 17, 2004, www.nytimes.com/2004/10/17/magazine/17BUSH.html?_r=1&oref=slogin.
7. Richard Posner, "Bad News," *New York Times Review of Books*, July 31, 2005; Jon Nichols, "Newspapers...and After?" *Nation*, January 29, 2007, 11; Daniel C. Hallin, *We Keep America on Top of the World: Television Journalism and the Public Sphere* (New York: Routledge, 1994), 133.
8. Douglas Little, *American Orientalism: The United States and the Middle East since 1945*, 3rd ed. (Chapel Hill: University of North Carolina Press, 2008), 29–42; Melani McAlister, *Epic Encounters: Culture, Media, and U.S. Interests in the Middle East, 1945–2000* (Berkeley: University of California Press, 2001), 201.
9. Philip M. Taylor, *War and the Media: Propaganda and Persuasion in the Gulf War* (Manchester, UK: Manchester University Press, 1992), 8; McAlister, *Epic Encounters*, 239; Zbigniew Brzezinski, "Terrorized by 'War on Terror,'" March 25, 2007, www.washingtonpost.com/wp-dyn/content/article/2007/03/23/AR2007032301613_p.
10. The 9/11 Commission, *The 9/11 Commission Report* (New York: W. W. Norton, 2004), 13.
11. Little, *American Orientalism*, 42; Paul S. Boyer, "When Foreign Policy Meets Biblical Prophecy," February 22, 2003, www.informationclearinghouse.info/article1583.htm.
12. David Stout, "Bush Says He Wants to Capture Bin Laden 'Dead or Alive,'" *New York Times*, September 17, 2001, www.nytimes.com/2001/09/17/national/17CND_BUSH.html; Bob Woodward, "A Course of Confident Action," *Washington Post National Weekly Edition*, December 2–8, 2002; *The Siege* (Edward Zwick, 1998). I am grateful to Helena Vanhala for this reference; *9/11 Commission Report*, 334.

13. John Anthony Maltese, *Spin Control: The White House Office of Communications and the Management of Presidential News* (Chapel Hill: University of North Carolina Press, 1992), 2.

14. Ron Suskind, *The One Percent Doctrine: Deep Inside America's Pursuit of Its Enemies Since 9/11* (New York: Simon & Schuster, 2006), 72–73; Maureen Dowd, "We Love the Liberties They Hate," *New York Times*, September 30, 2001.

15. Caryn James, "Television, Like the Country, Loses Its Footing," *New York Times*, November 4, 2001; Dana Milbank, "Patriotism's Price," *Washington Post National Weekly Edition*, February 17–23, 2003.

16. *Onion*, October 11–17, 2001; Margaret Talbot, "Losing the Home Front," *New York Times Magazine*, December 22, 2002, 13; Jonathan Raban, "September 11: The View from the West," *New York Review of Books*, September 22, 2005, 8; Paul S. Boyer, "Duct Tape Madness," February 18, 2003, http://hnn.us/articles/1268.html; Toni Morrison and Cornel West, "Blues, Love and Politics," *Nation*, May 24, 2004, 22.

17. David E. Sanger, "Taking on Another War, Against Mixed Messages," *New York Times*, November 4, 2001; Wilfried Mausbach, "Forlorn Superpower: European Reaction to the American Wars in Vietnam and Iraq," in *Iraq and the Lessons of Vietnam*, ed. Lloyd C. Gardner and Marilyn B. Young (New York: New Press, 2007), 66; Tom Zeller, "Trading in Conflict," *New York Times*, December 9, 2001.

18. Howard Kurtz, "The Information War Has Begun," *Washington Post National Weekly Edition*, February 25–March 3, 2002, 30; Richard Cohen, "Bush: Safely in Denial," *Washington Post National Weekly Edition*, July 19–25, 2004, 27.

19. The White House group included Karen Hughes; Ari Fleischer; Mary Matalin, the counselor to the vice president; James Wilkinson, deputy director of communication; Anna M. Perez, counselor to the national security advisor; Charlotte Beers, undersecretary of state for public diplomacy; Richard Boucher, assistant secretary of state for public affairs; Victoria Clarke, assistant secretary of defense for public affairs; and Alistair Campbell, head of the London Coalition Information Center. Elizabeth Becker, "In the War on Terrorism, A Battle to Shape Opinion," *New York Times*, November 11, 2001; Emily S. Rosenberg, "Rescuing Women and Children," in *History and September 11th*, ed. Joanne Meyerowitz (Philadelphia: Temple University Press, 2003), 85.

20. Rampton and Stauber, *Weapons of Mass Deception*, 25–36.

21. The concern regarding the Office of Strategic Influence was focused on the likelihood that such propaganda intended for foreign audiences would end up back in the United States, which had been prohibited by Congress since 1948. Thomas E. Ricks, "Defense Department Divided Over Propaganda Plan," *Washington Post*, February 21, 2002; Thomas E. Ricks, "Rumsfeld Kills Pentagon Propaganda Unit," *Washington Post*, February 27, 2002; "Rumsfeld's Roadmap to Propaganda," October 30, 2003, National Security Archive, www.gwu.edu/~nsarchiv/NSAEBB/NSAEBB177/index.htm.

22. "National Security Strategy of the United States," 2002.

23. Thomas E. Ricks and Vernon Loeb, "War Without End," *Washington Post National Weekly Edition*, February 24–March 2, 2003; Michael Isikoff and David Corn, *Hubris: The Inside Story of Spin, Scandal, and the Selling of the Iraq War* (New York: Crown Publishers, 2006), 25.

24. Glenn Kessler, "Chilly Winds Abroad," *Washington Post National Weekly Edition*, September 16–22, 2002, 7; Ellen Hale, "Global Warmth for U.S. after 9/11 Turns

to Frost," *USA Today*, August 14, 2002; Bruce Ackerman, "What About the Constitutional Case for War?" *Washington Post National Weekly Edition*, August 26–September 1, 2002, 32; Sheldon Rampton and John Stauber, *The Best War Ever: Lies, Damned Lies, and the Mess in Iraq* (New York: Tarcher/Penguin, 2006), 5.

25. Isikoff and Corn, *Hubris*, 78–79; Rampton and Stauber, *Weapons of Mass Deception*, 53–56; Daniel Benaim, Vishesh Kumar, and Priyanka Motaparthy, "TV's Conflicted Experts," April 21, 2003, *Nation*, 2003, 6–7.

26. Isikoff and Corn, *Hubris*, 29, 33; Rampton and Stauber, *Best War Ever*, 17.

27. "Deputy Secretary Wolfowitz Interview with Sam Tannenhaus, *Vanity Fair*," May 9, 2003, www.dod.mil/transcripts/2003; Barton Gellman and Dafna Linzer, "No Bush Critics Allowed," *Washington Post National Weekly Edition*, April 17–23, 2006, 15; Brian Knowlton, "Bush Steps Up Push for War Resolutions," October 9, 2002, *International Herald Tribune*; Max Frankel, "The Washington Back Channel," *New York Times Magazine*, March 25, 2007, 47.

28. Jim Rutenberg and Robin Toner, "Critics Say Coverage Helped Lead to War," *New York Times*, March 22, 2003; Frank Rich, *The Greatest Story Ever Sold: The Decline and Fall of Truth from 9/11 to Katrina* (New York: Penguin, 2006), 68; University of Maryland Program on International Policy Attitudes, "Misperceptions, the Media, and the Iraq War," October 2003, http://65.109.167.118/pipa/pdf/oct03/IraqMedia_Oct03_rpt.pdf.

29. George W. Bush, "President Discusses the Future of Iraq," February 26, 2003, www.whitehouse.gov/news/releases/2003/02/20030226-11.html, see www.georgewbushlibrary.gov; Editorial, "Mr. Cheney on Iraq," *Washington Post National Weekly Edition*, September 2–8, 2003; Thomas E. Ricks, "Ready, Set...," *Washington Post National Weekly Edition*, March 10–16, 2003, 6–7.

30. Jonathan Schell, "The Case Against the War," *Nation*, March 3, 2003, 11–23; Bob Woodward, *Plan of Attack* (New York: Simon & Schuster, 2004), 228.

31. James Mann, *Rise of the Vulcans: The History of Bush's War Cabinet* (New York: Penguin, 2004), 343–49; Michael Dobbs, "Where's the Smoking Gun?" *Washington Post National Weekly Edition*, December 16–22, 2002, 16.

32. Karen DeYoung, "The Undoing of Colin Powell," *Washington Post National Weekly Edition*, October 16–22, 2006, 6–10; Rich, *Greatest Story*, 264.

33. Nicholas Lemann, "Order of Battle," *New Yorker*, November 18, 2002, 42; Sheryl Gay Stolberg, "Congress Makes Law, Not War," *New York Times*, March 23, 2003; Isikoff and Corn, *Hubris*, 150.

34. Dana Milbank, "Why Let the Facts Get in the Way?" *Washington Post National Weekly Edition*, October 28–November 3, 2002, 13; James Risen and David Johnston, "Split at C.I.A. and F.B.I. on Iraqi Ties to Al Qaeda," *New York Times*, February 2, 2003.

35. Thomas E. Ricks, *Fiasco: The American Military Adventure in Iraq* (New York: Penguin, 2006), 96–100; Christopher Marquis, "Bush and Democrat Invoke 1962 Cuban Crisis as Model," *International Herald Tribune*, October 9, 2002; Joseph Wilson, "Republic or Empire?" *Nation*, March 3, 2003, 4–5.

36. Evelyn Nieves, "Pressure Is Building to Avoid Using Military Force," *Washington Post National Weekly Edition*, December 9–15, 2002, 7; National Public Radio, February 16, 2003; *Reliable Sources* (CNN, January 26, 2003); Rampton and Stauber, *Best War Ever*, 149–51.

37. Sheryl Gay Stolberg, "Congress's War on France Is Just Starting," *New York Times*, March 16, 2003; Jack Thomas (*Boston Globe*), "A War of Words—against France,"

Milwaukee Journal Sentinel, March 2, 2003; Mausbach, "Forlorn Superpower," 79; Mary Nolan, "Anti-Americanism and Anti-Europeanism," in *New American Empire*, ed. Gardner and Young, 122.

38. Nancy Franklin, "Must-See Saddam," *New Yorker*, March 10, 2003, 30; Rutenberg and Toner, "Critics Say"; W. Lance Bennett, Regina G. Lawrence, and Steven Livingston, *When the Press Fails: Political Power and the News Media from Iraq to Katrina* (Chicago: University of Chicago Press, 2007), 43.

39. Nicholas Lemann, "After Iraq," *New Yorker*, February 12–24, 2003, 70–71; Andrew J. Bacevich, *The New American Militarism: How Americans Are Seduced by War* (New York: Oxford University Press, 2005), 28; *The Today Show* (NBC, January 28, 2003); Robert G. Kaiser, "The United States Risks Isolation and a Loss of Key Allies," *Washington Post National Weekly Edition*, March 24–30, 2003, 9.

40. *Gladiator* (Ridley Scott, 2000); Ricks, *Fiasco*, 116; Michael R. Gordon and General Bernard E. Trainor, *Cobra II: The Inside Story of the Invasion and Occupation of Iraq* (New York: Pantheon Books, 2006), 164–77.

41. Carl Hulse and Eric Schmitt, "Pentagon Strokes Lawmakers Every Morning and They Seem to Like It," *New York Times*, March 29, 2003.

42. Peter J. Boyer, "The New War Machine," *New Yorker*, June 30, 2003, 55–71; John M. Broder, "Sober Replies to Speculative Questions," *New York Times*, April 4, 2003; Elisabeth Bumiller, "Even Critics of War Say the White House Spun It With Skill," *New York Times*, April 20, 2003.

43. Thom Shanker and Eric Schmitt, "Rumsfeld Says Iraq Is Collapsing," March 22, 2003, *New York Times*; David Von Drehle, "Rumsfeld Wrestles With History," *Washington Post National Weekly Edition*, November 21–27, 2005, 6.

44. Ricks, *Fiasco*, 371.

45. Elisabeth Bumiller, "Administration Is Heeding Lessons of First Gulf War," *New York Times*, March 24, 2003; R. W. Apple, Jr., "Lessons of the Past for Bush on Leading a Nation at War," *New York Times*, March 25, 2003; Richard W. Stevenson and Elisabeth Bumiller, "In Speech to Military Aides, Bush Shies from Quick End," *New York Times*, March 27, 2003; Adam Nagourney and David E. Sanger, "Bush Defends the Progress of the War," *New York Times*, April 1, 2003; David E. Sanger and William E. Schmidt, "Bush Offers Optimism to Cheering Marines," *New York Times*, April 4, 2003.

46. "Support for Bush Surges at Home," *New York Times*, March 22, 2003; Nathaniel Fick, *One Bullet Away: The Making of a Marine Officer* (Boston: Houghton Mifflin Company, 2005), 251.

47. Todd S. Purdum and Jim Rutenberg, "Reporters Respond to Pentagon's Frontline Welcome Mat," *New York Times*, March 23, 2003; David Carr, "War News From MTV and People Magazine," *New York Times*, March 27, 2003; Boyer, "The War Machine," 55–71; Colby Buzzell, *My War: Killing Time in Iraq* (New York: G. P. Putnam's Sons, 2005), 140; *Connections* (NPR, March 21, 2003).

48. David Carr, "Reporters' New Battlefield Access Has Its Risks as Well as Its Rewards," *New York Times*, March 31, 2003; "Spinning to War" (BBC World Service, August 4, 2003).

49. Pew Research Center's Project for Excellence in Journalism, "Embedded Reporters: What Are Americans Getting?" April 3, 2003, www.journalism.org/node/211.

50. Rampton and Stauber, *Weapons of Mass Deception*, 180–81.

51. CBS, April 9, 2003.

52. Nancy Franklin, "News Under Fire," *New Yorker*, April 4, 2003, 94–95; Charles McGrath, "Bomb," *New York Times Magazine*, April 3, 2003, 15–16.

53. After an extended legal fight, the Defense Department released photos of caskets returning from Iraq in April 2005 in response to Freedom of Information Act requests by Ralph Begleiter, a professor of communications at the University of Delaware and a former CNN correspondent. National Security Archive, "Return of the Fallen," April 28, 2005, www.gwu.edu/~nsarchiv/NSAEBB/NSAEBB152/index.htm; David Carr, "Telling War's Deadly Story At Just Enough Distance," *New York Times*, April 7, 2003; Ghaith Abdul-Ahad, Kael Alford, Thorne Anderson, and Rita Leistner, *Unembedded: Four Independent Photojournalists on the War in Iraq* (White River Junction, VT: Chelsea Green, 2005); Paul Rutherford, *Weapons of Mass Persuasion: Marketing the War against Iraq* (Toronto: University of Toronto Press, 2004), 110.

54. Nagourney and Sanger, "Bush Defends the Progress of the War"; Dexter Filkins, "Some Iraqis Grateful to U.S. But Wary of Any Changes," *New York Times*, April 9, 2003; Ricks, *Fiasco*, 124–25.

55. Julie Salamon, "New Tools for Reporters Make War Images Instant But Coverage No Simpler," *New York Times*, April 6, 2003; Michael Massing, "The Doha Follies," *Nation*, April 21, 2003, 24; David Carr, "Reporters' New Battlefield Access."

56. Jacques Steinberg, "TV Viewers Are Riveted, And Overwhelmed, Too," *New York Times*, April 7, 2003; Geoffrey Nunberg, "War-Speak Worthy of Milton and Chuck Norris," *New York Times*, April 6, 2003.

57. Mamoun Fandy, "Global Perspectives," *Washington Post National Weekly Edition*, April 7–13, 2003, 21; Susan Sachs, "Arab Media Portray War as Killing Field," *New York Times*, April 4, 2003; Judith Sylvester and Suzanne Huffman, *Reporting from the Front: The Media and the Military* (Lanham, MD: Rowman & Littlefield, 2005), 86–87, 193–97; *Control Room* (Jehane Noujaim, 2004).

58. Alessandra Stanley, "As the Conflict in Iraq Deepens, So Does the Debate About Coverage," *New York Times*, March 30, 2003; Jim Rutenberg, "Cable's War Coverage Suggests a New 'Fox Effect' on Television Journalism," *New York Times*, April 16, 2003.

59. Alessandra Stanley, "In Hoopla Over a P.O.W., A Mirror of U.S. Society," *New York Times*, April 18, 2003; Patrick Rogers et al., "Saved From Danger," *People*, April 21, 2003, 54–59; Dana Priest, William Booth, and Susan Schmidt, "Saving Private Lynch," *Washington Post National Weekly Edition*, June 23–29, 2003, 8–10; Daphne Eviatar, "The Press and Private Lynch," *Nation*, July 7, 2003, 18–20; Melani McAlister, "Saving Private Lynch," *New York Times*, April 6, 2003; Nancy Gibbs, "The Private Jessica Lynch," *Time*, November 17, 2003, 24–33; Project for Excellence in Journalism, "Jessica Lynch: Media Myth-Making in the Iraq War," June 23, 2003, www.journalism.org/node/233.

60. Sean Aday, John Cluverius, and Steven Livingston, "As Goes the Statue, So Goes the War: The Emergence of the Victory Frame in Television Coverage of the Iraq War," *Journal of Broadcasting & Electronic Media* 49 (2005): 314–31; Michael R. Gordon, "Faulty Intelligence Misled Troops at War's Start," *New York Times*, October 20, 2004; Sylvester and Huffman, *Reporting from the Front*, 182.

61. David Sanger, "Bush's Next Role," *New York Times*, April 8, 2003; Mark Leibovich and Roxanne Roberts, "Few Hawks Are Crowing about Iraq," *Washington Post National Weekly Edition*, April 14–29, 9; Mike Allen and Karen DeYoung, "The White House Works to Close a Communication Gap," *Washington Post National*

Weekly Edition, April 7–13, 2003, 9; "Excerpts from Remarks by Bush and Blair," *New York Times*, April 8, 2003.

62. John F. Burns, "Pillagers Strip Iraqi Museum of Its Treasures," *New York Times*, April 13, 2003.

63. "US Will Recruit Civilians to Run Interim Government," *New York Times*, April 11, 2003; the president's speech was broadcast on Iraqi TV on April 10, 2003; Susan J. Douglas, "Daily Show Does Bush," *Nation*, May 5, 2003, 24.

64. Steven Lee Myers, "Doubt and Death on Drive to Baghdad," *New York Times*, April 13, 2003; Peter Maas, "Good Kills," *New York Times Magazine*, April 20, 2003, 34; CNN, *War in Iraq: The Road to Baghdad*, DVD (AOL Time Warner, 2003).

65. Steven R. Weisman, "And in Iraq, Trying to Plant a Seed," *New York Times*, November 9, 2003; Elizabeth Becker, "The United States' Message of a Humanitarian War Is Faltering in the Arab World," *New York Times*, April 5, 2003.

66. Walter Gibbs, "Scowcroft Urges Wide Role for the U.N. in Postwar Iraq," *New York Times*, April 9, 2003; Susan Sachs, "Yemen Says 2 in Cole Attack Are Among 10 Qaeda Escapees," *New York Times*, April 12, 2003; Philip Shenon, "Administration Reduces Level of Terrorism Alert to Yellow," *New York Times*, April 17, 2003; David Barstow and Robin Stein, "Is It News or Public Relations? Under Bush, Lines Are Blurry," *New York Times*, March 13, 2005.

67. Greg Retsinas, "A Rally at Ground Zero for the Troops," *New York Times*, April 11, 2003; David M. Halbfinger with John W. Fountain, "Across the U.S., Elation Wrestles with Anxiety," *New York Times*, April 13, 2003; Adam Nagourney and Janet Elder, "Americans See Clear Victory in Iraq, Poll Finds," *New York Times*, April 15, 2003.

68. Rich, *Greatest Story*, 88–91.

69. Washington Post-ABC Poll, July 9–10, 2003, *Washington Post National Weekly Edition*, July 21–27, 2003.

70. Tom Zeller, "The Iraq–Qaeda Link," *The New York Times*, June 20, 2004; Bob Woodward, "The Facts Got in the Way," *Washington Post National Weekly Edition*, October 9–15, 2006, 6; Frank Rich, "Pfc. Jessica Lynch Isn't Rambo Anymore," *New York Times*, November 9, 2003; David Johnston, "CIA's Estimates About Iraq's Bioweapons Were Built on Sand," *New York Times*, July 11, 2004; Dana Priest and Glenn Kessler, "Cheney's Obsession," *Washington Post National Weekly Edition*, October 6–12, 2003, 6.

71. Peter Slevin and Dana Priest, "Unexpected Chaos," *Washington Post National Weekly Edition*, July 28–August 3, 2003, 8–9; George Packer, *The Assassin's Gate: America in Iraq* (New York: Farrar, Straus & Giroux, 2005), 184.

72. William Langewiesche, "Welcome to the Green Zone," *The Atlantic*, November 2004, 60–88; see also Rajiv Chandrasekaran, *Imperial Life in the Emerald City: Inside the Green Zone* (New York: Knopf, 2006).

73. AP, "Pentagon: Planting Stories in Iraqi Press Was Within Law," October 19, 2006, www.editorandpublisher.com; Jeff Gerth, "Military's Information War Is a Vast and Secret Mission," *New York Times*, December 11, 2005; Peter Maas, "Professor Nagl's War" *New York Times Magazine*, January 11, 2004, 38.

74. Jim Hoagland, "Tailor-Made for the CIA," *Washington Post National Weekly Edition*, February 21–27, 2005, 5; Peter J. Boyer, "Downfall," *New Yorker*, November 20, 2006, 63; Isikoff and Corn, *Hubris*, 314.

75. Joshua Partlow, "Friend or Foe?" *Washington Post National Weekly Edition*, March 5–11, 2007; Thomas E. Ricks and Ann Scott Tyson, "Unseen Casualties," *Washington Post National Weekly Edition*," May 14–20, 2007; Greg Jaffe, "As Pentagon's Top Gun Stresses Need for Speed, Strategic Debate Grows," *Wall Street Journal*, May 17, 2005; Bennett, Lawrence, and Livingston, *When the Press Fails*, 72–107.

76. Rich, *Greatest Story*, 129–30, 156–58, 193–95.

77. Dana Milbank, "Rhetoric and Resolve," *Washington Post National Weekly Edition*, May 3–9, 2004, 13; Rich, *Greatest Story*, 177.

78. Rampton and Stauber, *Best War Ever*, 28–29; David Barstow, "Behind Analysts, Pentagon's Hidden Hand," *New York Times*, April 20, 2008.

79. Julian E. Barnes, "The Iraq War Movie: Military Hopes to Shape Genre," *Los Angeles Times*, July 7, 2008, www.latimes.com/news/nationworld/nation/la-na-armyfilms7–2008u=jul07.0.2815991.story; *In the Valley of Elah* (Phil Haggis, 2007).

80. *Fahrenheit 9/11* (Michael Moore, 2004); Robert Brent Toplin, *Michael Moore's Fahrenheit 9/11: How One Film Divided a Nation* (Lawrence: University Press of Kansas, 2006).

81. "The Downing Street Memo," July 23, 2002, *Sunday Times* (UK), May 1, 2005; George Packer, "The Lessons of Tal Afar," *New Yorker*, April 10, 2006, 63.

82. "President Outlines Strategy for Victory in Iraq," November 30, 2005, www .whitehouse.gov/news/releases/2005/11/2005130–2.html, see www.georgewbushlibrary .gov; David E. Sanger, "Bush Gives Plan for Iraq Victory and Withdrawal," *New York Times*, December 2, 2005; Scott Shane, "In Bush Victory Call, Echoes of an Analyst's Voice," *New York Times*, December 4, 2005.

83. Helen Thomas, "Lap Dogs of the Press," *Nation*, March 27, 2006, 18.

84. Michael R. Gordon and David S. Cloud, "Rumsfeld Memo Proposed Major Policy Shifts in Iraq," and "Rumsfeld Memo of November 6, 2006," *New York Times*, December 3, 2006.

85. George Packer, "The Home Front," *New Yorker*, July 4, 2005, 48–59.

86. Bob Woodruff, "To Iraq and Back" (ABC, February 27, 2007); Lizette Alvarez, "Jane, We Hardly Knew Ye Died," *New York Times*, September 24, 2006; Donna St. George, "Tug of War," *Washington Post National Weekly Edition*, December 4–10, 2006, 6; Sara Corbett, "The Women's War," *New York Times Magazine*, March 18, 2007, 46.

87. Fred Kaplan, "The Professional," *New York Times Magazine*, February 10, 2008, 92.

88. Ricks, *Fiasco*, 166; Buddhika Jayamaha, Wesley D. Smith, Jeremy Roebuck, Omar Mora, Edward Sandmeier, Yance T. Gray, and Jeremy A. Murphy, "The War as We Saw It," *New York Times*, August 19, 2007; Sgt. Omar Mora and Staff Sgt. Yance Tell Gray were killed by insurgent bombs in Iraq in September 2007.

89. Thomas Powers, "Iraq: Will We Ever Get Out?" *New York Review of Books*, May 29, 2008, 14; Steve Coll, "The General's Dilemma," *New Yorker*, September 8, 2008, 34–47.

90. Richard A. Clarke, *Against All Enemies: Inside America's War on Terror* (New York: Free Press, 2004), 283; Michael T. Klare, "Imperial Reach: The Pentagon's New Basing Strategy," *Nation*, April 25, 2005, 13–18; Ken Silverstein, "Parties of God," *Harper's*, March 2007, 33–34; James A. Baker III and Lee H. Hamilton, *The Iraq Study Group Report*, www.usip.org/isg/iraq_study_group_report/report/1206/iraq_study_group_report.pdf; Project for the New American Century, "Rebuilding

America's Defense: Strategy, Forces and Resources for a New Century," September 2000, http://newamericancentury.org/Rebuilding/AmericasDefenses.pdf.

91. George Packer, "Planning for Defeat," *New Yorker*, September 17, 2007, 56; John F. Burns and Dexter Filkins, "For Once, President and Generals See the Same War," *New York Times*, December 1, 2005.

92. McClellan, *What Happened*, 204–6.

93. University of Maryland Program on International Policy Attitudes, "Misperceptions, the Media and the Iraq War," October 2, 2003; Andrew Hoskins, *Televising Wars: From Vietnam to Iraq* (New York: Continuum International Publishing Group, 2005), 48–49.

94. Sylvester and Huffman, *Reporting from the Front*, 151.

95. Anthony Swofford, "The Unknown Soldier," *New York Times Magazine*, March 30, 2003, 18–19.

96. Rob Walker, "Battle Cries," *New York Times Magazine*, April 6, 2008, 22.

97. Walter LaFeber, "Contradiction," *Washington Post National Weekly Edition*, October 14–20, 2002, 22.

98. Rich, "Operation Iraqi Infoganda."

99. Lori Montgomery, "The Price of Liberty," *Washington Post National Weekly Edition*, May 14–20, 2007, 6.

100. Dan Baum, "The Casualty," *New Yorker*, March 8, 2004, 71.

101. Thomas Hargrove, "Third of Americans suspect 9–11 government conspiracy," www .scrippsnews.com/911poll.

102. James Fallows, *Blind into Baghdad: America's War in Iraq* (New York: Vintage, 2006), 222; Seymour M. Hersh, "Up in the Air," *New Yorker*, December 5, 2005, 44; Bob Woodward, "State of Denial," *Washington Post National Weekly Edition*, October, 23–29, 2006, 33; James Bamford, "The Man Who Sold the War," *Rolling Stone*, November 2005, www.rollingstone.com/politics/story/_/id/8798997.

Conclusion

1. George W. Bush, "Remarks by the President to the Philippine Congress," October 18, 2003, www.whitehouse.gov/news/releases/2003/10/print/20031018–12.html, see www .georgewbushlibrary.gov.

2. David E. Sanger, "Bush Cites Philippines as Model in Rebuilding Iraq," *New York Times*, October 19, 2003; Sydney J. Freedberg, Jr., "Federalism Can Avert Civil War in Iraq," *National Journal*, February 14, 2004, 474–76.

3. Choe Sang-Hun, "Korean War's Lost Chapter: South Korea Says U.S. Killed Hundreds of Civilians," *New York Times*, August 2, 2008.

4. Walter Cronkite, "What Is There to Hide?" in *The Gulf War Reader: History, Documents, Opinions*, ed. Micah L. Sifry and Christopher Cerf (New York: Times Books, 1991), 381.

5. Emily S. Rosenberg, *A Date Which Will Live: Pearl Harbor in American Memory* (Durham, NC: Duke University Press, 2003), 18.

6. George W. Bush, "President's Address to the Nation," September 11, 2006, www .whitehouse.gov/news/releases/2006/09/20060911–3.html, see www .georgewbushlibrary.gov.

BIBLIOGRAPHY

Archives and Manuscript Collections

John F. Kennedy Library, Boston, Massachusetts
    Hilsman, Roger. Papers.
    Sorenson, Theodore C. Papers.
    Thompson, James C. Papers.
Library of Congress. Manuscript Division, Washington, DC
    Clapper, Raymond. Papers.
    Cortelyou, George B. Papers.
    Creel, George. Papers.
    Davis, Elmer. Papers.
    MacLeish, Archibald. Papers.
    Root, Elihu. Papers.
    Storey, Moorfield. Papers.
    Sweetser, Arthur. Papers.
    Taft, Robert A. Papers.
    Taft, William Howard. Papers.
    Tumulty, Joseph. Papers.
National Archives and Records Administration, Archives II, College Park, Maryland
    Record Group 44 Office of Government Reports
    Record Group 59 Department of State
    Record Group 63 Committee on Public Information
    Record Group 111 Office of the Chief Signal Officer
    Record Group 208 Office of War Information
    Record Group 330 Secretary of Defense
Franklin D. Roosevelt Library, Hyde Park, New York
    Roosevelt, Franklin. Papers.
        Official File

Presidential Secretary Files
Winant, John. Papers.
Harry S. Truman Library, Independence, Missouri
Elsey, George. Papers.
Moullette, John. Papers.
Nash, Philleo. Papers.
Quirk, James T. Papers.
Ross, Charles. Papers.
Truman, Harry S. Papers.
Official File
Staff Member and Office Files
Jackson, Charles W. Files
Wisconsin Historical Society, Madison, Wisconsin
Chappelle, Dickey. Papers.
Hall, Wilson. Papers.

Published Primary Sources

The 9/11 Commission. *The 9/11 Commission Report.* New York: W. W. Norton, 2004.

Acheson, Dean. *Present at the Creation: My Years in the State Department.* New York: W. W. Norton, 1969.

Adams, Henry. *The Education of Henry Adams.* Boston: Houghton Mifflin, 1961.

Baker, James A., III, and Lee H. Hamilton. *The Iraq Study Group Report.* www.usip. org/isg/iraq_study_group_report/report/1206/iraq_study_group_report.pdf.

Barrett, Edward W. Oral History Interview, July 9, 1974. www.trumanlibrary.org/ oralhist/barrette.htm.

Bernays, Edward L. *Biography of an Idea: Memoirs of a Public Relations Counsel.* New York: Simon & Schuster, 1965.

Bourne, Randolph. *The History of a Literary Radical.* New York: S. A. Russell, 1956.

Bresnahan, Roger J. *In Time of Hesitation: American Anti-Imperialists and the Philippine-American War.* Quezon City, Philippines: New Day Publishers, 1981.

Broun, Heywood. *The A.E.F.: With General Pershing and the American Forces.* New York: D. Appleton and Company, 1918.

Browne, Malcolm W. *Muddy Boots and Red Socks: A Reporter's Life.* New York: Times Books, 1993.

Bush, George W. Public Speeches and Radio Addresses. www.whitehouse.gov/news/ releases. See www.georgewbushlibrary.gov.

Butler, Smedley D. *War Is a Racket.* New York: Round Table Press, 1935.

Buzzell, Colby. *My War: Killing Time in Iraq.* New York: G. P. Putnam's Sons, 2005.

Caputo, Philip. *A Rumor of War.* New York: Ballantine Books, 1977.

Chandrasekaran, Rajiv. *Imperial Life in the Emerald City: Inside the Green Zone.* New York: Knopf, 2006.

Chase, Edna Woolman, and Ilka Chase. *Always in Vogue*. Garden City, NY:
Doubleday, 1954.

Chase, Harold W., and Allen H. Lerman, eds. *Kennedy and the Press: The News
Conferences*. New York: Thomas Y. Crowell Company, 1965.

Committee on Public Information. *German War Practices*. Edited by Dana
C. Munro, George C. Sellery, and August C. Krey. 1917.

Creel, George. *How We Advertised America*. 1920. Reprint, New York: Arno Press,
1972.

Davis, Charles Belmont, ed. *Adventures and Letters of Richard Harding Davis*. New
York: Charles Scribner's Sons, 1918.

Fick, Nathaniel. *One Bullet Away: The Making of a Marine Officer*. Boston:
Houghton Mifflin, 2005.

Goodman, Jack, ed. *While You Were Gone: A Report on Wartime Life in the United
States*. New York: Simon & Schuster, 1946.

Grant, Ulysses S. *Personal Memoirs*. Vol. I. New York: Century Company, 1895.

Herring, George C., ed. *The Pentagon Papers: Abridged Version*. New York:
McGraw-Hill, 1993.

Higgins, Marguerite. *War in Korea: The Report of a Woman Combat Correspondent*.
Garden City, NY: Doubleday, 1951.

Johnson, Lyndon B. *Public Papers of the Presidents, 1963–1969*. www.presidency.ucsb.
edu/index.php.

Judy, Will. *A Soldier's Diary*. Chicago: Judy Publishing Company, 1930.

Knox, Donald. *The Korean War: Pusan to Chosin: Oral History*. New York:
Harcourt, Brace Jovanovich, 1985.

Lester, Robert E., ed. *Vietnam, the Media and Public Support for the War: Selections
from the Lyndon B. Johnson Library*. 11 microfilm reels. Bethesda, MD: University
Publications of America, 1986.

Library of America. *Reporting Vietnam, Part II: American Journalism 1969–1975*.
New York: Library of America, 1998.

———. *Reporting World War II, Part II: American Journalism 1944–1946*. New York:
Library of America, 1995.

Lin, Maya. *Boundaries*. New York: Simon & Schuster, 2000.

Link, Arthur, ed. *The Papers of Woodrow Wilson*. Vol. 63. Princeton, NJ: Princeton
University Press, 1990.

Luce, Henry. *The American Century*. New York: Farrar and Rinehart, 1941.

Lydgate, William A. *What Our People Think*. New York: Thomas Y. Crowell,
1944.

Mauldin, Bill. *Up Front*. 1945. Reprint, New York: W. W. Norton, 1995.

McClellan, Scott. *What Happened: Inside the Bush White House and Washington's
Culture of Deception*. New York: Public Affairs, 2008.

McKinley, William. *Public Papers of the Presidents, 1897–1901*. www.presidency.ucsb.
edu/index.php.

———. *Speeches and Addresses of William McKinley: From March 1, 1897 to May 30,
1900*. New York: Doubleday & McClure, 1900.

Morgan, H. Wayne, ed. *Making Peace with Spain: The Diary of Whitelaw Reid, September–December 1898*. Austin: University of Texas Press, 1965.

National Security Archive. "Rumsfeld's Roadmap to Propaganda," October 30, 2003. www.gwu.edu/~nsarchiv/NSAEBB/NSAEBB177/index.htm.

Nixon, Richard. *The Memoirs of Richard Nixon*. New York: Grosset and Dunlap, 1978.

———. *Public Papers of the Presidents, 1969–1974*. www.presidency.ucsb.edu/index.php.

Packer, George. *The Assassin's Gate: America in Iraq*. New York: Farrar, Straus & Giroux, 2005.

Palmer, Frederick. *America in France*. New York: Dodd, Mead and Company, 1919.

Pew Research Center's Project for Excellence in Journalism. www.journalism.org.

Project for the New American Century. "Rebuilding America's Defense: Strategy, Forces and Resources for a New Century." September 2000. http://newamericancentury.org/Rebuilding/AmericasDefenses.pdf.

Roosevelt, Franklin D. *Public Papers of the Presidents, 1933–1945*. www.presidency.ucsb.edu/index.php.

Roosevelt, Theodore. *Public Papers of the Presidents, 1901–1909*. www.presidency.ucsb.edu/index.php.

Safire, William. *Before the Fall: An Inside View of the Pre-Watergate White House*. Garden City, NY: Doubleday, 1975.

Sevareid, Eric. *Not So Wild a Dream*. New York: Atheneum, 1976.

Steinbeck, John. *Once There Was a War*. New York: Viking Press, 1958.

Stewart, Sidney. *Give Us This Day*. New York: W. W. Norton, 1986.

Suid, Lawrence H., and David Culbert, eds. *Film and Propaganda in America: A Documentary History. Volume IV: 1945 and After*. Westport, CT: Greenwood Press, 1991.

Trafton, William Oliver. *We Thought We Could Whip Them in Two Weeks*. Edited by William Henry Scott. Quezon City, Philippines: New Day, 1990.

University of Maryland Program on International Policy Attitudes. "Misperceptions, the Media, and the Iraq War." 2003. http://65.109.167.118/pipa/pdf/oct03/IraqMedia_Oct03_rpt.pdf.

U.S. Army. General Staff. *Korea Handbook*. Washington, DC, 1950.

U.S. Congress. Senate. Turner, George. "Speech." January 22–23, 1900.

U.S. Department of Defense. "Deputy Secretary Wolfowitz Interview with Sam Tannenhaus, Vanity Fair," May 9, 2003. www.dod.mil/transcripts/2003.

U.S. Department of State. "Address by the Secretary of the Treasury." July 22, 1944. *Department of State Bulletin*. XI. July 30, 1944.

———. Dean Acheson. "The Place of Bretton Woods in Economic Collective Security." March 23, 1945. Department of State Publication 2306.

U.S. National Security Council. "National Security Strategy of the United States." September 2002. www.whitehouse.gov/nsc/nss. See www.georgewbushlibrary.gov.

Truman, Harry S. *Public Papers of the Presidents, 1945–1953*. www.presidency.ucsb.edu/index.php.

Wilson, Woodrow. *President Wilson's State Papers and Addresses*. New York: Review of Reviews Company, 1918.

———. *Public Papers of the Presidents, 1913–1921*. www.presidency.ucsb.edu/index.php.

Worcester, Dean C. "Some Aspects of the Philippines Question." November 15, 1899. Hamilton Club of Chicago. Serial Publications. No. 13.

Zwick, Jim, ed. *Mark Twain's Weapons of Satire: Anti-Imperialist Writings on the Philippine-American War*. Syracuse, NY: Syracuse University Press, 1992.

Newspapers and Magazines

Atlantic Monthly

Chicago Daily News

Christian Science Monitor

Collier's

Harper's

International Herald Tribune

Life

Los Angeles Times

McClure's Magazine

Milwaukee Journal Sentinel

Nation

National Journal

New Republic

Newsweek

New York Herald Tribune

New York Review of Books

New York Times

New Yorker

Onion

People

Rolling Stone

Saturday Evening Post

Time

USA Today

U.S. News and World Report

Wall Street Journal

Washington Post

Films

Advance of the Kansas Volunteers at Caloocan. 1899.

Bataan. 1943.

The Birth of a Nation. 1915.

Casablanca. 1942.

Every 2½ Minutes. 1944.

Fahrenheit 9/11. 2004.

Gladiator. 2000.

Glory Brigade. 1953.

Gone With the Wind. 1939.

The Green Berets. 1968.

Hearts and Minds. 1974.

Hearts of the World. 1918.

In the Valley of Elah. 2007.

Mission to Moscow. 1943.

One Minute to Zero. 1952.

Pershing's Crusaders. 1918.

Rambo: First Blood Part II. 1985.

Sergeant York. 1941.

Shoulder Arms. 1918.

The Siege. 1998.

Spirit of '43. 1943.

Star Spangled Rhythm. 1942.

The Steel Helmet. 1951.

Tarzan Triumphs. 1943.

This Is the Army. 1943.

The Training of Colored Troups. 1918.

The Unbeliever. 1918.

Why Korea. 1951.

Why Vietnam. 1965.

Why We Fight: Prelude to War. 1942.

Books and Articles

Abdul-Ahad, Ghaith, Kael Alford, Thorne Anderson, and Rita Leistner.
Unembedded: Four Independent Photojournalists on the War in Iraq. White River
Junction, VT: Chelsea Green, 2005.

Adams, Michael C. C. *The Best War Ever: America and World War II*. Baltimore:
Johns Hopkins University Press, 1994.

Aday, Sean, John Cluverius, and Steven Livingston. "As Goes the Statue, So Goes
the War: The Emergence of the Victory Frame in Television Coverage of the Iraq
War." *Journal of Broadcasting & Electronic Media* 49 (2005): 314–31.

Allen, Michael J. " 'Help Us Tell the Truth about Vietnam': POW/MIA Politics
and the End of the Vietnam War." In *Making Sense of the Vietnam Wars: Local,
National, and Transnational Perspectives*. Edited by Mark Philip Bradley and
Marilyn B. Young, 251–75. New York: Oxford University Press, 2008.

Almond, Gabriel A. *The American People and Foreign Policy*. 1950. Reprint,
New York: Frederick A. Praeger, 1960.

Anderson, David L., ed. *Facing My Lai: Moving Beyond the Massacre*. Lawrence:
University Press of Kansas, 1998.

——, ed. *Shadow on the White House: Presidents and the Vietnam War, 1945–1975*.
Lawrence: University Press of Kansas, 1993.

Appy, Christian. *Patriots: The Vietnam War Remembered from All Sides*. New York:
Penguin Books, 2003.

Arlen, Michael. *The Living Room War*. New York: Penguin Books, 1968.

Bacevich, Andrew J. *The New American Militarism: How Americans Are Seduced by
War*. New York: Oxford University Press, 2005.

Barnet, Richard J. *The Rockets' Red Glare: When America Goes to War: The Presidents
and the People*. New York: Simon & Schuster, 1990.

Baughman, James L. *Henry R. Luce and the Rise of the America New Media*. Boston:
Twayne Publishers, 1987.

——. *The Republic of Mass Culture: Journalism, Filmmaking, and Broadcasting in
America since 1941*. Baltimore: Johns Hopkins University Press, 1992.

Beisner, Robert L. *Twelve Against Empire: The Anti-Imperialists, 1898–1900*. Chicago:
University of Chicago Press, 1985.

Bennett, Todd. "Culture, Power, and *Mission to Moscow*: Film and Soviet-American
Relations during World War II." *Journal of American History* 88 (September
2001): 489–518.

Bennett, W. Lance, Regina G. Lawrence, and Steven Livingston. *When the Press
Fails: Political Power and the News Media from Iraq to Katrina*. Chicago:
University of Chicago Press, 2007.

Bennett, W. Lance, and David L. Paletz, eds. *Taken By Storm: The Media, Public
Opinion, and U.S. Foreign Policy in the Gulf War*. Chicago: University of
Chicago Press, 1994.

Bernays, Edward L. *Propaganda*. 1928. Reprint, Port Washington, NY: Kennikat
Press, 1972.

Bernhard, Nancy E. "Ready, Willing, Able: Network Television News and the
    Federal Government, 1948–1953." In *Ruthless Criticism: New Perspectives in
    U.S. Communication History*. Edited by William S. Solomon and Robert
    W. McChesney. Minneapolis: University of Minnesota Press, 1993.
——. *U.S. Television News and Cold War Propaganda, 1947–1960*. Cambridge:
    Cambridge University Press, 1999.
Bird, Kai. *The Chairman: John J. McCloy and the Making of the American
    Establishment*. New York: Simon & Schuster, 1992.
Blum, John Morton. *V Was for Victory: Politics and American Culture during World
    War II*. New York: Harcourt, Brace Jovanovich, 1976.
Boyer, Paul S. *By the Bomb's Early Light: American Thought and Culture at the Dawn
    of the Atomic Age*. New York: Pantheon, 1985.
——. "Duct Tape Madness." 2003. http://hnn.us.articles/1268.html.
——. "When Foreign Policy Meets Biblical Prophecy." February 22, 2003.
    www.informationclearinghouse.info/article1583.htm.
Brands, H. W. *Bound to Empire: The United States and the Philippines*. New York:
    Oxford University Press, 1992.
Breitman, Richard. *Official Secrets: What the Nazis Planned, What the British and
    Americans Knew*. New York: Hill & Wang, 1998.
Brewer, Susan A. *To Win the Peace: British Propaganda in the United States during
    World War II*. Ithaca, NY: Cornell University Press, 1997.
Bryce, James. *The American Commonwealth*. Vol. 2. 3rd ed. New York: Macmillan,
    1899.
Capozzola, Christopher. *Uncle Sam Wants You: World War I and the Making of the
    Modern American Citizen*. New York: Oxford University Press, 2008.
Casey, Steven. *Cautious Crusade: Franklin D. Roosevelt, American Public Opinion,
    and the War against Nazi Germany*. New York: Oxford University Press, 2001.
——. *Selling the Korean War: Propaganda, Politics and Public Opinion, 1950–1953*.
    New York: Oxford University Press, 2008.
Chernus, Ira. "Operation Candor: Fear, Faith, and Flexibility." *Diplomatic History*
    29 (November 2005): 779–809.
Clarke, Richard A. *Against All Enemies: Inside America's War on Terror*. New York:
    Free Press, 2004.
Cohen, Lizabeth. *A Consumer's Republic: The Politics of Mass Consumption in
    Postwar America*. New York: Vintage Books, 2004.
Cohen, Warren I., and Nancy Bernkopf Tucker, eds. *Johnson Confronts the World:
    American Foreign Policy, 1963–1968*. New York: Cambridge University Press, 1994.
Conway-Lanz, Sahr. "Beyond No Gun Ri: Refugees and the United States Military
    in the Korean War." *Diplomatic History* 29 (January 2005): 49–81.
Costigliola, Frank. *France and the United States: The Cold Alliance, 1941–1990*.
    New York: Twayne Publishers, 1992.
Cull, Nicholas J., David Culbert, and David Welch, eds. *Propaganda and Mass
    Persuasion: A Historical Encyclopedia, 1500 to the Present*. Santa Barbara, CA:
    ABC-CLIO, 2003.

Daniels, Roger. *Prisoners Without Trial: Japanese Americans in World War II*.
New York: Hill & Wang, 1993.

DeBauche, Leslie Midkiff. "Melodrama and the World War I Film." In *The Bounds of Representation: Censorship, the Visible, Modes of Representation in Film*. Edited by Leonardo Quaresima, Alessandra Raengo, and Laura Vichi. Undine, Italy: VI International Film Studies Conference, University of Udine, 1999.

———. *Reel Patriotism: The Movies and World War I*. Madison: University of Wisconsin Press, 1997.

Doerries, Reinhard R. *Imperial Challenge: Ambassador Count Bernstorff and German-American Relations, 1908–1917*. Chapel Hill: University of North Carolina Press, 1989.

Doherty, Thomas. *Cold War, Cool Medium: Television, McCarthyism, and American Culture*. New York: Columbia University Press, 2003.

———. *Projections of War: Hollywood, American Culture, and World War II*.
New York: Columbia University Press, 1993.

Dower, John W. *War Without Mercy: Race and Power in the Pacific War*. New York: Pantheon Books, 1986.

Emery, Michael. *On the Front Lines: Following America's Foreign Correspondents across the Twentieth Century*. Washington, DC: The American University Press, 1995.

Entman, Robert M. *Projection of Power: Framing News, Public Opinion, and U.S. Foreign Policy*. Chicago: University of Chicago Press, 2004.

Faust, Drew Gilpin. "'We Should Grow Too Fond of It': Why We Love the Civil War." *Civil War History* 50, no. 4 (2004): 368–81.

Fink, Carole, Phillipp Gassert, and Detlef Junker, eds. *1968: The World Transformed*. New York: Cambridge University Press, 1999.

Fisher, James T. "A World Made Safe for Diversity: The Vietnam Lobby and the Politics of Pluralism, 1945–1963." In *Cold War Constructions: The Political Culture of United States Imperialism, 1945–1966*. Edited by Christian G. Appy, 217–37. Amherst: University of Massachusetts Press, 2000.

Fousek, John. *To Lead the World: American Nationalism and the Cultural Roots of the Cold War*. Chapel Hill: University of North Carolina Press, 2000.

Freeland, Richard M. *The Truman Doctrine and the Origins of McCarthyism: Foreign Policy, Domestic Politics, and Internal Security, 1946–1948*. New York: New York University Press, 1985.

Fried, Richard M. *The Russians Are Coming! The Russians Are Coming!: Pageantry and Patriotism in Cold-War America*. New York: Oxford University Press, 1998.

Gardner, Lloyd C. *Safe for Democracy: The Anglo-American Response to Revolution, 1913–1923*. New York: Oxford University Press, 1984.

———. *Spheres of Influence: The Great Powers Partition Europe, from Munich to Yalta*. Chicago: Ivan R. Dee, 1993.

Gardner, Lloyd C., and Marilyn B. Young, eds. *Iraq and the Lessons of Vietnam*.
New York: New Press, 2007.

———, eds. *The New American Empire*. New York: New Press, 2005.

Gordon, Michael R., and General Bernard E. Trainor. *Cobra II: The Inside Story of the Invasion and Occupation of Iraq*. New York: Pantheon Books, 2006.

Gould, Lewis L. *The Presidency of William McKinley*. Lawrence: University Press of Kansas, 1980.

Goulden, Joseph C. *Korea: The Untold Story of the War*. New York: Times Books, 1982.

Griffith, Robert. "The Selling of America: The Advertising Council and American Politics, 1942–1960." *Business History Review* 57 (Autumn 1983): 388–412.

Gullace, Nicoletta F. "Sexual Violence and Family Honor: British Propaganda and International Law during the First World War." *American Historical Review* 102 (June 1997): 714–47.

Halberstam, David. *The Best and the Brightest*. New York: Random House, 1972.

Hall, Mitchell K. *Crossroads: American Popular Culture and the Vietnam Generation* Lanham, MD: Rowman & Littlefield, 2005.

Halliday, Jon, and Bruce Cumings. *Korea: The Unknown War*. New York: Pantheon, 1988.

Hallin, Daniel C. *The Uncensored War: The Media and Vietnam*. New York: Oxford University Press, 1986.

—— *We Keep America on Top of the World: Television Journalism and the Public Sphere*. New York: Routledge, 1994.

Hammond, William M. *Reporting Vietnam: Media and Military at War*. Lawrence: University Press of Kansas, 1998.

Hannigan, Robert. *The New World Power: American Foreign Policy, 1898–1917*. Philadelphia: University of Pennsylvania Press, 2002.

Hedges, Chris. *War Is a Force That Gives Us Meaning*. New York: Public Affairs Press, 2002.

Heiss, Mary Ann. "The Evolution of the Imperial Idea and U.S. National Identity." *Diplomatic History* 26 (Fall 2002): 511–40.

Herring, George C. *America's Longest War: The United States and Vietnam, 1950–1975*. 2nd ed. New York: Alfred A. Knopf, 1986.

Hilderbrand, Robert. *Power and the People: Executive Management of Public Opinion in Foreign Affairs, 1897–1921*. Chapel Hill: University of North Carolina Press, 1981.

Hixson, Walter L., ed. *The United States and the Vietnam War*. New York: Garland Publishing, 2000.

Hoff, Joan. "The American Century: From Sarajevo to Sarajevo." *Diplomatic History* 23 (Spring 1999): 285–320.

——. *A Faustian Foreign Policy: From Woodrow Wilson to George W. Bush: Dreams of Perfectibility*. New York: Cambridge University Press, 2008.

Hoganson, Kristin. *Fighting for American Manhood: How Gender Politics Provoked the Spanish-American and Philippine-American Wars*. New Haven, CT: Yale University Press, 1998.

Honey, Maureen. *Creating Rosie the Riveter: Class, Gender, and Propaganda during World War II*. Amherst: University of Massachusetts Press, 1984.

Horne, John, and Alan Kramer. *German Atrocities, 1914: A History of Denial*. New Haven, CT: Yale University Press, 2001.

Horton, Gerd. *Radio Goes to War: The Cultural Politics of Propaganda during World War II*. Berkeley: University of California Press, 2002.

Hoskins, Andrew. *Televising Wars: From Vietnam to Iraq*. New York: Continuum International Publishing Group, 2005.

Isikoff, Michael, and David Corn. *Hubris: The Inside Story of Spin, Scandal, and the Selling of the Iraq War*. New York: Crown Publishers, 2006.

Jablon, Howard. *David M. Shoup: A Warrior against War*. Lanham, MD: Rowman & Littlefield, 2005.

Jackall, Robert, ed. *Propaganda*. New York: New York University Press, 1995.

Jowett, Garth, and Victoria O'Donnell. *Propaganda and Persuasion*. Beverly Hills, CA: Sage Publications, 1986.

Kaplan, Amy. *The Anarchy of Empire in the Making of U.S. Culture*. Cambridge, MA: Harvard University Press, 2002.

Kaplan, Richard L. "American Journalism Goes to War, 1898–2001: A Manifesto on Media and Empire." *Media History* 9, no. 3 (2003): 209–19.

Karnow, Stanley. *In Our Image: America's Empire in the Philippines*. New York: Random House, 1989.

Karp, Walter. *The Politics of War*. New York: Franklin Square Press, 2003.

Kaufman, Burton I. *The Korean War: Challenges in Crisis, Credibility, and Command*. New York: McGraw-Hill, 1997.

Kazin, Michael, and Joseph A. McCartin, eds. *Americanism: New Perspectives on the History of an Ideal*. Chapel Hill: University of North Carolina Press, 2006.

Keene, Jennifer D. *Doughboys, the Great War, and the Remaking of America*. Baltimore: Johns Hopkins University Press, 2001.

Kennedy, David. *Freedom from Fear: The American People in Depression and War, 1919–1945*. New York: Oxford University Press, 1999.

———. *Over Here: The First World War and American Society*. New York: Oxford University Press, 1980.

Kennedy, Paul. *The Rise and Fall of the Great Powers: Economic Change and Military Conflict from 1500–2000*. New York: Random House, 1987.

Kimball, Warren. *The Juggler: Franklin Roosevelt as Wartime Statesman*. Princeton, NJ: Princeton University Press, 1991.

Kimble, James J. *Mobilizing the Home Front: War Bonds and Domestic Propaganda*. College Station: Texas A&M University Press, 2006.

Kinnard, Douglas. *The War Managers*. Hanover, NH: University Press of New England, 1977.

Knightley, Phillip. *The First Casualty: The War Correspondent as Hero and Myth-Maker from the Crimea to Kosovo*. Baltimore: Johns Hopkins University Press, 2002.

Knock, Thomas J. *To End All Wars: Woodrow Wilson and the Quest for a New World Order*. Princeton, NJ: Princeton University Press, 1992.

Koppes, Clayton R., and Gregory D. Black. *Hollywood Goes to War: How Politics, Profits and Propaganda Shaped World War II Movies*. Berkeley: University of California Press, 1987.

Kramer, Paul. *The Blood of Government: Race, Empire, the United States and the Philippines*. Chapel Hill: University of North Carolina Press, 2006.

——. "Race-Making and Colonial Violence in the U.S. Empire: The Philippine-American War as Race War." *Diplomatic History* 30 (April 2006): 169–210.

LaFeber, Walter. *America, Russia, and the Cold War, 1945–2006*. 10th ed. New York: McGraw-Hill, 2008.

——. *The American Search for Opportunity, 1865–1913*. New York: Cambridge University Press, 1993.

——. *The Deadly Bet: LBJ, Vietnam, and the 1968 Election*. Lanham, MD: Rowman & Littlefield, 2005.

Lasswell, Harold. *Propaganda Technique in World War I*. 1927. Reprint, Cambridge, MA: MIT Press, 1971.

Leech, Margaret. *In the Days of McKinley*. New York: Harper & Brothers, 1959.

Linn, Brian McAllister. *The Philippine War, 1899–1902*. Lawrence: University of Kansas Press, 2000.

Lippmann, Walter. *Public Opinion*. 1922. Reprint, New York: Free Press, 1965.

Lipstadt, Deborah. *Beyond Belief: The American Press and the Coming of the Holocaust*. New York: Free Press, 1986.

Little, Douglas. *American Orientalism: The United States and the Middle East since 1945*. 3rd ed. Chapel Hill: University of North Carolina Press, 2008.

Logevall, Fredrik. *Choosing War: The Lost Chance for Peace and the Escalation of War in Vietnam*. Berkeley: University of California Press, 1999.

Lorence, James J. *Screening America: United States History Through Film Since 1900*. New York: Pearson, 2006.

Lykins, Daniel L. *From Total War to Total Diplomacy: The Advertising Council and the Construction of the Cold War Consensus*. Westport, CT: Praeger, 2003.

MacArthur, John R. *Second Front: Censorship and Propaganda in the Gulf War*. Berkeley: University of California Press, 1993.

MacMillan, Margaret. *Paris 1919: Six Months That Changed the World*. New York: Random House, 2001.

Maltese, John Anthony. *Spin Control: The White House Office of Communications and the Management of Presidential News*. Chapel Hill: University of North Carolina Press, 1992.

Manela, Erez. *The Wilsonian Moment: Self-Determination and the International Origins of Anticolonial Nationalism*. New York: Oxford University Press, 2007.

Mann, James. *Rise of the Vulcans: The History of Bush's War Cabinet*. New York: Penguin, 2004.

Marling, Karal Ann, and John Wetenhall. *Iwo Jima: Monuments, Memories, and the American Hero*. Cambridge, MA: Harvard University Press, 1991.

May, Glenn Anthony. *A Past Recovered*. Quezon City, Philippines: New Day, 1987.

May, Lary. *The Big Tomorrow: Hollywood and the Politics of the American Way*. Chicago: University of Chicago Press, 2000.

McAlister, Melani. *Epic Encounters: Culture, Media, and U.S. Interests in the Middle East, 1945–2000*. Berkeley: University of California Press, 2001.

McGovern, Charles F. *Sold American: Consumption and Citizenship, 1890–1945*. Chapel Hill: University of North Carolina Press, 2006.

Merritt, Russell. "D.W. Griffith Directs the Great War: The Making of Hearts of the World." *Quarterly Review of Film Studies* (Winter 1981): 45–65.

Millett, Allan R., and Peter Malowski. *For the Common Defense: A Military History of the United States of America*. New York: Free Press, 1994.

Millis, Walter. *The Martial Spirit*. 1931. Reprint, Chicago: Ivan R. Dee, 1989.

Mintz, Steven and Randy Roberts, eds. *Hollywood's America: United States History Through Its Films*. St. James, NY: Brandywine Press, 1993.

Mock, James R., and Cedric Larson. *Words That Won the War: The Story of the Committee on Public Information, 1917–1919*. Princeton, NJ: Princeton University Press, 1939.

Moeller, Susan D. *Shooting War: Photography and the American Experience of Combat*. New York: Basic Books, 1989.

Mueller, John E. *Policy and Opinion in the Gulf War*. Chicago: University of Chicago Press, 1994.

——. *War, Presidents and Public Opinion*. New York: John Wiley & Sons, 1973.

Murray, Stuart, and James McCabe. *Norman Rockwell's Four Freedoms*. New York: Gramercy Books, 1993.

Murray, Williamson, and Allan R. Millett. *A War To Be Won: Fighting the Second World War*. Cambridge, MA: Belknap Press, 2000.

Musser, Charles. *The Emergence of Cinema: The American Screen to 1907*. New York: Charles Scribner's Sons, 1990.

Neff, Mark. "The Politics of Sacrifice on the American Home Front in World War II." *Journal of American History* 77 (March 1991): 1296–1318.

Nelson, Richard Alan. *A Chronology and Glossary of Propaganda in the United States*. Westport, CT: Greenwood Press, 1996.

O'Leary, Cecilia Elizabeth. *To Die For: The Paradox of American Patriotism*. Princeton, NJ: Princeton University Press, 1999.

Paterson, Thomas G. *Meeting the Communist Threat: Truman to Reagan*. New York: Oxford University Press, 1988.

Pérez, Louis A. Jr. *The War of 1898: The United States and Cuba in History and Historiography*. Chapel Hill: University of North Carolina Press, 1998.

Pierpaoli, Paul G. Jr. *Truman and Korea: The Political Culture of the Early Cold War*. Columbia: University of Missouri Press, 1999.

Ponder, Stephen. "The President Makes News: William McKinley and the First Presidential Press Corps, 1897–1901." *Presidential Studies Quarterly* 24 (Fall 1994): 823–37.

Rampton, Sheldon, and John Stauber. *The Best War Ever: Lies, Damned Lies, and the Mess in Iraq*. New York: Tarcher/Penguin, 2006.

——. *Weapons of Mass Deception: The Uses of Propaganda in Bush's War on Iraq*. New York: Tarcher/Penguin, 2003.

Rawls, Walton. *Wake Up America! World War I and the American Poster*. New York: Abbeville Press, 1988.

Rich, Frank. *The Greatest Story Ever Sold: The Decline and Fall of Truth from 9/11 to Katrina*. New York: Penguin, 2006.

Ricks, Thomas E. *Fiasco: The American Military Adventure in Iraq*. New York: Penguin, 2006.

Roeder, George H. Jr. *The Censored War: American Visual Experience during World War Two*. New Haven, CT: Yale University Press, 1993.

Rosenberg, Emily S. *A Date Which Will Live: Pearl Harbor in American Memory*. Durham, NC: Duke University Press, 2003.

———. "Rescuing Women and Children." In *History and September 11th*. Edited by Joanne Meyerowitz, 81–93. Philadelphia: Temple University Press, 2003.

Rosenberg, Jonathan. "For Democracy, Not Hypocrisy: World War and Race Relations in the United States, 1914–1919." *International History Review* 21 (September 1999): 592–625.

Rutherford, Paul. *Weapons of Mass Persuasion: Marketing the War against Iraq*. Toronto: University of Toronto Press, 2004.

Rydell, Robert. *All the World's a Fair: Visions of Empire at American International Expositions, 1876–1916*. Chicago: University of Chicago Press, 1984.

Samuel, Lawrence R. *Pledging Allegiance: American Identity and the Bond Drive of World War II*. Washington, DC: Smithsonian Institution Press, 1997.

Sanders, Michael, and Philip Taylor. *British Propaganda in the First World War, 1914–1918*. London: Macmillan, 1982.

Schaffer, Ronald. *America in the Great War: The Rise of the War Welfare State*. New York: Oxford University Press, 1991.

Schmitz, David F. *The Tet Offensive: Politics, War, and Public Opinion*. Lanham, MD: Rowman & Littlefield, 2005.

Schoonover, Thomas. *Uncle Sam's War of 1898 and the Origins of Globalization*. Lexington: University Press of Kentucky, 2003.

Seelye, John. *War Games: Richard Harding Davis and the New Imperialism*. Amherst: University of Massachusetts Press, 2003.

Shaw, Angel Velasco, and Luis H. Francia, eds. *The Philippine-American War and the Aftermath of an Imperial Dream, 1899–1999*. New York: New York University Press, 2002.

Shaw, Tony. *Hollywood's Cold War*. Amherst: University of Massachusetts Press, 2007.

Sheehan, Neil. *A Bright Shining Lie: John Paul Vann and America in Vietnam*. New York: Random House, 1988.

Sifry, Micah L., and Christopher Cerf, eds. *The Gulf War Reader: History, Documents, Opinions*. New York: Times Books, 1991.

Small, Melvin. *Antiwarriors: The Vietnam War and the Battle for America's Hearts and Minds*. Wilmington, DE: Scholarly Resources, 2002.

———. *At the Water's Edge: American Politics and the Vietnam War*. Chicago: Ivan R. Dee, 2005.

Spector, Ronald H. *After Tet: The Bloodiest Year in Vietnam*. New York: Free Press, 1993.

Sperber, A. M. *Murrow: His Life and Times*. New York: Freundlich Books, 1986.

Sproule, J. Michael. *Propaganda and Persuasion: The American Experience of Media and Mass Persuasion*. Cambridge: Cambridge University Press, 1997.

Steele, Richard W. *Propaganda in an Open Society: The Roosevelt Administration and the Media, 1933–1941*. Westport, CT: Greenwood Press, 1985.

Stevens, John D. "When Sedition Laws Were Enforced: Wisconsin in World War I." *Transactions of the Wisconsin Academy of Sciences, Arts, and Letters* 58 (1970): 39–60.

Stueck, William. *Rethinking the Korean War: A New Diplomatic and Strategic History*. Princeton, NJ: Princeton University Press, 2002.

Suskind, Ron. *The One Percent Doctrine: Deep Inside America's Pursuit of Its Enemies Since 9/11*. New York: Simon & Schuster, 2006.

Sweeney, Michael S. *The Military and the Press: An Uneasy Truce*. Evanston, IL: Northwestern University Press, 2006.

Sylvester, Judith, and Suzanne Huffman. *Reporting from the Front: The Media and the Military*. Lanham, MD: Rowman & Littlefield, 2005.

Taylor, Philip M. *Munitions of the Mind: A History of Propaganda from the Ancient World to the Present Day*. Manchester, UK: Manchester University Press, 2003.

——. *War and the Media: Propaganda and Persuasion in the Gulf War*. Manchester, UK: Manchester University Press, 1992.

Tebbel, John, and Sarah Miles Watts. *The Press and the Presidency: From George Washington to Ronald Reagan*. New York: Oxford University Press, 1985.

Tobin, James. *Ernie Pyle's War: America's Eyewitness to World War II*. New York: Free Press, 1997.

Toplin, Robert Brent. *History by Hollywood: The Use and Abuse of the American Past*. Urbana: University of Illinois Press, 1996.

——. *Michael Moore's Fahrenheit 9/11: How One Film Divided a Nation*. Lawrence: University Press of Kansas, 2006.

Turner, Kathleen J. *Lyndon Johnson's Dual War: Vietnam and the Press*. Chicago: University of Chicago Press, 1985.

Vaughn, Stephen. *Holding Fast the Inner Lines: Democracy, Nationalism, and the Committee on Public Information*. Chapel Hill: University of North Carolina Press, 1980.

Voss, Frederick S. *Reporting the War: The Journalistic Coverage of World War II*. Washington, DC: Smithsonian Institution Press, 1994.

Ward, Larry Wayne. *The Motion Picture Goes to War: The U.S. Government Film Effort during World War I*. Ann Arbor, MI: UMI Research Press, 1985.

Weinberg, Gerhard L. *A World At Arms: A Global History of World War II*. New York: Cambridge University Press, 1994.

Westbrook, Robert B. *Why We Fought: Forging American Obligations in World War II*. Washington, DC: Smithsonian Books, 2004.

Whitfield, Stephen J. *The Culture of the Cold War*. Baltimore: Johns Hopkins University Press, 1996.

Williams, Walter L. "American Imperialism and the Indians." In *Indians in American History: An Introduction*. Edited by Frederick E. Hoxie and Peter Iverson, 231–49. Wheeling, IL: Harlan Davidson, 1998.

Winkler, Allan. *The Politics of Propaganda: The Office of War Information, 1942–1945*. New Haven, CT: Yale University Press, 1978.

Winter, Thomas. "The Training of Colored Troops: A Cinematic Effort to Promote National Cohesion." In *Hollywood's World War I: Motion Picture Images*. Edited by Peter C. Rollins and John E. O'Connor, 13–25. Bowling Green, OH: Bowling Green State University Popular Press, 1997.

Woodward, Bob. *Plan of Attack*. New York: Simon & Schuster, 2004.

Wyatt, Clarence. *Paper Soldiers: The American Press and the Vietnam War*. New York: W. W. Norton, 1993.

Wyman, David S. *The Abandonment of the Jews: America and the Holocaust, 1941–1945*. New York: Pantheon Books, 1984.

Yergin, Daniel. *The Prize: The Epic Quest for Oil, Money and Power*. New York: Touchstone, 1992.

Young, Marilyn B. *The Vietnam Wars 1945–1990*. New York: HarperPerennial, 1991.

Zeiger, Susan. *In Uncle Sam's Service: Women Workers with the American Expeditionary Force, 1917–1919*. Ithaca, NY: Cornell University Press, 1999.

Zieger, Robert H. *America's Great War: World War I and the American Experience*. Lanham, MD: Rowman & Littlefield, 2001.

INDEX